OKLAHOMA

To
Jack T. Conn, Billy M. Jones, Robert B. Kamm,
Paul F. Lambert, and W. Roger Webb:
FRIENDS

OKLAHOMA
LAND OF THE FAIR GOD

ODIE B. FAULK

Windsor Publications, Inc.—History Book Division

Publisher: John M. Phillips
Editorial Director: Teri Davis Greenberg
Design Director: Alexander D'Anca

Staff for *Oklahoma: Land of the Fair God*
Senior Editor: Michelle Hudun
Editor, Text: Lane A. Powell
Director, Corporate Biographies: Karen Story
Assistant Director, Corporate Biographies: Phyllis
    Gray
Editor, Corporate Biographies: Judith Hunter
Editorial Assistants: Kathy M. Brown, Laura
    Cordova, Marcie Goldstein, Marilyn Horn, Pat
    Pittman, Sharon Volz
Designer: J.R. Vasquez
Layout Artist, Text: Ellen Ifrah
Layout Artist, Corporate Biographies: Mari
    Catherine Preimesberger
Sales Representatives, Corporate Biographies: Curtis
    Courtney, Angie Cardner, Nita Hawley, Jo Mohr,
    Barbara Whitaker

Library of Congress Cataloging-in-Publication Data

Faulk, Odie B.
    Oklahoma land of the fair God.

    Bibliography: p.
    Includes index.
    1. Oklahoma—History. 2. Oklahoma—Description and
travel. 3. Oklahoma—Industries. I. Franks, Kenny
Arthur, 1945-   . Partners in progress.
II. Lambert, Paul F. III. Title.
F694.F38   1986   976.6   86-1573
ISBN 0-89781-173-9

Advisory Committee
Governor George Nigh
Senator Bernice Sheddrick
Representative Jim Barker
Lee Alan Smith
James Leake
Ralph McCalmont
John Williams
Bill McLean
C.J. Silas
Morrison Tucker
E.L. Gaylord
Fred Olds
Charles Banks Wilson
Betty Price
Dr. Lawrence Boger
Bob Allen
Dr. Larry Zenke
Dr. Donald Wright
Quintus Herron
Jim Monroe

Endpapers
Bison, longhorn cattle, elk, and other endangered species are protected at the Wichita Mountains Wildlife Refuge near Lawton. Photo by Jim Argo

Preface
A crew drilling for oil in Beckham County is pictured during the 1980s. Oil is a major Oklahoma industry that has resulted in countless jobs for residents both in the oil industry itself, as well as related companies. Photo by Jim Argo

Contents

Preface

Most of us, when we think of Oklahoma, picture an outline of its shape, the Red River curling across the southern edge, the sides forming almost a rectangle, and the Panhandle jutting westward in a long, thin extension. Usually we can tell we have crossed one of these boundaries into another state only by a highway marker that notes the fact, for the borders are imaginary lines on a geographer's map; except for the Red River, these lines do not exist in any concrete way. In reality, Oklahoma is far more than an outline—it is a state of mind that exists in the hearts and minds of a people who are positive, vibrant, dynamic, and hospitable.

Some people have suggested that the Sooner State was settled by the castoffs and dregs of other states: Indians shoved out of almost every part of the United States, along with farmers who had failed elsewhere, businessmen who had gone bankrupt, and ne'er-do-wells unable to fit into society. Such may have been the case in a few instances, but the majority of those who moved to Oklahoma were energetic, imaginative, and ambitious and were filled with sinew, spirit, and a hope for the future.

In Oklahoma these immigrants found variety in nature—as well as in themselves. The elevation ranges from a few hundred feet above sea level to almost a mile; some of it is flat, arid plains country, while other parts are mountainous and covered with towering pines. Yet it was the people that proved to be Oklahoma's greatest natural resource, for they transformed the region from a frontier into a bountiful and productive state in a remarkably short time. In the process they performed deeds of daring and valor, as well as dishonesty and dishonor. Today Oklahoma is a land rich in past, present, and future. Its history stretches back three-quarters of a century before the landing of the celebrated English settlers on the Eastern seaboard, while its growth and prosperity appear unlimited in the future.

This volume is intended as an introduction to the varied, beautiful land that is Oklahoma. It is not a scholarly treatise opening new avenues of research, but rather a summary and synthesis of the 400-plus years of the state's past, a look at the present, and an overview of its potential. It is intended for the newcomer, the tourist, and the student, a short volume wherein they may find a ready source of information about the sweep, the color, and the pageantry of Oklahoma's history, while the longtime resident may discover in it new reasons for loving the state.

In writing this book I incurred numerous debts to librarians, particularly at The Oklahoma Historical Society and the Western History Collections of the University of Oklahoma. I especially thank Dr. Bob Blackburn and his staff in the Publications Division of The Oklahoma Historical Society, while Drs. Paul Lambert and Kenny Franks of the Oklahoma Heritage Association likewise provided information as well as encouragement and counsel. I also note with deep gratitude the help in research I received from Dr. Carl N. Tyson, a scholar who regrettably left Oklahoma's academic community to prosper in the world of business. My thanks also go especially to those who read the manuscript and offered suggestions, particularly to Dr. Norbert Mahnken of Oklahoma State University, Dr. Don Green of Central State University, and the late Dr. John W. Morris of the University of Oklahoma. In addition, I offer my appreciation to those students who sat through my classes in Oklahoma history and from whom I learned more than I taught.

My wife Laura, as usual, read proof, suggested ways to improve the work, and gave support in numerous ways, and to her goes much of the credit for seeing this book into print.

In every person's life there comes some moment when friends are doubly appreciated, people who take positive steps to help when help is most needed. I was fortunate at such a moment in my life to have several people who truly proved themselves to be friends in the finest sense of the word: Jack T. Conn, Billy M. Jones, Robert B. Kamm, Paul F. Lambert, and W. Roger Webb. No words can convey to these men how much I appreciate them and how much their friendship has meant to me.

Odie B. Faulk
Muskogee, Oklahoma
January 1986

CHAPTER I

Land of Contrast

*F*rancisco Vásquez de Coronado in 1535 came to New Spain, as Mexico was then known, where he had become governor of a large province. Born in Salamanca, Spain, into a family of the minor nobility, he was fair of countenance and light of hair, a handsome young man who had been named a courtier to the king and had been presented at court and enjoyed the viceroy's favor and knew the advantages of wealth and cosmopolitan life.

His comfortable existence changed dramatically in 1540 when he accepted command of a large expedition which was to search for the Seven Cities of Cíbola, a land rumored to contain great wealth somewhere to the north in the *tierra incognita* (the unexplored area north of settlements in Mexico). With 336 Spanish troops and hundreds of Indian allies, he marched into present-day Arizona and New Mexico, there to fight battles with Pueblo Indians and suffer great hardships—to discover only rumors of yet another wealthy kingdom, the Gran Quivira, which supposedly lay somewhere to the east and north of the pueblos of New Mexico. There, according to the Indians, even the humblest peasant ate from golden dishes, the streets were paved with silver, and the chief each afternoon took a nap under a tree adorned with golden bells that tinkled musically when the breeze blew.

From central New Mexico, Coronado and his followers marched for more than thirty days to the east during the spring of 1541, arriving at last at Palo Duro Canyon (near the present Amarillo, Texas). There he sent most of his army back to New Mexico while he marched on to Quivira, taking with him thirty horsemen, six footmen, and several Indian guides. On June 1 they set out riding north, as he wrote, "by the needle" (using a magnetic compass, he would have taken a route slightly east of north). On this course they made about eight miles a day, bringing them by mid-June to the Panhandle of pres-

Opposite page
This redbud tree blooms
during the spring on
Talimina Scenic Drive in
eastern Oklahoma. The
redbud is the official state
tree of Oklahoma. Photo by
Jim Argo

Above
Broken Bow Reservoir in
McCurtain County is one
of Oklahoma's newest
lakes, created in 1969 by
the United States Corps of
Engineers. The lake was
formed by the damming of
Mountain Fork River and
is a favorite of state hunters and fishermen. Photo
by Jim Argo

This artist's interpretation of Francisco Vásquez de Coronado depicts the "Knight of Pueblo and Plains" as he might have looked at the time of his explorations. Courtesy, Bill Ahrendt

falo], for, as I told your Majesty, these animals are very wild and ferocious." On these plains there were no trees, and the men cooked their food as would the pioneers of a later age, over a fire using buffalo chips as fuel. In addition, because there were no major rivers in the area, they were "without water for many days."

As these Spaniards suffered across the High Plains, they little realized that this land one day would be part of the great state of Oklahoma, nor could they know the diversity of the geography of that future state. All they saw was a level sameness, for they were crossing the area that later would be known as the Great Plains. This is a land formed by silt carried out of the Rocky Mountains by a multitude of rivulets, creeks, and rivers. The first feature these Spaniards noticed was the absence of trees. Next they commented about the grass. The vegetation most associated with the southern Great Plains usually was called "shortgrass," for the subsoil did not hold sufficient moisture to allow the growth of the extensive root systems needed by taller grasses. The more level the ground, the more the grass dominated. However, where this land was broken, other types of plants grew: gnarled mesquite trees, some thorny shrubs, and cactus, while along the few creeks of the area tall cottonwoods reached for the sky. These towered above the blue (or buffalo) grass, which was the home of wild hogs, white-tailed deer, pronghorns (antelope), wild turkeys, prairie dogs, ground squirrels, and millions of field mice and jackrabbits. Also, there were dozens of varieties of birds to add a dash of color, a warble of song, and a sudden thrashing of wings.

The best-known native animal to feed on this shortgrass was the American bison, or buffalo. Across the vast plains there was no predatory animal that by itself was capable of killing these great shaggy beasts. A buffalo bull made a formidable enemy, for he often weighed a ton, and with horns and hooves he could fight off most any attacker. Moreover, buffalo were difficult to surprise, for when the herd grazed an old cow usually stood guard, quick to hear anything approaching (these animals had keen hearing). Buffalo were also good runners; only a fast horse could keep up with a stampeding herd. In addition, they were equally commendable swimmers, capable of crossing

ent-day Oklahoma.

This area—in the vicinity of the present towns of Hardesty, Adams, and Tyrone—was extremely flat, an ocean of short grass when Coronado saw it, and everywhere buffalo grazed. "The country where these animals roamed was so level and bare," wrote one of Coronado's men in his journal, "that whenever one looked at them one could see the sky between their legs, so that at a distance they looked like trimmed pine tree trunks with the foliage joining at the top." Coronado's supplies were so depleted by this time that he and his men were reduced to living almost exclusively on buffalo meat secured, Coronado declared in a letter to Charles V, King of Spain, "at the cost of some of the horses slain by the cattle [buf-

Left
This Wichita Indian village, located in central Oklahoma during the 1850s, resembled the villages visited by Coronado during his expedition of 1541. Courtesy, The Oklahoma Historical Society (OHS)

Below
The Oklahoma High Plains was a region of vast grasslands, few trees, and little water. At times it was a garden producing wild flowers and abundant grasses; at other times it was a drought-stricken semi-desert, a formidable land that was the last frontier conquered by non-Indian settlers. Photo by Jim Argo

Right
This mural of an Osage warrior by Monroe Tsa-Toke can be found in the Wiley Post Historical Building in Oklahoma City. OHS

Opposite page, top Winds in the Oklahoma Panhandle have carved the Dakota sandstone of the area into many unusual shapes, including this one called "The Wedding" or "The Three Sisters." The formation is near Black Mesa State Park in Cimarron County. Photo by Jim Argo

Opposite page, bottom American bison, or buffalo, once inhabited the Great Plains in herds of more than two million animals. Today, due to massive extermination of the species following the Civil War, only small herds exist on carefully protected wildlife refuges. Photo by Jim Argo

any river to escape an enemy or reach a new feeding ground. On the plains of western Oklahoma, as well as in Kansas and Texas, these buffalo spent their lives grazing contentedly, wallowing in sand to clean themselves, drinking from creeks and streams, and increasing in numbers.

The plains country is a windy region, with winds that freeze in winter, parch in summer, and bring seasonal rains in spring and fall that turn it into a vast marsh on occasion. The area has a "continental weather pattern" (according to modern meteorologists); it gets the extremes of weather conditions known on the North American continent. The storms of spring bring tornadoes, hail, and rain, while the "northers" of winter bring sleet and blinding snowstorms. In the summer winds blow from the south into the nearby Rocky Mountains to melt the snow cover and bring silt-laden water rushing down to form yet another layer on the plains.

The Panhandle of Oklahoma is situated almost exactly between the Arkansas and the Red rivers, the two major rivers that drain the state. Because the Panhandle is the highest part of the state, sloping downward to the southeast from almost 5,000 feet to approximately 300 feet above sea level, these two rivers run in that direction. Since the western two-thirds of the state's land is soft and sandy, the rivers do not cut deep and jagged banks, but rather meander in snake-like fashion as they flow toward the Mississippi. On their way across the state they are fed by other rivers: the Arkansas receives the flow of the Verdigris, the Grand (also known as the Neosho), the

Illinois, the Cimarron, the Canadian, and, at the border of Arkansas, the Poteau. The Red is joined and increased in size from the north by the Washita, the Blue, and the Kiamichi and from the northwest and northeast by the Elm Fork and North Fork, the Prairie Dog Town Fork, and the Salt Fork.

As these rivers approach the eastern portion of Oklahoma, their channels become narrower and better defined, for the land is more resistant to erosion. This portion of Oklahoma consists of rolling hills and minor outcroppings of sandstone. Once the treeless plains give way to prairie and hills, the rivers flow through the Cross Timbers (running north and south almost through the middle of the state). This is an area of

One of Oklahoma's more lovable inhabitants is the prairie dog. A large village is preserved at the Wichita Mountains Wildlife Refuge near Lawton. Photo by Jim Argo

Oklahoma's weather is often unpredictable and frequently severe. The heart of "Tornado Alley," central Oklahoma usually ranks high in the nation in instances of tornadoes each year. Courtesy, National Severe Storms Laboratory, National Oceanic and Atmospheric Administration

blackjack and post oak intermingled with mesquite and smaller shrubbery, while along the rivers' banks cottonwoods give way to long-leaf pine, giant live and white oaks, and finally to stately cypress and pecan groves. In extreme eastern Oklahoma, where the rainfall is heavy, Spanish moss occasionally hangs from the branches of these tall trees. Open patches of ground are covered with Indian paintbrushes, sunflowers, and honeysuckle. Wood bison, a smaller cousin of the great beasts of the high plains, graze these areas along with white-tailed deer, while squirrels chatter and fuss at them from the branches of the trees. Frogs, field mice, and lizards keep a wary watch for hawks and owls.

Contrasting with the plains to the west are the mountains of southern and eastern Oklahoma. The mightiest chain, known to geographers as the Interior Highlands, is a western extension of the Ozarks and consists of the Boston Mountains, the Cookson Hills, and the Ouachita Mountains; the Ouachitas contain several curving ridges known as the Kiamichi, Winding Stair, Poteau, and San Bois Mountains. In the south-central part of the state are the Arbuckles, while to their west are the Wichitas. The Wichita Mountains rise 3,000 feet from the plains and are rich in minerals; for centuries water eroded the earth of these hills, carrying mineral deposits to the Red River and coloring its waters a rusty tint (from which the river received its name). The highest point in Oklahoma, however, is located not far from where Coronado and his treasure-seeking soldiers crossed the Panhandle. Known as Black Mesa, it is not a mountain, but rather was formed by a lava flow some 10,000 years ago and juts 4,978 feet above sea level.

The exact date when humans first entered into what is now Oklahoma is unknown, shrouded in the obscurity of unrecorded history. Archaeologists believe that Paleo-Indians came to the region about 15,000 B.C., bringing with them bone tools and spear points. They were gatherers of fruits, nuts, and berries and hunters of the wooly mammoth. Somewhere between 1500 B.C. and A.D. 500 came the introduction of the bow and arrow, pottery, and basket weaving, and the Native Americans of this time lived in semi-permanent villages near which they cultivated corn. Archaeological digs at village sites have uncovered ornamental pen-

dants, hairpins, shell and bone necklaces, pottery, arrow points, and cooking pits. They had a fully developed religion, and they buried their dead wth artifacts which they thought would be needed in the after-life.

Between A.D. 500 and A.D. 1350 (known as the Gibson Period) Oklahoma's Indian inhabitants lived in fixed settlements, relied heavily on agriculture, and had developed techniques to fire pottery. They developed trade routes to obtain items they could not produce: to the Gulf Coast for shells, to the Great Lakes for copper and pipestone, and to Nevada and New Mexico for certain types of pottery. A class of artisans produced goods for trade, while a priestly class ruled all aspects of life. The priests were given lavish funerals with burial offerings placed in great mounds (some books refer to these Native Americans as the "Mound Builders").

About 1350, however, came a severe period of drought, causing the breakup of large villages and an end to the practice of mound building as the priestly class declined in importance. Between 1350 and the appearance of Europeans, several advances in pottery-making techniques introduced the use of finely ground mussel shells, mica, and sand as additives to the clay base to improve the tempering of pottery. Stone knives were manufactured, and tools made from bison and deer bone became more common-

Several important archaeological sites are located near present-day Ponca City. Ferdinandina, purportedly the first white settlement in Oklahoma (although in reality a Wichita Indian Village), Bryson Paddock, and Uncas have all produced important finds for archaeologists. This pot was uncovered at the Uncas site. Photo by Jim Argo

place. In the remains of villages built in eastern Oklahoma during this period bison bones are prevalent, indicating that the inhabitants either hunted farther west or the buffalo ranged farther east. This also was the period when Indians began to decorate their clothing, which was made from animal hides, and to weave textiles.

The principal tribes in Oklahoma at the time Coronado made his trek across the Panhandle were adapted to the area and the climate in which they lived. In the southeastern part of the state lived a Caddoan confederation, woodland Indians who supported themselves by hunting and farming. They tended muskmelons, plums, cherries, white grapes, and mulberries, all of which grew bountifully with little or no care. They killed the game that inhabited the forest, and they processed salt for trade. The Caddos were especially noted for their friendliness. They usually welcomed guests by washing their visitors' hands and feet, feeding them well, and giving them the best accommodations in the village. Included among the Caddos were several different groups of Indians related by a common language and tradition: the Natchitoches (in

Left
The artisans of Spiro produced elaborate ceramics and engraved animal bones for trade and for the ornamentation of their leaders. This replica of an effigy pipe is similar to many found at the Spiro Mounds Archaeological State Park by archaeologists excavating the site. Photo by Jim Argo

Above
In eastern Oklahoma, a culture of town builders flourished from A.D. 800 to 1400. Centered near the present-day town of Spiro, these prehistoric people conducted trade with tribes throughout North America, built mounds for ceremonies and houses, and carried out extensive agriculture in the fertile valley of the Arkansas River. Courtesy, Donald R. Johnson

Top, right
These women cultivate corn in a field near the Spiro Mounds. Controlling farmlands, trade routes, and the manufacture of finished goods, the Spiro leaders ruled a large area west of the Mississippi River for some 600 years. Courtesy, Donald R. Johnson

Above
Southeastern Indian traders meet with Spiro leaders to negotiate trade agreements. Courtesy, Donald R. Johnson

Opposite page, bottom
Black Mesa, the highest point in Oklahoma, is located in the northwestern corner of the Oklahoma Panhandle. Photo by Jim Argo

The Caddo Indians were living in the area that became the state of Oklahoma at the time of the first contact with white explorers. Artist George Catlin depicted them gathering wild grapes during his travels in the west in the early 1800s. Courtesy, The Thomas Gilcrease Institute of American History and Art, Tulsa, Oklahoma

present Louisiana), the Cadohadacho, and the Hasinai.

Upriver from the Caddos along the Kiamichi River were the Wichita Indians, a second Caddoan confederation that included the Taovaya, Tawakoni, Yscani, Waco, and Kichai. Originally these Indians lived in northern Oklahoma along the Arkansas River, but they migrated southward when the Osage began moving into northern Oklahoma from present-day Missouri. The Wichitas lived in permanent villages and, like the Caddos, had an economy based on farming and hunting. Generally these two confederations lived in peace, neither relying on raiding and warfare for economic gain. Likewise they lived in peace with the Pawnee, who lived to their north and who also were a farming-hunting tribe.

A second major group of Indians, related by the Siouan language they spoke, were the Osage and Quapaw tribes. They carved

a homeland for themselves in northeastern Oklahoma, living in permanent villages. They cultivated corn and squash, and supplemented their diet by hunting buffalo to the west during the summer. This annual trek was a time of great pleasure, for they returned laden with dried meat to be eaten during the winter, and with hides for clothing, and bones to be carved into implements. Generally these Indians, a tall, well-formed people, were feared by the plains tribes because of their courage and their zest for combat.

In the broken country and plains of western Oklahoma lived the Lipan Apaches, eastern cousins of the warlike tribes of the desert Southwest. These were Uto-Aztecan people, speaking an Athapascan language who apparently had migrated to the region sometime between A.D. 900 and A.D. 1200 from northwestern Canada. Nomadic and fierce, the Lipan Apaches quickly carved a

20

stronghold for themselves on the plains from the Arkansas River south to central Texas, following the buffalo and living in temporary shelters known as wickiups. In physical appearance they were taller than average Indians height, and they were noted orators. Like their neighbors to the east they wove baskets and made pottery, but principally lived by raiding other tribes. Traveling in small bands, because the land would not support large numbers, they followed whatever war leader inspired their confidence. They attacked suddenly, swooping down on unsuspecting Indian villages, seizing all corn, beans, and other food and capturing women and children. They were noted for their cruel and warlike nature, their strength and endurance, and their ability to spread terror among other tribes—except the Osage, whom the Apaches learned to respect as hard fighters.

Change came slowly for these tribes. Decades would slip past with no noticeable change in their economy, their technology, or their society. With no calendar to tell them another year had passed, they dated the events of their lives by the season, a successful hunt, a drought, a raid. Time passed with quiet monotony as they contended with each other and with nature for subsistence, their daily lives almost exactly the same as those of their ancestors. Theirs was not a bleak, brutish existence, for they knew the pleasures of the hunt and the harvest, the generous providence of natural bounty, and the satisfaction of geographic beauty. Yet life for them was uncertain when game grew scarce, the rains were sparse, crops failed, or battles went against them. They suffered from disease, from periodic famine, from man's inhumanity to man. Such an existence was all they had ever known, however, and within it they found reason for hope, for laughter, for dreams.

The years of sole Indian ownership of Oklahoma ended in 1541 with the hoofbeats of an animal never before seen in the area— the horse. Riding these strange beasts were Spaniards, the men of Francisco Vásquez de Coronado, who came looking for streets paved with silver and listening for the sounds of golden bells tinkling in trees. They came searching for the Gran Quivira and the Seven Cities of Cíbola, little noticing—or caring—about the agricultural potential of the land beneath their horses'

hooves, the diversity of geography, or the rights of the native races of the land through which they rode.

Some tantalizing evidence exists that Coronado and his men were not the first Europeans to visit Oklahoma. At Heavener and elsewhere in the state there are carvings on stone which may be pictographs (a form of writing used in the era before the invention of the alphabet). These may have been made by Vikings in the thirteenth or fourteenth centuries or even by visitors from lands bordering the Mediterranean who came as early as 500 B.C. Archaeologists, however, disagree among themselves about the meaning of these pictographs. About Coronado's trek there is no doubt, for his report is detailed and exact.

This painting by C. Wimar shows the impact the horse had on the Osage Indians. Given the greater mobility and speed of horsepower, these Indians could range out on the Great Plains, hunting and warring to expand their influence. OHS

CHAPTER II

European Entanglements

Hernándo de Soto led the Spanish group that explored from Florida to Oklahoma and Texas. Reproduced from De Soto and the Conquistadores *by Maynard. Longmans, Green & Company, New York (1930)*

Coronado and his hand-picked band of thirty mounted Spaniards, along with his footmen and Indian guides, quickly crossed the Oklahoma Panhandle at their slow pace of eight to ten miles each day. Entering Kansas, they continued moving about ten degrees east of north, a route that brought them eventually to the Arkansas River near the present town of Ford. At that point a guide declared he recognized the river and said that the golden city he had described was only a short distance to the northeast.

No doubt with quickening heartbeats, the Spanish explorers crossed the Arkansas and began moving along the north bank of the river at an increased pace of twelve to fifteen miles a day. Three days later, on July 2, 1541, they met natives from Quivira hunting buffalo. Coronado's guide, Sopote, was able to converse with the friendly Quivirans. Riding with these people, Coronado and his band went to the main settlement. What they found there was greatly disappointing. True, the countryside was green and rolling; true, there were trees along the banks of the stream; and true, a few cultivated fields showed great agricultural potential. Yet there were no golden plates, no streets paved with silver, no king holding stately court. Rather, there was a Wichita Indian village of dome-shaped grass huts, filled with tattooed Indians wearing few clothes, little different in appearance from the natives Coronado had seen elsewhere. His seventy-seven-day ride from New Mexico had been for naught.

Eventually Coronado had an interview with the chief of the Wichita tribe, "a man already aged" who wore a metal amulet around his neck (probably of meteoric origin). The chief said there were similar villages in the surrounding countryside, none possessing anything that the Spaniards would consider of value. All the Indians lived in huts of wood and grass construction, all hunted buffalo, and all tended small fields.

Nowhere was there gold or silver or turquoise.

In great disappointment Coronado secured guides from among the Wichitas to lead his group back to New Mexico. This trip was made in almost a direct line from Kansas to the Pueblo country around Albuquerque, which once again brought the party across western Oklahoma. On this part of his trip, Coronado wrote a description of the plains Apaches. He noted that these nomads lived almost exclusively on buffalo meat, that from the hides of these shaggy beasts came the Indians' clothing and tepees, and that they bartered buffalo hides with the eastern tribes for agricultural products. Reunited with the rest of his party in New Mexico, Coronado returned empty-handed to Mexico to report to the viceroy in the spring of 1542.

While Coronado was yet in New Mexico that spring, Fray Juan de Padilla, a Franciscan priest, expressed a desire to return to Kansas to Christianize the Wichita Indians and bring them under the domination of the Spanish king. With Coronado's approval, he selected one soldier to accompany him—Andres do Campo, whose name would indi-

cate a Portuguese background. Also accompanying Padilla were two Mexican Indians who had taken the vows of lay brothers, Lucas and Sebastián.

The Wichita Indian guides, the priest, Campo, and the two lay brothers returned to Quivira and spent the summer of 1542 seeking converts. Their success was so small that the priest, hearing of the Kaw (or Kansa) Indians to the east, determined to take his gospel message there. On the journey however, the small party was ambushed. During the struggle, Fray Juan de Padilla was killed and the other three—Campo, Lucas, and Sebastián—were captured and held as slaves for almost a year. Their masters probably were Kaw Indians who worked them but did not treat them badly. Nor did they watch their captives too closely, for in the summer of 1543 the three managed to slip away, walking south toward Mexico.

As they crossed Oklahoma the brothers took turns carrying a large wooden cross as a sign of penitence. Along this route they were joined by a dog that apparently preferred Spanish to Indian allegiance. This animal proved invaluable, by catching rabbits and other small game when the small party could not beg something to eat from the Indian tribes they encountered. Five long years of walking took them across Oklahoma, Texas, and northern Mexico, and finally in 1548 they reached safety at the Spanish town of Panuco (present Tampico, Mexico). During their heroic trek, they pioneered a road to the north far shorter than the one followed by Coronado, but it was not to be used by other Spaniards.

At the same time Coronado was crossing Oklahoma in search of the Gran Quivira, another Spanish expedition led by Hernándo de Soto was heading westward from Tampa Bay, Florida, after landing there on May 25, 1539. After discovering the Mississippi River, De Soto and his army crossed into Arkansas—and perhaps the extreme eastern border areas of Oklahoma. De Soto's private secretary, Rodrigo Ranjel, noted in his journal that the area abounded with corn, pumpkins, beans, wild game, and fish, and frequently members of the expedition killed woodland buffalo for meat. Ranjel's narrative also noted that many Indian villages were protected by stockades. At one point De Soto's expedition apparently was within 200 miles of Coronado and his men, but neither knew of the other's presence.

Eventually De Soto despaired of finding wealth, for he had reached the edge of the plains country where he found food harder to secure. Therefore he and his men turned back in 1541 to winter on the banks of the Mississippi. There De Soto died of a fever on May 21, 1542. Luís de Moscoso assumed command, and after many adventures brought 320 survivors safely to Panuco (Tampico) in 1543. The official report of the De Soto-Moscoso expedition was similar to that made by Coronado: to the north there was no gold, no silver, nothing of wealth, just natives willing to fight for their supplies of food. Spaniards therefore had no reason to return to the region that would become Oklahoma.

Gradually during the remainder of the sixteenth century, Spanish settlement crept northward from the central valley of Mexico until, in 1598, a finger of settlement was thrust northward into New Mexico. This colony was founded by Juan de Oñate, who hoped to discover the wealth that Coronado might have overlooked. Thus in 1601, with New Mexico firmly established as a colony, Oñate led a full-scale expedition to the northeast, paralleling Coronado's trek to

René Robert Cavelier, Sieur de la Salle, made the first complete exploration of the Mississippi River, discovering its mouth in 1682. He thenceforth claimed all lands drained by the river for King Louis of France. Reproduced from A History of the Mississippi Valley by Spears and Clark. A.S. Clark & Company, Cleveland (1903)

Kansas and reaching the same Wichita Indian village. His report of this expedition was similar to Coronado's: "What I am sure of," he wrote, "is that there is not any gold nor any other metal in all that country." The Oñate foray across Oklahoma to Kansas brought to an end the early period of Spanish exploration. Everyone was convinced that no riches were to be found in the area, and there was an excess of good farm land elsewhere. A quiet century would follow leaving the Indians undisturbed in directing their own affairs.

In the late seventeenth century, René Robert Cavelier, Sieur de la Salle, was responsible for the return of Europeans to Oklahoma. Born in France in 1643, La Salle immigrated to Canada where he gained a reputation as a woodsman and leader of men. Hearing of a great river to the south, he gradually became obsessed with a desire to be the discoverer of its mouth. This dream he realized on April 9, 1682, when he stood near the Gulf of Mexico at the mouth of the Mississippi River—"The Father of Waters"—and intoned the ritual formula for taking possession of new lands:

In the name of the most high, mighty, invincible, and victorious Prince, Louis the Great, by the grace of God, King of France, and of Navarre, Fourteenth of that name, I ... have taken, and do now take ... posses-

sion of this country of Louisiana.
Oklahoma, which was drained by the Mississippi, thus was aclaimed by the French.

Even as he fulfilled one dream, La Salle conceived another: he wanted to plant a settlement at the mouth of the Mississippi to ensure that the vast territory he called Louisiana would forever remain French. In 1685, however, his ships carrying colonists missed the mouth of the Mississippi (which was hidden in a mass of delta islands), and he planted his settlement on the coast of Texas at Matagorda Bay. This settlement, which he named Fort Saint Louis, proved ill-fated. In the spring of 1687 La Salle was killed by unhappy colonists, and within a short time the local Indians overran the little settlement.

The French were determined to settle on the Gulf Coast, however, and in 1699 Iberville le Moyne established a settlement at Biloxi. Three years later came another colony at Mobile. Le Moyne's intent was to make profits by trading European goods to the Indians for furs and by sending out his own trappers to gather more pelts. Then in 1712, Louis XIV decided to give Louisiana to a private businessman for development. This enterprising Frenchman, Antoine Crozat, was in charge of settling the area between Biloxi and the Mississippi to the west. In return for the investment, Crozat expected to reap profits from the fur trade, and to introduce French goods into the Spanish colo-

Above
This painting by O.C. Seltzer illustrates the fur traders and trappers of Oklahoma and the West. Courtesy, The Thomas Gilcrease Institute of American History and Art, Tulsa, Oklahoma

Left
French coureurs du bois, *or runners of the woods, were often illegal Indian traders who conducted extensive trade with the Wichita and Comanche Indians of Oklahoma. Reproduced from* The Story of Oklahoma *by Wright. Webb Publishing Company (1929)*

26

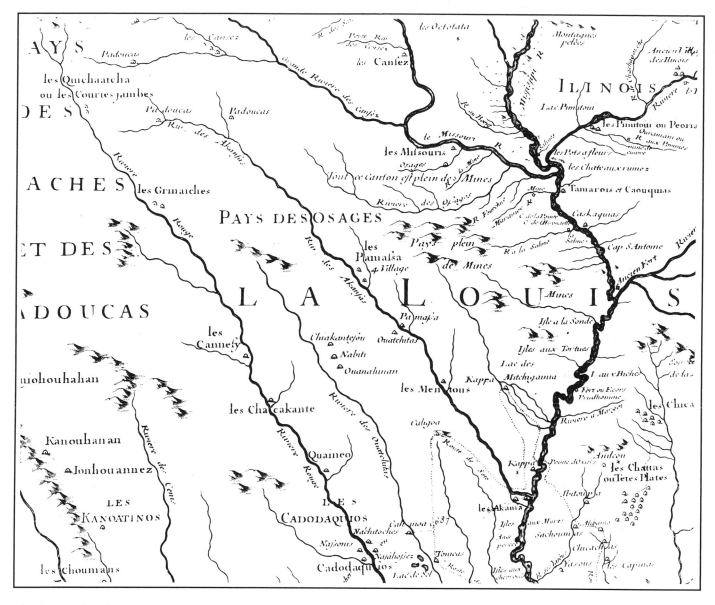

les Cansez
R
Poste Raw
des Canses
les Octotata
Montagnes
pelées
Ancien ville
des Illinois

AYS
Padoucas
les Quichaatcha
ou les Courtes jambes
DES
Padoucas
Grande Riviere des Cansez
le Missouri R
les Cansez
Mississipi R
I L I N O I S
Lake Pimitoui
Riviere Ici
les Pimitoui ou Peoria
Ouramam ou
R aux Hommes

ACHES
les Grinaiches
Riviere des Akansas
les Missouris
Osages
Tout ce Canton est plein des Mines
Riviere des Osages
les Pots a fleur
les Chateaux rumez

PAYS DES OSAGES
R Fourche
Mine
E de la Ponte
E de Missouille
Tamarois et Caouquias
Cascaquias

ET DES
Rouge
les Pamalsa
4 Village
Pays plein de Mines
R a la Saline
les Salines
Cap S. Antone
Riviei

ADOUCAS
LA
LO
U
I
S
Pamassa
Isle a la Sonde
Mines
Ancien Fort

uiohouhahan
les Cannesy
Chiakantesou
Nabiti
Ouatchitas
Ouanahinan
Kappa
Mitchygama
Isles aux Tortues
Lac des
Lau x Biches
de la

Kanouhan an
les Chatcakante
Riviere des Ouatchitas
les Men tous
Calujoa
Fort ou Ecors Prudhomme
Riviere a Margot
les Chica

Jonhouannez
Quaineo
Riviere Rouge
Kappa
Ponte de vou
Andeou
les Chattas
ou Tetes Plates

LES
KANOATINOS
LES
CADODAQUIOS
Calumoa 687
Nachitoches en
les Akania
Isles aux Mures
Sachoumas
Alibamu
Hutou ya

les Choumans
Cadodaquios
Nasonis
Najahossez
Tonicas
Lac de Sel
Roote
Isles aux chenous
Chicachas
Yasous
les Capinas

nies in Mexico (although this was strictly forbidden by Spanish laws that held that all goods sold in New Spain had to come only from the mother country). Nevertheless, Le Mothe Cadillac, Crozat's governor in Louisiana, received orders to make this effort.

As leader of the crucial first expedition, Governor Cadillac selected the daring and enterprising Louis Juchereau de St. Denis, a native of Canada fluent not only in Spanish but also in several Indian dialects. In 1713 St. Denis led a small party of French traders up the Red River. That autumn he traded with the Natchitoches Indians, reconnoitered the area, and established a trading post named for the local natives. Possibly he explored into the present Oklahoma before traveling in 1714 across Texas to the Rio Grande to attempt trade with Spaniards. He was arrested, however, as a foreign intruder,

his goods were confiscated, and he was taken to Mexico City for questioning by the viceroy.

The sudden appearance of Frenchmen in Texas caused Spanish officials to order the colonization of East Texas, a task undertaken in 1716. Two years later, San Antonio was settled as a halfway station between Spanish outposts on the Rio Grande and those in East Texas. Eventually San Antonio would become the center of Spanish activity in Texas. That same year Bienville le Moyne founded New Orleans, which would become the capital of French Louisiana.

In the three decades that followed, Spanish and French officials in Louisiana and Texas contended for supremacy in trade with the Indians of the Great Plains, especially those in North Texas and Oklahoma. This was done partly for the profits involved,

This French map of 1718 shows the locations of the Mississippi Valley and Plains tribes when contacted by French traders and trappers operating out of New Orleans. Courtesy, Library of Congress, Geography and Map Division

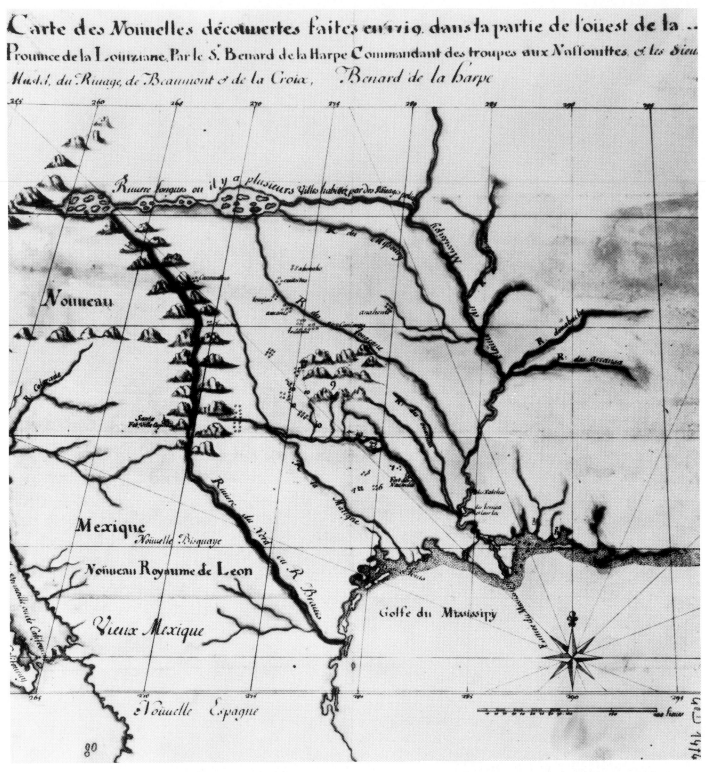

but more for the loyalty and military support of these tribes. European colonists, Spanish and French, were so few in number that the nation which won the loyalty of the Indians would dominate the area. In short, the Indians of Oklahoma had become pawns in a game of imperial rivalry for mastery of the interior of North America.

In this contest the French proved superior.

French traders, called *coureurs du bois* (literally "runners of the woods"), used the Mississippi and its lower tributaries, the Red and the Arkansas, as highways into Oklahoma. Soon canoes, pirogues, and flatboats were plying these streams carrying French guns, ammunition, knives, axes, beads, cloth, ribbon, and assorted trade goods upriver to be traded for bales of muskrat, beaver, and other furs, even tanned buffalo robes, which made their way to New Orleans and eventually to France to be used to make fashionable clothes. Each French trader was an agent of empire for his distant king, for the government of the region had changed.

In 1717 Louis XV revoked the charter given Antoine Crozat, awarding it to John Law, a refugee from Scotland, who used it as the basis for one of the greatest swindles in history. Forming the "Louisiana Company," Law began selling stock and from the income gained from sales, he began paying handsome dividends—and then sold yet more stock at even higher prices. Law was hailed as a financial genius—until 1721 when the "Mississippi Bubble" burst and Law fled France. Thereafter Louisiana was a royal colony administered by a governor appointed by the crown.

During and after the frenzied period of Law's company, sons of France were quietly roaming the Mississippi Valley—and Oklahoma—trading and expending French influence among the Indians. In 1719 Charles Claude du Tisne went up the Mississippi to the Missouri River to open trade with the Osage and Missouri Indians. Then, moving southwest into northern Oklahoma, Du Tisne visited Wichita villages along the Arkansas (near the present Newkirk). His goal was to reach New Mexico for he had hopes of opening trade with Spanish settlers there.

Another trader, Bénard de la Harpe, came from New Orleans in the spring of 1719 to Indian villages along the Red River in eastern Oklahoma. La Harpe there dispatched one of his aides, the Sieur du Rivage, westward to explore the possibility of opening trade with Spaniards at Santa Fe. In June 1719 Du Rivage reported that he had visited Wichita villages on the Red River, given presents to the Apaches he encountered, and had met a tribe of newcomers to western Oklahoma, the Comanches.

La Harpe, meanwhile, had moved north from the Red to the Canadian to the Arkansas River (at the future site of Haskell in Muskogee County), where he found Indian villages with some 7,000 natives living in "dome-shaped houses of straw and reeds covered with earth." In their fields they raised corn, beans, pumpkins, and "prodigious quantities" of tobacco. In the vicinity they hunted bear and deer, and there was good fishing in the river. Each October the

tribe hunted buffalo in the plains to secure a winter's supply of meat and a year's supply of hides. Already the horse had become a part of their culture. La Harpe noted that the Wichitas were "unable to do without them either in war or hunting." He wrote that the Wichitas were "people of good sense, cleverer than the nations of the Mississippi, but the fertility of the country makes them lazy. They are always sitting around their chief and usually they think only of eating, smoking and playing." After two pleasant days of being feasted, La Harpe left, instructing one of his men to "carve on a post the arms of the king and the company and the day and year of taking possession." In his report he recommended that the Louisiana Company should establish a permanent trading post with these friendly Indians, using this as a base from which to open trade with the plains natives.

La Harpe was so impressed with Du Rivage's report about the Comanches that he determined to make a personal visit westward "to make an alliance with [them] . . . in order to shorten the way into New Mexico . . ." Going up the Arkansas, he paused at every Indian village along the way to give presents of guns, powder, shot, knives, and hatchets to the chiefs, and he spoke of the advantages of friendship with France.

La Harpe was not alone in visiting the Comanches and Apaches, for other French *coureurs du bois* had learned the route from Louisiana to western Oklahoma. Such visits alarmed Spanish officials in Texas and New Mexico, for they feared that if the French gained total influence among these tribes the natives might drive all Spaniards out of the region. Moreover, the French were trading firearms and alcoholic beverages to the Indians, which was prohibited by Spanish law. When these officials complained to the viceroy, the Marquis de Casafuerte, however, he decided (from the security of his office in Mexico City) that French trade with the plains Indians was harmless, and chose to ignore the threat.

French officials in Louisiana regarded the opening of trade with the plains Indians as extremely significant. Du Tisne was called for a personal report to Governor Bienville, who in the early 1720s decided to attempt an alliance with the Comanches. He named Etienne Venieard, Sieur du Bourgmont, to head another expedition to western Oklahoma. Bourgmont was a dashing adventurer married to an Indian and fluent in several dialects. After months of preparation, Bourgmont set out in February 1723, arriving in the Comanche country in the spring of 1724 and making contact with several bands of the tribe. These lords of the plains proved friendly to the Frenchman, and some of the chiefs returned to New Orleans with Bourgmont where they were given guns, ammunition, and steel knives.

These new weapons of war, along with the ones they acquired in trade with the French, so strengthened the Comanches that they grew more powerful than the neighboring Apaches, and the balance of power on the plains was upset. The Comanches, cousins of the Arapaho, originally had lived in the Rocky Mountains, but about the turn of the eighteenth century they had emerged onto the plains to capture mustang horses. Mounted on these and equipped with French weapons, they started moving south in search of a better homeland. In 1706 they made their first recorded appearance at Santa Fe, and by 1743 they had moved as far south as San Antonio, driving their Apache enemies before them. Spaniards in Texas bore the brunt of French trade with the Comanches, for Spaniards steadfastly had refused to supply any tribe with firearms. Almost without realizing it, the Spaniards thereby were forced into a disastrous alliance with the Apaches, who were desperately seeking some way to combat the advancing Comanches.

French influence with the plains tribes continued to grow, thanks to the efforts of remarkable frontiersmen such as Bénard de la Harpe, who reached Santa Fe in 1724. Other French explorers crossed Oklahoma to arrive at the foothills of the Rocky Mountains by mid-eighteenth century, placing themselves in the good graces of the natives along the way because of their non-restrictive trade policies. They would sell anything—firearms, firewater, ammunition, gunpowder, and knives, along with mirrors, beads, ribbons, and vermilion. They liberally gave gifts and cultivated friendships, and thus through their economic policies they were an instrument of imperial destiny for France. In 1741 Fabry de la Bruyere set out in company with soldiers and trappers in an attempt to map the route from Louisiana to Santa Fe. He ascended the Arkansas to the Canadian River and pushed up it to the

point near the present boundary between McIntosh and Hughes counties, but there he was halted by shallow water and sandbars.

By the mid-eighteenth century French influence in Oklahoma had become so significant that many Indian tribes had forsaken their old ways to become commercial fur hunters. Bales of fur came out of Oklahoma each year by pirogue and flatboat on the Arkansas and Red rivers. The French left behind children who were part European, as well as place names including Poteau, San Bois, Fourche Maline, Cavanal, Sallisaw, Bayou Menard, Verdigris, Salina, and Vian Creek (originally known as Bayou Viande). The French flag also flew over Wichita villages on the Canadian and Arkansas rivers. Like the Spaniards in Texas who allied with the Apaches, however, the Frenchmen who traded in Oklahoma had identified themselves too closely with one tribe, the Wichita, who were bitter enemies of the powerful Osage nation. As Osage attacks increased from the north, Wichita bands gradually moved south to form two new villages on the Red River: San Bernardo, in present Jefferson County, Oklahoma, and San Teodoro, in what is now Montague County, Texas. By 1749 only one Wichita village was still on the Arkansas: Fernandina (near the present Newkirk). Fernandina fell before an Osage onslaught in 1757, and the residents moved south to San Bernardo and San Teodoro. There they built palisaded walls around their towns, and they sought an alliance with the masters of the plains, the Comanches.

The Osages, Wichitas, and Comanches were pushing Spaniards in Texas hard. A year after Fernandina fell to the Osages, the Comanches destroyed a Spanish mission built for Apaches at San Saba, Texas. That raid in 1758 triggered a Spanish reprisal the following year when the viceroy in Mexico City determined to avenge what he saw as an insult to Spanish honor. In August of 1759 Colonel Diego Ortíz de Parilla led a force of 380 soldiers and more than 100 Apache allies north to strike the Comanches. Arriving at the Red River in October, Parilla found the Comanches and their Wichita allies inside a palisaded fort surrounded by a moat, over which flew a French flag. A Spanish charge proved fruitless, and general fighting ensued. That evening Colonel Parilla counted his casualties

The Plains Apache Indians were fierce rivals of the Comanches and Wichitas during the period of French control of Oklahoma. OHS

and learned that his Apache allies had stolen many of his horses and had escaped into the night. Parilla wisely chose to retreat, leaving behind the eleven cannons so laboriously brought from San Antonio and which proved unable to batter down the walls of the Indian fort.

Parilla's report of French influence among the plains Indians caused considerable consternation among officials in Mexico City. Yet the Indians so outnumbered Spanish soldiers on the northern frontier that it was hopeless to think of total war as a solution. Swallowing his pride, the governor of Texas hired Athanase de Mézières, a French trader from Louisiana, who persuaded the Comanches to return the cannons abandoned by Parilla.

Spanish fears of French influence on the plains tribes ended in 1762. The close of the Seven Years' War (known in America as the French and Indian War) saw England victorious in Canada, India, and the Continent. Spaniards, who had been dragged into this conflict on the side of France, suffered the loss of Florida to England, while France lost so decisively it feared the hated British would get all former French colonies in North America. To compensate Spain for the loss of Florida—and to prevent England from taking it—France gave Spain all the Louisiana Territory west of the Mississippi River, thereby making Oklahoma Spanish once again.

During the next four decades the region was under Spanish rule, although the traders coming up the Red and Arkansas rivers were Louisianans of French descent—the sons and grandsons of the *coureurs du bois* who had opened the region to trade. The governor at New Orleans tried to halt the traffic in guns for which the Wichitas had been famous, and their prosperity began to wither away, as did their power and influence as traders and allies of the Comanches.

During this last phase of European ownership, Oklahoma was still a source of furs, but on a declining scale.

It was during this period that Bénard de la Harpe's dream of using Oklahoma as a highway of commerce to New Mexico finally was realized. In September 1786 Governor Domingo Cabello y Robles of Texas called Pedro Vial to his office and hired him to open a road from San Antonio to Santa Fe. Vial, a Frenchman from Louisiana, went north from San Antonio to San Bernardo and then up the Red River to its source, reaching Santa Fe on May 26, 1787, after traveling more than 1,100 miles. The following year Vial made a similar journey from Santa Fe to the village on the Red River, from there to Nacogdoches in East Texas, and then to San Antonio.

The route Vial pioneered from Santa Fe to the Wichita village on the Red River was used by some traders who went from New Mexico to San Bernardo and then on to New Orleans. Thereafter a regular traffic soon developed between Louisiana and New Mexico. Huge two-wheeled carts, little changed from those used in biblical days, came squealing down from Santa Fe loaded with woolen blankets, piñon nuts, even furs, and returned carrying imported items needed in the west. Spanish coins were used to pay for food and lodging along the way, and today treasure hunters still find gold and silver coins *(pedazos de ocho)* buried near the banks of the Red River.

Such was the nature of European Oklahoma: a place where golden villages were sought, where Spaniards and Frenchmen battled for Indian loyalties, and where roads crossed the region. This era came to an end not because Spaniards or Frenchmen desired it, but because of events in Europe. The kaleidoscope of history was turning in Paris, Madrid, London, and Washington, and this would determine Oklahoma's future.

CHAPTER III

Oklahoma Becomes American

Thomas Jefferson ignored congressional opposition when he began negotiations to obtain the Louisiana Purchase for the United States. When the purchase was made, Oklahoma and the Trans-Mississippi West was added to the United States, more than doubling the size of the young country. Courtesy, Western History Collections, University of Oklahoma Library

*T*he revolution which began in France in 1789 was a fire that burned fiercely. Within three years it brought Louis XVI and Marie Antoinette to the guillotine, and France moved from monarchy to republic and then to anarchy. Out of the ashes of this social fire in 1799 came Napoleon Bonaparte, an emperor with visions of restoring his nation to greatness as a colonial power. Casting his eyes to the south, he saw a weak Charles IV on the throne of Spain, a king who had abdicated the day-to-day affairs of government to Prince Manuel Godoy. Napoleon summoned Charles IV and Prince Godoy north to inform them that he wished Louisiana returned to France. On October 1, 1800, they drafted and signed the secret Treaty of San Ildefonso, which retroceded Louisiana to France.

With Louisiana again French—on paper—Napoleon quickly moved to take actual possession. In November 1801 he sent his brother-in-law, Marshal V.E. LeClerc, with an army of 10,000 men to suppress a slave rebellion against French ownership of Haiti and then to occupy Louisiana. When LeClerc arrived on the island of Santo Domingo, he found the former slaves united and ready for war under the leadership of Toussaint L'Overture. At first the battles were won by Frenchmen, and L'Overture was captured by intrigue (later to die in a French prison in the Alps).

However, LeClerc's soldiers had no experience with tropical diseases, particularly yellow fever. Unaccustomed to the ravages of this scourge, they died in incredible numbers. More and yet more troops arrived from France only to become infected and die, as did LeClerc. After 27,000 men had been sent to the New World and Haiti still had not been reconquered, Napoleon at last realized he would have to grant the island-nation its independence. Nor could he spare additional men to occupy Louisiana, for by

1802 war with England again loomed. The French emperor clearly understood that when this war began, England, with its control of the seas, could easily take Louisiana from him. Determined that the hated "nation of shopkeepers" would not own this territory, he decided to sell it to the United States, commenting early in 1803:

I know all the value of Louisiana . . . . A few lines of a treaty have given it back to me, and hardly have I recovered it when I must expect to lose it. But if I lose it, it will be dearer one day to those who compel me to abandon it [England] than to those to whom I wish to deliver it [the United States].

In the United States, almost since it was recognized as an independent nation, Americans had been casting covetous eyes on Spanish Louisiana, and particularly the port of New Orleans. Frontiersmen in the backcountry of Tennessee and Kentucky were floating their produce down the Mississippi to that city for shipment to the East Coast. Spanish officials periodically halted this flow of goods, causing the frontiersmen to complain loudly to their national government. By 1801 the newly installed president, Thomas Jefferson, was listening—and hoping for an opportunity to make a change.

Jefferson heard of the secret Treaty of San Ildefonso and, at first, watched to see what move the French might make. When nothing happened—because of yellow fever in Haiti— he decided at last to act. In January of 1803 he asked the Senate to name James Monroe as minister extraordinary with authority to work with Robert Livingston, the American minister in France, to seek the purchase of New Orleans from Napoleon. The Senate concurred, and Congress voted a secret appropriation of two million dollars for such a purchase.

In France, war with England was rapidly approaching. Early in March, Napoleon told the British ambassador that France must have ownership of the island of Malta or war with England would result. War obviously was what he would get, and both nations began feverish preparations. Thus on April 10 Napoleon told his finance minister, the Marquis Francois de Barbe-Marbois, "I renounce Louisiana. It is not only New Orleans that I cede; it is the whole colony without reserve." The next day Robert Livingston was told that

the United States was to be the unwitting beneficiary of European intrigues.

James Monroe arrived the following day, April 12, armed with orders from Jefferson to attempt to buy New Orleans. It was Livingston, however, who conducted most of the negotiations with Barbe-Marbois. Napoleon had told Barbe-Marbois that he would accept fifty million francs; the marquis, hoping to impress his emperor, doubled that amount when he made his first offer to Livingston. The American minister countered with an offer of twenty million francs. Back and forth the haggling went until at last a figure of sixty million francs was set—with the United States requesting twenty million francs to indemnify Americans who had claims against France. This final sum, in total, amounted to fifteen million dollars. When the agreement was signed on April 20, 1803, Livingston commented, "We have lived long, but this is the noblest work of our lives."

That noble work proved a headache for President Jefferson when the treaty reached his desk. He had long maintained that the national government had only those powers specifically granted it in the Constitution— and nowhere in that document did it state that the government could acquire territory. Yet he strongly wanted Louisiana. All his life he had idealized agriculture as a way of life, for he thought farming developed moral and political virtue in people. He therefore wanted the United States to be a land of yeoman farmers, and the Louisiana Territory, he believed, would provide sufficient land for the farms needed by Americans for the next 500 years. Caught in this dilemma, Jefferson first considered a constitutional amendment to authorize the purchase; the amendment would also have provided for creating an Indian state in part of the Louisiana Territory. Yet Jefferson knew that amending the Constitution took time, perhaps years, and he had no time. He was continually receiving letters from Livingston urging quick ratification of the treaty before Napoleon's fertile mind found another use for Louisiana.

Jefferson therefore sent the treaty to the Senate. That body concurred that, although the Constitution did not specifically state that the nation had the right to acquire territory, this right was inherent in national sovereignty, and the treaty was ratified. On December 15, 1803, American commissioners were in New Orleans to take possession from Frenchmen, who only a short time before had themselves taken ownership from Spaniards. The ceremony of raising the American flag was then repeated at other places, such as St. Louis, in the months that followed. The land later to be known as Oklahoma (except for its Panhandle) had become part of the United States.

The Louisiana Purchase immediately brought new problems, however. The actual boundaries of the area were unclear, for neither Spain nor France had ever drawn specific lines separating Louisiana from Texas and New Mexico. The French negotiators who sold the territory to the United States recognized the vagueness of this boundary, Napoleon himself commenting, "If an obscurity did not already exist, it would, perhaps, be good policy to put one there." By this he meant that the United States thereby was free to claim as much Spanish territory as it could defend. After the transfer to American ownership, the Spanish commissioners at New Orleans, Manuel Salcedo y Salcedo and the Marques de Casa Calvo, withdrew west of the Sabine River (the present boundary between Louisiana and Texas) to await developments.

Jefferson wanted to quickly determine the limits of the land he had bought. Even before the purchase, his curiosity had led him to propose an exploratory party into the American West, resulting in the expedition of Meriwether Lewis and William Clark, who trekked to the mouth of the Columbia River in Oregon and back to St. Louis between 1804 and 1806. Simultaneously Jefferson sent explorers into the Southwest to learn the sources and courses of the Red and Arkansas rivers, important in setting a boundary between American and Spanish territory. No exact maps existed, and knowledge was a weapon that negotiators could use to advantage.

In April 1804 Congress appropriated $3,000 for Sir William Dunbar and Dr. George Hunter to lead the expedition in search of the rivers' headwaters, but the effort failed. The two scientists were blocked by Spaniards in Texas, who did not want Americans to gain a favorable boundary settlement. Therefore Dunbar and Hunter spent the money exploring for four months in the Quachita River Valley of Arkansas, an area already settled by American frontiersmen. Although Dunbar and Hunter made no geographic discoveries, they did gather valuable scientific information.

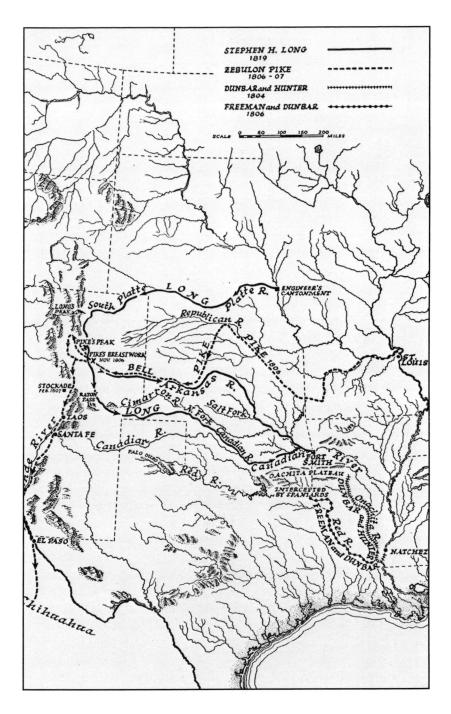

Before Jefferson could send yet another expedition westward, General James Wilkinson, commander of American forces in Louisiana, ordered young Lieutenant Zebulon Montgomery Pike into the region to search for the headwaters of the Arkansas and to open commerce with the plains Indians. Wilkinson's reasons for sending Pike are unclear, but the general was heavily involved with former Vice-President Aaron Burr, who perhaps had thoughts of taking some Spanish territory by force.

Lieutenant Pike set out from St. Louis on July 15, 1806, going west by way of the

This map shows the routes of the American explorers in the Great Plains from 1804 to 1819. OHS

Lieutenant Zebulon M. Pike, the "lost pathfinder," led the first American expedition across the Great Plains in 1806. His assistant, Lieutenant James B. Wilkinson, was the first American to record his travels through Oklahoma. OHS

Missouri and Osage rivers. He was accompanied by James B. Wilkinson, son of the general, twenty-three whites, and fifty-one Osage and Pawnee Indians. Turning south at the mouth of the Osage River, the group arrived at Osage villages near the Lake of the Ozarks. From there they made their way northwestward to Pawnee villages on the Republican River (near the present Kansas-Nebraska border). Pike found the Pawnees unfriendly, having recently been visited by a 600-man Spanish force from New Mexico commanded by Lieutenant Colonel Facundo Melgares. A Spanish flag flew over the village, and around the chiefs' necks were Spanish medals, but Pike persuaded the Pawnees to replace the Spanish flag with the flag of the United States. He and his party then rode to the Arkansas River, reaching it near the present town of Great Bend, Kansas. At that point, because

young Wilkinson was seriously ill, he and six men were allowed to begin a return trip to the Mississippi by way of the Arkansas River.

Pike subsequently pushed into Colorado, discovered the peak that today bears his name, and turned south into New Mexico. There he was captured by Spanish soldiers, taken to Santa Fe and then to Chihuahua City for questioning, and finally marched across Texas to Louisiana, arriving there on July 1, 1807.

Meanwhile, Lieutenant Wilkinson and his six companions were struggling down the Arkansas River and crossing the northeastern part of Oklahoma. They started downriver on October 28, 1806, hoping to reach friendly Indians or traders before the winter became too harsh, but their boats immediately ran aground on sandbars and ice. Soon they abandoned their boats, each man carrying a gun, a buffalo robe, and a few cups of corn. Two weeks later they reached the site of the present Wichita, Kansas. There they decided to try the river once more, and ten days were consumed in felling trees and fashioning canoes. Again, however, the boats snagged on sandbars and ice. Moreover, the canoe holding the major part of their food and ammunition overturned, and these essential supplies were lost.

As the men crossed into Oklahoma they seemed doomed, but there they were befriended by Osage Indians who offered to kill fresh meat for them while they rested in an Osage camp. While there, Wilkinson was told that Tuttasuggy, an Osage chief, was ill and needed medical attention. Wilkinson agreed to help, traveling on November 30 by mule to an Osage village located near the present Ponca City. This marked the first entrance of an official American exploration in what soon would be the Indian Territory.

On December 1, Wilkinson and his six companions resumed their journey, fighting ice on the river day after weary day. They rested for three days at the mouth of the Salt Fork River, Wilkinson using the time to write in detail on the hunting habits of the Osages and the location of their villages. On December 10, they were at the site of Sand Springs, pausing there to make a small side journey up the Cimarron River, which Wilkinson labeled the Saline because the Osages gathered salt along its marshes. By December 23, the party rested at an

This portrait of Chief Clermont was painted by George Catlin. Clermont led his band of Great Osages from central Missouri to northeastern Oklahoma to conduct fur trading with the Chouteaus at the Three Forks region. OHS

Osage village at the confluence of the Verdigris and Grand rivers. There Wilkinson took another side trip, this time sixty miles up the Verdigris to the Osage village of Chief Clermont (near present Claremore). Clermont was the hereditary chief of the Great Osage, but when he was a child his place had been assumed by Pawhuska (White Hair) with the aid of Pierre Chouteau, a trader working out of Missouri. Pierre's halfbrother Auguste Chouteau, a merchant living in St. Louis, had been given a monopoly on trade with the Osages in 1794, but in 1802 his license was revoked by the governor-general of Louisiana. Unwilling to lose this profitable trade, he sent his halfbrother Pierre to persuade the

Osages to leave their traditional homeland in Missouri to live along the banks of the Arkansas in Oklahoma, and some 3,000 Osages agreed to move, driving out both Caddos and Wichitas.

Leaving the Three Forks area where Muskogee eventually would grow, Wilkinson and his party on December 29 arrived at "a fall of near seven feet perpendicular" (Webbers Falls). At last, on January 7, 1807, the weary travelers arrived at Arkansas Post (where the Arkansas joins the Mississippi). There their journey ended.

The reports of Pike and Wilkinson left President Jefferson still without exact knowledge about the Arkansas and Red rivers, and he was so anxious to learn the

Osage Chief Pawhuska settled his band in north-central Oklahoma on the fringe of the Great Plains. OHS

geography of the area that he had already sent another expedition into the region. In April 1806, Thomas Freeman and a party that included Captain Richard Sparks and Peter Custis moved up the Red River to Natchitoches, Louisiana. Late in May, Freeman set out upriver with thirty-seven men in two flatboats and a pirogue.

They immediately encountered great hardship, for just above Natchitoches was the Great Raft, a logjam extending more than seventy miles along the river. Sweating and cursing, they cut their way through this maze of wood following the serpentine course of the river. Adding to their misery was the fear of what lay ahead, for on June 8 Freeman received word that a large Spanish army was moving up from San Antonio to intercept the Americans and prevent their exploring and mapping the Red River. When at last Freeman's party reached the Great Bend of the Red, they were warned by Caddo Indians that Spaniards were in the area.

The two parties met on July 28. Captain Francisco Viana and 150 Spanish soldiers were waiting near the site of Wichita Falls, Texas. Freeman, faced with a superior force, agreed to turn back, and after a harsh return journey reached the Mississippi River in August 1806. Although the expedition had failed to find the source of the Red, it had mapped 635 miles of the river

and had gathered a considerable amount of scientific information about the region.

Less interested in knowledge than profits were the civilian traders who, like the Chouteau brothers, began working in Oklahoma at this time. When Lieutenant James Wilkinson was making his way down the Arkansas in January 1807, he met James Bogy and a party of traders coming upriver. Bogy had secured a license to trade with the Osages, and had loaded a boat with goods. At the Three Forks area Bogy ascended the Verdigris a short distance, erected log cabins, and began trading for pelts. Despite the conflict between the tribes contending for supremacy in the region, he would stay.

In 1811 another official American expedition would venture into Oklahoma, this one led by George Champlin Sibley, son of John Sibley, who was in charge of the Red River and Sulphur Fork Indian Factory, a licensed trading post in Louisiana. Sibley, who was to solicit the plains Indians' friendship for the United States, first visited the Osages, then went to the Great Salt Plains and explored the Salt Fork River (in present Alfalfa County). In the process he made copious notes about the geography of the region.

Despite the many explorations, Oklahoma largely remained a mystery to map makers. Moreover, the headwaters of the Red and Arkansas rivers still had not been discovered. Despite this scarcity of hard knowledge, the United States and Spain, once the Napoleonic wars ended in 1815, negotiated their way toward an agreement about the boundary separating the Louisiana Territory and Texas. When finally signed, the Treaty of 1819 (also known as the Adams-Onís Treaty) provided for the boundary to begin three marine leagues out in the Gulf of Mexico, proceed up the south or west bank of the Sabine River to its intersection with the 32nd parallel, go due north to the Red River, move west along its south or west bank to its intersection with the 100th meridian, run due north to the Arkansas, proceed along its south or west bank to its source, then run due north to the 42nd parallel, and follow that parallel to the Pacific Ocean. The American desire to have total ownership of the Sabine, Red, and Arkansas rivers (rather than run up the middle of each river, as usually was the case in drawing boundaries) stemmed from earlier difficulties with Spain over the right of transit on the Mississipi. No such quarrel could

develop if the United States totally owned these rivers. From this eventually would come Oklahoma's complete ownership of the Red, which it shares as a boundary with Texas (a point that became extremely important when oil was discovered in the bed of the river).

Following this treaty the United States naturally needed to learn the source of the Arkansas and Red rivers and to have these streams mapped accurately. Sent to accomplish these tasks was Major Stephen Harriman Long. During the summer of 1820, Long, accompanied by nineteen soldiers and Dr. Edwin James, a scientist, journeyed first to the source of the Arkansas, and then into Oklahoma, leaving half his command to float down the Arkansas under the leadership of Captain John R. Bell. In Oklahoma, Long mistook the Canadian for the Red River and set out down it, eventually reaching the Arkansas and joining with Captain Bell to continue into Arkansas Territory, which had been created the previous year. Once again Oklahoma had been penetrated by Americans.

In his report Long asserted, as had Pike, that the Great Plains constituted a "Great American Desert" on which only a nomadic population could live. He argued that the region was forever unfit for habitation by people depending on agriculture for a living, saying that, although some of the soil was fertile and that some timber and water were present in isolated spots, the area could never be of any value—except as a buffer to prevent too wide a dispersement of the American population. In short, Long saw the Great American Desert as a barrier to westward expansion. Because of his pessimistic report, few frontier Americans wanted to move there.

Nevertheless, the United States was the owner of this vast expanse of land, and it occurred to some national leaders that, if farmers could not exist there, it might be an ideal place to remove all Indians living east of the Mississippi. As early as 1803 Thomas Jefferson had written of the possibility of

*Right
This map was part of
Stephen Long's report. It
clearly shows the area la-
beled the "Great American
Desert" crossing western
Oklahoma. Courtesy, The
Thomas Gilcrease Institute
of American History and
Art, Tulsa, Oklahoma*

*Opposite page, top
During Stephen Long's ex-
pedition across the central
Great Plains, the explorer
contacted several Indian
tribes. An important tribe
located strategically in
eastern Kansas was the
Kansas or Kaw Indians.
Here warriors of the tribe
attempt to impress Long
and his men with a war
dance. Courtesy, The
Thomas Gilcrease Institute
of American History and
Art, Tulsa, Oklahoma*

*Opposite page, bottom
The report of Stephen
Long's expedition in the
Great Plains was illustrated
with views of the lands that
they crossed and of the explorers themselves. Here
the caravan marches
through the foothills of the
Rocky Mountains in east-
ern Colorado, heading
south to Oklahoma. Cour-
tesy, The Thomas Gilcrease
Institute of American History and Art, Tulsa,
Oklahoma*

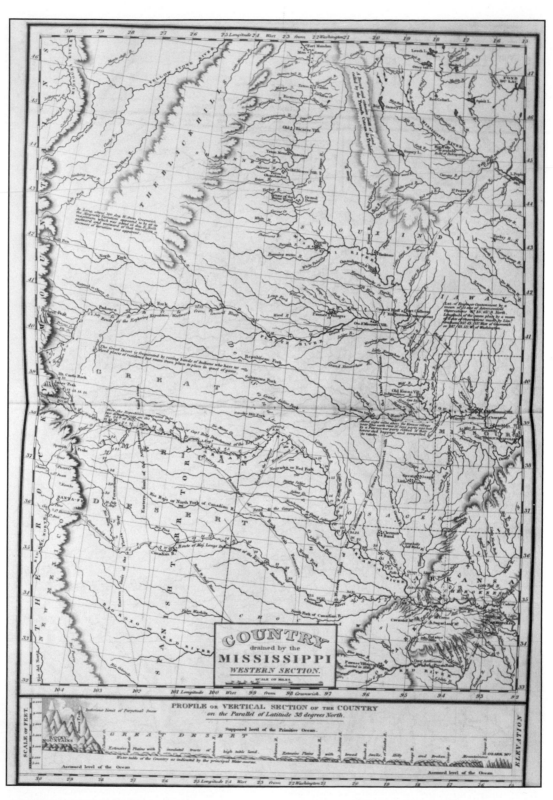

using part of the Louisiana Purchase as a home for eastern Indians. Little came of this suggestion until 1823 when Secretary of War John Calhoun began worrying with the problem of what to do with these Native Americans.

Calhoun drafted a plan for removing all eastern Indians to the Great American Des-

ert, noting that 53,625 Cherokees, Creeks, Choctaws, and Chickasaws still owned 33,573,176 acres in Georgia, Alabama, Mississippi, North Carolina, and Tennessee, while 5,000 Seminoles owned a sizable portion of Florida. These Indians, Calhoun suggested, should be removed to an "Indian Territory." President James Monroe, in pre-

senting this plan to Congress in his annual message on January 27, 1825, stated that it would "promote the interests and happiness of these tribes," to which "the attention of the Government has long been drawn with great solicitude." In 1830 Congress agreed with this proposal, setting aside the Indian Territory and requiring all non-Indians within that area to leave unless specifically licensed to trade with the Indians. However, some Indians from the eastern states already had been forced to move to the territory long before Congress legislated the policy as a national goal.

CHAPTER IV

The Indian Territory

Pushmataha was principal chief of the Choctaw Nation prior to and during removal. He allied his tribe to the United States during the War of 1812 and the Creek Wars, winning the admiration of General Andrew Jackson. OHS

*A*t the time of the adoption of the Articles of Confederation during the midst of the American Revolution, one of the most hotly debated issues involved the western land claims of the various states. Some, such as Maryland and Pennsylvania, had definite western limits, while others, such as Virginia and Georgia, laid claim to almost unlimited acres in the West. By July 1778, eight states had signed the Articles, but New Jersey, Delaware, and Maryland refused until all states had ceded their claims to the western lands. Representatives from Maryland argued that the Revolution was a common effort, and therefore the western lands should be a common heritage. The Continental Congress responded in 1780 by asking those states with land claims in the West to surrender them. New York shortly thereafter led the way, followed by Virginia and most other states with claims. Thereupon the Articles of Confederation were ratified. Not until 1802, however, did Georgia finally cede its western land claims, and then only with the provision that the national government extinguish all Indian land titles within that state.

In the northern part of the United States, the policy of removal (or extermination) moved forward rapidly. By the end of the War of 1812, most of the Northeast and some of the Northwest Territory had been cleared of native inhabitants. In the Southeast, however, most of the so-called Five Civilized Tribes—the Cherokees, Creeks, Choctaws, Chickasaw, and Seminoles—were stoutly resisting white encroachment. A few of their number had surrendered and had moved westward, especially among the Cherokees. One small group from this tribe had moved to Texas perhaps as early as 1813 onto land allotted them by the Spanish government in that province (but to which no land title was given). Another slightly larger body of Cherokee had settled in Arkansas.

Yet the majority of the members of the

This chickie, or Seminole Indian dwelling, was similar to most used by that tribe and others of the Five Civilized Tribes prior to their adoption of white ways. OHS

Five Civilized Tribes desired to stay on their traditional lands, and devised several strategies to remain there. They cooperated with the national government, hoping for protection from citizens of the various states. They signed treaties whereby they surrendered part of their lands in order to be guaranteed ownership of their remaining traditional lands. The Cherokees, for example, signed away parts of North Carolina, South Carolina, Tennessee, Kentucky, and Alabama in order to retain acres in eastern Tennessee and northern Alabama.

Another strategy of the Five Civilized Tribes was to adopt white ways in the hope of winning acceptance by their non-Indian neighbors. They adopted white dress and white patterns of farming, owned slaves, sent their children to school, welcomed missionaries and became Christians, and fought on the American side in the War of 1812. Despite these policies, they found no white acceptance—and little federal protection. Land-hungry frontiersmen, land speculators, and gold hunters looked with greed and envy on the fertile acres owned by the Indians, and gradually a series of laws were enacted in Georgia, Alabama, and Mississippi designed to force the Indians westward. Everywhere there was the argument that the federal government had not lived

up to its commitment, made during the ratification of the Articles of Confederation, to remove the Indians. Thus the Indians, despite their resistance, gradually lost skirmish after skirmish to retain their homelands. They lost in state legislatures, in Congress, and finally in the courts.

The first major removal resulted from a meeting of leaders of one group of Cherokees, American officials, and the headmen of the Osages. At this meeting in St. Louis in 1808, the Osage agreed to cede all their land east of a line running directly south from Fort Clark (on the Missouri River) to the Arkansas River. Included in this cession was almost all of the land within the present state of Arkansas north of the Arkansas River, as well as a significant portion of the present state of Missouri. The following January, President Jefferson gave permission for the Cherokees to send exploring parties westward to examine and reconnoiter "the country on the waters of the Arkansas and White rivers, and the higher up [farther upriver] the better, as they will be longer unapproached by our [white] settlement." According to this treaty of removal, heads of Cherokee families were to receive 640 acres, while those not heads of families, called "poor warriors" in the treaty, were to receive "one rifle and ammunition, one blanket and one brass kettle, or in lieu of the brass kettle, a beaver trap." In addition, the government said it would provide flat-bottomed boats to aid any Cherokee moving west.

By the terms of this treaty, such emigration was voluntary, but by 1817 there were some 2,000 Cherokees who moved westward from Tennessee and Georgia into present Arkansas. In their new homeland, east and north of present Fort Smith (between the Arkansas and White rivers), they began erecting homes, clearing land, and planting crops, and in 1813 Major William L. Lovely was sent by Colonel R.J. Meigs, Cherokee Indian agent in Tennessee, to serve as sub-agent to the Western (or Arkansas) Cherokees.

The major problem with this scheme of removal was that the Osages still were contesting for ownership of the land onto which the Cherokees settled. As early as 1814 Subagent Lovely was recommending that a military post be opened on the Arkansas River to keep peace in the region. By the summer of 1816, with no troops yet posted and intertribal warfare more intense than ever, Lovely called for a meeting at the Three Forks area (the present Muskogee) between the Arkansas Cherokees and the Southern Osage. At this council Lovely asked Chief Clermont and the Osages to cede yet another vast tract of land, more than seven million acres, to the United States. On July 9 the Osage chiefs signed the accord agreeing to what became known as Lovely's Purchase. This involved the land bounded on the east by the old Osage line, on the south by the Arkansas River, on the west by the Verdigris River up to the falls, then in a straight line northeast to the saline springs on the Grand River, and from there due east to the Osage line. The Cherokees would become owners of this new land, said Lovely, and thereby peace would return to the region. Lovely did not live to see his hope realized, for he died shortly after securing the purchase that would bear his name.

In the summer of 1817, with warfare still raging between the two tribes, American commissioners met with Eastern Cherokee chiefs to persuade them to remove to Arkansas, thereby throwing their old homeland open to white settlement. The Cherokees agreed, and in return were promised payment for their costs of removal and military

protection in their new homeland. As a result of this treaty, another 4,000 Cherokees would remove westward in the next two years, bringing the total number of Cherokees in Arkansas to some 6,000, and in 1817 Fort Smith would be erected at the junction of the Arkansas and Poteau rivers at a place known as Belle Point.

Yet the strife between the Cherokees and Osages continued to rage, so much so that on September 25, 1818, the United States signed a treaty with the Osages at St. Louis in which the Osages reconfirmed their agreement to Lovely's Purchase made in 1816. This tract then was given to the Arkansas Cherokees as a hunting ground and as a path to the plains for killing buffalo. The hope was that this would bring peace, but soon the Osage and Cherokee nations were at war once again. Because of this, in 1822 Colonel Matthew Arbuckle, commanding officer at Fort Smith, recommended that a garrison be placed at the mouth of the Verdigris River to keep peace in the region.

Orders to this effect were issued early in 1824, and on April 9 Colonel Arbuckle marched his 7th Infantry troops upriver, and on April 22 selected the location of what became known as Fort Gibson, named in honor of Colonel George Gibson, then commissary general of subsistence. Colonel Arbuckle also sent troops to the Red River near its junction with the Kiamichi River to found Fort Towson, named for Nathan Towson, a hero of the War of 1812. Fort Gibson eventually proved to be the most useful post, for it was located near where several major confrontations would occur and because it was situated on three navigable streams (the Arkansas, the Grand, and the Verdigris). Fort Towson proved difficult to supply because the Red River often was unnavigable. In 1825 a road was surveyed to connect Forts Smith and Gibson, paralleling the present route of U.S. 64. Later a road was opened between Forts Smith and Towson, while other roads, really little more than cart paths, were opened across other parts of southeastern Oklahoma.

At the same time the government was persuading the Osages to cede land for Cherokee settlement, it was also pressuring the Quapaws to sign away a huge strip of their homeland. This cession, signed in 1818, defined a tract of land bounded on the south by the Red River and on the

Right
This sketch of Fort Towson, located near the Red River in southeastern Oklahoma, shows the parade ground and barracks of the troops. This post was abandoned in the 1830s as the frontier of the Five Civilized Tribes moved westward. OHS

Below
Reconstruction of the Fort Gibson Stockade was completed during the 1930s. This post is the oldest military fort in Oklahoma. OHS

Malmaison, *the plantation home of Greenwood LeFlore in Mississippi, showed the degree of civilization of the mixed-blood members of the Five Civilized Tribes. When the Choctaw Nation was removed to Indian Territory, LeFlore chose to remain in Mississippi rather than move with his people. OHS*

north by the Canadian and Arkansas rivers. In claiming that this huge area (almost one-third of the present Oklahoma) had become open to settlement by eastern tribes, however, the government ignored the legitimate claims of many other tribes to parts of this land, including the various Caddoan people and, in the west, the roving bands of plains tribes. However, with this treaty signed by the Quapaws, the federal government increased its pressure on the Five Civilized Tribes to remove westward.

Moreover, Congress in 1820 further defined the boundaries of what was increasingly becoming an "Indian Territory." When it passed the Enabling Act for Missouri to enter the Union as a state, Congress set 36°30' north latitude as the dividing point between Missouri and Arkansas. The Indian Territory thus was the area between the Red River and 36°30' north latitude and between the western edge of Arkansas and the 100th meridian.

After some Cherokees recognized the inevitable and began moving westward, part of the Choctaw Nation followed suit. For two decades the white settlers of Mississippi had been pressing the federal government to open Choctaw lands to settlement, and in 1820 Chief Pushmataha represented the tribe in negotiating with General Andrew

Jackson, spokesman for the United States. By terms of the Treaty of Doak's Stand, signed in 1820, the Choctaws, in return for part of their traditional homeland, were given the recently ceded Quapaw Strip (from the Red River north to the Canadian and Arkansas and east into present Arkansas). Any Choctaw warrior who would move west was to be given a rifle, a bullet mold, one year's supply of ammunition, a blanket, a kettle, and money to cover the value of the improvements he had made on the land he left behind. About one-fourth of the tribe eventually left under the terms of the Treaty of Doak's Stand.

Immediately after this treaty was signed, whites in Arkansas protested that it gave away large amounts of land already settled by them. Congress in 1824 responded by defining the western boundary of Arkansas as beginning forty miles west of the southwestern boundary of Missouri and then running due south to the Red River. This pleased whites in Arkansas but greatly disturbed the Choctaws who had removed westward. In 1825 a delegation of Choctaws went to Washington to protest, resulting in yet another agreement, this one setting the western boundary of Arkansas at 100 paces west of Fort Smith and then running due south to the Red River. Thereby the Choctaws re-

Left
William McIntosh, the principal chief of the Lower Creeks, signed away by treaty the majority of his tribe's lands in Georgia in 1825. He was condemned to death by a tribal council and executed by a band of tribesmen outside his home at Indian Springs, Georgia. OHS

Below
During the first century following contact with whites, the Indians of the Southeastern United States accepted many of the ways of the whites. Log houses made of cut logs replaced the thatched huts of earlier days, and iron implements made cultivation easier. Courtesy, Western History Collections, University of Oklahoma Library

gained a forty-mile strip of territory. They were also promised $6,000 a year "forever," a removal of all whites from Choctaw lands, and prevention of any future white settlement on land belonging to the Choctaws.

Also in 1825 the Osage were induced to cede their remaining land in Oklahoma. In 1808, 1816, and 1818 they had made agreements to surrender land, and each time they vowed to live in peace with their neighbors. Yet these promises had always been broken and incessant warfare had raged. The opening of Forts Smith and Gibson failed to bring peace to the region. In 1825, however, faced with rising debts to other tribes and with declining numbers, the Osage, represented by Chiefs Clermont and Pawhuska, agreed to cede all their remaining land except for a reserve fifty miles wide along the southern border of Kansas from the 95th to 100th meridian.

Next to feel the pressure to move were the Creeks. Already in 1814, by the Treaty of Fort Jackson, they had lost domain along the Coosa and Tallapoosa rivers because some of the tribe had fought against the United States during the War of 1812 (the so-called "Red Sticks"). In 1818 they had been forced to cede another fifteen million acres, largely in Georgia. These two losses caused a majority of the tribe to oppose any further cessions—even to oppose talks that might possibly lead to cessions. In 1824 the will of the majority was demonstrated by a tribal order decreeing the death penalty for any Creek who proposed selling land to the whites. Yet within the tribe there were members who foresaw the inevitability of a move westward. This faction was led by William McIntosh, a half-breed related to the governor of Georgia. McIntosh believed the Creeks would prosper only when removed from white influences and pressures. Twice in the early 1820s he tried to sell tribal lands in exchange for a new domain in the West, but both times he was thwarted by conservative Creeks.

In 1824 the United States government, under pressure from Georgians to remove the Creeks, approached the tribe about selling some of its land. McIntosh and his followers indicated a willingness to negotiate, and the Treaty of Indian Springs was signed on February 12, 1825. This provided for the purchase of all Creek lands in Georgia and eastern Alabama in return for land between the Arkansas and Canadian rivers in the

Indian Territory, along with a cash bonus of $400,000.

Although the Treaty of Indian Springs was signed only by McIntosh and fifty other Creeks, the government was so desperate to remove the Creeks from Georgia that it chose to recognize this as binding and sent it to the Senate for ratification. Within a month the Senate voted its approval, causing consternation in the Creek tribal council. The council immediately sent a delegation to Washington to protest that the treaty was illegal, while simultaneously ruling that McIntosh was guilty of treason and subject to the death penalty (as stipulated by Creek law in 1824). On April 30, 1825, a large group of warriors surrounded McIntosh's home. Everyone inside, except McIntosh and one other signer of the treaty, was allowed to leave, after which the house was set afire. When the two men emerged, they were shot. The Creeks always maintained that this was a legal execution, not murder.

President John Quincy Adams, who took

Chilly McIntosh was the son of William McIntosh and the leader of the pro-removal faction of the Creek Nation. OHS

Sequoyah developed a syllabary for his tribesmen, making them among the most literate people in the world at that time. OHS

office on March 4, 1825, also thought the Treaty of Indian Springs was fraudulent, and he nullified it. Public opinion in Georgia, however, was against the Creeks, and finally the tribal leadership realized that bloodshed was inevitable unless some new accord was reached. Therefore a delegation was sent to Washington in the spring of 1826, and a new treaty was signed on April 26, voiding the Indian Springs treaty, but stipulating that most of the Creek lands in Georgia were to be exchanged for a new home for the tribe along the Canadian River plus an immediate cash settlement of $217,600 and an annual allotment of $20,000. In addition, the government was to furnish transportation for this move westward. The McIntosh Creeks, as that faction was called, were to be moved westward at government expense, to settle on unoccupied land somewhere west of the Mississippi River, and to receive $100,000.

The McIntosh Creeks were the only members of that tribe to move immediately. Led by Roley McIntosh, son of the slain chief, this group began settling along the west bank of the Verdigris River early in 1828. The government purchased the improvements made by Auguste and Pierre Chouteau, and after the McIntosh tribe moved there, the old Chouteau trading post became the Indian Agency headquarters. The McIntosh group was fortunate, because the site was near Fort Gibson, giving them protection from the still-belligerent Osages. By 1830 more than 2,000 Creeks were living at this site between the Verdigris and Grand rivers. The majority of the Creek Nation resisted removal, however, and moved from Georgia to settle on remaining tribal lands in Alabama.

During this same period, the government was having problems with white encroachment onto Cherokee lands in present Arkansas. At the time of Lovely's Purchase, the Cherokees were granted the land for hunting and as a path to the plains for pursuing buffalo. By the early 1820s, however, continued white settlement in that area caused the Cherokees to fear that the arrangement might be threatened. In 1822 they sought a congressional guarantee of their right to this land, but nothing was done. Again in 1826 they made the same request of Congress. This caused whites, some of whom were living illegally on the land encompassed by Lovely's Purchase, to petition Congress, through

the Arkansas territorial legislature, for the area to be opened to white settlement. When Congress agreed, settlers rushed in, and almost overnight Lovely's Purchase was transformed into Crawford County by the Arkansas territorial legislature.

The Western Cherokees were shocked and dismayed by this action, as it left them surrounded by white settlers and with no outlet to the plains. They again sent a delegation to Washington to protest that by terms of the Treaty of 1818 they had been promised an outlet to the west. One member of this delegation was Sequoyah, who already had gained fame for the Cherokee syllabary he had invented. The result was a new treaty signed on May 6, 1828, which provided for an exchange of Cherokee land in Arkansas for a new home bounded on the north by the southern border of Kansas, on the south by the fork formed by the Arkansas and Canadian rivers, and on the east by the western boundary of Arkansas. The treaty also promised the Cherokees a permanent outlet to the west, and provided for the removal of all whites from the Indian Territory. The Cherokees were to be paid for all the improvements they had to leave behind in Arkansas and they were given fourteen months to make the move.

When the provisions of this treaty were announced to the Western Cherokees, many of them threatened to inflict on the negotiators the same punishment meted out to

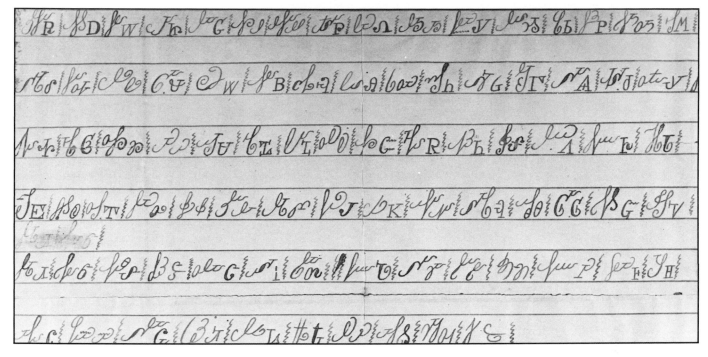

William McIntosh by the Creeks—death. In the face of a binding treaty, however, they had no recourse and began preparations to leave. Simultaneously, the whites in what had been Crawford County did not want to move eastward. Their anger was appeased somewhat by the grants of land made them to the east in Arkansas, and they likewise packed to move, spurred in part by the government's threat that any white not out of the Indian Territory by December 27, 1828, would forfeit any claim to land in Arkansas.

The treaty of 1828 had one additional feature: it sought to reward the genius of one Cherokee: Sequoyah. Born about 1770 in the village of Taskigi, Tennessee, Sequoyah was the son of the trader named Nathaniel Gist. His mother, who was part Cherokee, was abandoned by her husband shortly before the birth of her child. Sequoyah used his Indian name until he approached manhood, at which time he assumed the name George Guess (as he understood his father's last name to be spelled). Crippled for life in a hunting accident, he became an excellent silversmith. As an adult his curiosity was piqued by "talking leaves," as he called books. In 1809 he determined to master this secret and apply it to his own people. After a dozen years of ridicule and insults, he invented a Cherokee alphabet of eighty-five or eighty-six characters, each representing a sound in the tribal language. In 1821 he demonstrated his invention before the Cherokee council, which

approved his work. Within two years thousands of Cherokees had mastered the syllabary, stimulating the printing of books and some newspapers in the Cherokee language, allowing Cherokees in the West to communicate fully with their kinsmen still in the East. In the treaty of 1828 the United States government recognized the importance of Sequoyah's work by awarding him $500 and adding another $1,000 for the Cherokees to buy a printing press.

As a result of the treaty of 1828, the Arkansas Cherokees rapidly moved into the Indian Territory, and they soon erected homes on their new land. Conflicts with the Osage continued, for some members of that tribe were still living on the land promised by the government to the Cherokees. Despite these clashes, the Cherokees cleared land and planted crops.

In their new homeland the Western Cherokees were joined in 1829 by Sam Houston. Born in 1793, Houston had grown to manhood in Tennessee, lived among the Cherokees there from 1809 to 1812, and was given the name "The Raven." Houston in 1819 became attorney general of Tennessee, then a congressman for four years, and finally governor of the state in 1827. In January of 1829 he married Eliza Allen, but in April that year he divorced her, resigned as governor, and fled to the Indian Territory to live among the Cherokees once again. Just a few miles northwest of Fort Gibson he erected Wigwam Neosho, a trading post,

Sequoyah's Cherokee alphabet is depicted in the scholar's own handwriting. Courtesy, The Thomas Gilcrease Institute of American History and Art, Tulsa, Oklahoma

and took a Cherokee wife, Talihina (or Tiana). Twice he represented the Cherokees in dealings with the federal government, traveling to Washington on their behalf. However, in 1831 he was defeated for membership on the tribal council, and the following year he moved to Texas (there to become a hero of the Texas Revolution and twice president of the Republic of Texas).

While the Western Cherokees were successfully settling the Indian Territory, their eastern kinsmen, along with members of the other Five Civilized Tribes, were having difficulties. In Georgia there was mounting white pressure on the Cherokees despite the 1827 tribal constitution patterned on that of the United States; this abolished "tribal government" and established a constitutional republic. The following year the Eastern Cherokees elected John Ross as principal chief. Ross, who was only one-eighth Cherokee, nevertheless adopted the viewpoint of the full bloods and worked diligently to prevent further land cessions or removal westward.

The governor and legislature were determined in 1828 to force a removal, however, and that year passed legislation which made tribal members subject to state laws and declared it illegal for Indians to testify against whites in court. Thus whites who took Indian lands were immune from prosecution because the Indian owners could not testify against them. When gold was discovered on Cherokee land in 1829, the legislature of Georgia declared it unlawful for the Cherokees to prospect for or to mine gold on their own land. That same year the legislature abolished the Cherokee government and announced that all Cherokee lands were the property of the state. The tribal council was forbidden to meet except to discuss removal westward. Another law, aimed at the missionaries working among the Cherokees, required any white living among the Indians to have a permit from state officials.

The Cherokees knew their rights were guaranteed them by treaty with the United States government, but the future was made clear to them when Congress on May 28, 1830, passed the Indian Removal Act, a response to the belief that the West was a "Great American Desert." The Indian Removal Act decreed that Indian lands in the East should be exchanged for land in the West. Although this law did not call for enforced removal, it did recommend it strongly

Right
Samuel Austin Worcester was a Methodist minister and missionary who contributed to the civilizing process of the Cherokee Indians. He suffered imprisonment in Georgia for refusing to obey state statutes that restricted missionaries in Indian lands. Worcester accompanied the Cherokees on the Trail of Tears. OHS

Opposite page, top
Sam Houston befriended the Cherokee Indians while a child in Tennessee. After a tumultuous career in Tennessee politics, Houston rejoined his blood brothers in the Indian Territory, taking a Cherokee woman for a wife and representing them in a conference held in Washington. Courtesy, Western History Collections, University of Oklahoma Library

Opposite page, bottom
John Ross was a one-eighth Cherokee Indian who led his people in the difficult times preceding and following removal to Indian Territory. He died in 1866, after unsuccessfully attempting to lead his tribe through the turmoil of the Civil War. OHS

and empowered the president to work for it. Two years later Congress passed a second Indian Removal Act further strengthening its recommendation of the forcible westward removal of all Indians east of the Mississippi River.

Among the Cherokees, thanks to their own inclination and to the work of dedicated missionaries, the tribe had an educated group of leaders who understood the workings of the American government and thus believed that one other route lay open to them: an appeal to the federal courts. When the state of Georgia in 1831 arrested eleven missionaries for preaching and teaching among the Cherokees without permits from the state, and subsequently sent two of these men, Samuel A. Worcester and Elizar But-

ler, to prison, the Cherokees made their appeal to the federal judiciary. Eventually this dispute reached the United States Supreme Court in the case *Worcester* v. *Georgia*, and in 1832 the Court ruled in favor of the Cherokees by declaring that their status as a "domestic dependent nation" meant that state laws could not be enforced in treaty-guaranteed Cherokee territory. Rulings of the Supreme Court were enforced by the executive branch of government, however, and President Andrew Jackson, a frontiersman from Tennessee, refused to carry out the ruling. Worcester and Butler stayed in the Georgia prison. Thereafter, the fate of the Indians was sealed. They would be moved, willingly or unwillingly, to the Indian Territory.

CHAPTER V

The Trail of Tears

Moshulatubbee, a full-blood Choctaw chief, led his people westward over the Trail of Tears to settle southeastern Indian Territory. Courtesy, Smithsonian Institution

By 1830 only a small part of the Five Civilized Tribes was living in the Indian Territory: some 6,000 Cherokees, 2,000 Creeks, and one-fourth of the Choctaws. The others were tenaciously clinging to their reduced homeland in the Southeast, many hoping that justice somehow would yet prevail. On the other side, however, were whites equally determined that these Native Americans would be moved westward—peacefully if possible, at bayonet point if necessary.

When faced with pressure to move, most Cherokees responded by asking that the provisions of their treaties with the United States be honored. They were instead met with a firm federal demand for removal. In October 1832 President Jackson's representative, E.W. Chesser, conferred with tribal leaders to state this demand clearly. Principal Chief John Ross personally headed a delegation to Washington to respond that the tribe would never consent to removal.

On this trip Ross learned that, although his voice carried weight in Cherokee councils, it had no impact in Washington. Born near Lookout Mountain, Tennessee, in 1790, Ross was the son of a Scottish father and a mother one-quarter Cherokee and three-quarters Scottish. His Indian name was Cooweescoowee, and he was educated by private tutors and then at Kingston Academy in Tennessee. His rise to prominence in the tribe began in 1819, when he was elected a member of the Cherokee National Council. Two years later he became president of the council, a position he held for five years. In 1822 he helped write the Cherokee constitution and was elected assistant chief. Then in 1827 he became principal chief, a position he held until 1839 (although he spoke Cherokee so poorly that he refused to make public speeches in that language. He spoke in English with an interpreter standing by his side to render his words into Cherokee).

Left
John Ridge had at one time opposed cession of tribal lands, but, seeing the inevitable, he signed the Treaty of New Echota, exchanging tribal holdings in Georgia for land in the Indian Territory. He was later assassinated by anti-Treaty supporters of John Ross. OHS

Far left
Major Ridge was leader of the Cherokee Treaty Party supporting removal to Indian Territory. Cherokees opposing removal assassinated him, his son, and nephew after they arrived in the Indian Territory in 1839. OHS

Despite his strong statements in Washington, Ross found several headmen willing to accept removal when the tribe met in council in May 1833. Major Ridge, his son John Ridge, and Elias Boudinot, who spoke for a significant minority of the tribe, suggested that Ross was fighting a losing battle and that the tribe should accept the inevitable. Called the Treaty Party, the Ridge-Boudinot group generally consisted of mixed-blood Cherokees, while the anti-removal group, Ross Party, as that faction was known, largely consisted of full-bloods. Major Ridge had earlier helped execute a headman who in 1808 had signed a treaty selling Cherokee lands, and his son John had been extremely outspoken for many years against removal. Boudinot, a nephew of Major Ridge and editor of the *Cherokee Phoenix,* had written rousing editorials denouncing federal bureaucrats, Georgia functionaries, and members of the tribe who were trying to remove the Cherokees to the Indian Territory. The three men gradually had come to believe, however, that removal was inevitable and that the tribe would prosper in the West (later there would be charges that these three men were bribed by the federal government to speak in favor of removal, but no evidence supports this).

In 1834 the state of Georgia showed its determination to be rid of the Cherokees by passing legislation calling for a survey of Cherokee land and opening it to white settlement by lottery. John Ross lost his property in this way. That same year the Georgia militia marched to New Echota, the Cherokee capital, and smashed the *Cherokee Phoenix* printing press. Such actions caused the Treaty Party to gain yet more followers.

This split in the Cherokee Nation emboldened the federal government. Late in 1835 officials of the Indian Office announced that a general council would be held in December that year at New Echota. To insure that a treaty resulted, federal officials had Ross arrested and held while negotiations were underway. The Treaty of New Echota, concluded on December 29, 1835, provided for a total cession of all Cherokee lands in the Southeast in return for five million dollars and land in the Indian Territory. Leaders of the Treaty Party agreed, although they were warned by the Ross Party that their signatures would constitute their death warrants.

Ross, when freed, protested the treaty and even went to Washington to lobby against its ratification. Nevertheless, the Senate accepted it, and President Jackson signed it into law, although Ross concluded that a majority of the Cherokee Nation would refuse to move. The followers of the Ridges and Boudinot, some 2,000 Cherokees, did emigrate voluntarily. They were paid for their cost of removal and given subsistence for their first year in their new home. The Treaty of New Echota promised them joint ownership of the Cherokee lands

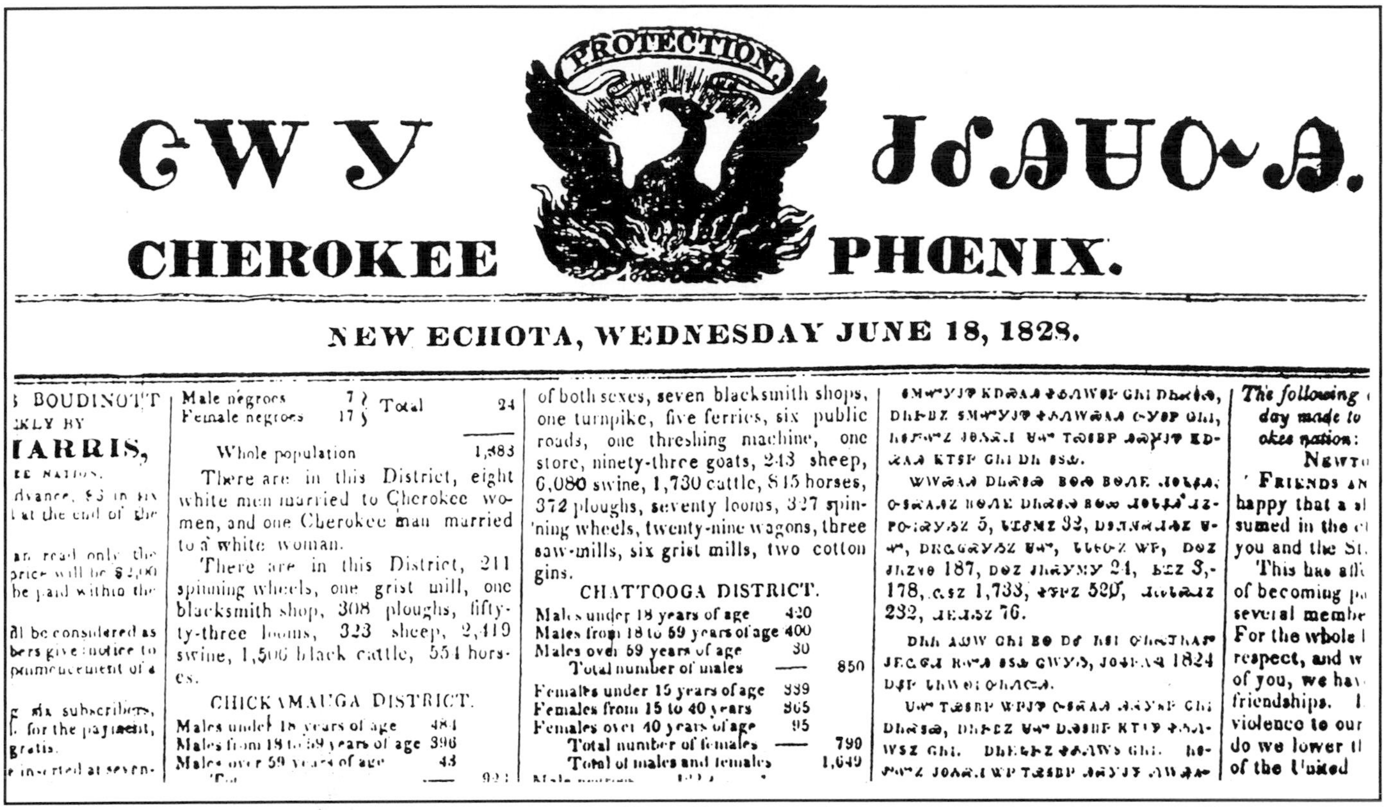

NEW ECHOTA, WEDNESDAY JUNE 18, 1828.

...S BOUDINOTT
...KLY BY
...IARRIS,
...EE NATION.
...dvance, $3 in six
...at the end of the
...an read only the
...price will be $2,00
...be paid within the
...all be considered as
...bers give notice to
...mmencement of a
...r six subscribers,
...for the payment,
...gratis.
...e inserted at seven-

Male negroes	7	Total	24
Female negroes	17		
Whole population			1,883

There are in this District, eight white men married to Cherokee women, and one Cherokee man married to a white woman.

There are in this District, 211 spinning wheels, one grist mill, one blacksmith shop, 308 ploughs, fifty-three looms, 323 sheep, 2,419 swine, 1,506 black cattle, 554 horses.

CHICKAMAUGA DISTRICT.

Males under 18 years of age	484	
Males from 18 to 59 years of age	396	
Males over 59 years of age	43	
T...	—	923

of both sexes, seven blacksmith shops, one turnpike, five ferries, six public roads, one threshing machine, one store, ninety-three goats, 243 sheep, 6,080 swine, 1,730 cattle, 815 horses, 372 ploughs, seventy looms, 327 spinning wheels, twenty-nine wagons, three saw-mills, six grist mills, two cotton gins.

CHATTOOGA DISTRICT.

Males under 18 years of age	420	
Males from 18 to 59 years of age	400	
Males over 59 years of age	30	
Total number of males	—	850
Females under 15 years of age	339	
Females from 15 to 40 years	365	
Females over 40 years of age	95	
Total number of females	—	790
Total of males and females		1,649

The following ...
day made to ...
...okee nation:
NEWTO...
FRIENDS AN...
happy that a ...
sumed in the ...
you and the St...
This has all...
of becoming p...
several membe...
For the whole ...
respect, and w...
of you, we hav...
friendships. I...
violence to our...
do we lower t...
of the United

Above
Pictured is a detail from the front page of the June 18, 1828, Cherokee Phoenix, *which was published at New Echota, Georgia, by Elias Boudinot. This unique newspaper, printed in both English and Cherokee, typified the level of culture attained by members of the Five Civilized Tribes. OHS*

Far right
Elias Boudinot, editor of the Cherokee Phoenix, *was an outspoken critic of efforts to sell tribal lands to the Americans, however, he joined with his uncle Major Ridge and his cousin John Ridge and signed the Treaty of New Echota. OHS*

already assigned in the Indian Territory, and they were allowed to buy an additional 800,000 acres (a strip of land twenty-five miles wide and fifty miles long—in present Kansas adjoining the state of Missouri—for $500,000). In addition, Article 2 of the treaty gave the tribe the Cherokee Outlet, a broad strip of territory stretching from the Cherokee land in northeastern Indian Territory west to the 100th meridian, providing them access to the buffalo plains.

Members of the Ross Party learned to their sorrow that the federal government indeed intended to enforce the Treaty of New Echota. General John E. Wool, a fatuous soldier of little competence more at home behind a desk than in the field, was sent in 1836 to begin the task of removing the Cherokee holdouts. At first Wool harangued the Cherokees to accept the inevitable, but when talking proved futile he erected fenced camps in which Cherokees arrested by his soldiers were held until a sizable party could be gathered and shipped westward. For two years Wool and his troops sent approximately 2,000 of the more than 16,000 Cherokees in Georgia to the Indian Territory. Wool and many of his soldiers hated this job; only Georgia militiamen proved enthusiastic for the task. Ross repeatedly requested delays and worked unceasingly to prevent

removal, but at last President Martin Van Buren grew impatient and sent General Winfield Sott to take command of 7,000 soldiers and speed up the process.

Scott, a competent soldier and humane man who tried to do an unpleasant job without causing undue hardship and suffering, coordinated his troops and began making wholesale arrests, but some of his troops

OKLAHOMA: LAND OF THE FAIR GOD

and many of the Georgia militia committed rape, robbery, and even murder. The Cherokees suffered from hunger and disease, and the death rate rose rapidly among the sick, the aged, and the young. In July 1838 Ross returned from another unsuccessful trip to Washington and found the suffering so intense that he dropped resistance as a weapon. He asked Scott to let the Cherokees themselves oversee their own removal. Scott agreed at once, and by August the *nuna dat suhn'yi*—Trail of Tears—was a reality. Waiting until the heat of summer had passed, Ross sent his people west by overland trail and by boat. Cholera and measles took a heavy toll. Among the dead was Ross' wife, who expired near Little Rock, Arkansas. By December 1838 the last party of Cherokees put Georgia behind to march toward the sunset of the Indian Territory. The Cherokees had been removed.

The following year, 1839, Mirabeau B. Lamar, president of the Republic of Texas (and former secretary to the governor of Georgia) determined to rid that nation of all its native inhabitants. Under his direction the Cherokees who had removed to Texas while it was owned by Spain were driven north into the Indian Territory. For the first time in some four decades the entire Cherokee Nation was together—but at a terrible price in human life.

As the Cherokees were fighting unsuc-

cessfully to stay in Georgia, the remainder of the Five Civilized Tribes were undergoing a similar experience. The first to remove entirely were the Choctaws. When Alabama and Mississippi enacted laws discriminating against Indians, the Choctaws began serious negotiations with the United States, and in September of 1830 the three district chiefs of the nation—Greenwood LeFlore, Moshulatubbee, and Nitakechi—signed the Treaty of Dancing Rabbit Creek. In return for all their lands in the southeastern United States, they were given land between the Red River on the south and the Canadian and Arkansas rivers on the north, and between the Arkansas border and the 100th meridian. The federal government agreed to transport the tribe and to furnish members with food for the first year after their removal. As many tribal members as possible would move "during the falls of 1831 and 1832," and the remainder would move during the autumn of 1833. Any tribal members not wishing to move were to receive individual allotments of land and become citizens of their state of residence. Finally, the federal government, represented in negotiations by Secretary of War John

Steamboats carried members of the Five Civilized Tribes to new homes in the Indian Territory during the Trail of Tears. Later the Arkansas River was an important supply route for the Indians and whites in the territory. OHS

The misery and grief of the Indians on the Trail of Tears is depicted in this painting by Echohawk. Family members lay a lost one to rest in the cold prairie, while even the trooper charged with their forced removal looks on with compassion. Courtesy, The Thomas Gilcrease Institute of American History and Art, Tulsa, Oklahoma

59

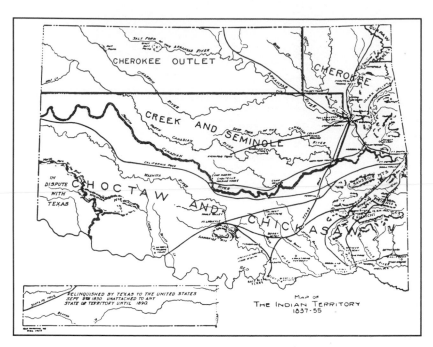

*This map shows the original lands of the Five Civilized Tribes following removal to Indian Territory from circa 1830 to 1855.
OHS*

Eaton and General John Coffee, promised the tribe that its new homeland would never, for any reason, be made part of a state or territory and that it would forever be governed by its own laws. This feature was to allay tribal fears that their experience in the Southeast would not be repeated if whites someday coveted their new home.

To aid in this removal, the government in 1831 opened an agency headquarters fifteen miles up the Arkansas River from Fort Smith. Agents of the Indian Office of the Department of War would help settle the Choctaws once they had completed their exodus. Less than thirty-six months were required to remove the sovereign Choctaw Nation to the Indian Territory, but there was intense suffering because of poor planning on the part of government functionaries and intensely cold weather. Almost half the 12,000 members of the tribe chose to remain in Mississippi and Alabama—only to meet discrimination and the eventual loss of their lands to whites who overran their acres with impunity. They would later move to the Indian Territory during the late 1830s and 1840s.

The same state laws that forced the Choctaws to move westward also affected the Creek Nation. Already that tribe had been forced out of Georgia into Alabama, and there was no enthusiasm for yet another move to join the McIntosh faction already in the Indian Territory. By 1832, however, the tribal leaders recognized that their days in the East were numbered, and a Creek delegation, headed by Opothleyahola, negotiated the Treaty of Washington signed on March 24. In return for ceding their lands in Alabama, the Creeks could either move to the Indian Territory to live on the land given to the McIntosh Creeks, or they could accept an allotment of land in Alabama (640 acres for a chief, 320 acres for every other head of a family), receiving the deed after five years. In return, the government agreed to pay the tribe $12,000 a year for five years and then $10,000 annually for fifteen years. Implied in this treaty was federal protection for those Creeks who chose to remain in Alabama, and only 630 members of the tribe agreed to removal. The others elected to stay in Alabama under the mistaken impression they were safe at last.

In the Indian Territory, inaccuracies in the maps setting boundaries of Creek and Cherokee lands caused conflicting claims among the tribes. Under the treaty of 1826, the Creeks were granted land along the Arkansas River near the mouth of the Verdigris; that same land also had been given to the Cherokees by a 1828 treaty. This dispute was settled in 1833 when the Cherokees agreed to allow Creek ownership of the disputed area. It was in this area around the Three Forks that the McIntosh Creeks had settled, and it was to this same area that the 630 Creeks who migrated in 1832 came.

Those who remained behind found their lot hard indeed. Their livestock was stolen, and whites took their homesteads by means both violent and fraudulent. The federal government did nothing even when peaceful Creeks were murdered while working their fields. Finally in 1836 the Lower Creeks unified under Chief Eneah Emothla to fight back. Alarmed Alabamans proclaimed a "Creek Rebellion" and appealed for federal troops, who were sent under command of General Winfield Scott. Scott was assisted by almost 2,000 Upper Creeks commanded by Opothleyahola; the Lower Creeks were defeated, and their suffering began in earnest. The 2,495 captives—men, women, and children, the sick and the aged—were bound in chains and sent westward, many of them dying during a winter march in 1836 to 1837. Another party of 300 captives was moved aboard a riverboat previously declared unsafe, and when it sank all of the Indians died.

At the same time the government demanded that the Upper Creeks remove westward despite their assistance in putting down the "Creek Rebellion." Opothleyahola led his people to the Indian Territory, with an estimated 3,500 Creeks perishing during the move. In the Indian Territory they chose to separate themselves from the earlier migrants of the McIntosh faction and settled farther south along the Canadian and Deep Fork creeks.

The Chickasaws, like the other Five Civilized Tribes, were also under great pressure to remove. During the early 1830s leaders of this tribe, recognizing that such a move was inevitable, sent a delegation west, but it failed to find a suitable home. Then in January 1837 a Chickasaw delegation met with leaders of the Choctaws at Doaksville (adjoining Fort Towson) to forge the Treaty of Doaksville, which provided for a Chickasaw home along the western edge of what had been Choctaw lands. This treaty also stipulated a unified Choctaw-Chickasaw tribal government (one clause stated that in cases of disagreement there would be an appeal to the President of the United States for settlement).

The removal of the Chickasaws was better managed and more orderly than other Indian relocations among the Five Civilized Tribes. Most Chickasaws had time to prepare, gathering their livestock and slaves and storing provisions for the trek. Moreover, the distance to be traveled was not as great for them as for the other four tribes. By 1840 the Chickasaws were living in their new home along the Washita River. Yet a majority of the tribe did not favor a unified government with the more numerous Choctaws, and this feature of the Treaty of Doaksville would cause trouble for several years.

The last of the Five Civilized Tribes to face removal were the Seminoles, a subgroup of the Creek Nation noted for their warlike ways. Traditionally they had lived in Florida, southern Georgia, and southern Alabama, welcoming to their ranks runaway slaves and those Creek warriors who had fought against the United States during the War of 1812 (the Red Sticks).

When the United States bought Florida from Spain in 1819, whites entering the area began demanding that the government remove the tribe. In 1832 James Gadsden, representing the United States, negotiated the Treaty of Payne's Landing, calling for

the Seminoles to remove to the Indian Territory as soon as a suitable home could be found. The tribe was given three years to make the move, and the government agreed to pay the cost of removal plus a one-time payment of $15,400 and an annual payment of $3,000 for fifteen years.

Osceola, a Seminole leader, spoke against this agreement. Born about 1800 on the Tallapoosa River in Georgia, Osceola was the son of William Powell, a Scottish trader, and a Creek wife. In 1808 his mother moved to Florida, there to associate with the Seminoles. Osceola, although still a youngster, fought at the Battle of Horseshoe Bend with the Red Stick Creeks, and in 1818 he was in the thick of fighting against American troops led by Andrew Jackson. In 1832 he lived near Fort King, Florida, and rose to prominence and tribal leadership among the Seminoles.

Late in 1832, under the terms of the Treaty of Payne's Landing, seven Seminole chiefs and Agent John Phagan journeyed to the Indian Territory to look for a home for the tribe. During this visit the delegation,

Osceola led the hostile Seminole Indians in the First Seminole War until his capture by General Thomas Jesup. He was succeeded by Billy Bowlegs in leading the futile attempt to repel Army troops and resist removal to Indian Territory. Courtesy, Western History Collections, University of Oklahoma Library

61

while at Fort Gibson, met with Creek leaders who offered to allow the Seminoles to settle on Creek lands. In February 1833 the two groups signed the Treaty of Fort Gibson, and the Seminole delegation returned home to prepare to move. During a discussion between American commissioners and Seminole leaders, some Seminole chiefs indicated their disagreement with the Treaty of Fort Gibson by refusing to touch a pen; Osceola did so by plunging his knife into the paper.

On December 28, 1835, Osceola and his followers killed Chief Emathla, one of the signers of the Treaty of Fort Gibson, along with Indian Agent Wiley Thompson. That same day Osceola's men surrounded 110 American soldiers near Fort King and killed 107 of them, triggering the six-year Seminole War. During this conflict Osceola achieved national prominence because of his victories in several major battles against American soldiers. On August 16, 1836, for example, he almost overwhelmed Fort Drane, Florida, leading to widespread criticism of the Army and especially of General Thomas Jesup. Jesup ordered Osceola captured under a flag of truce, which was accomplished on October 21, 1837. First imprisoned at Fort Marion, Florida, Osceola later was moved to Fort Moultrie, South Carolina, where he died on January 30, 1838, of mysterious causes. A majority of the tribe surrendered in the spring of 1839

and were moved westward, leaving only a few small bands to continue guerrilla warfare against the United States (until the government allowed them to remain in Florida; this war cost twenty million dollars and the lives of 1,500 soldiers).

While the Seminole War was in progress, the government moved peaceful Seminoles and captive warriors to the Indian Territory and by 1842 there were some 3,000 Seminoles living on Creek lands between the southern and northern forks of the Canadian River.

During the movement of the Five Civilized Tribes to the Indian Territory, the federal government also moved two additional tribes there: the Quapaw (who once had claimed ownership of the land that eventually belonged to the Choctaws and Creeks) and the Senecas (who at one time had lived in New York). Both tribes had suffered a drastic reduction in numbers since their first contact with whites. In the 1600s the Senecas had been a major part of the six-nation Iroquois Confederacy. Yet they were crushed during the wars of the eighteenth century, and had been overrun during the white settlement of the Ohio Valley. By the 1830s the tribe numbered only a few hundred and was living on a reservation in Ohio. In 1831 the government decided to move them to the Indian Territory because whites wanted their 90,000-acre reservation, and by treaty that year the Senecas agreed to give up that land

During the Leavenworth Dragoon Expedition of 1834, artist George Catlin painted this encounter between the dragoons, riding in ordered pairs; the Comanche Indians; and a herd of bison. Courtesy, The Thomas Gilcrease Institute of American History and Art, Tulsa, Oklahoma

in return for 130,000 acres between the Grand River and the southwest boundary of Missouri (north of the Cherokee preserve). Another small party, the Seneca-Shawnee (Mixed Band), was brought to the area after an 1832 agreement.

The Quapaws likewise had once been a numerous people, but the population had been reduced by wars with whites and with other Indians. In 1818 they had ceded the land they owned in Oklahoma for a reservation in Arkansas, then had been removed south of the Red River where they lived with the Caddos. This proved an unhappy time for the Quapaws, for the Caddos gave them marginal land that was flooded annually by the Red River. Moreover, the humid, balmy climate produced fevers that killed hundreds of Quapaws. In desperation the 300 survivors illegally returned to Arkansas to find homes on abandoned land and to petition the federal government for relief. In May 1833 they signed a treaty granting them a reserve of 96,000 acres between the Missouri and Grand rivers (north of the Seneca land). With their own home assured them, the Quapaw gradually ended their wandering about the Indian country and settled on their lands.

When the tribes newly moved to the Indian Territory came into conflict with the Indians already on the land, they turned to the federal government for assistance, and federal agents tried to negotiate a compromise. A major conflict, for example, occurred between the Osages and Cherokees, and it continued until all the Osages moved north into Kansas (about 1840). More serious than this, however, were the frequent raids on newcomers by the Comanches, Wichitas, Kiowas, and Kiowa-Apaches.

The Wichitas, a Caddoan tribe, considered the prairies of central Oklahoma to be their hunting grounds, while the Comanches coveted the buffalo and antelope roaming the plains. The Comanches lived along the upper reaches of the Canadian, Red, and Cimarron rivers, and were closely allied with the Wichitas, who inhabited the middle section of the Red River. Frequently the two tribes joined to form hunting and war parties that raided south into Texas and even deep into Mexico. The Kiowas and Kiowa-Apaches, equally possessive and fierce, roamed western Oklahoma and the Texas Panhandle, also joining the Comanches on occasion to form raiding parties. All four tribes considered hunting

United States dragoons, in field dress (on horseback) and parade dress (on foot), made the difficult journey across southern and western Oklahoma during the summer of 1834. Commanded by General Henry Leavenworth, this expedition suffered intensely from disease and heat. OHS

parties of the Five Civilized Tribes to be intruders and attacked them, and they journeyed to the eastern part of the Indian Territory to attack villages established by the newcomers. In addition, all four of the plains tribes were enemies of the Osages, which compounded the difficulty of keeping the peace. As long as such raids were small and infrequent, the government tried to ignore them. But when raids grew large and numerous, the government was compelled to take action.

Such an occasion arrived in 1832, and a federal commission led by Governor Montfort Stokes of North Carolina and accompanied by United States Indian Commissioner Henry L. Ellsworth met with the Cherokees and Osages to settle old disputes and to avoid future bloodshed. Noted writer Washington Irving accompanied this commission and wrote about its adventures in his delightful *A Tour on the Prairies.* Yet despite the visit of the Stokes Commission, war soon erupted between the Osages and the plains tribes. In the summer of 1833 the Osages, led by Chief Clermont, located an unprotected Kiowa village near the Wichita Mountains and attacked. When the war party returned eastward with some fifty scalps, it left the village strewn with dead bodies and burning tepees. The federal government felt compelled to take action, as a general war might result—and thereby delay the removal of the Five Civilized Tribes.

To demonstrate the might of the United States government, General Henry Leavenworth, who recently had taken command of the region from the ailing General Matthew Arbuckle, ordered the erection of three camps on the frontier. These were Cantonment Leavenworth, near the mouth of the Washita River, and Camps Arbuckle and Holmes on the Canadian River. General Leavenworth in 1834 personally inspected the frontier with a large body of troops drawn from Forts Gibson and Towson. One member of this party was artist George Catlin, who preserved the history of the region through the medium of his canvas. This party first marched west to the Washita River, intending to move further west to confer with the Comanches and Kiowas. At the Red River, however, General Leavenworth and more than half his men became ill, and Colonel Henry Dodge assumed command.

Dodge marched west to hold a meeting with the Kiowas, Comanches, and Wichitas, exchanging prisoners ransomed from the Osages for Osages and white captives held by the plains tribes. One individual released was the son of Judge Arthur Martin, who had been captured by the Kiowas after his father was killed near the site of the present Madill, Oklahoma. At this time Dodge had fewer than 200 healthy soldiers with him, so when negotiations were completed he hastily retreated to Fort Gibson, returning late that summer to learn that General Leavenworth had died from his illness.

At Fort Gibson a conference was held between representatives of the plains tribes who had accompanied Dodge back to the post and leaders of the Cherokees, Creeks, Choctaws, Delawares, Osages, and Senecas. Little was accomplished, but all agreed to meet again the following year.

The meeting in 1835, a large affair, was held in August at Camp Mason, a new post established by General Matthew Arbuckle on the western edge of the Cross Timbers beside the Canadian River (in present Cleveland County). Arbuckle (returned to command in place of the deceased Leavenworth) and Montfort Stokes represented the United States. Indian leaders at the conference represented the Cherokees, Creeks,

Choctaws, Delawares, Osages, Senecas, and Quapaws, and there were delegations present from the Comanches, Kiowas, and Wichitas. A general treaty resulted in which the tribes in the eastern part of the Indian Territory were granted the right to travel and hunt on the western prairies and plains. Only the Kiowas refused to sign this agreement (in 1837 they would be forced to agree to it, as would the plains Apaches with whom the Kiowas had become allies). Yet despite the assurances contained in this treaty, warfare continued between the plains Indians and the woodland tribes recently removed to the Indian Territory.

The other newcomers to the Indian Territory during the 1820s and 1830s, other than a few licensed traders, were the soldiers who came to man Army posts such as Gibson, Towson, Leavenworth, Washita, Arbuckle, and Cobb. Many of these posts proved short-lived, like Fort Coffee, which was erected on the banks of the Arkansas between Forts Smith and Gibson in 1834 to control illegal liquor traffic. Despite the presence of the cannon at this post, whiskey continued to move upriver, and Fort Coffee was abandoned in 1838. Fort Gibson remained the major military installation in the Indian Territory until the eve of the Civil War.

Duty at these posts was hard and dangerous for the soldiers. The men erected their quarters themselves, cutting logs or quarrying stone, moving these to the desired location, and erecting them according to plans drawn by their officers. They fought malaria and bilious fevers, ate government hardtack and bacon, escorted supply wagons, scouted new territory, and sometimes fought Indians or white renegades—all for eight dollars a month. Little wonder that so many of them deserted at the first opportunity.

By 1840 almost all Indians who once lived east of the Mississippi River had been removed westward, and the people of the United States hailed this as a great national achievement. In the process all of present-day Oklahoma (except the Panhandle) had been allotted by treaty to one tribe or another. Yet in this land there was no celebrating, for the nations were struggling to reestablish themselves economically in their new homeland and to heal the tribal divisions between those who had fought removal and those who had accepted it as inevitable.

Top
The third mural, Indian
Immigration, *covers Okla-
homa's history from 1820
to 1885. Courtesy, Charles
Banks Wilson*

Above
The fourth mural, Settle-
ment, *covers Oklahoma's
history from 1870 to 1906.
Courtesy, Charles Banks
Wilson*

These colorful Indian murals by artist Monroe TsaToke can all be found in the Wiley Post Historical Building in Oklahoma City. The upper left illustration depicts a Kiowa chief, the upper right illustration is a Kiowa woman with her child, in the lower left, is a Kiowa fancy dancer, and in the lower right is a Comanche chief. OHS

Right
This untitled work by Monroe Tsa-Toke, of an Indian with a pipe, is also a mural in the Wiley Post Historical Building in Oklahoma City. OHS

Below
Indian Friendship, *by James Auchiah, is another mural in the Wiley Post Historical Building in Oklahoma City. OHS*

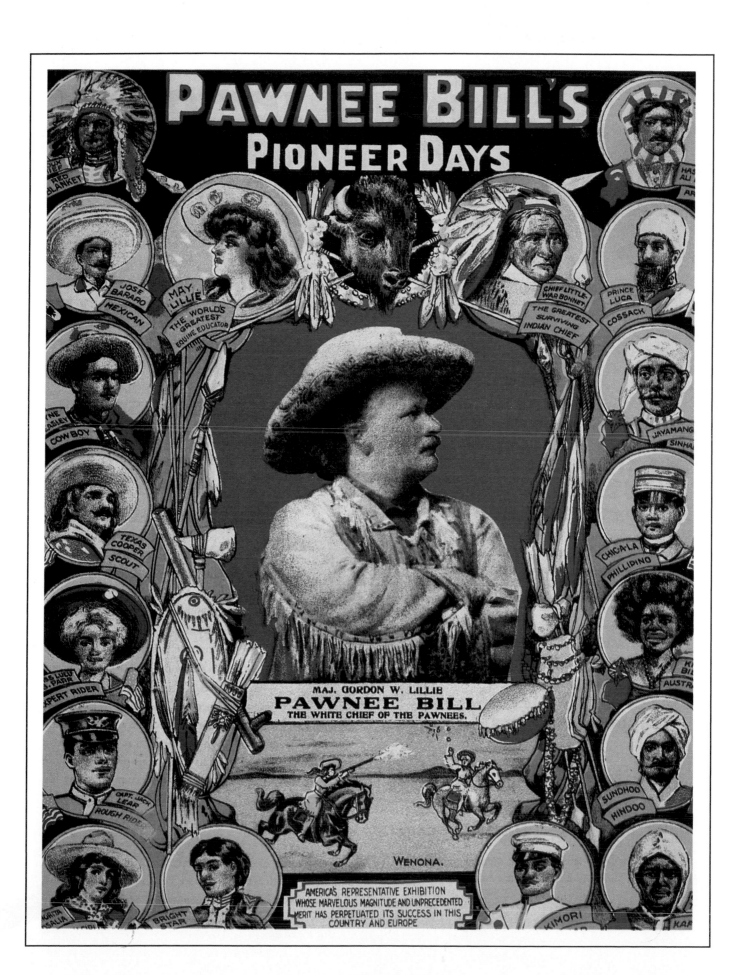

CHAPTER VI

Indian Republics in a New Land

The Cherokee National Female Seminary was established at Park Hill to educate the young women of the tribe. Following the strict Mount Holyoke regimen, the faculty and students of the school established an educational tradition that remains to this day at Northeastern Oklahoma State University, which occupies some of the school's former buildings. Courtesy, Western History Collections, University of Oklahoma Library

*T*he Native Americans removed to the Indian Territory in the second, third, and fourth decades of the nineteenth century arrived in their new homeland eager for a time of tranquility in which to reestablish their tribal identities. They were refugees from years of persecution and struggle with whites, and they came in search of peace. Tranquility was elusive, however, for within most of the tribes there were conflicting factions vying for positions of leadership.

The most seriously divided of the Nations were the Cherokees, who were split into three factions: the Old Settlers, consisting of those tribesmen who had moved to Arkansas and then to the Indian Territory prior to 1830; the Treaty Party, made up of the Ridges, Boudinot, and their followers who had removed westward voluntarily; and the Ross Party, who had taken part in the Trail of Tears. The federal government apparently hoped that, once in the Indian Territory, the entire Nation would be dominated by the Treaty Party, but Ross and his adherents were too numerous and too bitter to accept this leadership. In fact, on June 22, 1839, Major Ridge, John Ridge, and Elias Boudinot were killed for signing the Treaty of New Echota (members of the Ross Party always insisted that these were legal executions, while adherents of the Treaty Party saw the deaths as brutal murders). Stan Watie, brother of the slain Boudinot, assumed leadership of the Treaty Party. It was Watie, who, after viewing his dead brother's face, said, "I will give ten thousand dollars for the names of the men who did this."

Born on December 12, 1806, south of New Echota, Georgia, Watie at birth was named Degadoga ("He Stands"), and was the son of a full-blood Cherokee named David Watie and Susanna Reese, a half blood. When his parents converted to Christianity he took the name Isaac S. Watie, later preferring to be known as Stand Watie. His father fought on the side of the

United States during the War of 1812 against the Red Stick Creeks at the Battle of Horseshoe Bend. Watie was educated at a Moravian mission school and then returned to a quiet existence on the family farm. In 1828 he entered Cherokee politics when he was chosen clerk of the Nation's Supreme Court under the constitution of 1827. In the confrontation between whites and Cherokees in Georgia, Watie played a small but active role, but gradually he came to believe in the inevitability of removal. In the Indian Territory, after his older brother Elias Boudinot and the Ridges were killed, Watie became the leading opponent of John Ross for almost three decades.

Following the death of the three leaders of the Treaty Party, Ross and his party seized power, but the principal chief found it necessary to have a bodyguard of 500 to 600 men almost all the time for fear of reprisal. In this bloody struggle for power, a constitution was drafted in 1839 at Double Springs, some ten miles north of Fort Gibson. The three sharply divided Cherokee factions were all present, but the constitution adopted at this meeting did not restore peace, and violence continued despite the efforts of would-be peacemakers within the tribe and the Army.

Several federal officials voiced the opinion that no accord could be reached among the various factions, and that separate reservations might be required. Legislation, introduced in Congress in 1846, resulted which would have separated the tribe. Fortunately, John Ross and a Cherokee delegation arrived in Washington before the bill could be passed. These men convinced President James K. Polk that a commission should be appointed to study the matter. Polk responded by naming William Armstrong, superintendent of Indian Affairs of the Western Territories, as chairman and Albion K. Parris and Edmund Burke as commission members.

For almost six months this presidential commission visited leaders of each faction and negotiated the Treaty of 1846. This recognized a United Cherokee Nation, reaffirmed the tribe's claim to its lands in the Indian Territory, pardoned past crimes by Cherokees, and granted funds (as compensation) to the families of the Ridges and Boudinot.

With peace restored, the tribal constitution of 1839 at last could be implemented.

The constitution provided for a two-house legislative body consisting of a National Committee of Sixteen (two members from each of the eight districts into which the Nation had been divided) and a council consisting of three members from each of the eight districts. Sitting together, the two houses were known as the National Council, with the principal chief, as executive, who had veto powers and who was aided by an assistant principal chief. The judiciary consisted of a supreme court and a circuit court system, while a treasurer was selected by the National Council. To maintain law and order justices of the peace would be appointed by the principal chief of each district, and each district elected its own sheriff. Under the new civil government, schools were opened, books and newspapers were printed, and churches were organized. In addition, the tribe established a Male Seminary in Tahlequah, capital of the Nation, and a Female Seminary at nearby Park

Stand Watie, leader of the Pro-Treaty party of the Cherokee Indians following the assassination of his brother, uncle, and cousin, led the Confederate Cherokees during the Civil War, rising to the rank of brigadier general of the Confederate Army. OHS

Hill.

Unfortunately a few members of the Cherokee Nation were unable to return to peaceful ways after the Treaty of 1846 was implemented. A report in the *Cherokee Advocate* in 1845 observed: "The great mass of the Cherokees remained uncorrupted and incorruptible. But some . . . became drunkards, some idlers, and others were seduced from the path of virtue and innocence. From among those last enumerated, may be found some of those depraved but unfortunate beings who, while indulging the habits and vices imbibed from the whites, commit the crimes that are occurring in our country." Several gangs of outlaw Cherokees had begun operating in the vicinity of the present Stilwell, spreading terror and destruction. The most famous of these groups was the "Starr Gang," captained by Thomas Starr and his brothers. For almost a decade this gang enjoyed success in thefts, robberies, and murders, but in 1858 gang members were gunned down by a Cherokee posse. Other outlaw bands met a similar fate, and peace gradually returned to the Cherokee Nation.

Yet horrible economic suffering during these same early years in the Indian Territory hampered a return to prosperity among the Cherokees and the Creeks. Fields had to

be cleared and planted, a process that took time. Many of the newcomers, not understanding that the region was subject to flooding, settled alongside streams, and in their first years frequently saw their homes washed away, their livestock drowned, and their crops ruined. The promised government rations either were not forthcoming or else were provided by some contractors so intent on cheating that much of what did arrive was rotten. Moreover, the climate proved unhealthy for the newcomers, and hundreds died of "bilious and intermittent fever" (malaria and typhoid). Proud people accustomed to refinements of living were forced to endure in rude shelters, subsist on whatever food could be gathered, and work long hours rebuilding farms and homes.

The Creeks arriving in the Indian Territory in the late 1830s benefitted from the pioneering work of the McIntosh branch of their Nation. This group, led by Roley McIntosh, son of the slain William McIntosh, arrived in the valley of the Verdigris years before the majority of the tribe and had laid out farms (utilizing slave labor). By the time the other Creeks arrived, the McIntosh faction had determined what crops would grow well in the area, and had food supplies on hand to aid the newcomers.

Once reunited in Oklahoma, the Creeks

After removal from Georgia to the Indian Territory, the Cherokee Indians set about the task of rebuilding their nation. Rose Cottage, near Park Hill, was the home of Principal Chief John Ross, who ably led his people through the dark post-removal days. Courtesy, Western History Collections, University of Oklahoma Library

reinstituted their traditional political system comprised of semi-independent towns, each with a village chief, and "Upper" and "Lower" nations with a hereditary chief ruling over each. Although the two divisions of the tribe had been enemies during the Alabama "Creek Rebellion," there was peace between them until the outbreak of the Civil War. The legislature for the Nation consisted of two houses, the upper house composed of "kings" representing the towns, and the lower house composed of one "warrior" from each town plus an additional "warrior" for every 200 people in each town. A principal chief was elected in the Upper and Lower nations by males over the age of eighteen, and a judicial system meted out justice. The Creek General Council met in present McIntosh County and were presided over by the two hereditary chiefs representing the Upper and Lower nations. Within this system the Creeks made rapid progress, with southern plantation homes rising where only a few years before had been trees and prairie grass. A few of the more prosperous Creeks, such as the McIntosh and Perryman families, farmed large acreages and sold surplus corn and other produce to the Army at Fort Gibson.

Because the Choctaws were the first of the Five Civilized Tribes to remove most of its members to the Indian Territory (by the early 1830s), this nation likewise was the first to produce a new written constitution. Adopted in 1834, it was a revision of a document first drafted in 1826. It divided the Choctaw Nation into three districts: Pushmataha, Moshulatubbee, and Okla Falaya (or Red River), each with its own chief elected for a four-year term (each limited to two terms). The tribal General Assembly consisted of nine members from each district and met annually, while a judicial body also was elected. Each district had a police force consisting of six "lighthorsemen." A bill of rights attached to this constitution assured every Choctaw citizen of the right to trial for any crime, and it guaranteed all males twenty-one years of age or older the right to vote. For a time the Choctaw capital was at Nanih Wayah (near present Tuskahoma), but in 1850 it was moved to Doaksville.

The three chiefs, sitting together, had the power to veto legislation (two of them constituted a majority); however, the assembly could override a veto by a two-thirds vote.

In the first election held in 1834, Nitakeechi was elected chief of the Pushmataha District, Joseph Kincaid chief for the Moshulatubbee District, and George Harkins (nephew of Greenwood LeFlore, who had remained in Mississippi) was chief of the Okla Falaya District. Progress under this system was rapid and the tribe became prosperous.

The Chickasaws, when forcibly moved to the Indian Territory in the late 1830s, were ordered, much against their will, to integrate with the Choctaw Nation. However, the Treaty of Doaksville, under which they received land in the western part of the Choctaw preserve, was specific on this point. The Choctaws simply added a fourth district, named Apuckshumnubbee, to their government for the Chickasaws, and they were given thirteen representatives in the General Assembly. The newcomers were un-

Colonel Zachary Taylor ordered the establishment of Fort Washita to protect the Five Civilized Tribes from marauding Plains Indians. OHS

John Jumper, Seminole principal chief, negotiated a treaty with the federal government and the Creek Nation for a separate homeland for his tribe in 1856. OHS

dians, Colonel Zachary Taylor, commanding the Department of the Southwest, ordered the establishment of Fort Washita at the mouth of that river in 1842. This lessened the threat of Comanche raids, and thereafter the Chickasaws began to prosper.

The Seminoles, unlike the other four members of the Five Civilized Tribes, had not been farmers in their original homeland, and they suffered greatly from what they considered to be harsh winters in the Indian Territory. They were a hunting people, and they resisted efforts to make them farmers in the Indian Territory. The greatest problem facing the Seminoles, however, was their Creek landlords. The Creeks were more numerous, given to agriculture, and owned slaves. The Seminoles traditionally had protected runaway slaves and had brought a number of blacks west with them. When the Creeks began claiming these blacks as slaves, difficulties erupted between the two tribes. To avoid clashes, the Seminoles tended to remain near Fort Gibson for a time, but by the mid-1840s they had begun to settle along the banks of the Canadian River near Little River. They never developed extensive farms or a written constitution, but lived in twenty-five scattered villages, each with its own chief and council of warriors. A general tribal council, headed by Chief Micanopy, met each year to make laws for the tribe although the Creek General Council had veto power over these laws. In 1856 the Seminoles, led by Chief John Jumper, negotiated a treaty in Washington with the chiefs of the Creek Nation and secured tribal autonomy. Afterward they built a new capital at Wanette (in present Pottawatomie County).

In moving west and reestablishing themselves in the Indian Territory, the Five Civilized Tribes, along with the Seneca, Ottawa, and other tribes, were aided by missionaries representing several Christian sects. In their enthusiasm to "civilize" the Indians, various church leaders lobbied the federal government for financial help, and on March 13, 1819, Congress established an annual fund of $10,000 to be used to employ "persons of good moral character" to instruct the Indians in agriculture and to teach their children reading, writing, and arithmetic. Naturally these funds were doled out to missionary organizations, such as the United Foreign Missionary Society, one of the principal lobbyists for this legislation.

happy with being forced to submit to the Choctaw laws, methods of policing, and judicial system, but were unable to change it until 1855. Then they were separated by formal agreement with the United States, and allowed to establish their own system of government, which proved similar to that of the Choctaws.

The Chickasaws also had to contend with the constant raiding of their lands by the fierce plains nomads. Because the Chickasaws were principally located in the Washita Valley on the western part of the Choctaw Nation, they lived so close to the plains that they were a tempting target for plains raiders. The Comanches and their allies, the Kiowas and Kiowa-Apaches, had major war trails leading south into Texas, and on these forays there were always a few warriors who would decide to turn east and raid the Chickasaws. To defend these peaceful In-

Bloomfield Academy was established prior to the Civil War to educate Chickasaw Indian women. OHS

Union Mission was the first missionary station established in Oklahoma. The first printing press and the first book printed in Oklahoma were located there. Photo by Jim Argo

The United Foreign Missionary Society was created on July 25, 1817, in New York City by representatives of the General Assembly of the Presbyterian Church, the General Synod of the Reformed Dutch Church, and the General Synod of the Associated Reform Church. Its purpose was "to spread the gospel among the Indians of North America . . . ." Once Congress began appropriating funds, the society sent Epaphras Chapman and Job P. Vinal, two Presbyterian missionaries, to explore the possibility of establishing a mission among the Cherokees then in Arkansas. The two men found, however, that a competitor had already staked a claim there—the American Board of Commissioners of Foreign Missions, founded in 1808 by four students at Andover Theological Seminary. Therefore Chapman and Vinal traveled on to the Osage country to select a site on the Grand River some twenty-five miles above the Arkansas.

On the return trip to New York City, Vinal died, leaving Chapman the task of beginning the work. Chapman realized that more was required than simply evangelizing the Indians, for by an act of Congress the federal funds were to be used to "civilize" the natives. So in recruiting for his mission, Chapman selected a farmer, a carpenter, a blacksmith, a physician, and women to teach domestic skills. When Reverend Chapman began his return trip, he and his fellow missionary, Reverend William F. Vaill, had seventeen adults and four children in their party. After some ten months of travel and hardship, they arrived in the Indian Territory on February 18, 1821. Their station was named Union Mission, and on August 27 they opened the first school in the Indian Territory with four Osage children. Soon thereafter Hopewell Mission, located farther north on the Grand River, was established.

Other missionaries soon came to the Indian Territory, some traveling with the Indians from the Southeast. The Western Cherokees, for example, had asked for missionaries in 1820, and the American Board responded by founding Dwight Mission in Arkansas, named in honor of Timothy Dwight, one of the board's members. When the Cherokees traded their land in Arkansas for new homes in the Indian Territory, Dwight Mission moved westward with them, as did Mulberry Mission, another American Board establishment founded in Arkansas. In the Indian Territory, Dwight Mission was located on Sallisaw Creek (in present Sequoyah County near the town of New Dwight), while Mulberry Mission was located near the present Stilwell. In 1829 Mulberry moved and was renamed Fairfield Mission. In 1830 the board established a third mission for the Cherokees called Forks of the Illinois because of its location on the Illinois River.

For a time there was wasteful duplication of effort between the missionaries of the American Board and the United Foreign Missionary Society. In 1826, however, the two societies were united into the American Board of Commissioners for Foreign Missions. As the Five Civilized Tribes began arriving in the Indian Territory in large numbers, missionaries were assigned to work with them. Each mission station tried to accomplish the same result: conversion of everyone to Christianity, schooling for the children, and vocational education for adults, along with medical assistance for the sick. For example, when the Creeks settled in the Three Forks area, the American Board assigned Abraham Redfield of Union Mission to serve the newcomers. In anticipation of his arrival in their midst, the Creeks built a two-room schoolhouse measuring 16-by-30 feet. This was the first Creek school in the territory.

Congregational missionary Samuel Austin Worcester traveled with the Cherokees over the Trail of Tears. Released from imprisonment in Georgia, Worcester established himself in the Indian Territory at Park Hill in 1835. Two years later he moved his printing press from Union Mission (where it had operated temporarily) to Park Hill to establish the leading center of both secular and religious training in the Cherokee Nation. Worcester annually published the *Cherokee Phoenix,* a newspaper partially in

the syllabary of Sequoyah, and the *Cherokee Almanac,* along with portions of the Bible in the Cherokee language. Worcester was a stern and devout leader who remained an influence among the Cherokees until his death in 1859.

The Moravians, who were not partners in the American Board, came to the Indian Territory and founded New Spring Place Mission in present Delaware County, while the Baptists also opened a mission in Delaware County and published religious material, including the *Cherokee Messenger.* Methodist circuit riders continually rode among the newly settled Indians to preach the gospel, as well.

Often these missionaries faced hostility from the traders licensed to work among the Indians, for the ministers constantly fought

Cyrus Byington was a missionary to the Choctaw Indians. He developed a written language for the tribe, translating the Bible and other written texts to help educate his adopted people. OHS

against the sale of whiskey in the territory. Occasionally there were feuds between contending denominations—and even fights within certain denominations. Nevertheless, the Indians realized their children needed schooling, and many of them converted to Christianity. Therefore the missionary work continued, and their schools increased in size and quality. By the mid-nineteenth century the Cherokees, Choctaws, and Creeks had made notable advances in agriculture, education, and comfortable living, while the Chickasaws were trying to overcome the disadvantage of living too near the plains raiders. Even the Seminoles were gradually making progress. The forced uprooting of these various tribes from their traditional homelands, according to one observer, had done "more at a single stroke to obliterate Indian ideas than could have been accomplished by fifty years of slow development." By 1850 these changes had been made, and the future looked bright for the newcomers to the Indian Territory.

Right
The oldest remaining church building in Oklahoma, Wheelock Mission was established in 1832 by the Reverend Alfred Wright to minister to the Choctaw Indians following their removal from Mississippi. Photo by Jim Argo

Opposite page, top
Following the removal of the Choctaw Indians to Indian Territory from Mississippi, the nation was divided into three districts. The elected chiefs from each district were provided houses by the federal government. This cabin, located near Swink, was one of the original homes built in the Indian Territory and is the oldest remaining home in the state. Photo by Jim Argo

Opposite page, bottom
The Choctaw National Capitol was located at Nanih Waya, near Tuskahoma. This building was first used for the tribe's house of representatives and later became a school for tribal children. OHS

Bottom
The Cherokee Nation was subdivided into several districts after removal to the Indian Territory. One of these districts had its council house and courthouse located near Gore. This replica depicts the style of construction prevalent in the Indian Territory before the Civil War. Photo by Jim Argo

CHAPTER VII

Broken Promises, Broken Dreams

The primary crossing of the Red River on the Texas Road was at Colbert's Ferry. The route of the Texas Road was later used by cattlemen driving herds northward into Kansas and Missouri, and the Missouri, Kansas & Texas Railway followed its path when the rail line was constructed from 1870 to 1872. Photo by Jim Argo

*T*he chance discovery of gold in January 1848 by an employee of John A. Sutter, feudal baron of the Sacramento Valley in California, directly affected events in the Indian Territory within a year. As word of the discovery spread across the United States, all sanity seemed to vanish from the public mind. As the *New York Herald* commented in a special edition:

Husbands are preparing to leave their wives, sons are parting with their mothers, and bachelors are abandoning their comforts; all are rushing head over heels toward the El Dorado on the Pacific.

Wherever and whenever men gathered that winter of 1848 to 1849, the talk was of California and the gold strike. By the spring of 1849 tens of thousands of eastern Americans were ready to depart for the gold fields to pick up the fortune they thought was awaiting them.

Businessmen in Fort Smith, Arkansas, knew that these Forty-Niners would spend large sums outfitting in any city that became known as a jumping-off point for an overland trail, so in late 1848 they called on General Matthew Arbuckle, commanding at Fort Smith, to win his support for the construction of a military road from Fort Smith to Santa Fe, New Mexico (where Forty-Niners could use the existing Gila Trail to reach California). The road would bring Fort Smith the business its merchants desired—and at federal expense. When Arbuckle gave his approval, local residents then went before the state legislature to solicit its support, and that body duly petitioned the Secretary of War to authorize a military expedition to open a wagon road from Fort Smith to Santa Fe by way of the Indian Territory. By spring of 1849 Congress had appropriated $50,000 for surveys from the Mississippi River to the Pacific Coast, and the Fort Smith route was in-

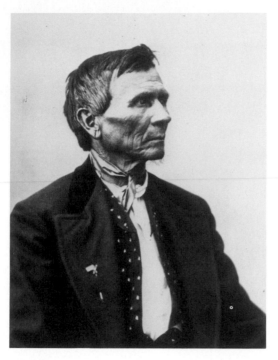 

cluded.

Some 2,000 emigrants gathered at Fort Smith that spring to take advantage of the military escort provided by the troops assigned to this survey, spending large sums and driving up the price of horses, mules, oxen, and food supplies. Commanding the infantry and dragoons was thirty-five-year-old Captain Randolph B. Marcy, a native of Massachusetts and a graduate of the United States Military Academy. His orders were to blaze a suitable trail across the plains and to escort the gold-seekers through the domain of the plains tribes.

Leaving Fort Smith on April 4, 1849, soldiers and civilians alike fought their way through a sea of mud caused by heavy rains in February and March. Startled residents of the Indian Territory, waiting for drier weather to plow and plant, could only stare in wonder as this wave of gold-seekers and soldiers struggled across their land. At last the column came to the Canadian River. There Marcy decided this stream would be an unavoidable signpost for future travelers and determined to follow it westward. This journey proved largely uneventful except for the wonder and excitement generated by the geological formation to be known as Rock Mary. Discovered on May 23 (in present Caddo County), it was named for seventeen-year-old Mary Conway, one of the travelers who was a cousin of President James Madison and granddaughter of a governor of Arkansas. Several junior officers of the

party raced to the crest, planted an American flag there, and named it Rock Mary in her honor. (In subsequent years this red fifty-foot-high sandstone formation served as a guidepost to travelers across the flat grasslands of that region.)

Arriving in Santa Fe on June 28, Marcy and the caravan had averaged thirteen miles a day. During the return trip, made without hindrance of civilians, Marcy tried a different route. From Santa Fe he went down the Rio Grande to the town of Dona Ana, then east to the Pecos River and across northwest Texas to enter the Indian Territory at the town of Preston, a ford on the Red River. From Preston his column proceeded to Fort Washita and thence to Fort Smith. Thereafter this route across the southern part of the Indian Territory, named Marcy's Trail in the captain's honor, would be the prinicipal route used by gold-seekers and settlers crossing from the mid-Mississippi Valley to the great West. The trail was also used by many Cherokees who also wanted a share of the riches so widely believed to be waiting in California.

Even the Butterfield Overland Mail, which on September 16, 1858, began operating stagecoaches from St. Louis to San Francisco, followed Marcy's Road. From Fort Smith westward, the Butterfield passed through what one traveler called "two hundred miles of the worst road God ever built." Waterman L. Ormsby, a reporter for the *New York Herald* who was on the first

The California Road blazed by Captain Randolph Marcy crossed western Oklahoma. Wagons journeying along the road left deeply cut wagon ruts in the sandstone of present-day Red Rock Canyon State Park near Hinton. Photo by Jim Argo

Rock Mary, a natural outcropping along the California Road, became a landmark for travelers crossing western Oklahoma. This drawing of the formation is by German artist H. Mollhouser, who accompanied Captain A.W. Whipple on an 1854 surveying expedition. OHS

stagecoach making this run, expressed fear of the Indians west of Fort Smith, but was surprised to find that Choctaws had been hired as station keepers and were excellent at their jobs. Ormsby wrote:

The night was beautifully clear and bright, and I was tempted to stay up and enjoy it; but I had become too much fatigued with the journey to be able to withstand the demands of somnolence, and wrapping myself up in my shawls, was soon obliviously snoring on the extended seats of the wagon. I awoke but once during the night, having been jolted into a position where my neck felt as if there was a knot in it. They had stopped at a station to change horses, and for the time not a sound could I hear. I had been dreaming of the Comanche Indians, and in the confusion of drowsiness first thought that the driver and the mail agent had been murdered, and that I, being covered up with blankets, had been missed; then I recollected that I had a pistol and thought of feeling for it; but finally I thought I would not stir, for fear the Indians would see me—when I was brought to my senses by a familiar voice saying "Git up there, old hoss," and found it was the driver hitching up a new team.

Ormsby might have been astonished to learn that his fear of Indians was matched by an Indian fear of whites—and of other Indians. During the decade of the 1850s the new owners of the Indian Territory were not left alone to develop the homes they had carved for themselves and their families. Constantly they were bothered by raids conducted by plains tribes, while the federal government was under pressure to remove even more Indians to the territory. The result was increased federal involvement in tribal affairs.

The Comanches were the principal raid-

This map of the Indian Territory shows the important routes and trails that crisscrossed the region prior to the Civil War. OHS

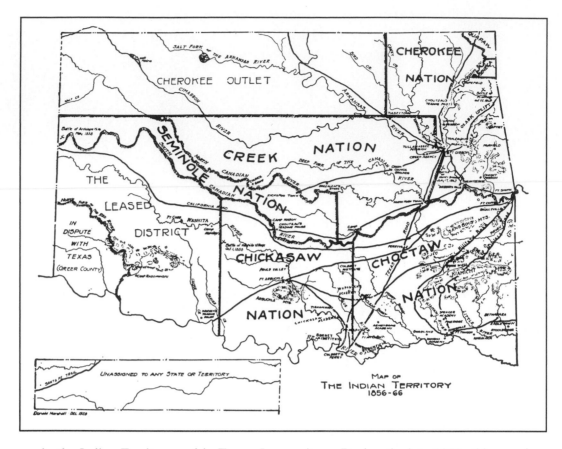

MAP OF
THE INDIAN TERRITORY
1856-66

ers in the Indian Territory and in Texas. In theory this tribe had a claim to land in the Lone Star State, but when Texas came into the Union it was granted ownership of all its public lands—and the state government wanted to remove these Indians from the state. In 1855 the federal government leased from the Choctaws and the Chickasaws the area between the Canadian and Red rivers in the southwestern corner of Oklahoma as a reserve onto which the plains raiders could be placed at some future date. In addition, the Army, to make its presence more visible to the plains tribes, established Camp Radziminski on Otter Creek (in present Kiowa County), and the following year opened Fort Cobb (at the site of the present town of Fort Cobb). At the insistence of the federal government, the Comanches were given a reservation in Texas in 1855, but were forced by irate civilians to leave four years later and were assigned to part of the Leased District. In theory they were to confine themselves there. In reality, however, they continued to raid south of the Red River and among the Five Civilized Tribes to the east.

The removal of the Comanches to north of the Red River signaled difficult years ahead for the inhabitants of the Indian Ter-

ritory. During the late 1850s this area increasingly was surrounded by whites who began looking with covetous eyes on lands supposedly given to the Indians in perpetuity. Texans were moving beyond the 98th meridian along the south bank of the Red River, and to the north, Kansas was being settled.

During the 1854 debate in Congress about the creation of Kansas Territory, the future of the Indian Territory was discussed. Senator Robert Johnson of Arkansas proposed that year that the Indian Territory also be considered for statehood. He wanted to divide the Indian Territory into three new territories: Cherokee, Muscogee (to consist of Creek and Seminole lands), and Chata (to be made up of Choctaw and Chickasaw lands). He suggested that the region be surveyed, that tribal members be given an allotment of acres, and that surplus lands be opened to settlement by non-Indians. When all three territories had sufficient settlers to meet the requirements for statehood, they would be reunited and admitted as the state of Neosho.

All tribes in the Indian Territory united in opposition to Senator Johnson's plan, asserting that they had been promised their new homelands would never be violated for any reason. Because of this strong opposition, as well as binding treaty obligations, Johnson's bill was not passed by Congress, but the idea did not die. The desire to break up the Indian republics to allow white settlement became dormant until some way could be found to void the government's treaty obligations to the tribes. Then came the Civil War, giving the government the excuse it was seeking.

As war clouds darkened the horizon of the United States in the late 1850s, the leaders of the Five Civilized Tribes found their position difficult. Slavery was traditional among them and was an established

Above
Stagecoaches like this one jolted and lurched along the crude trail across southeastern Oklahoma during the heyday of the Butterfield Overland Mail route. OHS

Left
During the heyday of the Santa Fe trade, the Santa Fe Trail which ran from Westport, Missouri, to Santa Fe, New Mexico, carried thousands of wagons and tens of thousands of draft animals. The Cimarron Cutoff crossed the northwestern corner of the Oklahoma Panhandle. In this photograph the ruts left by the wagons still remain on the Oklahoma prairies. Photo by Jim Argo

part of their agricultural pattern. Thus their sympathies were Southern. It was Southerners, however, who had driven them from their traditional homelands in Georgia, Alabama, Tennessee, Florida, and Mississippi. On the other hand, the federal government was protecting them in their new homes, but newly elected President Abraham Lincoln held abolitionist views and spoke openly of allowing white settlement in the Indian Territory. Then, with the outbreak of war in April 1861, the federal government withdrew its troops from all posts in the Indian Territory, thereby admitting it could not protect the Indians from Confederate attacks. Lincoln and his advisers did not want the Indian Territory to be swallowed by the South, but defense of Eastern states seemed far more important to them.

The newly organized Confederate States of America wanted the Five Civilized Tribes as allies. The Indian Territory could be a useful buffer against a Union invasion of Texas, as well as a strategic staging area should Southern forces invade Kansas. In Texas the secession convention early in 1861 sent delegates to ask the Five Civilized Tribes to ally with the Confederacy. In February these delegates found the Choctaws, Chickasaws, Creeks, and other tribes willing to side with the Confederacy. The Texas delegates were unable to secure a favorable response, however, from Chief John Ross of the Cherokees.

Ross moved slowly because he did not want to act emotionally. He feared what might befall his tribe should the Union win the war. Moreover, he knew that many

Albert Pike, pictured in Masonic regalia, negotiated treaties of alliance between the Five Civilized Tribes and the Southern Confederacy in 1861. He later commanded the Indian troops involved in the Battle of Pea Ridge in 1862. OHS

Cherokees, particularly the full bloods of the anti-treaty party, were cool toward the South. The old division within the tribe caused by the Treaty of New Echota, which had forced the Cherokees to move westward, had already been reopened. In 1859 the Reverend Evan Jones restructured the Keetoowah Society a pro-Union, abolitionist organization, while Stand Watie and his followers organized chapters of the Knights of the Golden Circle to promote a pro-slavery and pro-Southern attitude in 1860. The Keetoowahs, known as "pins" because of the emblem their members wore, were openly fighting the "Knights" by late 1860, and the Cherokees were a divided people once again, although Ross was able to postpone a decision to align the Cherokees with either side during the summer of 1861.

The withdrawal of federal troops from the territory decided the issue, for shortly afterward a Confederate force from Texas arrived. Many Indians who had wanted to remain neutral—and even many who were pro-Union—thereupon were forced to accept the South and to take up arms. Realizing this advantageous position, Southern officials acted quickly. Albert Pike, a lawyer at Little Rock, Arkansas, who had handled some legal matters for the Choctaws and was trusted by the Civilized Tribes, was sent by the South to make treaties with these nations as well as with the plains tribes, treaties that would ally them with the Confederacy.

Arriving at Tahlequah early in the summer of 1861, Pike began negotiations with the Cherokees. When Ross dragged these talks on with no end in sight, Pike left and in the next several weeks signed treaties with the other four Civilized Tribes. These assured their friendship for the Confederacy in return for perpetual Southern recognition of the Indians' title to their lands. Journeying on, Pike concluded similar agreements with the plains tribes, even with the Comanches, who promised to raid into Union Kansas rather than Confederate Texas. Returning then to Tahlequah, Pike in October concluded a Southern alliance with the Cherokees. Ross reluctantly had decided, following early Confederate victories in the war, that his tribe had to come to terms with the South—although many Cherokees were opposed to his actions.

Pike's treaties called for the Indians to raise troops for the South: one regiment of

Cherokees, another of Choctaws and Chickasaws, and a third from the Seminoles and Creeks. The Confederacy, in return, would provide equipment and pay and would protect the Indian Territory from Union invasion, in addition to paying the annuities which the United States previously had paid the tribes. The Five Civilized Tribes quickly kept their end of the bargain by raising 5,000 soldiers. Prominent among their leaders was Stand Watie, who on July 12, 1861, was commissioned a colonel in the Confederate Army.

The first battle in which Indian troops were engaged was against their fellow tribesmen. This resulted because Opothleyahola, the Creek leader, was unhappy with the treaty signed by his tribe with Pike. He had been absent when the negotiations had taken place, but his signature had been placed on the document. Upon his return he refused to recognize any alliance with the

Douglas H. Cooper was Indian agent to the Choctaw and Chickasaw Indians prior to the Civil War, and later commanded the Department of Indian Territory for the Confederacy during the war. His defeat at the Battle of Honey Springs jeopardized Confederate control of the Indian Territory. OHS

Confederacy, and those Upper Creeks faithful to him, along with their families, livestock, and slaves, began gathering at his plantation, where they retreated to a camp on the Deep Fork of the Canadian River. There he and his followers, who also included some Delawares, Seminoles, Shawnees, and Comanches, came to be known as the "Neutral Indians," and they decided to remove to Kansas, setting out November 5. By this time his following numbered some 6,000 men, women, and children.

Unfortunately for them, the pro-Confederate Indians refused to allow neutrality. On November 15, 1861, Colonel Douglas Cooper, a former Choctaw agent, set out with a force of 1,400 Indians and Texans to stop them from reaching Kansas and to recover the Creek treasury that Opothleyahola possessed. Cooper's scouts soon located the Neutrals, and on November 19 the Battle of Round Mountain (the first battle of the Civil War in Indian Territory) was fought. Opothleyahola's warrior's were fighting for the welfare of their families. Led by two Seminoles, Billy Bowlegs and Alligator, they defeated Cooper's Confederates while Opothleyahola led the Neutrals farther north to a new camping place at Caving Banks (Chusto-Talasah) on Bird Creek.

Cooper was determined to force Opothleyahola's people to join the Confederacy, so reinforced by a regiment of Cherokees early in December he again sent out scouts to locate the Neutrals, and on December 9 a second engagement was fought. The Neutrals used the natural fortifications at Caving Banks to good advantage, and the Confederates were driven back a second time. Before Cooper could take further action, his regiment of Cherokees withdrew, and the Confederate leader retreated to Fort Gibson to reorganize.

Cooper remained steadfast in his determination to overwhelm the Neutrals and make them join the Confederacy, and when he was reinforced by 1,500 Confederates from Van Buren, Arkansas, commanded by Colonel James McIntosh, he again took the field during the third week in December. Marching up the Verdigris River from Fort Gibson, McIntosh located the Neutrals northeast of Caving Banks at a place called Chustenahlah (near the present Skiatook). There on December 26 the Neutrals twice turned back Confederate charges, but a third assault destroyed the resistance of the tired and under-supplied Neutrals. That night a fierce blizzard blanketed the area, and the freezing chill numbed Opothleyahola's followers, who were without shelter. McIntosh followed those Neutrals who escaped capture as they fled toward Kansas, harassing them and capturing stragglers. Hundreds died before reaching Union lines, and many of the survivors lost limbs to frostbite. Eventually some members of this Neutral column would return to the Indian Territory in Union uniforms.

With Opothleyahola's followers gone, the Confederacy reigned supreme in the Indian Territory—but only for a short time. The North recovered quickly from its early defeats in the Trans-Mississippi West and organized a large army for a sweep into Arkansas in the spring of 1862. Led by General Samuel Curtis, this force crossed southern Missouri to confront Confederate defenders in Arkansas commanded by General Sterling Price. Faced with this Union threat, Major General Earl Van Dorn, commanding Confederates in the West, ordered Brigadier General Albert Pike to take all forces from the Indian Territory and join Price to confront Curtis' force. Pike, who had been given overall command of the Indian Territory, was headquartered at Fort Davis (named for Confederate President Jefferson Davis) located on the southwest side of the Arkansas River at the Three Forks area (in present Muskogee County).

Pike responded to Van Dorn's orders by taking all his Indian forces into Arkansas, leaving the territory without defense—in violation of the agreements he had negotiated (these had stipulated that no Indian troops would be withdrawn from the territory without permission of the tribal governments, which was never secured). Van Dorn's hope for a quick victory over Union forces in Arkansas was not realized. At the Battle of Pea Ridge, fought on March 6 to 8, 1862, the Confederates sustained heavy losses and had to retreat. The Indian regiments fought bravely and well, Stand Watie and his Cherokees captured a Union artillery battery, but Van Dorn in his report slighted their contribution. This so enraged Pike that he withdrew to the southern part of the Indian Territory to establish Fort McCulloch on the west side of the Blue River (in present Bryan County), leaving Douglas Cooper in command at Fort Davis.

Cooper's position never became secure.

Colonel John Drew's Confederate Indian troops deserted en masse to the enemy twice during the Civil War, once before the battle of Caving Banks, and then prior to the fall of Tahlequah. He did, however, lead his Cherokees valiantly and well throughout the war. OHS

The Confederate defeat at Pea Ridge left him without adequate men and supplies to defend the northern part of the Indian Territory. Union officials realized Cooper's weakness, and in April 1862 the "Indian Expedition" was organized to regain control of the territory. This expedition consisted of troops from Kansas and other Northern states along with volunteers from Opothleyahola's followers. Commanded by Colonel William Weer, a Kansan, this force on June 2 set out down the Grand River from Baxter Springs, Kansas.

Once in the Indian Territory, Weer's command constantly was harassed by Stand Watie's Cherokees until on July 3 the two forces met in open battle at Locust Grove. For a time it seemed Watie and his men

would repel the Union invaders, but a withering Yankee cannon fire broke the Confederate line and insured a Northern victory. Following this victory, Weer sent one column to occupy Fort Gibson and another to take Tahlequah. The fort fell easily, but Tahlequah was well defended. For a time it seemed that siege of the Cherokee capital would be necessary, but the full-blood Cherokee regiment of Colonel John Drew deserted to the Union side, leaving the town open. On July 12 Weer's troops occupied Tahlequah without firing a shot. Chief John Ross and his family, who were in Tahlequah, thereupon moved to Philadelphia, Pennsylvania, where he helped organize Unionists in the Indian Territory through his agents.

The Confederate defeats at Locust Grove, Fort Gibson, and Tahlequah made it appear that nothing could stop Weer from marching all the way to the Red River; however, the column halted of its own accord. Many of Weer's soldiers were unhappy at the thought of advancing further into the Indian Territory because Watie's cavalry was harassing their detachments, and they feared their line of supply from Kansas (and their line of retreat, if that became necessary) would be cut if they advanced toward the Red River. Moreover, a rumor was circulating among the Federals that a Confederate force equal in size to their own was across the Arkansas at Fort Davis. When Weer argued at Tahlequah for an advance, he was charged with insanity and disloyalty by Colonel Frederick Salomon of Wisconsin and a band of Union officers and men; they relieved Weer of command and then retreated to Kansas during the summer of 1862. This gave the Confederates time to reorganize, and Stand Watie, elected Cherokee chief by pro-Southern members of the tribe, was able to spread terror in southern Kansas and southwestern Missouri by raiding undefended towns. Watie also burned Ross' home at Park Hill, Rose Cottage, as well as the Cherokee capitol building in Tahlequah.

By the fall of 1862 the situation in the Indian Territory was degenerating toward chaos. William A. Phillips, aided by agents sent by John Ross, organized the pro-Federal Indian Home Guard, and was spreading fear among Confederate Indians along the Verdigris River. And William C. Quantrill had arrived from Kansas in mid-1862 with his band of cutthroats, called irregulars, to

Far right
Colonel Tandy Walker
commanded the Confed-
eracy's Second Indian
Brigade, composed of
Choctaws, Chickasaws, and
Caddos, during 1864 and
1865. OHS

Below
The Battle of Honey
Springs was the largest
Civil War engagement
fought in the Indian Terri-
tory. The Union victory in-
sured that Indian Territory
would not remain in the
hands of the Confederacy.
This marker was erected by
the United Daughters of
the Confederacy to honor
the Confederate soldiers
who fought in the battle.
Photo by Jim Argo

wreak havoc. Despite Watie's efforts to provide order and stability in the Cherokee and Creek country, the area was suffering from its own miniature civil war and from lawlessness.

Union planners then decided to recapture the Indian Territory, and in October 1862 General James G. Blunt led a Federal column into the area from Arkansas. Douglas Cooper, still officially in command of Confederate forces north of the Canadian River, moved his troops to Fort Wayne, a post first established in 1838 (in northeastern Adair County) but moved a few months later to present Delaware County and abandoned in 1842. His hope was to make a thrust into Kansas, diverting Blunt's forces there to protect that area. Blunt learned of Cooper's presence, made a forced march, and engaged the Confederates in battle on October 22. During the one-hour contest near old Fort Wayne,

the Federals tried to engulf Cooper's troops, but failed. Cooper was able to retreat, but his defeat effectively opened the Cherokee country to Union control—and it encouraged the full-blood Cherokees to ally with the North.

The pro-Union Cherokees met in National Council at Cowskin Prairie in February 1863, elected Thomas Pegg acting chief, reasserted that John Ross was the legitimate chief of the Cherokees, repudiated the treaty with the Confederacy, declared Stand Watie's Confederate Cherokee government illegal, confiscated all the property of pro-Confederate Cherokees, and freed all slaves in the tribe. When pro-Confederate Cherokees called for a National Council to meet at Webbers Falls on April 25, Colonel William A. Phillips, commanding the Union Indian Brigade at Fort Gibson, crossed the Arkansas and attacked the pro-Southerners, who fled in disorder. Thereafter until the end of the Civil War, there were two Cherokee governments contending for supremacy, with Union sympathizers in the majority.

Desperate for supplies, on May 28 Watie led his pro-Southern troops to attack a Federal supply train steaming to Fort Gibson. There he met defeat, as he did again in June when he attempted to capture a Union wagon train. Watie then retreated to Honey Springs, a Confederate supply depot on the Texas Road south of Three Forks, where he joined forces with Douglas Cooper to rally their troops for an attack on Fort Gibson, which was seen as the key to the Union presence in the Indian Territory.

At Fort Gibson, General Blunt and his troops crossed the Arkansas below the mouth of the Grand and engaged Watie and Cooper on July 17. Heavy rains preceded this Battle of Honey Springs, and the Confederates had allowed their gunpowder, already of inferior quality, to become damp—to their great disadvantage during the fighting. Blunt used the large number of cannons he had brought to good advantage, and after bitter fighting the Confederate line broke. At Webbers Falls the local residents listened to the echoes of cannon fire and learned the outcome of the battle when retreating Confederates were followed by Union troops who burned the town.

Late in August 1863, when General William Steele and a Confederate force approached Fort Gibson, Blunt again came out to do battle. The Federals followed part of Steele's troops to Perryville, and there defeated the Confederates and destroyed their supply depot. More Confederate supplies were lost at North Fork Town, and on September 1 a Union force captured Fort Smith, thereby closing the upper Arkansas to any Confederate traffic. The fall of Fort Smith signaled the end of any real hope for a Southern victory in the region—and signaled the onset of great suffering. Roving bands of thieves and killers, especially the men of William Quantrill, cloaked themselves behind the Confederate flag and spread terror in the territory. Medical supplies and food were in desperately short supply.

Early in 1864 the Confederacy made a last attempt to reassert its authority. Two new Indian units were formed: the First Indian Cavalry Brigade, composed of Cherokees, Creeks, Seminoles, and Osages and commanded by Stand Watie, who was promoted to brigadier general; and the Second Indian Cavalry Brigade, composed of Choctaws, Chickasaws, and Caddos and commanded by Colonel Tandy Walker. Watie thereby became the only Indian general on either side during the Civil War. Although he was openly critical of the Confederacy for abandoning its Indian allies, Watie and his men continued to fight. They conducted guerrilla raids that thrust deep into Union territory, and they had some notable successes. At Cabin Creek on September 18 to 19, 1864, they captured 250 Federal supply

Colonel William A. Phillips led the Union Indian Home Guard and was a stalwart friend of Indian refugees devastated by the war. OHS

wagons and distributed food to needy Indian refugees.

Despite such limited successes, the South was defeated. On April 9, 1865, Robert E. Lee admitted the inevitable and surrendered his army to Ulysses S. Grant at Appomattox Courthouse in Virginia. Some Confederates in the Trans-Mississippi West swore to continue the war indefinitely, but in May General Edmund Kirby Smith, commander of the department, surrendered. In mid-May the Indian Territory leaders of the various tribes called for a united meeting at Council Grove to discuss a course of action, but disbanded when threatened with Union force. Meeting again at Camp Napoleon (on the Washita River), these leaders agreed to unite in negotiations with the United States. On June 23, 1865, General Stand Watie formally surrendered his troops, the last Confederate force to quit the field. At long last the bloody war was over.

CHAPTER VIII

Reconstruction and Pacification

After federal law was extended to the Indian Territory following the days of lawlessness after the Civil War, a common event was the caravan of marshals and prisoners en route to court in Fort Smith. Harper's Weekly *illustrated this in its May 15, 1875, issue. Courtesy, Western History Collections, University of Oklahoma Library*

Not all residents of the Indian Territory had allied with the Confederacy during the Civil War, but all would suffer in the decade that followed. The eleven states that had seceded would feel the presence of federal troops and basic changes in their laws, but none of them would endure the hardships imposed on the natives of the Indian Territory. Some Northern leaders not only wanted vengeance for Indian participation in the rebellion, but also to destroy tribal government and to nullify tribal ownership of land.

Residents of Kansas were most interested in breaking up the reservations. They were bitter at the destruction and death caused by raiders operating out of the Indian Territory, and they wanted retribution. In addition, they wanted tribes still in Kansas moved to the Indian Territory, leaving Indian land in Kansas open to white settlement. Some Kansans wanted to end the concept of Indian reservations completely, forcing all heads of families to take an allotment and opening the remaining acres to white homesteading. Such a desire had been voiced during the Civil War by Senators Samuel Pomeroy and James Lane of Kansas, who in 1862 had proposed that treaties with the Five Civilized Tribes be voided and the Indians of Kansas moved to the Indian Territory. Congress passed this measure in 1863, and it became the basic plan for reconstruction of the Indian Territory.

The blow was delivered in the fall of 1865. Leaders of the Five Civilized Tribes, with chiefs from the Osage, Wichita, Caddo, Seneca, Shawnee, Quapaw, and Comanche nations, met with federal officials at Fort Smith in September. Representing the United States were Dennis Cooley, Commissioner of Indian Affairs; Elijah Sells, Superintendent of the Southern Superintendency; General William S. Harney, representing the Army; Colonel Ely Parker, a Seneca mixed-blood; and Thomas Wistar, a mem-

Pro-Southern Cherokee delegates to the Fort Smith conferences included, from the left, John Rollin Ridge, Saladin Watie, Richard Field, E.C. Boudinot, and W.P. Adair. OHS

ber of the Society of Friends. In his opening statement Commissioner Cooley told the Indians that by joining the Confederacy they had "lost all rights to annuities and lands," that their treaties had been voided, and that their tribal laws no longer were valid. Each tribe would have to negotiate a new treaty with the United States, free all slaves, and cede a portion of their lands for use by other tribes.

The Indians were stunned by the severity of this pronouncement. This was especially hard on the Cherokees, for its pro-Union tribal government had already confiscated the property of all Cherokees who had sided with the Confederacy. John Ross and others spoke so vehemently against the proposals that no treaties could be negotiated immediately, and the conference recessed to resume in Washington the following year. At the conclusion of the meeting in Fort Smith, simple treaties were signed wherein the Indians renewed their allegiance to the United States.

The fall and winter of 1865 to 1866 was a time of terrible suffering in the Indian Territory. Few crops had been planted the previous spring, and hunger took a heavy toll. Survivors, suffering from malnutrition, fell prey by the hundreds to cholera, which

ravaged the refugee camps. When at last the survivors of the Cherokee, Creek, and Seminole tribes returned home, it was to find waste and destruction; contending armies had stripped the countryside of livestock, knocked down fences, and burned homes, while unplowed fields had returned to grass and weeds. Moreover, those tribes which had split into Northern and Southern factions during the war (Cherokee, Creek, and Seminole) faced internal quarrels that still pitted brother against brother.

In the negotiations in 1866 the United States was represented by Commissioner Cooley, Elijah Sells, Colonel Parker, and Secretary of the Interior James Harlan. The quarrelsome Cherokees sent two delegations, one headed by an ill John Ross, the other by Stand Watie and several pro-Southern Cherokees who were demanding that the Cherokee tribe be divided into two separate nations. The Choctaws and Chickasaws were served by Peter Pitchlynn, the Southern Creeks by D.N. McIntosh, the Northern Creeks by Chief Oktarsars Harjo Sands, and the Seminoles by John Chupco. Because of differences within the tribes, the Indians were negotiating from a position of weakness, while the American negotiators were united in their desire to force the Indians to give up part of their lands.

Four treaties were signed—one with the Creeks, one with the Cherokees, another with the Seminoles, and one with the Choctaws and Chickasaws. Known as the Treaties of 1866, these four agreements sharply reduced tribal prerogatives. Slavery was ended and the freedmen ordered adopted into the tribes. All five nations had to agree to allow railroads to build across the territory, and there was agreement in principle to an intertribal government for the territory. The contending Cherokee delegations agreed to a single treaty when the federal government promised to restore the confiscated property of the pro-Confederates. The most crushing feature of these treaties was the loss of land. The Cherokees had to cede their 800,000 acres in Kansas, while the federal government assumed de facto ownership of the Cherokee Outlet. The Cherokees were forced to agree that the government could settle other tribes in the Outlet and in what had been the principal Cherokee reservation as the need arose. The Seminoles had to sell their land to the government for fifteen cents an acre, but they did receive a new reservation of 200,000 acres in the western section of the Creek Nation—which they had to buy at fifty cents an acre. Creek lands were sharply reduced. The tribe lost more than three million acres in the western half of their reserve for the government's price of thirty cents an acre. The Choctaws and Chickasaws sold what had been known as the Leased District to the government for $300,000.

The signing of the Treaties of 1866 saw life in the Indian Territory drastically changed. No longer were the Indians masters of their own destiny, makers of their own laws, or sole owners of vast stretches of land. No longer were their constitutions the sole foundation on which their governments operated. In addition, they had to overcome chaotic economic and social conditions. Using the same stoicism with which they faced removal and resettlement in the 1830s, they set about rebuilding homes, fencing land, and plowing and planting, and they began healing the wounds of tribal divisions during the Civil War.

In the Cherokee Nation the old hatreds had been intensified by the war, and they had divided along the old lines: those who had opposed the Treaty of New Echota and who had supported the Union on one side,

Daniel N. McIntosh commanded a Confederate Creek regiment during the Civil War. He later represented his tribe during the treaty conferences at Fort Smith in 1866. OHS

and those who had favored the treaty and had supported the South on the other side. When John Ross died unexpectedly on August 1, 1866, while negotiating in Washington, the situation grew worse. Strangely, however, some of his followers joined adherents of Stand Watie to form the Union Party in 1867, and thereafter this group for almost two decades would control the tribe despite opposition from a hard-core band of disciples of John Ross.

The end of serious factionalism among the Cherokees in 1867 marked the beginnings of economic recovery for the tribe. Aided by missionaries sent by Presbyterians, Baptists, and Moravians, the Cherokees rebounded quickly, and by the early 1870s prosperity was returning. Schools were established for Cherokee children, crops were replanted and herds rebuilt, and their courts restored social order.

The Creeks, who also had been divided by removal and by the Civil War, were unable

Right
The Cherokee National Capitol, Tahlequah, was constructed in 1870 as part of the reconstruction effort following the Civil War. It was used following statehood as the Cherokee County Courthouse. OHS

Opposite page, top
The Indian Territory provided a haven for outlaws during the post-Civil War period. Belle Starr and Blue Duck were among the many famous and not-so-famous criminals who found refuge during the pre-statehood period. OHS

Opposite page, bottom
A favorite hideout of criminals in the Indian Territory was Robber's Cave near Wilburton. At one time frequented by the likes of the James brothers, Belle Starr, and other notorious fugitives, the cave is now preserved as a state park. Photo by Jim Argo

Below
Freedmen of the Five Civilized Tribes were a major point of conflict between the United States and the tribes. The federal government demanded that the freedmen be included as members of the tribes, while the Indians adamantly opposed their enrollment as tribal members. OHS

to restore peace and harmony so quickly. Samuel Checote, a Confederate veteran, was elected primary chief in 1867, but Union sympathizers within the tribe refused to accept him. This led to open warfare within the tribe in the early 1870s, and federal troops were required to restore order. For more than two decades thereafter, only the presence of soldiers at nearby Fort Gibson prevented continued violence. With such quarrels openly evident, it was difficult for the tribe to return to prosperity, although a new tribal constitution, adopted after Chief Checote's election, did allow tribal leaders to effect some progress. Under this organ of government, the tribal reserve was divided into six judicial districts with a supreme court at Muskogee providing ultimate resolution to disputes, while companies of light-horsemen provided police protection. The Creeks were a hard-working and ambitious people, and by 1880 their fields again were green, thousands of horses and cattle grazed their pastures, and schools educated their children.

The Seminoles suffered most terribly from factionalism. At the end of the Civil War they were moved to a new reserve and began rebuilding—only to learn that they were still on Creek land. They bought another 175,000 acres from the Creeks at one dollar an acre. Yet on this land there was no peace, for the Seminoles were still divided according to Civil War loyalties: John Chupco and the pro-Union forces against John Jumper and the pro-Confederates. Living apart from one another, each band developed its own government until the 1880s, when the division mended and the tribe began cataloging its laws; although the statutes were never published. As a people the Seminoles had never liked farming, and because of their several moves and political divisions they were hesitant to begin tilling the soil on their new reservation. Only the threat of starvation at last forced them to begin planting and harvesting, but prosperity did not visit the Seminole part of the Indian Territory.

Ironically the tribes that suffered the least during reconstruction were the two that had supported the Confederacy most strongly: the Choctaws and Chickasaws. Their lands in the southern part of the territory were least touched by war, and the tribes were not divided by factionalism after the conflict ended. Therefore life in these two nations was not disrupted economically or socially. Moreover, they were able to sell coal from mines in their land when railroads built through, and the range cattle industry came to the Chicksaw Nation.

In the immediate aftermath of the war, while the various Civilized Tribes were attempting to rebuild, the Army had returned to occupy posts such as Fort Gibson, but there were so few troops that they did little to restore order. Until 1870 Army officers acted as agents to the tribes, after which they were returned to civilian agents—often

OKLAHOMA: LAND OF THE FAIR GOD

Right
Isaac C. Parker, the "law west of Fort Smith," served as United States judge for the Western District of Arkansas for twenty-one years. During his tenure he won the title of the "hanging judge." OHS

Far right
United States deputy marshals enforced federal law in the Indian Territory and Oklahoma Territory. One of the most famous was Bill Tilgham. OHS

Northern carpetbaggers seeking personal enrichment rather than interested in helping the Indians. In 1874 control of the Five Civilized Tribes was centralized as the Union Agency, which the following year opened its headquarters at Muskogee.

Another major problem during this era was the status of the freedmen. These former slaves did not receive land, although they were reluctantly granted citizenship by all the Five Civilized Tribes except the Chickasaws. Many of the freedmen squatted on land in the territory. Without money—and largely without hope—some freedmen turned to stealing as a means of livelihood. To control them, vigilante law was exercised by members of the Five Civilized Tribes, a practice that sometimes led to abuses and needless cruelty. Some freedmen, caught with a stolen horse, cow, or hog, were executed on the spot, while many were severely flogged for lesser offenses. Eventually the blacks settled near one another for self-protection, a practice that led to the development of several all-black communities.

Controlling the white outlaw bands operating in the territory proved more difficult. In the immediate post-Civil War years the Indian Territory was being ravaged by roving bands of outlaws, restless veterans trained in the recent conflict in hit-and-run tactics, killing, and robbery. Such notorious figures as the James brothers, the Younger gang, and the Daltons regarded the territory as a good hideout and as a place where theft could be committed without fear of capture,

while homegrown outlaws such as Ned Christie contributed to the lawlessness. Indian courts had jurisdiction only over issues involving Indians, but not over crimes committed by whites—even those involving a white against an Indian. These cases, along with cases involving federal laws, had to be tried in the nearest United States District Court.

Immediately after the Civil War the nearest federal court was at Van Buren, Arkansas; Indians had to ride many miles and miss days of work to appear there. Tribal leaders therefore urged the government to establish a district court at Muskogee where the Union Agency was located. On March 3, 1871, the government transferred the court for the Western District of Arkansas, whose jurisdiction included the Indian Territory, to Fort Smith. Judge William Story presided during the next three years, but his effectiveness was terminated when he was called before a congressional committee to explain how $714,000 had been spent in his district in just three years. Following Story's resignation, President Grant appointed Isaac C. Parker to the bench, and the situation changed dramatically.

For twenty-one years following his appointment in 1875, Judge Parker was known as "the law west of Fort Smith" and as "the hanging judge." More than 13,000 prisoners would be arrested in the Indian Territory and taken to Fort Smith for judgment, and Parker was a stern, puritanical man who did not flinch in handing out the death sentence—151 of them, of whom eighty-three were executed. Parker was described by contemporaries as "white of hair and beard, with pink cheeks and slightly rotund," a man "with a twinkle in his eye and a little contagious chuckle which always made [youngsters] think of Santa Claus."

The United States marshals served as Parker's executives, assigning warrants and writs to be served by deputies in the field. They worked in bad weather and good, in extreme cold and stifling heat. They expected violence, for few criminals in "the Nations" wanted to be brought before Judge Parker. These deputy marshals also performed their work for no salary, only fees. Each received seventy-five cents a day to feed his prisoners, ten cents a mile for travel, and two dollars for each paper served. If in the course of duty he killed a man, he not only lost his fees, but also had to pay

jurisdiction, and conflicts between them and the district court at Fort Smith were common. Once in 1872 a group of deputy marshals entered a Cherokee court to arrest the defendant, Ezekial Proctor, who was on trial for killing an Indian; the marshals wanted him for killing a white man. When the Cherokees refused to give up their prisoner, guns were drawn and fired until seven deputy marshals and four Cherokees were dead. Despite such quarrels, however, Judge Parker and the Federal District Court at Fort Smith did reduce outlawry in the Indian Territory.

The tribes removed to the Indian Territory from Kansas added to the confusion and uncertainty in the area. Kansas was experiencing a growing demand for land, especially that assigned to various tribes of Indians, owing to passage of the Homestead Act in 1862, the tendency of many people

Among the ablest of the deputy marshals who served in the Indian Territory was Bass Reeves (pictured at the far left). He earned a reputation as being fearless, and he always brought in his man. OHS

burial expenses. This work was extremely hazardous—sixty-five deputy marshals lost their lives in the line of duty—yet good men continued to serve, men such as Bill Tilghman, Chris Madsen, and Charlie Colcord. Blacks such as Grant Johnson, Bass Reeves, and Ike Rogers served with equal valor and honesty—but without the fame that came to their white counterparts.

The Indian courts were jealous of their

to move west after the end of the Civil War, and almost unlimited immigration from Europe, along with the introduction of pioneering techniques and inventions, such as barbed wire, the windmill, the sod house, and drought-resistant kinds of wheat. To clear lands for white settlers the government decided to move these natives to the Indian Territory, and after 1865 a steady stream of new exiles flowed there.

Additional Indian reservations were established following the Civil War in the
Indian Territory. Indians
from as far away as Cali-
fornia and Washington
were removed to Oklahoma
to free lands for non-Indian
settlers. OHS

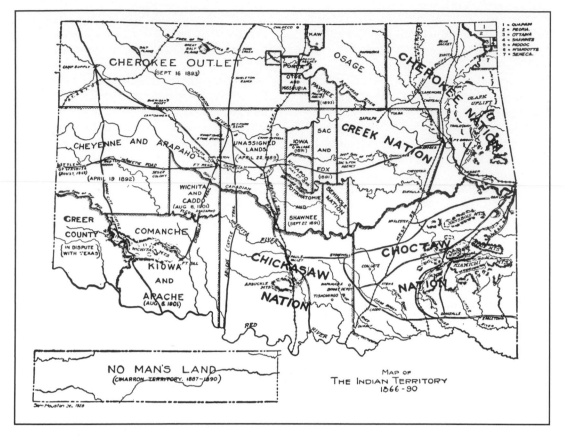

So many whites had already encroached on the reserves these Indians had in Kansas that it required little inducement by the government to get them to move southward. First to arrive in the territory were the Pottawatomies, who in 1867 were settled between the Canadian and the North Canadian (west of the Seminoles). Just to the north of the Pottawatomies the so-called Absentee Shawnees were given a small reserve, as were the Iowa, while the Sac and Fox also were removed in 1867 to a reserve west of the Creek Nation between the Cimarron and North Canadian rivers.

Another tribe forced from Kansas was the Osage. Residents of the Sunflower State wanted the Osage land, which had been given to the tribe by the federal government in exchange for the reserve given to the Cherokees in the Indian Territory that once had been the home of the Osage Nation. As a result, in 1870 Congress heeded Kansans' demand for removal of the Osages by passing an act creating a new reservation for the tribe in the Indian Territory. The Osages accepted this move peacefully because, five years earlier, they had signed a treaty which, in principle, agreed to their removal southward. They bought title to a reservation in the Indian Territory from the Cher-

okees with the money paid them for their land in Kansas, bounded on the east by the 96th meridian and on the west by the Arkansas River. Individual Osages who wanted to remain in Kansas, accept a homesteader's allotment, and adopt white ways were allowed to remain in that state, but their acres were overrun by whites and they were cheated out of their land. They soon joined the remainder of the tribe in the Indian Territory. Ironically, it was an area their ancestors had left at the insistence of the federal government.

Kansans were still not content, however, and soon they wanted the reserves that belonged to all remaining Indians inside their borders. Yet to yield were the Kansas (or Kansa, or Kaw). Linguistically related to the Osages, the Kansas were given 100,000 acres in 1872 along the Arkansas River in the northwest corner of the Osage Reservation.

In Nebraska the Pawnee tribe found its situation similar to that faced by Indians in Kansas. Their reservation along the Loup River had been created in 1857, but almost immediately settlers and the territorial government began lobbying for their removal elsewhere to allow white settlement. In addition, the Pawnees faced frequent raids by the warlike Sioux. Because of this—and lured by tales of happy natives in the Indian Territory—the Pawnees agreed in 1872 to cede their reservation in Nebraska in return for a new home along Black Bear Creek between the Arkansas and Cimarron rivers. Congress failed to appropriate the promised funds for this move, but it was made anyway between 1873 and 1874.

The Ponca, another tribe in Nebraska, faced the same pressures, and in 1876 its members agreed to removal. Arriving in the Indian Territory in 1877, they lived for a time with the Quapaws, then received a tract of land along the western bank of the Arkansas. A few years later the Oto and Missouri tribes were moved to a home just south of the Ponca. By the 1880s this area along the Arkansas had been designated the Ponca Agency, and to it came yet another displaced people, the Tonkawas. A Caddoan folk, the Tonkawas had been moved in 1859 from Texas to the Leased District, but there they suffered continual abuse from the more warlike Kiowas and Comanches. In 1884 they were allowed to resettle along the Salt Fork of Arkansas (northwest of the Poncas).

The area inhabited by the Senecas and Quapaws was also used to settle several small bands of dispossessed Indians. Between 1865 and 1880 the Wyandottes, Peorias, Miamis, and Ottawas were located peacefully in this region, receiving land taken from the Quapaws and Senecas for their part in the Civil War. In 1873 that part of the Modoc tribe that had followed Captain Jack into rebellion in northern California and southern Oregon was given 4,000 acres taken from the Eastern Shawnees who had been settled there during the 1830s.

As new tribes arrived in the territory, the Bureau of Indian Affairs created individual agencies to watch over them. Gradually some of these were closed, their duties transferred to central agencies or to sub-agencies. By 1889 there were eight agencies operating: the Kiowa-Comanche Agency at Fort Sill, the Sauk and Fox Agency near present Stroud, the Darlington Agency near Fort Reno (for the Cheyenne-Arapaho), the Wichita-Caddo Agency near Anadarko, the Quapaw (or Neosho) Agency near present Miami, the Union Agency at Muskogee (for the Five Civilized Tribes), the Osage Agency at Pawhuska, and the Ponca Agency near present Ponca City.

While the tribes in the eastern and north-ern parts of the Indian Territory accepted these changes peacefully—if not happily—the warlike and fierce raiders of the plains refused to accept white authority or adopt white ways. Theirs was a nomadic existence, their economies based on raiding in addition to the slaughter of buffalo. The government attempted to settle these tribes on reservations by diplomacy, but military conquest proved the only permanent solution.

At the end of the Civil War, peace-longing congressmen and officials in the Indian Office, along with representatives of various religious denominations, still hoped for an easy solution to the threat posed by the plains Indians. At their insistence a council was called with tribal leaders of the Kiowas, Cheyennes, Arapahos, and Comanches to meet in October 1865 near present Wichita, Kansas. Known as the Little Arkansas Council, because of the stream running nearby, the plains tribes ceded all their lands north of the Arkansas River to the United States, promising to limit their wanderings to the Panhandle of Texas, the western part of present Oklahoma, and southwestern Kansas and to be no threat to white settlers. However, this treaty proved of short duration and the tribes continued their raids into Kansas and Texas.

Two years later, Congress sent yet another commission west to negotiate at Medicine Lodge Creek in southern Kansas. Chiefs of the Kiowas, Comanches, Kiowa-Apaches, Cheyennes, and Arapahos gathered to confer with Commissioner of Indian Affairs Nathaniel Taylor, John Henderson, Samuel F. Tappan, General W.S. Harney, General Alfred Terry, and Colonel C.C. Augur. The American commissioners warned the nomadic Indians that, with the movement of white farmers onto the plains and the eventual slaughter of the buffalo, they soon would be forced to turn to agriculture themselves, supplementing their diet with government-issued beef. In response Kiowa Chief Satanta summed up the feelings of the tribes gathered there: "I love to roam over the wide prairies, and when I do it, I feel free and happy, but when we settle down we grow pale and die." Comanche Chief Ten Bears spoke in a similar vein:

I was born upon the prairies, where the wind blew free, and there was nothing to break the light of the sun. I was born where there were no enclosures, and where every-

Left
Lieutenant Colonel George Armstrong Custer led the Seventh Cavalry in an assault on the Cheyenne camp of Black Kettle in the winter of 1867. OHS

Far left
Major General Philip Sheridan, Civil War hero and commander of the military department of the Missouri, was charged with the subjugation of the Cheyenne and Arapaho Indians in the winter of 1867 to 1868. OHS

Bottom, left
A Cheyenne Indian camp in western Oklahoma is shown following the defeat of the tribe at the hands of the Seventh Cavalry in 1867. OHS

Below
Black Kettle, a Cheyenne peace chief, survived the Sand Creek Massacre in Colorado, but fell during Custer's attack on his village during the Battle of the Washita. Courtesy, Western History Collections, University of Oklahoma Library

thing drew a free breath. I want to die there, and not within walls.

Despite these plaintive calls for freedom, the American commissioners already had decided that the Indians would have to give up yet more land, accept small reservations, allow railroads to be built, and permit whites on what had been Indian land. In return they would receive houses, schools, churches, and instruction in agriculture. The Kiowas and Comanches were to be settled in the Leased District, while the Cheyennes and Arapahos were to have a reserve in the

Cherokee Outlet.

Once the Treaty of Medicine Lodge was completed, the Indians returned to their old habits of following the buffalo and raiding. With the onset of winter, they went into winter quarters believing that the Army, as usual, would not undertake a campaign then. Yet Major General Philip Sheridan, commanding the Department of the Missouri, was angered that the tribes paid so little heed to the treaty just concluded, and he determined to punish them, particularly the Cheyennes of Chief Black Kettle. This tribe, driven from Colorado in 1864 follow-

ing the infamous Chivington Massacre at Sand Creek, was not living on their reservation in the Cherokee Outlet between the Cimarron and Arkansas rivers. Instead they had moved south to settle on the North Fork of the Canadian and along the Washita River. Early in 1868 Sheridan ordered his soldiers to establish a post later named Fort Supply on Beaver and Wolf creeks (in western Woodward County) from which they could mount a winter campaign.

Troops massed at Fort Supply when it opened in November 1868. Heavy snows began to fall just as scouts returned to report that Black Kettle and the Cheyennes were encamped on the upper Washita River. Lieutenant Colonel George A. Custer and eleven troops of the 7th Cavalry set out, not waiting for reinforcements, and on the morning of November 27 the impetuous Custer led his men into Black Kettle's village. This engagement, later known as the Battle of the Washita, was a victory for the Army. Black Kettle and more than 100 Cheyenne men, women, and children were killed, hundreds of Indian horses were shot,

Above
General Custer's captives from Black Kettle's camp are pictured being escorted to Camp Supply following the Battle of the Washita. Courtesy, Western History Collections, University of Oklahoma Library

Top
Custer's Demand, *a painting by Charles Schreyvogel, depicts the soldier's order for the surrender of the Cheyenne and Arapaho Indians in the spring of 1868. Courtesy, The Thomas Gilcrease Institute of American History and Art, Tulsa, Oklahoma*

105

Above
Fort Reno was established in 1874 to assist the agents at the Darlington agency in controlling the Cheyenne and Arapaho Indian reservations. Courtesy, Western History Collections, University of Oklahoma Library

Below
Federal Indian agents appointed by President Grant to carry out his "Peace Policy" were members of the Society of Friends. Brinton Darlington is seated in the center and Lawrie Tatum stands at the far right. OHS

and the village and its supplies were destroyed, while fifty Indians were captured. Custer, however, as he later would do at the Little Big Horn, had divided his command, and thirty soldiers commanded by Major Joel Elliott were killed. This winter strike so disheartened some Cheyennes that they, along with some Arapahos and Kiowas, moved onto the reservations to which they had been assigned—and stayed there.

Sheridan continued this massive winter campaign, striking the Kiowas and the Comanches, leading to the establishment of a reserve for them near the site of Fort Cobb. In addition, Sheridan established Camp Wichita, which soon was renamed Fort Sill. With its completion, the Army's cordon of

posts stretched from Fort Supply to Fort Sill, a valiant—if vain—attempt to keep the plains tribes from raiding into Texas. That same year the Cheyennes and Arapahos were assigned to a new reservation on the North Fork of the Canadian River (north of the Kiowa-Comanche reservation and west of the 98th meridian) by presidential proclamation. The agency for this reservation was first located at Pond Creek, but in 1870 it moved to become the Darlington Agency. Fort Reno would be built near this agency in 1874.

Despite this winter campaign and the building of new forts, the Comanches still roamed the plains and raided into Texas. Particularly inclined to this life was one band of the tribe, the Kwahadi, led by Chief Quanah Parker. The son of Chief Pete Nokona and Cynthia Ann Parker, a captive white girl who lived among the tribe more than twenty years, Quanah Parker was the bold, resourceful leader of a proud, free, and fierce people. Joining Parker and his Kwahadis were Kiowas and their leaders Satanta, Big Tree, and Satank. They likewise scorned farming and the confined life of the reservation.

When Ulysses S. Grant was inaugurated as president in 1869, he turned over administration of the reservations and agencies to members of various religious denominations, hoping the Native Americans would become Christianized and forego their old habits, customs, and economic system to live in harmony with whites. This became known as Grant's "Quaker Policy" because the Society of Friends (Quakers) played a prominent role in its implementation. As part of this plan, Lawrie Tatum, a Quaker from Indiana ignorant of Indian customs but long on brotherly love, was placed in charge of the Comanches and Kiowas at Fort Sill. Good-hearted and honest, Tatum could not control the reservation or halt the raiding. When he admonished one chief to keep his young men from joining forays south of the Red River, the chief told him that if he wanted these attacks to cease he would have to move Texas far away so his warriors could not find it.

One major cause of Indian raiding during this period was the slaughter of the buffalo, an animal which played a key role in the economic system of these tribes. Prior to the 1870s buffalo had been hunted by Indians, and professional hunters had killed them to feed railroad crews. In addition, sportsmen came from afar to hunt the beasts. There was a small commerical market for hides, which were used (with the hair on) as robes in sleighs and carriages. Despite the killing done to 1870, however, no one thought the animal was in any danger of extinction, for all attempts to tan buffalo hides into commercial-grade leather had produced a spongy product of little value. As late as 1869 one herd crossing the tracks delayed a Kansas Pacific train for nine hours.

With the discovery of a tanning process in Germany in 1871, the price paid for a single hide soon jumped to as much as three dollars, and a boom rapidly developed. Soon the techniques of the trade had also been developed. A hunter—the one doing the shooting—was the leader of a party. He hired as many men as he thought he needed to skin the buffalo he killed. A party might include as many as fifteen skinners, normally greenhorns who wanted to learn the business. Hunters at first used a Springfield .50 caliber Army rifle loaded with seventy grains of powder and a swedge ring ball. Soon, however, almost all of them switched to the .50 caliber Sharps rifle, which seemed made especially for killing buffalo. This was a large, heavy weapon designed not for the saddle but for a man hunting on foot. Its killing range, 600 yards, was so great that one Indian was moved to remark that the weapon "shoots today and kills tomorrow."

When a hunter sighted a herd, he approached it from downwind, for buffalo had a keen sense of smell. Once near the herd, the hunter aimed for a bull and shot it, hoping the others would mill about rather than stampede. When a herd did mill—the hunters called this a "stand"—the hunter often could kill a dozen or more of the beasts before the others began to run. Soon there were conflicting claims as to who had killed the most buffalo. One report claimed that Tom Dixon had killed 120 buffalo in one stand and that in a period of one month and five days he had slaughtered 2,173 of these shaggy beasts. Because of such wholesale slaughter, the northern herd (north of the Arkansas River) began to thin, and hunters went to Fort Dodge to ask the commanding officer about hunting south of the Arkansas in violation of treaties with the Indians.

Quanah Parker, a half-blood Comanche, led the Kwahadi Comanches in their transition from Plains nomads to reservation Indians. OHS

"Boys," replied the commanding officer, "if I were a buffalo hunter, I would hunt where the buffalo are." They did, and soon the southern herd also was thinning toward extinction.

The result of this slaughter was increased pressure on the plains tribes to leave their reservations to raid. Texans, in turn, complained loudly to Washington about these incursions, but officials there dismissed the assertions of these former Confederates. Finally in 1871 General William T. Sherman, commanding general of the Army, decided to inspect the region to determine the truth. In north Texas he saw the devastation wrought by the raids, and there near Fort Richardson he narrowly missed being killed by one party of marauders. A wagon train just hours away was attacked, seven people were killed, and their bodies were mutilated.

Sherman went directly to Fort Sill, there to meet Kiowa Chief Satanta and hear him brag about having led this raid. Sherman arrested him, along with Chiefs Satank and Big Tree, and sent them to Texas to stand trial. Satank was shot while trying to escape, while Satanta and Big Tree were convicted and sentenced to death. Their sentences were commuted, however, by the reconstruction governor of Texas, and they were imprisoned at Huntsville—only to be pardoned by that same governor in 1873. Satanta and Big Tree immediately led more raids in revenge for their captivity. Satanta

was captured on one such raid, brought to trial, and again was sentenced to prison. Four years later he committed suicide rather than spend his years in the Texas State Penitentiary.

Nevertheless, the raids continued, and by 1874 Quanah Parker and his Comanches, along with the Kiowas, had the frontier of north Texas aflame with their incursions. In response the government declared that all Indians off the reservation were renegades and subject to punishment, and the Secretary of War ordered the Army to capture them. The result was a five-pronged attack called the Red River Campaign, centering on the Panhandle of Texas (near Palo Duro Canyon). The maneuver involved Colonel Ranald S. MacKenzie, coming north with a large force; from Fort Sill came another body of troops; coming from the northeast was a third body of troops led by Colonel Nelson A. Miles; a fourth contingent of men marched from Fort Union, New Mexico; while a fifth column marched east from central New Mexico. More than 3,000 soldiers were engaged in this effort.

In the course of this campaign, carried out during the winter of 1874 to 1875, fourteen battles were fought. In one of these, an engagement at Tule Canyon, Captain (later General) Adna R. Chaffee made military history by shouting to encourage his soldiers, "If any man is killed, I will make him a corporal." By the spring of 1875 the Co-

manches' spirit had been broken. They were largely without horses and provisions, and most of their women and children had been captured and taken to Fort Sill. In small groups the warriors began trickling into that post to surrender. On June 2, 1875, Quanah Parker and more than 400 Kwahadis admitted defeat and laid down their arms at Fort Sill. Seventy-five Comanche and Kiowa leaders were arrested, tried, and sentenced to imprisonment in Florida, a few years later to be returned to their people at Fort Sill.

With the conquest of the Kiowas and Comanches, the Indian wars in the territory at last came to an end. Reluctantly they began scratching the earth to grow food for themselves and their families, for the paltry rations given them by the government were inadequate. They would be joined at Fort Sill in 1894 by Geronimo and proud Apache survivors of the wars in Arizona, but by that time the day of sole Indian ownership of the territory was past.

CHAPTER IX

Iron Horses and Longhorn Cattle

Frederic Remington sketched this stampede of Texas longhorns. A common occurrence on the trail drives from Texas to Kansas, the stampede was only one of many hazards that made the life of a cowboy exciting and brief. Courtesy, Bob L. Blackburn

*I*n the years immediately following the end of the Civil War, the eastern part of the United States was industrializing and urbanizing rapidly, and the people there needed a reliable system of transportation. The Far West would be connected to the booming East by a transcontinental railroad in 1869 with the completion of the Union Pacific, but the Indian Territory, with its native population, small towns, and lack of manufacturing, was slower to see rails laid.

Transportation had long been a problem in the region. The Arkansas and its major tributaries had provided ready highways for commerce, but these streams were inconsistent, rising and falling rapidly depending on rainfall and snow melt. The Red River similarly was a moody mistress for steamboats and flat-bottomed skiffs. Thus the Indian Territory at the end of the Civil War had no reliable system of transport other than wagons, but these slowed—and often stopped—when rains turned the few roads into quagmires of mud.

Between 1870 and 1880 the Army Corps of Engineers worked to improve navigation on the Arkansas and Red rivers, and goods did move by steamboat up the Red to the mouth of the Washita and up the Arkansas as far as Wichita, Kansas. The boats used on these streams were not the floating pleasure palaces that plied the Mississippi; rather they were sternwheelers of extremely shallow draft, woodburning carriers of freight and frontiersmen. There were always problems. Low water could halt transport or strand boats on sandbars.

By this period the railroad had proved to be the best means of moving people and freight. It represented the future, and the right to lay tracks across the Indian Territory was part of the Treaties of 1866, despite the protests of the various nations. Most Indian leaders did not want railroads crossing their lands for fear they would bring whites to the region, whites who would demand the

right to settle in the area and thereby threaten Indian control. The directors of several railroads were interested in pushing track across the territory because they hoped to get land bonuses in it and because this area lay between Kansas and Texas as well as between Arkansas and Colorado. The Cherokees would resist rail construction through their land, but to no avail; the snorting and puffing and shrill whistle of the iron horse soon would be heard in a country that previously had known only the wagon and buckboard.

The first line to push onto Indian lands was the Missouri, Kansas, and Texas (usually called the Katy), a branch line of the Union Pacific that operated in the states for which it was named. The owners of the line hoped to get three million acres in land subsidies within the Indian Territory, but Congress late in 1866, when it granted permission for the Katy to build across this area, could not give the land bonus because the area was not part of the public domain. Nevertheless, the Katy worked rapidly in order to forestall competition, and by 1870 the roadbed had been surveyed and track was being laid, largely following the old Texas Road from southeast Kansas to the Red River near the mouth of the Washita (at Colbert's Ferry). As the Katy built

southward, the towns of Chouteau, Gibson Station, Muskogee, Eufaula, McAlester, and Atoka became terminal points. By January 1873 locomotives were pulling freight and passenger cars across the Indian Territory in a north-south direction.

At the same time, the St. Louis and San Francisco, usually called the Frisco, was entering the territory on an east-west route. A subsidiary of the Atlantic and Pacific chartered to run between St. Louis and San Francisco, the Frisco began laying track through the Quapaw reservation west of the Missouri boundary in May 1871 and reached the Katy's tracks by September 1. At this strategic junction, where a city was bound to grow, there was a major quarrel. The Cherokee Nation, which opposed the laying of tracks through its lands, passed a law requiring one square mile to be reserved at every railroad station with lots sold only to Cherokee citizens. Elias C. Boudinot, son of the slain Cherokee leader and an influential mixed-blood Cherokee who served as attorney for several railroad interests, tried to gain control of 1,000 acres at the junction of the Frisco and Katy in order to start his own town, which he named Vinita in honor of sculptress Vinnie Ream. The Cherokee National Council disallowed Boudinot's claim, took control of the area, and renamed

These men are bridge building on the Wichita Falls and Northwestern Railroad, a branch line of the Missouri, Kansas, & Texas Railroad in western Oklahoma. Courtesy, Western History Collections, University of Oklahoma Library

the town Downingville in honor of Prinicpal Chief Lewis Downing. During the quarrel between the Nation and Boudinot, the Vinita Hotel, which Boudinot had built, was burned by his opponents. (Later the town's name would be changed back to Vinita.)

For almost a decade the Frisco's tracks ended at Vinita, but in 1882 the road was extended to a Creek village called Tulseytown (later to become the modern city of Tulsa) at the junction of the Arkansas and Cimarron rivers. In the latter part of the nineteenth century the line would build across to Oklahoma City, and in 1896 it would extend on to Quanah, Texas.

Another major railroad to enter the Indian Territory in this period was the Atchison, Topeka, and Santa Fe, better known simply as the Santa Fe. A branch line headed south into the territory in 1886 from Arkansas City, Kansas. Once its tracks entered the Indian Territory, Santa Fe officials immediately began lobbying in Washington to have the region through which it ran, the so-called Unassigned Lands in the center of the Indian Territory, opened to white settlement.

The Rock Island, yet another major carrier, built on a north-south line across the

Pictured is a Rock Island locomotive of the 1880s. The Chicago, Rock Island & Pacific Railroad was constructed through Oklahoma Territory in 1890, following the route of the Chisholm Trail. A branch line ran east to west across the state. OHS

territory in 1890, while the Choctaw, Oklahoma, and Gulf (later to become part of the Rock Island) in 1894 laid tracks from El Reno to Oklahoma City and southeast to McAlester by the following year. There it joined company track that ran on east to Wister. The track between McAlester and Wister had been laid in 1888 by a small line named the Choctaw Coal and Railway Company to transport the growing amount of coal being mined in the Choctaw Nation. The firm went bankrupt in 1891 and was acquired by the Rock Island.

The Kansas and Arkansas Valley connected Fort Smith, Arkansas, with Coffeyville, Kansas, while yet another line laid track from Fort Smith to Paris, Texas, in the early 1880s, crossing the Choctaw Nation. Other small lines in the territory included the Split Log; the Kansas City, Fort Scott, and Gulf; the Fort Smith and El Paso; and the Chicago, Kansas, and Nebraska. Most of these were eventually absorbed by one or another of the major lines. By 1903 more than 2,500 miles of track crisscrossed the area that became Oklahoma.

While various railroad companies were hurriedly constructing lines across the Indian

Territory, another major industry was developing: the cattle business. The animal involved in this business was the Texas longhorn, a direct descendant of the unseemly, lanky animals brought by Spanish conquistadors to the New World and then driven north from Mexico into Texas. By the 1820s, when Americans began moving into that area, the longhorn was running wild in south Texas, for it had found conditions there ideal: the climate was mild, the grass grew tall, and predatory animals were few. Domestic cattle brought by Anglo-Texans interbred with the longhorn, producing a different animal with almost unlimited color variations: brindle, blue, mouse-colored, duns, brown, cream, yellow in several shades, black, white, red, and splotchy combinations. Weighing about 800 pounds by age four, with some grizzled veterans of ten tipping the scales at 1,000 pounds, the longhorn was big at the shoulders, flat-ribbed, and thin at the hips. The animal's body was so long that the back frequently swayed as it walked. Packers asserted the animal was "all legs and horns," but there was considerable beef on his large frame—though much of it was stringy and tough. Cowboys declared that the longhorn, despite its independence and mean nature, was the best animal ever devised for trail driving. These long-legged animals had tough hoofs, great endurance, and the ability to walk up to sixty miles without water, farther than cattle of improved blood—the "high grade" stuff of a later period. A natural rustler, the longhorn seemed to thrive on almost any plant it could get into its mouth. His long legs carried him tirelessly over great distances, and he was unaffected by heat, hunger, and the unmelodious singing of cowboys. These virtues compensated in part for the distressing inability of the breed to produce quality beef.

When Texans returned from the Civil War, their Confederate currency was worthless and their economy was wrecked, but they did have beef—millions of longhorns free to anyone who could round them up in the brush country or buy them at four to five dollars a head. This was beef that would bring forty to fifty dollars a head at northern and eastern markets, although Texas had no rail connections. In 1866 a few enterprising Texans attempted to drive cattle through highly populated areas of the Indian nations, destroying crops and infect-

Joseph G. McCoy built cattle pens at the small Kansas town of Abilene for the herds of cattle from Texas he hoped to attract. He later was active in early Oklahoma Territory politics, narrowly being defeated for congressional delegate in 1890. OHS

ing milk cattle with splenic fever. Better known as "Texas fever," this disease spread by ticks carried on the longhorns; the hardy Texas cattle were immune. The tribes in the Indian Territory brought pressure to halt the longhorn drives across their lands, as did farmers in Arkansas, Missouri, and eastern Kansas.

It was twenty-nine-year-old Joseph G. McCoy who provided a solution. He persuaded the Kansas Pacific Railroad to build to the middle of Kansas, beyond the farmers' frontier (and west of the lands of the Five Civilized Tribes through which cattle were trailed northward), and establish loading pens there. This caused the birth of Abilene, Kansas, for merchants, gamblers, and assorted others flocked to the railhead to separate the cowboys from their pay. To publicize this railhead, McCoy hired Jesse Chisholm, a mixed-blood Cherokee, to pioneer a trail south and tell Texas cattlemen of this place to market their cattle. In 1867, the first year this trail was open, 35,009 cattle were marketed at Abilene, but in the next four years more than a million longhorns would be loaded there to be shipped to packing houses in Kansas City or Chicago. Each spring a river of beef would run north from Texas up the Chisholm Trail to Abilene, or up the Western Shawnee Trail, which in the Indian Territory started at Boggy Depot and ran to Sedalia, Missouri,

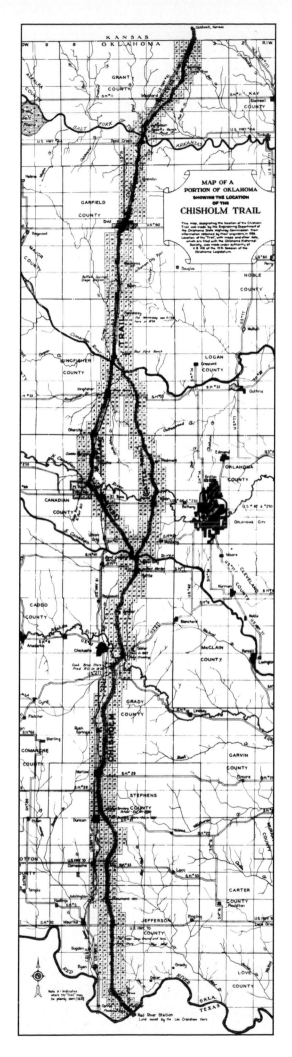

Left
Jesse Chisholm had been a trader in the Indian Territory and, along with Black Beaver, blazed a trail from Texas to Kansas. The Abilene Trail would eventually be renamed the Chisholm Trail. OHS

Far left
A map of the Chisholm Trail in western Oklahoma was drafted by the Oklahoma Department of Highways in the 1930s to locate the route of the trail and to preserve its heritage. OHS

and later to Baxter Springs, Kansas.

As the farmers' frontier advanced beyond Abilene and as the Santa Fe built across southern Kansas, other cities briefly boomed as "cowtowns": Newton, Wichita, Ellsworth, and then Dodge City, the "Queen of the Cow Town" from 1876 until the closing of the frontier about ten years later. The Great Western Trail was opened in 1876, running from south Texas north to the Red River (west of present Childress at Doan's Store) and then proceeding north across the Indian Territory.

Cattle drives across the Indian Territory and the profits realized by Texas cattlemen soon gave rise to a new industry north of the Red River: cattle grazing and ranching on Indian lands. Vast tracts owned by the Five Civilized Tribes were vacant because no tribesmen were farming them, and on this land grew blue stem and gramma grasses rich in the nutrients cattle needed to fatten. Interspersed among the grass-covered hills were creeks usually containing water, even during dry summer months. The climate was colder than in Texas, but cattlemen soon learned that this was an advantage; cattle that wintered in the Indian Territory lost their ticks, which could not

Left
A trail drive was divided into two main sections—the herd of cattle, often numbering 2,000 head, and the horse remuda, with 50 to 100 head of horses for the drovers. Securing sufficient water for such a large number of animals was often difficult in western Oklahoma. OHS

Opposite page, top
In the Indian Territory Indians worked as cowboys. These herders were Caddos and Kickapoos from central Oklahoma. Courtesy, Western History Collections, University of Oklahoma Library

Opposite page, bottom
Cowboys are pictured having dinner on the trail. Trail driving quickly became an established art during the decade following the Civil War. A well-trained unit of approximately fifteen men could easily handle upwards of 2,000 cattle on the three-month trail to Kansas. OHS

stand the cold weather. Thus the cattle no longer were carriers of splenic fever. Cattlemen who could claim rights in the Nations either by blood or by marriage crowded into the region, while some Indians took up ranching themselves.

The largest pasture of fine grass in the territory was the Cherokee Outlet, a 6.5 million-acre strip of land extending along the southern boundary of Kansas from the Arkansas River to just west of present Laverne. Prior to 1879 Texas drovers often paused in this area to fatten their cattle before taking them on to Abilene or Dodge City. If the market was glutted, the longhorns were held at the Outlet until prices rose. In 1879 the Cherokees decided to seek payment for grazing rights and began charging ten cents a head for pasturing cattle there. The cost per head rose rapidly, for the Cherokees quickly realized the value of this pasturage. For a time grazing rights reached one dollar a head, but soon fell back to about forty cents. In 1883 the cattlemen using this area decided to organize. At Caldwell, Kansas, that year they organized the Cherokee Strip Live Stock Association to prevent illegal grazing in the Outlet, to halt rustling there, and to negotiate with the Cherokees for a favorable contract. This was reached that same year: $100,000 per year rental for a period of five years. The agreement was renewed in 1888 at a fee of $200,000 per year. A lease

signed, the Association fenced the Outlet into pastures, subleasing plots to individual cattlemen who paid two cents per acre rental to the Association, which in turn paid the Cherokees. Within a short time most other tribes in the Indian Territory had made profitable leases with cattlemen—to the benefit of both.

Life within these leased tracts was hard. Ranchers erected only temporary quarters, paying young cowboys twenty-five to thirty dollars a month for long days of hard work. The Indians did not police these areas, and the states of Kansas and Texas had no jurisdiction in the territory. Therefore the Cherokee Strip Live Stock Association or individual ranchers had to perform the functions of government and try to protect life and property.

The typical cowboy of that era wore heavy woolen trousers; a woolen shirt whose sleeves were held up by sleeve garters; a large hat that protected him from rain, snow, and hot sun; a neckerchief knotted around his neck to be pulled up to cover his nose in wintry cold or blowing dust; and boots that fitted well into stirrups. Only in winter did the cowboy don a coat, for it tended to bind his arms and hold in the heat. Instead he wore a vest in which he kept his watch, his tobacco, and any coins he might possess. He took great care in selecting the gloves he wore year-round, which usually were of buckskin. His boots were a

Branding calves in the Indian Territory was a yearly event. Roundups were coordinated by cattlemen's associations, and mavericks were distributed to association members. Courtesy, Western History Collections, University of Oklahoma Library

source of great pride, although he tended to be awkward in them when not on horseback. Finally, he wore chaps made of heavy leather and fitting as a second pair of trousers, to protect his legs from thorns. Somehow chaps became a symbol of the trade to newcomers, who wanted to "look like cowboys."

Because most of the young men coming into the occupation had read lurid tales of what their life was supposed to be like, they also wanted a pistol to strap around their waists. In practice, the weapon most often proved a bother, just extra weight to be carried, for few cowboys had the money to buy the ammunition needed for practice to become expert shootists. Gradually most young range workers discarded the weapon except when they went to town and wanted to look like cowboys.

Another item of great pride to a cowboy was his saddle. This was designed as a place for long hours of work, so it was much like a chair, but with a horn for roping. On the average these saddles weighed thirty pounds. Each cowboy was expected to provide his own saddle; thus selling it meant he was totally broke and without prospects.

Perhaps it was long hours in the saddle that made the cowboy quiet, bottling up his emotion even among his closest friends. When he did talk, it was a salty language born from his occupation. For example, one old cowboy, when asked late in life to what he attributed his longevity, replied, "Try to get your beefsteaks three times a day, fried in taller [tallow]. Taller is mighty healing,

and there's nothing like it to keep your stomach greased-up and in good working order." This life also produced a raw sense of humor that appreciated the ignorance of greenhorns and the ever-present danger. Once in the Cherokee Outlet, when a horse rolled over on its rider and killed him, the foreman and the other five cowboys in the group dug a shallow grave on a hillside. With the body placed, the foreman solemnly asked the group, "Does anybody know the right words to say?" When no one answered, the foreman commented, "Well, throw some dirt on the son of a gun, and let's get back to work."

The cowboy found his life filled with monotony and hard work. Cattle had to be tended, for the brutes had a knack for getting themselves into trouble. They had to be pulled from quicksand, eased out of barbed wire, and dragged out of mud. They had to be doctored and helped during calving time. Barbed wire fences had to be strung and repaired—a particularly nasty job. Post holes had to be dug and wire strung. Harness had to be kept in repair, saddles mended, and other equipment looked after. Horses had to be broken—"gentled" was the word cowboys used, but "broken" was more apt, for about one in five horses had to be almost ruined before it could be ridden, while one in a hundred could never be ridden. Nor did the cowboy have a favorite horse he loved above all other animals—that was a fiction of the pulp writers. Because these horses were grass fed, the cowboy had to change mounts frequently.

Broken bones and death were constant threats. To be thrown from a horse meant bruises at the least; often it meant a broken leg, usually set improperly. One kick from a temperamental horse could kill, while a simple ride across the countryside could mean death if the horse was sufficiently mean to deliberately run under a low tree limb at high speed. A terrified herd stampeding at night could bring injury or death to a cowboy in a hundred ways; "stompede" was the cowboy pronunciation of a word one old-timer defined as "one jump to their feet and another jump to hell." Equally hazardous was an unexpected blizzard in winter which could trap a cowboy on the range where he might freeze to death. Sleeping on hard ground brought arthritis to many a cowpoke, and it exposed them to rabies from the bite of infected skunks and other wild animals. Even the simple act of roping could result in the loss of a finger or two if these were caught between rope and saddle horn when a thousand-pound steer hit the end of the rope. Little wonder that the average working life of a cowboy was only seven years.

Yet young men continued to seek out the life, 20 percent of them black and 10 percent of them Indian. To them no other life seemed to hold such romance, such glamour, such chance for glory. Their occupation continued unchanged into the twentieth century, for the rich grass in the Indian and Oklahoma territories attracted ranchers even after the dramatic changes that were to unfold in the years between 1887 and 1907.

Frederic Remington made a brief trip to Indian Territory as an artist and writer in the 1880s. While there he sketched the branding of cattle to be issued to the Cheyenne and Arapaho Indians for their subsistence. Part of the fees charged by these and other tribes for the right of crossing their reservation was a number of cattle for meat. OHS

OKLAHOMA

CAPT. PAYNE'S

OKLAHOMA COLONY

Will move to and settle the Public Lands in the Indian Territory before the first day of December, 1880. Arrangements have been made with Railroads for

LOW RATES.

14,000,000 acres of the finest Agricultural and Grazing Lands in the world open for

 # FREE HOMES

For the people—these are the last desirable public lands remaining for settlement.

Situated between the 34th and 38th degrees of latitude, at the foot of Washita Mountains, we have the finest climate in the world, an abundance of water, timber and stone. Springs gush from every hill. The grass is green the year round. No flies or mosquitoes.

The Best Stock Country on Earth.

The Government purchased these lands from the Indians in 1866. Hon. J. O. Broadhead, Judges Jno. M. Krum and J. W. Phillips were appointed a committee by the citizens of St. Louis, and their legal opinion asked regarding the right of settlement, and they, after a thorough research, report the lands subject under the existing laws to Homestead and Pre-emption settlement.

Some three thousand have already joined the colony and will soon move in a body to Oklahoma, taking with them Saw Mills, Printing Presses, and all things required to build up a prosperous community. Schools and churches will be at once established. The Colony has laid off a city on the North Fork of the Canadian River which will be the Capital of the State. In less than twelve months the railroads that are now built to the Territory line will reach Oklahoma City. Other towns and cities will spring up, and there was never such an opportunity offered to enterprising men.

MINERALS!

Copper and Lead are known to exist in large quantities—the same vein that is worked at Joplin Mines runs through the Territory to the Washita Mountains, and it will be found to be the richest lead and copper district in the Union. The Washita Mountains are known to contain **Gold and Silver.** The Indians have brought in fine specimens to the Forts, but they have never allowed the white men to prospect them. Parties that have attempted it have never returned.

In the early spring a prospecting party will organize to go into these Mountains and it is believed they will be found rich in GOLD AND SILVER, Lead and Copper.

The winters are short and never severe, and will not interfere with the operations of the Colony. Farm work commences here early in February, and it is best that we should get on the ground as early as possible, as the winter can be spent in building, opening lands and preparing for spring.

For full information and circulars and the time of starting rates, &c., address,

T. D. CRADDOCK,
General Manager,

GEO. M. JACKSON,
General Agent,

CHAPTER X

The Run
for Land

*A*mong the Choctaw delegates to Washington in 1866, when the tribe was negotiating a new treaty following the end of the Civil War, was Allen W. Wright, who first suggested that the Indian Territory be renamed "Oklahoma." Wright derived the name from two Choctaw words: *okla*, meaning people, and *homa* (or *huma*), meaning red. Oklahoma, he suggested, would be an appropriate name for a land that was "home of the red man." In 1869 a bill was introduced in Congress to effect this change, but the word usually was applied only to the empty part of the area. The remainder continued to be known as the Indian Territory, an officially designated but unorganized territory.

The Treaties of 1866 had contained provisions whereby the Indian Territory might become organized—and thus introduced into the state-making process. Delegates from the various tribes were to work out the details in conference, their expenses paid by the federal government. This intertribal council met at Okmulgee in 1867 and again in 1869, but no plan of organization emerged. Then, with the introduction of a bill in Congress to create a "Territory of Oklahoma," the tribal leaders met yet again in 1870. This time they drafted a document known as the "Okmulgee Constitution." This established a framework for a governmental union of all tribes in the territory (even including a bill of rights), but it made no mention of the United States. Subsequently the various tribes refused to ratify this document, nor was it accepted by Congress. Each year thereafter until 1876, when Congress ceased appropriating funds to pay the costs involved, the intertribal council met, but no satisfactory plan for organizing the territory could be reached. Indian leaders feared such organization would be a first step to abolishing tribal governments and allowing whites into the area, thereby ending Indian control of their own destinies.

Allen W. Wright, a Choctaw chief, first proposed the name "Oklahoma" for the Indian Territory in 1866. OHS

This fear was well-founded, for there were thousands of landless whites who wanted fertile acres on which to homestead. By the late 1870s most of the West had been carved into separate territories, and the good farming and ranching lands were settled. Only in the Indian Territory could these people see unoccupied acres suitable for farming. Naturally they coveted this land, and they began clamoring for Congress to open it to settlement. Joining landless whites in this demand were railroad officials anxious to see more settlers on the land—farmers and ranchers who would buy and sell and require rail shipments. Equally anxious to see the Indian Territory opened were merchants in the adjacent states of Kansas and Texas, businessmen who knew such an opening would expand their trade territory. Congressmen favoring business and railroad interests responded to the pressure, and legislation periodically was introduced to throw the land open to settlement.

Indian leaders, particularly among the Five Civilized Tribes, naturally opposed white settlement. They knew that if the unassigned lands were opened to homesteading, white frontiersmen would not be satisfied. Soon they would demand an end to the reservations, the alloting of a homestead to each Indian head of family, and the opening of the remainder to non-Indian settlement.

Thereby tribal governments would end—and with this the way of life the Indians had come to know in their territory. Ranchers joined Indian leaders in protesting the opening of the Unassigned Lands, they were grazing their herds for small fees on these acres. Missionaries and eastern humanitarians also insisted that the opening of the territory would represent further despoliation of the Indians. Others fighting the opening included a horde of government bureaucrats, who feared a loss of influence—and their jobs; licensed traders, beef contractors, and merchants doing business with the Indians; and whiskey peddlers illegally supplying alcoholic beverages to the red owners of the land.

Not content to wait for Congress to act, Elias C. Boudinot, the mixed-blood Cherokee who had attempted to organize the town of Vinita, was convinced that progress for Indians in the territory would come only with breaking up the reservations, alloting homesteads to tribal members, and opening the remaining land to white settlement. Of particular interest to him was the tract of some two million acres taken from the Creeks and Seminoles at the end of the Civil War as a home for Indians from other parts of the United States, but never used for that purpose. This vast block was known as the Unassigned Lands (and, increasingly, as the Oklahoma District).

In 1878 Boudinot failed to lobby through Congress an Oklahoma Territory Bill, which would have opened the Unassigned Lands to white settlement. Therefore he tried another way to accomplish his goal. On February 17, 1879, he published an article in the *Chicago Times* in which he argued that fourteen million acres of land in the Indian Territory were legally a part of the public domain. He wrote that this land had been taken from various tribes to be used for the resettlement of other Indians, but had never been so employed and so had reverted to the public domain. With the article was a map he had prepared that showed what he considered the area open to homesteading: the Unassigned Lands, Greer County (then part of Texas but later added to Oklahoma), and parts of the Comanche, Kiowa, Wichita, and Cheyenne-Arapaho reservations.

Reprinted widely, Boudinot's article triggered the "Boomer" Movement, composed of whites anxious to settle in the Indian Territory. One leader who emerged in 1879

was Charles C. Carpenter, who previously had led prospective settlers onto Sioux lands in the Black Hills of South Dakota. Carpenter began speaking publicly of taking whites into Oklahoma, causing leaders of the Five Civilized Tribes, along with several Indian agents, to protest loudly to Washington.

President Rutherford B. Hayes issued a stern warning to these prospective settlers to stay out of the territory, a warning relayed by General Phil Sheridan, commander of the Department of the Missouri. This show of opposition caused Carpenter to abandon his effort, and his followers dispersed.

David L. Payne proved less easily discouraged in his drive to open the Indian Territory. Born in Indiana in 1836, Payne, after an average education, became a frontier guide in the process visiting the Indian Territory several times. After service in the Civil War, he was elected to the Kansas Legislature and then became a captain in the 19th Kansas Cavalry. Then, settling in Wichita, he again served in the Kansas legislature, after which he became a doorkeeper for the House of Representatives in Washington, D.C. When he lost that position, he returned to Kansas and became leader of the Boomer Movement ("booming" the opening of the Indian Territory). During the next several years he supported himself by charging a fee of two, three, or even five dollars for membership in his "colony."

Payne proved persistent in his efforts. Several times he led colonists into what he called Oklahoma, only to be turned back by the Army. He also took the government to court at Fort Smith, Arkansas, and he hired a newspaperman from Chicago to write his

Elias C. Boudinot, the son of the assassinated leader of the Treaty Party of Cherokees, called for the opening of the Unassigned Lands to non-Indian settlement and the eventual statehood for the Indian Territory. OHS

The Intertribal Council, held in Okmulgee in 1878, attempted to create a territorial government for the Indian Territory. Lack of support from the Five Civilized Tribes led to the failure of the movement. OHS

123

biography in order to stir interest in his efforts. Because of his work the border towns of Kansas grew as prospective homesteaders moved to them to be near Oklahoma should it be thrown open. In addition, Boomer camps sprang up along the Red River in Texas. Several times the secretaries of the War and Interior departments urged Congress to enact laws making it a criminal offense to trespass on Indian lands, but Congress never complied.

On November 28, 1884, while Payne was organizing yet another attempt at colonization, he died suddenly at Wellington, Kansas. His lieutenant, W.L. Couch, aided by Samuel Crocker, inherited leadership of the movement, and in December of that year Couch led several hundred followers to the future site of Stillwater and began constructing crude houses. Bitter wintry cold prevented a full force of soldiers from arriving until January 25, 1885, when Colonel Edward Hatch and 350 soldiers came from Fort Reno. Hatch chose to starve out Couch

Left
Milton W. Reynolds took the nickname "Kicking Bird" from a Cheyenne Indian friend. He was one of the leading publicists of the Boomer movement, later settling in Edmond, Oklahoma, to operate a newspaper shortly before his death. OHS

Far left
William L. Couch was David Payne's lieutenant, who, upon Payne's death, succeeded to the leadership of the Boomer movement. He was later elected Oklahoma City's first mayor and died following a claim dispute. OHS

and the Boomers rather than fight, and they were escorted back to Kansas.

While the Boomers were attempting to gain a foothold, legal or otherwise, their story was being spread aross the country in newspapers. Particularly active in this effort was Milton W. Reynolds, who wrote extensively about what he labeled "The Land of the Fair God." Often writing under his Indian name, "Kickingbird," Reynolds did much to spread the word about the fertility and richness of Oklahoma.

At last Congress could ignore the situation no longer. Even Secretary of the Interior Henry M. Teller changed his mind after Couch's abortive effort to settle at Stillwater. On January 30, 1885, Teller recommended that the Oklahoma District be thrown open to settlement. The Indian appropriation bill passed on March 3 that same year authorized the president to negotiate with the Cherokees, Creeks, and Seminoles for land to be homsteaded. Four years later the negotiations were completed: the Creeks ceded their unoccupied lands for $2,280,000, while the Seminoles received $1,912,942. President Benjamin Harrison signed the act and proclaimed that the lands would be opened on April 22, 1889. David Payne's dream had come true.

Yet there still was the question of the

method by which the two million acres would be allotted to settlers. By 1889 there were tens of thousands of people wanting land. Governmental officials knew that on the day of the opening there would be chaos as these land-hungry individuals fought each other for a homestead. At last the bureaucrats decreed a land run. On March 23 President Harrison issued a proclamation stating that this run would commence at high noon on April 22; that the acreage would be subject to the provisions of the Homestead Act of 1862, which allowed a settler to acquire 160 acres; and that no person inside the Oklahoma District prior to noon on April 22 could legally homestead. Sections 16 and 36 in each township (of thirty-six square miles) were set aside for the benefit of public schools, and thus were not open to settlement, and the Secretary of the Interior was instructed to make provisions for appropriate townsites not exceeding 320 acres each. Finally, the Army was instructed to supervise the run and keep out those who tried illegally to enter the area prior to the run. Such people were known as "Sooners," and some estimates of their numbers run as high as 30 percent of all would-be settlers.

From all parts of the United States people came to participate in the run, camping

in Wichita and Arkansas City in southern Kansas, and Dallas, Fort Worth, and Gainesville in north Texas while they waited. A banner on one wagon in Kansas summed up the hard life of the pioneer and the hopes these people had for their new promised land: "Chintz-Bugged in Illinois, Sicloned in Nebraska, White-Capped in Indiana, Baldnobbed in Missouri, Prohibited in Kansas. Oklahoma or Bust!"

As the day of the opening neared, the ban on whites in the Indian Territory was lifted temporarily so the Boomers could camp along the outer boundary of the Oklahoma District rather than wait in Kansas or Texas. To the appointed places they came, and there they prepared for the run. Some chose to make the dash in wagons loaded with everything they owned; others decided they could make better time on horseback; still others chose to ride the Santa Fe, which had fifteen passenger trains ready to haul them. Because those coming up from the South first would have to cross the Canadian River, a treacherous stream, most Boomers chose to make their entry from the north.

A reporter for the *Arkansas City Traveler* headlined his story of that momentous run "An Empire Opened in a Second," describing how a cavalry sergeant stood beside an American flag and shouted, "Let'er Go Gallagher!" What followed was a mad stampede of 60,000 or more people. They ran for glory—and land. By dusk that evening almost the entire two million acres had been claimed by individuals planting wooden claim stakes, each about two feet long. Some who made the race got nothing for their effort, while occasional disputes flared over who had reached a particular town lot

or quarter section first. There were also some who made the run to a favored spot, only to find someone whose horse was not sweaty, and angry cries of "Sooner" were hurled, a charge that immediately meant a fight. There was violence—and ironically one of those who died in such a quarrel was William Couch.

"Cities" sprang into existence that afternoon. "Born grown" were Oklahoma City, Norman, Guthrie, Edmond, and Kingfisher. By the following morning each sported shops, stores, and banks operating out of tents, and within a few days some enterprising individuals had wooden buildings erected.

In the rush to open this area to settlement the federal government unfortunately had made no provision for any type of government. The settlers survived by invoking vigilante law where necessary and by following a form of rough democracy. They acted as if there was constituted authority and elected city councils, mayors, and chiefs of police. In the effort to keep the peace these officials were aided at times by United States marshals and by the soldiers in the area.

The need for legitimate government was belatedly solved when Congress, on May 2, 1890, passed the Oklahoma Organic Act which joined the Oklahoma District with "No Man's Land" to form the Oklahoma Territory. No Man's Land was that strip of territory that constitutes the present Panhandle of Oklahoma that had not been made part of Texas, Kansas, New Mexico, or Colorado, and thus was without any government. In the post-Civil War period it had been the home of so many outlaws that

for a time it was called Robber's Roost. Beginning in 1886 it had been settled by cattlemen and a few farmers, and they enforced vigilante justice. The following year they petitioned Congress for organization as the "Territory of Cimarron," but Congress ignored the area until 1890 when it was joined to the Oklahoma Territory.

The Organic Act of 1890 provided for the president to appoint a governor and three federal district judges who, sitting together, constituted a territorial supreme court. The legislature was to be composed of a lower house of twenty-six members and an upper house of thirteen members. There were to be seven counties in the territory: Logan, Oklahoma, Cleveland, Payne, Kingfisher, Canadian, and Beaver (all of the Panhandle), and Guthrie was designated the territorial capital. Until the legislature enacted a code of laws, Oklahoma Territory was to be governed by the laws of Nebraska. The Organic Act also provided that as Indian reservations were thrown open to white settlement, that land would be added to the Oklahoma Territory.

In making appointments to the seven territorial offices, President Harrison caused some hard feelings in Oklahoma by naming five people from out-of-state: George W.

Harrison Avenue, Guthrie, on June 22, 1889, two months after the land run, shows the rapid development of that city. Already the wood-frame buildings were being replaced by brick structures, and soon streetlights would be installed. OHS

Steele of Indiana as governor; Warren Lurty of West Virginia as United States marshal; and Edward B. Green of Illinois, Abraham J. Seay of Missouri, and John Clark of Wisconsin as supreme court justices. Robert Martin of El Reno and Horace Speed of Guthrie were appointed as secretary of the territory and as United States District Attorney. Steele, born in 1839, was an old friend of the president, a lawyer, a Civil War veteran, and a former congressman. When he arrived by train in Guthrie for inauguration on May 22, 1890, the disgruntled cries about carpetbag officials temporarily quieted. An hour-long parade, which included a contingent of girls from Miss Williams' horseback riding class, moved from the railroad depot to the temporary capitol and ended with a round of speeches in which Steele said, "I am determined as far as in my power to make my coming here both lucky to myself and lucky and useful to the people of Oklahoma."

Because of his Army service Steele was accustomed to giving orders, and within a month he had county government functioning and the United States marshal had taken a census indicating almost 60,000 people in the territory. Elections for legislative seats were held on August 5, and the Republican Party gained a slight majority: fourteen of the twenty-six House seats and six of the thirteen positions in the Council (as the upper chamber was called). The Democrats elected eight and five respectively, while the People's Alliance Party, better known as the Populists, was represented by four in the House and two in the Council. The close split between the two major parties enabled the Populists to enjoy considerable power: one of its members was chosen Speaker of the House and another President of the Council.

The territorial legislature, which convened on August 27, had much to do during its first session. Most needed was a code of laws, but the legislators instead spent endless hours debating about the permanent location of the capital. The logical choices were Guthrie and Oklahoma City because they were the two largest towns, each with about 5,000 people. When Governor Steele vetoed a bill that would have moved the capital to Oklahoma City, disgruntled legislators voted to move it to Kingfisher, a town of about 1,200 people; Steele likewise vetoed that. The capital would remain in Guthrie, but the debate would continue.

The governor did sign other acts passed by the legislature: one to create a territorial university at Norman, another to begin an agricultural and mechanical college at Stillwater, and yet a third opening a normal (teacher training) college at Edmond. The legislature also made provisions for a system of public schools and appropriated $50,000 for salaries, books, and supplies. In November it elected David A. Harvey as Oklahoma's delegate to Congress; in winning the office, Harvey defeated Joseph G. McCoy, the man who had opened the cattle market at Abilene.

The Territorial University was founded in Norman in 1890. This is the first administration building of the University of Oklahoma, pictured in 1900. OHS

Steele, who was resented as an outsider and hated for filling the appointive positions with non-Oklahomans, did persuade the federal government to allocate $47,000 to purchase food for the needy in the territory, and he convinced officials of the Santa Fe to send $10,000 worth of wheat to farmers to be used as seed (to be repaid when the first crop was harvested). Both these efforts were popular, for a drought in the summer of 1890 had left thousands in dire need.

Governor Steele, however, never wanted to make Oklahoma his home. Rather, he preferred to return to Indiana and be re-elected to Congress. Thus on October 3, 1891, he resigned. Later he would say, "Well sir, when I got there I found matters in pretty bad shape. Civil laws had been laid down . . . but there were no officers to enforce these laws . . . . Peace and order was restored and today the people out there are civilized and prosperous. The only thing they pine for is excitement."

While Steele was yet in office, a second land run occurred, for the day of unoccupied Indian lands was ending. In 1889 President Harrison appointed a commission to negotiate with tribes for unassigned lands. This commission was composed of General Lucious Fairchild, Judge Alfred M. Wilson, and John F. Hartrauft. When Fairchild and

Hartrauft resigned, they were replaced by David H. Jerome and Warren Sayre. This group, known as the Cherokee Commission or Jerome Commission, persuaded the Sauk and Fox, the Shawnee, the Iowa, and the Potawatomie to open 868,414 acres to white settlement. The run for this land on September 22, 1891, was marked by the same excitement as the opening of the Unassigned Lands two-and-a-half years earlier; 20,000 people, three times the number of claims available, rushed in. The addition of this territory allowed the expansion of Payne, Cleveland, and Logan counties and the creation of Lincoln and Pottawatomie counties.

The Jerome Commission then turned its attention to the Cheyenne and Arapaho tribes, and in October 1890 persuaded these tribes to accept allotments. The remainder of what had been reservation land, more than four million acres, was sold to the government for one and a half million dollars, and it was opened by run on April 19, 1892. Only 25,000 people took part in this rush, as the western portion of this land was thought too dry for farming. Much of it was not homesteaded in the run, but eventually would be settled and transformed into farms and ranches. Many of those who chose to locate in that area were Mennonites, and

On September 16, 1893, over 100,000 people partici-pated in the largest land run held in Oklahoma, that for the Cherokee Outlet. OHS

through their industry they showed the rich promise of this land. From the Cheyenne-Arapaho lands came Blaine, Dewey, Roger Mills, Custer, Washita, and Day counties, while Kingfisher and Canadian counties were expanded. (Day County would later be abolished by the constitutional convention.)

Next came the greatest run of all, that into the Cherokee Outlet. The Jerome Commission tried to negotiate with the Cherokees for this land in 1889, but the tribe refused an offer of a dollar twenty-five an acre. At that time the Cherokees were receiving an annual rental of $200,000 for this area from cattlemen, and one group of ranchers was offering them three dollars per acre for the Outlet if the Cherokees could get permission from the government to sell it. This was refused, and in 1891 the president ordered the cattlemen out of the Outlet, thereby denying the Cherokees any revenue from it. Giving in to the pressure, the Cherokees reluctantly sold the 6,220,854-acre Outlet on December 19, 1891, for $8,595,736—about a dollar forty an acre. The Pawness and Tonkawas had also been persuaded to take allotments and open the remaining parts of their reservations to white settlement, so when the great run occurred on September 16, 1893, there were almost six-and-a-half-million acres to be converted into farms and ranches. Congress, however, decreed that the settlers had to pay for this land, a fee that ranged from a dollar twenty-five an acre in the western portion to two dollars and fifty cents an

acre in the east.

Approximately 100,000 people gathered from across the United States to race for the 40,000 homesteads available, and rumors flew thick and fast as the great day neared. Some said that no trains would be allowed to make the run, others that the trains would be allowed to move at only five miles an hour. According to one story, only wagons drawn by a team of white horses and driven by red-headed girls could participate. In camps water sold for five cents a cup, and dry sandwiches hauled out from Wichita or Arkansas City sold at exorbitant prices. This was the last great block of land to be opened, and Kansas merchants tried to make as much money as possible.

The race was to begin at noon on September 16, the start to be signaled by Army troops discharging a firearm at each appointed place. At Hennessey someone fired a gun five minutes early, and the crowd surged into the Outlet. At Arkansas City, Kansas, a pistol shot sent 5,000 horses running eleven minutes before noon. Troops at both places tried to stop the Boomers, but their efforts were futile. Two hours after the race began, all was quiet. The land had been claimed, and Woodward, Woods, Garfield, Grant, Noble, Kay, and Pawnee counties had been created. The opening of the Cherokee Outlet was the last great run, although there was one small dash for land in 1895 when the Kickapoo reservation was opened to settlement.

No opening occurred in 1896, but Okla-

In 1901 southwestern Oklahoma was settled by a lottery system. More than 165,000 registered for 15,000 claims at El Reno (pictured) and Lawton. OHS

homa did expand that year when the Supreme Court ruled that what had been Greer County, Texas, belonged to Oklahoma. The question involved was which branch of the Red River constituted the main bed of the stream. Texans claimed that the North Fork was the main channel, while Oklahomans naturally asserted that the South Fork was the main channel (and therefore the correct boundary between them). On March 16, 1896, the Supreme Court ruled in favor of Oklahoma. Texans living on the land were allowed to claim their homesteads and file for an additional quarter section at one dollar per acre.

Yet another major tract of Indian land was opened to white settlement in 1901, some two million acres taken from the

Kiowas, Comanches, Caddos, Wichitas, and Apaches. This time the government chose not to have a run because of the lawlessness and disorder that had been associated with previous openings. Instead, this land was opened by lottery. Any adult, male or female, could register for a quarter section at Fort Sill or Fort Reno. Between June 9 and July 28 more than 165,000 hopefuls registered for the drawings, which were held between July 29 and August 5. Cards were drawn from the boxes until the 1,500 homesteads had been taken—and any single woman who won immediately received several proposals of marriage. Next came a drawing for the right to buy lots in the three townships of Lawton, Hobart, and Anadarko. The proceeds from this sale,

Following the lottery of 1901 towns were established at Hobart, Anadarko, and Lawton. In Hobart the first settlers lived in tents, causing the town to be called "Ragtown." The Guthrie Daily State Capital set up a newspaper and correspondence stand to provide news-hungry settlers with a connection to the outside world. Courtesy, Western History Collections, University of Oklahoma Library

Left
Whenever three pioneers got together on the American frontier, it was said, they would immediately clamor for territorial status. In Oklahoma the population of the Unassigned Lands soon after the run exceeded 50,000. This political rally held at Lexington was one of many calling for the establishment of an Oklahoma Territory. Courtesy, Western History Collections, University of Oklahoma Library

Opposite page, top
The first substantial home of many Oklahoma settlers was a dugout. Courtesy, Museum of the Great Plains, Lawton, Oklahoma

Opposite page, bottom
Civic improvements came shortly after the opening of the Unassigned Lands and the settlement of towns. Telephone lines had been strung, and streets were being prepared to be paved in Oklahoma City soon after the turn of the century. Courtesy, Bob L. Blackburn

some $700,000, were given to the three new counties (Kiowa, Comanche, and Caddo) to be used to erect county buildings and to run the county governments until taxes could be collected.

Finally in 1906 came the opening of the Big Pasture Reserve in southwestern Oklahoma, consisting of land belonging to the Comanches and Kiowas that had not been included in the lottery of 1901. Totaling 505,000 acres, it was sold at public auction in 160-acre tracts for an average of ten dollars per acre. No individual could purchase more than one quarter section. In the years between 1901 and 1906 some additional small parcels of land were opened through the closing of the Ponca, Kansa, and Missouri-Oto reservations; tribal members received allotments, and the remaining acres were opened. The Osages likewise received allotments, but inasmuch as that Nation had a deed to its lands (by purchase from the Cherokees), there was no surplus for white settlement; each Osage received approximately 500 acres as an allotment.

During these runs, lotteries, and auctions, two sections in each township generally were withheld for the support of public education, and other blocks of land were reserved for the Wichita Mountain National Forest and for Fort Sill. The income from leasing these school lands helped finance the 1,000 public schools that were open in Oklahoma by 1900. These openings caused the population of the territory to grow from some 60,000 in 1890 to more than 400,000 by 1900.

For these new citizens of Oklahoma Territory, life at first proved hard. Usually those who settled on the land fell into one of three categories: farmers, some of them destitute and seeking a place to begin anew or else well-to-do farmers, moving to escape the extreme temperatures of the north; speculators making every run in order to get land for quick sale; and people with little purpose, drifters and irresponsible vagrants who never lived long in one place. Most were young men desperately intent on making a success in the new land, for they realized the frontier was closing and that Oklahoma might be their last chance for inexpensive land. Descriptions of these settlers range from "polite but crude" to "secretive and talkative." In their new homeland they suffered from shortages of fuel and building materials, they knew loneliness and isolation, and they toiled long hours to clear and plow fields, erect fences, and put up some type of shelter, generally a sod dugout. Many came without furniture, and thus their new accommodations were rough-hewn and makeshift.

Once in Oklahoma they struggled to get a crop in and then tried to eke out an existence until harvest time. When drought came, as it frequently did, many of the men left the farm to seek employment in town while their women and children remained behind to walk along the creeks gathering plums, berries, wild greens, and black haws. As one pioneer woman recalled, "We ate mulberries that first spring that grew wild on the creek, and we had so many I never

Marshall McCully, a homesteader in the Cherokee Outlet, constructed this sod house on his claim in present-day Major County. The structure is now preserved and operated as a historic site by the Oklahoma Historical Society. OHS

liked them since." Gradually their lot improved as crops were harvested and sold. As that same pioneer woman remembered, "It was hard going at first, but we got a little ahead every year, until we added to our one room, and even had nice furniture. I kept some chickens, we had our own cow, a garden, and lived very well. Our menu never varied much—corn bread, sorghum molasses, and a lot of gravy—but we stayed healthy." One sign that a family was doing more than "getting by" was when it moved out of a dugout into a frame house.

During the first years in the Cherokee Outlet the only crop that seemed to do well was turnips, and people often ate these three times a day. Housewives taxed their cooking abilities trying to find new ways to prepare turnips. One story that was often told concerned a man from Enid who, on a trip to Oklahoma City in the fall of 1894, came down to the hotel restaurant for breakfast and, without looking at the menu, absentmindedly told the waitress, "I believe I'll have my turnips fried this morning."

Those who settled in the towns fared somewhat better, although their lot was not easy. There were quarrels over ownership of lots, and, as in Oklahoma City, rival township companies causing endless arguments over titles. Some who made the run hoped to get choice lots which could be sold quickly at a handsome profit, but most came with the intention of building a home and business. A few merchants arrived with train carloads of lumber and merchandise, and in a few days they had wooden stores open and doing a brisk business. Other less prosperous storekeepers had to make do in tents for weeks and even months. And there were a

few scoundrels intent on fleecing the new settlers—as, for example, the well-dressed man who arrived in Guthrie with a large iron safe; placing a board across two barrels, he erected a large sign stating that his "bank" was open and then, after taking in thousands of dollars in deposits, departed the territory never to be seen again. Most town dwellers, like their counterparts on farms, worked hard, put aside a few dollars each month, and gradually saw their lot improve.

Suffering perhaps more than any other group were the blacks who came to Oklahoma seeking a new home where they might find social equality. Blacks long had been associated with the region, for they had come as slaves to the Five Civilized Tribes, as runaways, and as soldiers. During the late 1870s many blacks fled Mississippi and Alabama to homestead in Kansas (the "Exodusters" they were called), and they had founded all-black communities such as Nicodemus (in central Kansas). A leader in this movement was Edward P. McCabe. Born in 1850 in Troy, New York, McCabe eventually reached Chicago, completed a law degree, and became a staunch Republican. Moving to Kansas, he worked hard for the party and at age thirty-three was named state auditor of Kansas. By the late 1880s, however, the town of Nicodemus was dying and McCabe's political power in Kansas was waning. He chose to migrate to the new Oklahoma Territory, as did many other blacks in Kansas. In this move they were aided by the Oklahoma Immigration Association, founded to help blacks move to the new territory.

Arriving in Guthrie in May of 1890, McCabe found rumors circulating that through his political connections in the Republican Party he was to be named governor, and Oklahoma was to be an all-black state. Such did not prove to be the case, however. McCabe's goal's were to show that black colonization would work and to carve out a new power base for himsef. His vehicle for both was the town of Langston, which he helped establish shortly after he arrived. His newspaper, the Langston City Herald, promoted black migration, instructed prospective settlers on the preparations they should make, and warned of frauds being perpetrated by fast-talking promoters on unsuspecting blacks. One typical fraud involved a promise that for thirty-five to fifty dollars land claims would be guaranteed, but after getting the money the promoters fled. McCabe did increase black immigration to Oklahoma. In 1890 there were approximately 22,000 blacks in the Oklahoma and Indian territories. By 1900 this figure had risen to 56,000.

Soon after his arrival in the Oklahoma Territory, McCabe became treasurer of Logan County. In 1894 he was named secretary of the Republican Territorial League, and three years later he became assistant territorial auditor. Moreover, he was able to persuade the legislature in 1897 to create a Colored Agricultural and Normal College at Langston so that blacks could secure an education. Despite McCabe's efforts, however, Langston's population gradually declined from a high of around 2,000 people to about 250 in 1907; only the presence of the college saved it from extinction. In 1907, with the coming of statehood and dominance by a white-oriented Democratic Party, McCabe left Oklahoma, his dream of a sanctuary where blacks would receive justice seemingly blocked.

For all Oklahoma's settlers, frontier life was not totally bleak. Long hours of hard labor made them appreciate small luxuries and opportunities for socializing. Revivals, community dances, all-night sings, communal Christmas observances—all made life more enjoyable by ending for a short time the loneliness of the new, hard land.

Outlaw gangs, however, did continue to disturb honest people both in the Oklahoma and Indian territories, finding the isolation and shortage of peace officers on the frontier to their liking. The Daltons, the Doolins, and the Starrs could hide in the Indian Territory after committing their crimes, but gradually the marshals and sheriffs caught up with them. Some outlaws were sent to prison in Kansas (Oklahoma Territory made an agreement with Kansas whereby prisoners were sent to the Kansas State prison at Lansing). Others were killed or driven out of the territory by peace officers such as Heck Thomas, Bill Tilghman, Chris Madsen, Charles Colcord, or Frank Canton. Shortly after the turn of the twentieth century, most of the outlaw gangs had disappeared.

Gradually the speculator and drifter moved from Oklahoma to seek elsewhere that which they would never find. Left behind were the solid, hard-working people who would build a dynamic culture and a vibrant economy. Yet troubling the solid citizens these years was a desire for total self-government free from carpetbag northern politicians appointed in Washington. They wanted statehood—and were willing to work for it.

Prosperity came slowly to Oklahoma settlers, but by the mid-1890s many farmers had progressed from sod house or dugout to a frame home. OHS

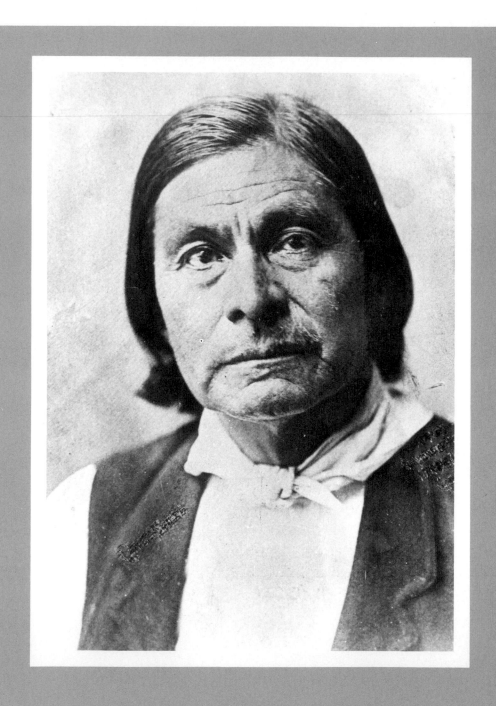

CHAPTER XI

Politics, White and Red

Chitto Harjo was the leader of the "Snake Indians" who opposed allotment and abolition of tribal governments in the 1890s. Harjo was arrested by federal marshals and United States cavalry in 1901. His followers were assigned allotments in the western portion of the nation, land that in the 1910s became valuable with the discovery of the Cushing Oil Field. OHS

Late in life George W. Steele, Oklahoma's first territorial governor, commented, "I did not expect to become permanently identified with Oklahoma, so I concluded to step aside and make room for someone who did." He submitted his resignation on October 3, 1891, but served until November 8 when Robert Martin, secretary of the territory, assumed the position of acting governor. Steele, who had intended to serve only five or six months, had completed seventeen months in office. He then returned to Indiana and was reelected to Congress. When he died in Marion, Ohio, in 1922, the flag in Oklahoma was flown at half-mast.

Martin's tenure was brief as acting governor—slightly less than three months. Born in Pennsylvania in 1833, Martin was a graduate of Westminster College in Ohio, a lawyer, a veteran of the Civil War, and a minor politician. He came to Oklahoma in 1889, settling at Harrison on the North Canadian River. Through old friends in Ohio (Senators John Sherman and William McKinley) he was appointed first secretary of the territory and thus became acting governor when Steele resigned. His duties as governor proved extremely light: issuing the Thanksgiving proclamation in 1891, signing the charter of a bank in Stillwater, and performing ceremonial duties on several occasions. When President Benjamin Harrison was considering names for a new territorial governor, Martin's name was taken from the list because the president thought him an extremely effective territorial secretary. Martin relinquished the office on February 2, 1892, and resided in Guthrie until his death in 1897.

When Steele resigned, the people of Oklahoma, tired of "carpetbagging," were loud in their demand that the president appoint a resident to the office and Harrison honored these demands—to some extent. He chose Abraham J. Seay, an associate justice of the territorial supreme court. Born in

The home of territorial governor Abraham J. Seay is preserved by the Oklahoma Department of Tourism and Recreation as an historic site. Located in Kingfisher, the Seay Mansion preserves a piece of Oklahoma's early history. Photo by Jim Argo

Virginia in 1832, Seay moved to Missouri with his family at age three, later finding success as a teacher, lawyer, judge, businessman, banker, and politician. A Republican, he was a Civil War veteran financially secure who wanted some appointive office. This came in 1890 when he moved to Oklahoma as an associate justice.

Inaugurated governor on February 2, 1892, Seay offended some Oklahomans by his appointment of non-residents to territorial jobs, which caused a split in the Republican Party in the territory: those supporting him and those opposing him. During his sixteen months in office, however, there was growth and change: the Cheyenne-Arapaho lands were opened to white settlement, an official territorial exhibit was sent to the Columbian Exposition in Chicago, and a legislative session was held during which Seay urged the upgrading of the territory's public schools. He also worked actively on behalf of higher education, and he pushed hard for statehood. In the election in the fall of 1892, no party emerged with a clear majority, and Seay proved unable to work in harmony with either house. His major accomplishment was to get $10,000 appropriated to buy "seeds for the Seedless." Seay was also noted for his favorable attitude toward

blacks and his unfavorable attitude toward "Jim Crow" laws, although some members of the legislature wanted to restrict the rights of blacks, as in several Southern states at this time. Yet Seay's tenure as governor was short because Grover Cleveland, a Democrat, was elected President in 1892. On May 10, 1893, Seay spoke at the inauguration of his successor, stating that he felt as if he were participating in the "graveyard ceremonies of . . . [my] own funeral." Afterward he devoted himself to his business interests, which included banks, hotels, and land. He died in 1915 and was buried in Kingfisher.

William C. Renfrow, the only Democrat—and Confederate veteran—to serve as territorial governor, was born in North Carolina in 1845. Moving to Arkansas after the Civil War, he lived there until 1889 when he moved to Norman to become majority stockholder in a bank and a local landowner. Taking office on May 10, 1893, Renfrow suffered few outcries of "carpetbagging," but his appointment of Democrats to many positions formerly held by Republicans did outrage many newspaper editors, most of whom were Republican. Especially outspoken was Frank Greer, publisher of the *Oklahoma State Capital* (later the *Daily*

State Capital) at Guthrie.

During Renfrow's four years in office the Cherokee Outlet, the Kickapoo Reservation, and Greer County became part of the territory. Despite working with a legislature sometimes dominated by Republicans, Renfrow secured legislation that in 1897 opened the Colored Agricultural and Normal School at Langston (now Langston University) and Northwest Normal School at Alva, and he pushed for creation of a territorial insane asylum at Norman. Moreover, Renfrow continually urged that the Oklahoma and Indian territories be combined and admitted as a state. The election of a Republican president in 1896 meant the end of Renfrow's administration, and on May 24, 1897, he saw his successor inaugurated. He then established the Renfrow Mining and Royalty Company to mine lead and zinc, and in 1920 went into oil exploration with his Mirindo Oil Company. He died in 1922 and was buried in Russellville, Arkansas.

With Republican William McKinley in the White House early in 1897, Cassius M. Barnes was appointed governor. Born in 1845 in New York, he grew to manhood in Michigan, where he trained as a telegrapher and went to work for Western Union at age twelve. During the Civil War he was a military telegrapher. After the war he moved to Arkansas, where he became involved in business and politics, then came to Oklahoma in 1889 as receiver for the United States Land Office at Guthrie. While the Democrats were in office, he studied law, was admitted to the bar, and was active in fraternal organizations such as the Masonic Lodge, the Knights of Pythias, and the Grand Army of the Republic. During the election of 1896, Oklahoma's Republicans split badly, and Barnes led the minority faction which did support McKinley's presidential bid, and on April 21, 1897, he was appointed governor.

The campus of Southwestern Oklahoma State University in Weatherford was established as a normal school during the administration of Governor Cassius M. Barnes. OHS

Barnes' main contribution as governor was the improvement of educational facilities in the territory. He encouraged the legislature to appropriate funds and erect buildings at the new normal school at Alva and at the Colored Agricultural and Normal College at Langston. He also persuaded the legislature in 1897 to create Southwestern Normal at Weatherford and in 1901 the University Preparatory School at Tonkawa (present-day Northern Oklahoma College), bringing to seven the number of territorial institutions of higher learning. Moreover, Barnes sought more funds for common school education and for better care of the insane, the aged, and the disabled. Working with Dennis T. Flynn, Oklahoma's delegate to Congress, Barnes secured in 1900 congressional passage of a Free Homes Bill. This allowed free settlement on unoccupied lands in the territory and canceled back payments owed to the government for homesteads taken in prior land runs, saving Oklahomans an estimated fifteen million dollars that otherwise would have been spent on land.

Continued feuding within Oklahoma's Republican ranks brought a delegation to Washington in 1901 petitioning that Barnes not be reappointed by President McKinley. To heal the party split, McKinley heeded the petition and appointed William M. Jenkins to succeed Barnes. Barnes retired to practice law in Guthrie—and later served two terms as its mayor. In 1910 he moved to Leavenworth, Kansas, and later to New Mexico, where he died in 1925. His body was returned to Guthrie for burial.

Jenkins, who had been secretary of the territory, was the first non-Civil War veteran to govern Oklahoma. As an adult he had practiced law in Iowa and Kansas until making the run for land in the Cherokee Outlet in 1893 and settling in a dugout in Kay County. A friend of President McKinley, he was appointed secretary of the territory in 1897. In this position he steered a neutral course between the two factions of the Republican Party. For this reason he was named governor on April 15, 1901, fol-

Territorial Normal School, later renamed Central State University, was the first territorial school of higher education to hold classes in the territory. Old North Tower is the symbol of this institution charged with training Oklahoma's teachers. OHS

lowing Barnes' ouster.

During Jenkins' short term in office, Oklahoma expanded with the opening of the Kiowa-Comanche and the Wichita-Caddo lands. Jenkins made needed reforms in the method of leasing school lands, including introducing an equitable system of appraising them for lease. When he attempted to remove certain members of various territorial boards governing the educational institutions, however, he ran afoul of the factional split in the Republican Party. In October 1901, only six months after his inauguration, formal charges were lodged with the Secretary of the Interior that Jenkins secretly owned stock in the Oklahoma Sanitarium Company of Norman and was profiting from its contract with the territory to care for the insane. At this point many of his political friends deserted him, and President McKinley had been assassinated. Theodore Roosevelt met with Jenkins on November 28, 1901, at the White House, and told him that while he did not consider him dishonest, he was indiscreet and could not continue in office. Two days later a presidential order formalized Jenkins' removal, stating that the governor had "an entire lack of appreciation of the duties of his office." Two years later an Oklahoma legislative investigation completely cleared him of any wrongdoing. He lived until 1941, most of that time in Sapulpa.

The territorial secretary, William C. Grimes, served a ten-day stint as acting governor while President Roosevelt searched for a candidate that would close the split in the Republican Party. When long-time Oklahoma resident Thompson B. Ferguson was appointed, Grimes returned to his duties as secretary. Ferguson, educated to be a teacher, had gradually turned his attention to journalism before making the run of 1889. However, he returned to Kansas soon afterward, coming back to Oklahoma in 1892 to establish the *Watonga Republican.*

Ferguson well understood the pitfalls of trying to reunite the Oklahoma Republican Party, for during Jenkins' term he had compared Oklahoma to a bronco, and on another occasion saying that to govern it "requires just as much bravery as it did to sail into Manila Bay, or to face the deadly Spanish Mausers at San Juan Hill."

After a quiet inaugural on December 9, 1901, Ferguson soothed partisan factions in the Republican Party by making all his

Thompson B. Ferguson served the longest term of office as Oklahoma's territorial governor, from 1901 to 1906. OHS

appointments on the basis of merit. Moreover, he moved to acquire the property and buildings at Fort Supply, recently abandoned by the Army, to be used to house the insane. This enabled him to end the contract with the Oklahoma Sanitarium Company in Norman, long a cause of quarrels. Ferguson worked hard to promote wise money management and sound financial planning, and he worked to secure additional funding for education, viewing with special pride the record $1,459,623 appropriated for common schools in 1904. He also wanted to cut the number of institutions of higher learning, however, stating, "One good Normal, one good University, one good Agricultural College is all that is required." The legislature pleased him in 1905 by enacting legislation allowing the consolidation of rural school districts. He also helped organize the territorial board of agriculture authorized in 1902. Ferguson was proud of Oklahoma, commenting in one report to the secretary of the interior that the territory was the "most progressive of any Western Commonwealth" and that "a story what would sound like a fairy tale might be truthfully written of the progress and advancement of the Territory of Oklahoma, the 'land of the Fair God.'"

Statehood might have been attained by Oklahoma during Ferguson's term had he not been opposed to joint statehood with the Indian Territory. He believed that consolidation of the two "would make Oklahoma a southern state" and "would fill her with southern people, a civilization many years behind our own." He might have been reappointed governor by Roosevelt had not an old friend of the president, Frank Frantz, wanted the job. Ferguson thus returned to private life on January 13, 1906, and continued to run his newspaper at Watonga until his death in 1921.

Frank Frantz, Oklahoma's last territorial governor, was also its youngest, coming to office at age thirty-seven. Born in Illinois in 1869, he had attended Eureka College in Illinois before moving to Oklahoma in 1894 to operate a lumber and hardware store at Medford. He subsequently moved to California and then to Arizona, enlisting in the Rough Riders in 1898. During the Spanish American War he so distinguished himself at San Juan Hill that he was given a battlefield promotion to captain—and earned the friendship of Theodore Roosevelt. Moving to Oklahoma in 1900, he settled at Enid to operate a hardware store and then, with Roosevelt's sponsorship, became postmaster there. In 1904 he became Indian agent to the Osage, a position involving great difficulties because oil and gas had been discovered on their lands, and many people sought entry onto their rolls to share in the wealth. In November 1905, because of his praiseworthy handling of this situation, Frantz was named governor.

Inaugurated on January 13, 1906, Frantz commented, "The lesson of the present day is progress with honor. The spirit in the very air is for fair play . . . . I shall try to be governor of all the people of the territory." No legislative sessions were held during his term, but he used the time to advantage. In one way or another he saved an estimated $200 million for the common school fund. At his urging the territory filed suits against the Rock Island and the St. Louis and San Francisco railroads to force them to lower their freight rates by 12 percent, and then he moved to prevent drilling for oil on school lands. Naturally these actions raised storms of political protest, and his last months in office were marked by bitter charges and denunciations. With passage of the Omnibus Statehood Bill on June 14, 1906, popular election of a governor was on the horizon, and Frantz was defeated as voters chose an almost totally Democratic slate. Frantz moved to Colorado to enter the oil business, returning to Tulsa in 1915 as head of the land department of Cosden Oil Company. (When Frantz was elected a member of the Oklahoma Hall of Fame in

1932, other inductees included Charles N. Haskell, who succeeded him as governor of Oklahoma, and William M. Jenkins, who had been removed as governor in 1901.)

The other office of importance to the entire Oklahoma Territory was the delegate to Congress. Territorial delegates could participate in debates but not vote. When Republicans convened in 1890 to nominate a candidate for this position, their choice was David A. Harvey, who would defeat his Democratic challenger on November 4. A little more than a year later, on January 25, 1892, Harvey introduced the first bill in Congress to make Oklahoma a state.

In 1892 Dennis T. Flynn won the Republican nomination for delegate to Congress and in the general election he defeated two others, nominated by the Democrat and Populist parties. Flynn had come to the territory during the run of 1889 to settle in Guthrie, and there he helped write the city charter. He would serve four terms as delegate to Congress and would be the dominant figure in one faction of the Republican Party in the territory. In 1893 Flynn quickly secured passage of an act giving Oklahomans more time to pay the government for their lands; poor crops and low prices had made it difficult for them to make their land payments in the allotted five years.

This measure made Flynn extremely popular, and he was easily reelected in 1894. Yet the growing discontent of farmers two years later at their hard lot and the depression then gripping the nation caused them to turn against Flynn. That year the Populists and the Democrats both nominated James Y. Callahan for territorial delegate, and he defeated Flynn. Callahan's service was undistinguished, and in 1898, following a return of general prosperity, Flynn was reelected.

Early in 1900 Flynn secured passage of a "Free Homes Bill," which allowed settlers in much of western Oklahoma to avoid paying a dollar twenty-five to a dollar fifty an acre for their homesteads. Thus in November that year he easily won reelection. Two years later Flynn chose not to seek reelection, whereupon Republicans nominated Bird S. McGuire of Pawnee. McGuire served as territorial delegate until statehood in 1907, winning reelection in 1904 and 1906, but his term was marked by bitter quarreling as statehood approached. McGuire, a Republican, favored the creation of a state out of Oklahoma Territory alone, while the Democrats favored joint statehood with the Indian Territory. When statehood became a reality, McGuire was elected to Congress from the First District, one of the few Republicans to win office in that election.

The sessions of the Oklahoma territorial legislature reflected the national struggle between Republicans and Democrats. During most of these years the Republicans controlled the legislature. However, when Democrats and Populists joined forces, the Democrats were able to control both houses of the legislature from 1896 to 1900, the lower house from 1900 to 1902, and the upper house from 1902 to 1904. During the seventeen years the area was a territory, there were several recurring issues: the location of the charitable or educational institutions, the permanent location of the capital, and school financing.

In the first territorial legislature the spoils were divided among several towns: Stillwater received the agricultural and mechanical college, Norman was granted the university, and Edmond received the normal school. No penitentiary was created because Ira N. Terrill, a Populist member of the first legislature (described by a fellow member as "A wild-eyed, vicious, beastly anarchist"), secured passage of a bill sending Oklahoma's prisoners to the Kansas State Penitentiary at Lansing. This was intended to save money for the territory. Ironically Terrill was among the first Oklahomans sent to Lansing, for on January 3, 1891, he was convicted of killing George M. Embrey, who had called him a Sooner. After serving his sentence, Terrill wrote a long poem whose title told what he thought had happened to Oklahoma: "A Purgatory Made of Paradise."

The permanent location of the capital was a continuing fight. The Organic Act of 1890 creating the territory had stated that the capital would temporarily be at Guthrie. In the first legislative session Guthrie naturally sought to retain this plum, but after a bitter fight the legislature in 1890 voted to move to Oklahoma City, an action vetoed by Governor Steele. The following year Congress passed an act prohibiting the Oklahoma legislature from moving the capital from Guthrie, but also forbidding the building of a capitol building. For the remainder of the territorial years the capital stayed at Guthrie, operating out of rented business buildings.

The Organic Act of 1890 made no provision for opening a public school system, however it did carry a federal appropriation

James Y. Callahan was elected territorial delegate to Congress on a Democratic-Populist fusion ticket in the election of 1896. He served a single term of office. OHS

of $50,000 for use in erecting a temporary system, and the Organic Act provided that two sections in each township were to be reserved for the support of education. In December 1890 the legislature used the $50,000 to create a system of elementary and high schools, and it authorized the election of local school boards to oversee the various school districts. The people who had rushed to Oklahoma held the traditional frontier view that education was valuable, and by the fall of 1891 more than 400 school districts were active with almost 10,000 students enrolled. In 1893, when the school lands were leased, more than $100,000 was secured, and with this money local school districts began making improvements.

These schools at first were raw and crude. Georgia Coffey Camp later recalled that her father, George Coffey, in 1893 opened a school in the Cherokee Outlet "in a one-room dugout . . . . with only a dirt floor and no furniture, no books, and no other supplies." He did this "with a few books of his own, Bibles, almanacs, and old papers brought by some fourteen students . . . ." In Kay County in 1894 Cora Waugh was persuaded to teach local students for three months for seventy-five dollars in a sod smokehouse loaned by a local farmer. Her daughter later recalled:

Seventeen pupils in grades one through eight sat on homemade benches. Slates and textbooks from Kansas schools were used. The March wind blew so much dirt into the schoolroom that the teacher and pupils could not remove their sunbonnets and straw hats. Outside, they played ball. A mother had sewn a string ball. A flat board was their bat.

Despite the hard conditions, these schools trained young Oklahomans to read and write, to do arithmetic, to mind their manners, and to perform as useful citizens. Improvements gradually were made, and soon a stream of young men and women were graduated from these early institutions.

While the lands of the Oklahoma Territory were being opened, while farms and ranches were being developed, while railroads were transporting agricultural produce out and manufactured goods in, while schools and churches were doing their work, and while territorial, county, and city officials were overseeing the growth of industry, roads, and farms, the residents of the Indian Territory were seeing an end to their dreams. No longer were the tribes independent nations existing within the boundaries of the United States and protected by treaties that guaranteed them sovereign status. Many Indians resisted these changes, but the federal government was dedicated to bringing them into the mainstream of American national life. Nevertheless by 1890 the various tribes still owned all the lands in the Indian Territory, and Indians held all political offices.

Passage of the Dawes Severalty Act of 1887 caused many non-Indians to believe that the reservations would soon be broken up by allotment and that surplus lands then would be available for settlement (although this act expressly exempted the Five Civilized Tribes from its provisions). The result was that by 1894 there were 250,000 non-Indians living in the Indian-Territory—with no schools of their own, no legal title to land, and few legal protections or restraints. In cities such as Tahlequah and Muskogee the tribal governments could maintain order, but in rural areas crime was rampant. Moreover, within each tribe a few dozen individuals controlled thousands of acres of the best land, while the remainder of the Indians lived at the subsistence level. Yet when the Jerome (or Cherokee) Commission, created in 1889, tried to discuss allotment of lands, the leaders of the Five Civilized Tribes expressed no interest in negotiating.

Congress responded in 1893 by creating the Dawes Commission (named for its chairman, Henry L. Dawes of Massachusetts) to negotiate allotment with the Five Civilized Tribes. The other members of this commission were A.S. McKennon and M.H. Kidd. When this commission arrived in the Indian Territory in February 1894 and met with delegates of the tribes at Checotah, the Indians flatly rejected allotment, feeling that this would lead to white domination of the lands promised to them by treaty and an end to their way of life. Subsequent meetings with individual tribal leaders also accomplished nothing, whereupon Congress in 1895 increased federal authority by en-

larging the number of federal courts in the Indian Territory to three. These courts were given authority over whites in the territory, as well as in cases involving the death penalty or long imprisonment. Sitting together in McAlester, these three judges also constituted an appellate court. Congress in March 1895 also provided for the surveying of the Indian Territory by the United States Geological Survey, a move obviously made in anticipation of allotment of individual homesteads.

Still the Five Civilized Tribes resisted. When the Dawes Commission met with tribal leaders at Eufaula in June of 1895, nothing could be accomplished. A year later Congress took more drastic action, authorizing the Dawes Commission to compile tribal rolls for the purpose of making allotments—with or without the help of the tribal governments. Included in this act was a statement that the United States would "establish a government in the Indian Territory which would rectify the many inequalities and discriminations now existing in said Territory and afford needful protection to the lives and property of all citizens and residents thereof." This was an obvious reference to the status of the many whites living in the territory.

The strong stance taken by Congress stimulated some tribal leaders to begin serious negotiations. First to accept the inevitable were the Chickasaws and Choctaws. Their leaders made one agreement in December 1896 at Muskogee. When this proved unacceptable to their followers, they negotiated another at Atoka the following April 23. This Atoka Agreement, the first break in the solid front of the Five Civilized Tribes, provided that timber and mineral-bearing tribal lands might be reserved for the benefit of the tribes and the remaining lands surveyed for allotment into homesteads and city lots. Moreover, it stipulated that tribal governments would survive for only an additional eight years past March 4, 1898, after which tribal members would be citizens of the United States. By this agreement the two tribes would lose both their reservations and their governments. The members of both tribes resisted ratifying the Atoka Agreement for a time, but eventually it was accepted—and spelled the end of separate Indian Nations and a separate Indian Territory. A similar agreement was reached with the Seminoles shortly afterward, and it

The Dawes General Allotment Act required that members of the Five Civilized Tribes be listed on tribal rolls and that each member of the tribes be allotted land in severalty to prepare the Indian Territory for statehood. This commission camp near Okmulgee was enrolling members of the Creek Nation prior to issuing them allotments. OHS

The Dawes Commission enrolled members of the Five Civilized Tribes prior to issuing them allotments. Taking to the field near Okmulgee to enroll members of the Creek Nation, the commission members posed for this photograph. OHS

was quickly ratified. Congress on July 1, 1898, accepted the Seminole settlement, making it the first fully implemented.

While the Choctaws and Chickasaws were dragging their heels at adopting the Atoka Agreement and while the Creeks and Cherokees were resisting allotments totally, Congress passed yet another measure signaling the end of the Indian Territory. The Curtis Act of June 28, 1898, was named for its author, Charles Curtis, a mixed-blood Kansa Indian (who later would be vice-president of the United States). This legislation destroyed the powers of the tribal governments by stipulating that the payment of tribal funds thereafter would be made directly to individual tribal members, and it ended the system of tribal courts by providing that everyone—red, black, and white—was subject to the laws of the United States or of the state of Arkansas. In addition, it called for a survey of tribal lands, the allotment of lands to individuals on the basis of tribal rolls compiled by the Dawes Commission, the erection of a system of schools open to all children, the leasing of tribal mineral lands by the secretary of the interior, the incorporation of towns in the territory, and voting by all citizens in these towns. All these provisions were to be fully effective at the end of eight years, and tribal government would cease on March 4, 1906.

Members of the Five Civilized Tribes fully understood the importance of the Curtis Act. In August 1898 the Choctaws and Chickasaws ratified the Atoka Agreement, and the Creeks and Cherokees conceded defeat in 1900. Agreements made with the last two tribes were ratified in 1901. These provided for an end to tribal government on March 4, 1906, ended tribal courts, and began liquidating tribal holdings. Some diehard members of the Cherokee tribe, organized as the Keetoowah Society, refused to appear to be enrolled by the Dawes Commission; claiming 5,000 members, the Keetoowah Society was composed largely of descendants of the anti-treaty party. It continues to be a force in northeastern Oklahoma to the present, although it has gradually become somewhat akin to a religion (or to a fraternal organization).

Using United States marshals and their deputies for protection, the Dawes Commission proceeded with the work of making tribal rolls. Henry L. Dawes was the nominal head of this commission until his death in 1903, but Tams Bixby, who became a member in 1897, actually directed most of the commission's work. The opposition was most violent among a faction of Creeks led by Chitto Harjo (also known as Crazy Snake). Harjo called a general council to meet late in 1900 for rebellious Creeks intent upon establishing their own Creek Nation and government, but Creek Chief Pleasant Porter used United States marshals to disperse the group. Then in January 1901 Harjo held his council and his followers tried to coerce tribal members not to accept allotments. This "Crazy Snake Rebellion" ended when the United States cavalry arrived and arrested ninety-four of the ringleaders. Tried at Muskogee, they were released after promising to accept allotment.

With or without Indian cooperation, the Dawes Commission proceeded in making

Pleasant Porter, Creek principal chief, served as president of the Sequoyah Statehood Convention in 1905. Although the movement to create the state of Sequoyah did not succeed, the Indian leadership of the Indian Territory did join the bandwagon to support single statehood for Oklahoma. OHS

tribal rolls in order to determine which individuals legally were entitled to land allotments. In 1905 Congress abolished the Dawes Commission, replacing it with the Commission to the Five Civilized Tribes, which operated until 1914. Between June 1898 and March 1907, when work was completed, this commission established that the Five Civilized Tribes held 19,525,966 acres (the Cherokees had 4,420,068 acres, the Choctaws 6,953,048, the Creeks 3,079,095, the Chickasaws 4,707,903, and the Seminoles 365,852). A total of 101,526 were enrolled (41,693 Cherokees, 25,091 Choctaws, 18,812 Creeks, 10,955 Chickasaws, 3,119 Seminoles, plus individuals from other tribes in that area), while more than 200,000 whites and blacks who sought enrollment—and land—were rejected. Almost sixteen million acres were allotted to those enrolled, and the remaining three-and-a-half million acres were opened to sale at public auction. Some tribal mineral lands were reserved, and the funds derived from the auction of mining rights were held in trust for the tribal members.

By March 4, 1906, when tribal government ceased among the Five Civilized Tribes, the Indian Territory was approaching a point where statehood seemed possible, as was the case in the Oklahoma Territory. The only question involved was whether there would be two states or one.

Soon to become citizens of the United States, the people of Oklahoma City are preparing for a genuine Fourth of July celebration

THE DAILY OKLAHOMAN

12,992
DAILY AVERAGE FOR MAY

LARGEST DAILY NEWSPAPER IN GREATER OKLAHOMA

VOL. 18. NO. 55   OKLAHOMA CITY, OKLAHOMA, SUNDAY, JUNE 17, 1906.   PRICE 5 CENTS

THE PRESIDENT HAS SIGNED THE STATEHOOD BILL

The Final Chapter of the Six Year's Legislative Battle to Make Oklahoma and Indian Territory a State Was Enacted Yesterday Afternoon at 3 O'clock in the Cabinet Room of the White House.

Chief Executive Signed the First Name "Theodore" With Gold Pen and "Roosevelt" With an American Eagle's Quill.

KOREA REVOLTS

JAPS ATTACK THE CITY BLOWING UP THE GATES AND RUSH IN TOWN

MANY PEOPLE KILLED

Koreans Appear to Be Well Armed and Offer Stiff Resistance to Onslaughter

SEE OWNERSHIP

ADVOCATES OF PUBLIC UTILITIES FIND BOAST IN GOVERNMENT OWNERSHIP OF CANALS

CALLS IT JOBBING SCHEME

Warm Debate Is Precipitated in Congress—La Follette Throws Out Warning By Arraignment of Republicans.

GERMANY REPRESENTED

MEN PROMINENT IN THE TWO TERRITORIES WITNESSED THE SIGNING OF THE BILL.

LAST CHANCE FOR ARIZONA

President Says the Opportunity For Statehood May Not Come to Arizona and New Mexico Again For a Score of Years and Congratulate the People of the New State of Oklahoma on the Gallant Fight Made For Admission to the Union—Pen Is Presented to the Oklahoma Historical Society.

IT IS FREE TRADE

REPUBLICAN PARTY MUST ACCEPT THE DOCTRINE OF TARIFF FOR REVENUE ONLY.

DEMOCRATS ARE VICTORIOUS

Purchase of Panama Supplies Is a Blacker For Protection and the Trusts.

CLOTH ASSAULTED

DASTARDLY DEED OF JAP SOLDIERS IN CATHEDRAL AT SEUL

WILL CAUSE TROUBLE

Case Will Be Put Up to the Mikado—Considerable Wrangling Over Commercial Affairs.

OKLAHOMAN INDEX

HOUSE SUMMARY

SENATE SPECIFIES WHAT AND HOW MATERIALS ARE TO BE BOUGHT

CANTEENS ARE DISCONTINUED

President Is the Arbiter in Matters Pertaining to Canal Supplies—Debate Limited

WEATHER FORECAST

CHAPTER XII

The Forty-Sixth Star

The Daily Oklahoman
*proudly announced Oklaho-
ma's statehood in this
front-page banner headline
published on Statehood
Day, November 16, 1907.*
OHS

A standing joke on the American frontier
was that when five people met in the wilderness they immediately began demanding
territorial status, and when the population
reached 100 they wanted statehood. Oklahoma's population was far more than this:
258,657 by 1890 and 790,391 by 1900.
Thus the area qualified in number of residents for statehood at an early date. It was
politics, not population, that delayed Oklahoma's admission to statehood.

In the Indian Territory there was little
sentiment for joint statehood with the Oklahoma Territory. Indian leaders feared that
whites would dominate all offices in a single
state government, but when they became
convinced that allotments and an end to tribal governments would be forced on them
they began work about 1902 to have the Indian Territory become the state of Sequoyah. In the Oklahoma Territory there were
no such worries, for the people there defi-
nitely wanted statehood. In December 1891
the first Oklahoma Statehood Convention
was held in Oklahoma City, and Sidney
Clarke prepared a memorial to Congress asking that the two territories be admitted as
one state. Introduced in Congress the following month the measure quickly died—
but the dream lived on.

During the 1890s several plans concerning statehood were discussed: single statehood for each territory; joint statehood for
the two; immediate statehood for Oklahoma
with the Indian Territory to be joined later;
statehood for Oklahoma with continued territorial status for the Indian Territory; and
postponing statehood for both territories until some future date. Partisan politics were
heavily involved in these debates because,
although the Republicans generally held a
majority of offices in the Oklahoma Territory, most observers felt that with the coming
of statehood the Democrats would win control of both territories. Thus national Republican leaders were not enthusiastic about

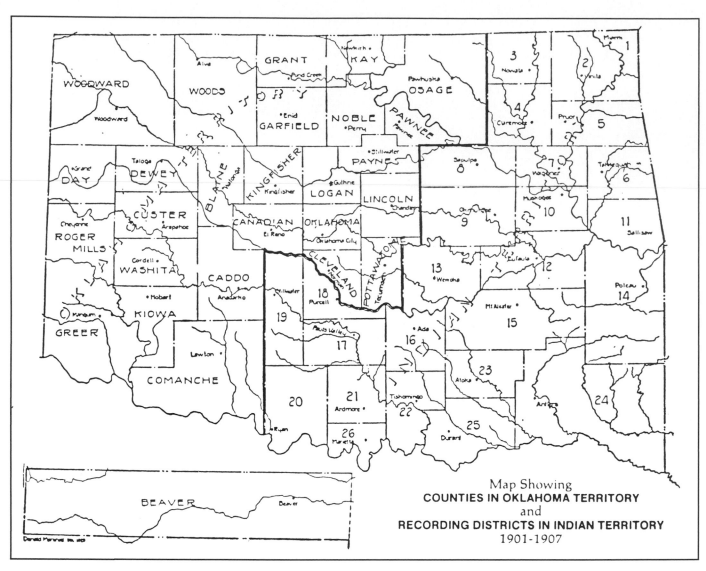

Map Showing
COUNTIES IN OKLAHOMA TERRITORY
and
RECORDING DISTRICTS IN INDIAN TERRITORY
1901-1907

At statehood Oklahoma Territory was divided into twenty-six counties (the Osage Indian Reservation would make an additional one), and the Indian Territory was divided into twenty-six districts. OHS

statehood for Oklahoma, while some Democrats tended to favor separate statehood in order that their party might gain four new seats in the Senate along with several new representatives in the House. A growing number of Republicans argued that with both territories as a single state their party might maintain its power, but party leaders listened to the debate and did nothing.

The pro-statehood forces in Oklahoma Territory annually pushed the introduction of bills in Congress calling for action. These bills usually died in committee as opponents pointed out how small Oklahoma was; however, this argument lost force as additional land was added to the territory with each new run, lottery, and auction. Opponents of Oklahoma statehood then killed the measure by noting the reluctance of the Indians toward joint statehood. As long as the tribes clung to their reservations and their tribal governments, little progress could be made

toward single statehood. The action of the Five Civilized Tribes Commission gradually reduced this argument, and by the early 1900s most Oklahomans favored single statehood as the best means of achieving a quick entrance into the Union.

In 1902 proponents of Oklahoma statehood tried to join their cause with Arizona's and New Mexico's push for admission, and an Omnibus Statehood Bill was introduced in Congress calling for the admission of all three as states. This failed, as did similar attempts in 1903 and 1904. Yet the persistence of this effort gradually convinced leaders in the Indian Territory that they must act quickly if they were to prevent unification of their area with Oklahoma.

At a meeting in Eufaula in 1902, representatives of the tribes formed an executive committee to study alternatives, but nothing came of the effort. Then in July 1905 tribal leaders issued a call for the election of dele-

This was the homestead allotment of Alexander L. Posey, a Creek Indian poet who served as secretary of the Sequoyah Statehood Convention. Courtesy, The Thomas Gilcrease Institute of American History and Art, Tulsa, Oklahoma

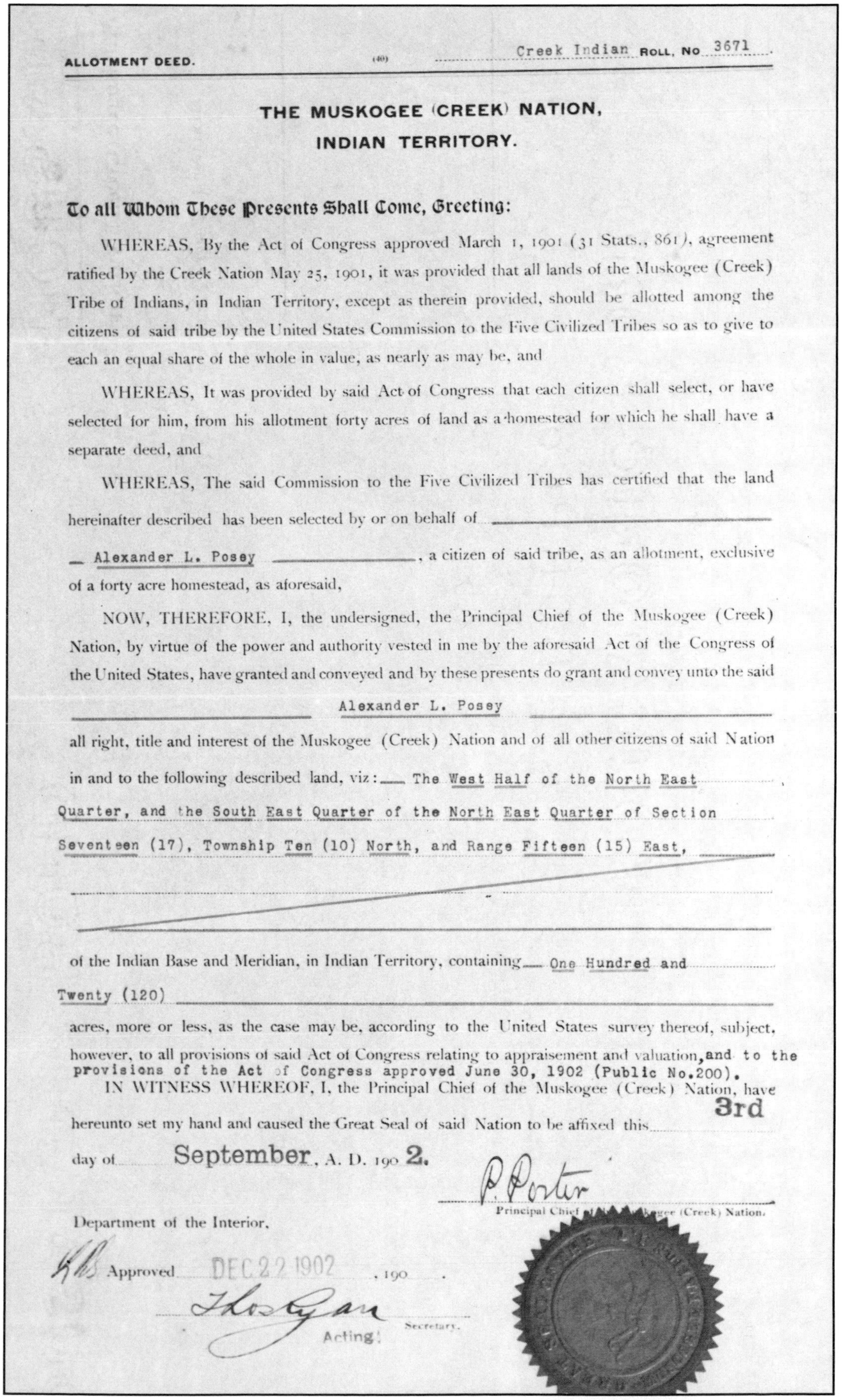

ALLOTMENT DEED. (40) Creek Indian ROLL. NO 3671

THE MUSKOGEE (CREEK) NATION,
INDIAN TERRITORY.

To all Whom These Presents Shall Come, Greeting:

WHEREAS, By the Act of Congress approved March 1, 1901 (31 Stats., 861), agreement ratified by the Creek Nation May 25, 1901, it was provided that all lands of the Muskogee (Creek) Tribe of Indians, in Indian Territory, except as therein provided, should be allotted among the citizens of said tribe by the United States Commission to the Five Civilized Tribes so as to give to each an equal share of the whole in value, as nearly as may be, and

WHEREAS, It was provided by said Act of Congress that each citizen shall select, or have selected for him, from his allotment forty acres of land as a homestead for which he shall have a separate deed, and

WHEREAS, The said Commission to the Five Civilized Tribes has certified that the land hereinafter described has been selected by or on behalf of _____

__ Alexander L. Posey _____, a citizen of said tribe, as an allotment, exclusive of a forty acre homestead, as aforesaid,

NOW, THEREFORE, I, the undersigned, the Principal Chief of the Muskogee (Creek) Nation, by virtue of the power and authority vested in me by the aforesaid Act of the Congress of the United States, have granted and conveyed and by these presents do grant and convey unto the said

Alexander L. Posey _____

all right, title and interest of the Muskogee (Creek) Nation and of all other citizens of said Nation in and to the following described land, viz:__ The West Half of the North East Quarter, and the South East Quarter of the North East Quarter of Section Seventeen (17), Township Ten (10) North, and Range Fifteen (15) East,

of the Indian Base and Meridian, in Indian Territory, containing__ One Hundred and Twenty (120) _____

acres, more or less, as the case may be, according to the United States survey thereof, subject, however, to all provisions of said Act of Congress relating to appraisement and valuation, and to the provisions of the Act of Congress approved June 30, 1902 (Public No.200).

IN WITNESS WHEREOF, I, the Principal Chief of the Muskogee (Creek) Nation, have hereunto set my hand and caused the Great Seal of said Nation to be affixed this **3rd**

day of **September**, A. D. 190 **2.**

P. Porter

Principal Chief of the Muskogee (Creek) Nation.

Department of the Interior.

Approved **DEC 22 1902** , 190 .

J. Hostyan

Acting Secretary.

Right
Green McCurtain, principal chief of the Choctaw Nation, also served as a vice-president of the Sequoyah Statehood Convention. OHS

Far right
Charles Nathaniel Haskell, a recently arrived resident of the Creek Nation, represented the Creek Indians at the Sequoyah Statehood Convention. He later served as delegate to the Oklahoma Constitutional Convention and was elected as the first governor of Oklahoma. OHS

gates to a constitutional convention, known as the Sequoyah Convention, to meet at Muskogee on August 21. Both white and red residents of the Indian Territory elected 182 delegates, the first time the two races had worked in harmony to achieve any major goal. Chief Pleasant Porter of the Creek Nation was elected president, and Alexander Posey, the noted Creek poet, was chosen its secretary. Five vice-presidents represented the various tribes: W.C. Rogers, for the Cherokees; Green McCurtain, for the Choctaws; John Brown, for the Seminoles; William "Alfalfa Bill" Murray, for the Chickasaws; and Charles N. Haskell, for the Creeks.

Haskell was a non-Indian railroad promoter and attorney who had moved to Muskogee in 1901 and who believed that statehood would benefit his commercial interests as well as those of the people of both territories. Thus he worked to convince the delegates that if separate statehood failed they should drop their opposition to single state-

hood with the Oklahoma Territory, thereby clearing the way for the area's admission to the Union. Murray, a thirty-six-year-old non-Indian who had moved to Tishomingo in 1898 and had married into the Chickasaw Nation, promoted the same ideas.

W.W. Hastings, a Cherokee, chaired the committee that drafted the proposed constitution. The document was a statement of Indian hopes and aspirations couched in terms similar to those of the American Constitution and the Bill of Rights. It called for creation of a state named Sequoyah with forty-eight counties, a two-house legislature, a supreme court and judicial system, and Fort Gibson as the capital (despite the fact that Muskogee offered to erect a capitol costing one million dollars if it was named the capital). After the convention adjourned Haskell and Murray led the campaign for popular ratification of the document, and in an election held on November 7, 1905, residents of the Indian Territory accepted the Sequoyah constitution by a vote of 56,279

Guthrie was to be the territorial capital until 1913, and the new state constitution had to provide for a system of public schools, to exclude alcoholic beverages from what had been the Indian Territory and the Osage Nation for twenty-one years, to accept the Fifteenth Amendment to the Constitution, and to submit the proposed state constitution to a popular vote. It also provided that the new state would have five seats in Congress until the next census (1910), and the federal government committed itself to paying Oklahoma five million dollars to help establish a public school system because no lands had been set aside in the Indian Territory for this purpose.

When the delegates convened in Guthrie on November 20, the Democrats were jubilant that they had won 100 of the 112 seats. When they organized, Alfalfa Bill Murray, also known as "Cocklebur Bill" Murray, was elected president, while Pete Hanraty of McAlester, representing the coal miners

William Henry "Alfalfa Bill" Murray, an inter-married Chickasaw Indian citizen, served his tribe at the Sequoyah Statehood Convention, then was elected president of the Oklahoma Constitutional Convention, voted the first Speaker of the Oklahoma House of Representatives, and later became governor of Oklahoma. OHS

Depicted is a panoramic view of the Oklahoma Constitutional Convention in Guthrie, with President William H. Murray standing at the podium on the left. OHS

to 9,073. Yet this document found little support in Congress, for the president and leaders in Washington had determined on single statehood. The movement for the state of Sequoyah had been worthwhile, however, for afterward Indian leaders honored their commitment not to oppose joint statehood further.

In December 1905, during the debate over the admission of the state of Sequoyah, five separate bills were introduced in the House of Representatives to admit the Oklahoma territories as a single state. When the bill to admit Sequoyah was killed, action began in earnest to pass an enabling act for single statehood, culminating in the Oklahoma Enabling Act on June 16, 1906. This provided for a constitutional convention consisting of fifty-five delegates from the Indian Territory, fifty-five from the Oklahoma Territory, and two from the Osage Nation.

there, was elected vice-president.

Kate Barnard, a young woman who had moved to Oklahoma in 1892 from her native Nebraska, significantly influenced the work of the convention, although she was not a delegate. An ardent reformer, she had fought for and secured higher wages for street workers in Oklahoma City and had helped organize them into the Federal Union, which affiliated with the American Federation of Labor. She also was closely identified with the progressive movement in Oklahoma. Because of her strong political base, she was able to exert pressure on the delegates to include provisions in the constitution such as compulsory education and a clause abolishing child labor in Oklahoma.

The debates and work of the convention lasted until March 1907 and touched on several burning issues that confronted the delegates: Jim Crow laws were not included

Above
The Oklahoma Constitu-
tional Convention was
convened in Guthrie in No-
vember 1906. Meetings
were held in the Guthrie
City Hall, pictured in
1906. OHS

Opposite page, left
Peter Hanraty served as
vice-president of the Okla-
homa Constitutional Con-
vention, and was later
elected the first chief mine
inspector of Oklahoma.
OHS

Opposite page, right
"Our Kate," Kate Barnard,
influenced the members of
the constitutional conven-
tion to pass provisions for a
department of charities and
corrections. She later
served as the first commis-
sioner of that department.
OHS

in the constitution for fear that these might cause it to be rejected by Congress or the president. Nothing was included concerning prohibition. Instead, a rider was attached calling for a referendum on the issue. Congressional districts were gerrymandered to the benefit of Democrats, for the few Republican delegates realized the new state probably would vote overwhelmingly Democratic. As a whole the constitution was designed to limit the power of governmental officials, to strengthen the hand of private citizens through the use of the initiative and referendum, to maintain some balance between the suppliers of governmental services and their users, and to exact the maximum amount of tax revenues from business and industry, while maintaining tight control over their activities.

The constitution contained provisions for a two-house legislature, a governor and other state officials who would serve four-year terms, and a judicial system with a five-member (later a nine-member) supreme court. Lingering memories of the appointment of carpetbaggers insured a provision for the popular election of almost every state official, including the secretary of state, clerk of the supreme court, state mine inspector, and even the state auditor. Because Oklahomans distrusted railroad officials, as did residents of many western states, the constitution provided for a strong

William Jennings Bryan, the Great Commoner, spoke on behalf of the progressive constitution passed by the constitutional convention. When submitted to a vote of the people of Oklahoma, the constitution passed overwhelmingly. OHS

Corporation Commission popularly elected; it would grant corporate charters and would have the authority to regulate businesses, such as railroads and utilities, with the public interest in mind. Moreover, the popular belief in the value and utility of education led the delegates to include a provision requiring vocational education in the public schools. The delegates also included a popularly elected statewide office, Commissioner of Charities and Corrections, which everyone understood would be filled by the reformer Kate Barnard.

Dividing the Indian Territory into counties and naming the county seats proved one of the most time-consuming duties of the convention, because almost every town aspired to be the seat of some county. Finally Bill Murray exerted his influence, obtained the resignation of several members of this committee, and then named Charles Haskell to chair it. Haskell and Murray had formulated the county boundaries in the Sequoyah Convention, so they used much of their work from that effort to draw Oklahoma's counties. In addition to creating the counties in the eastern half of the new state as they exist today (naming one county for Haskell

and another for Murray), this committee also subdivided the five large western counties of Woodward, Beaver, Woods, Comanche, and Greer. Subsequently two additional counties were created (Harmon County out of southwestern Greer County in 1909 and Cotton County in 1914 out of the southern part of Comanche County), bringing the total to seventy-seven counties in Oklahoma.

When the convention adjourned on March 15, 1907, everyone expected that Governor Frantz would call for a vote on the constitution within twenty days, but he delayed, saying the work of the convention would not be complete until an official copy of the document had been filed with the secretary of the territory. Murray continued to hold the constitution—he claimed—in an iron strongbox in his home; apparently he wanted to gauge public reaction to the document, and particularly the reaction of President Roosevelt, before filing a final copy with the territorial secretary.

There were many Republicans at the state and national level who were displeased with the constitution. In fact, some minority members of the convention drafted a second constitution that omitted many of the reform features of the majority document. President Roosevelt, when he saw the original, had comments that reportedly were unprintable and suggested several changes in the document. In addition, Woods County citizens who were unhappy at the way their county had been carved into smaller counties filed suit and persuaded a judge to issue an injunction halting ratification.

In the midst of this turmoil Alfalfa Bill Murray called the convention back into session to make some of the changes suggested by President Roosevelt. Meanwhile, the Oklahoma Territorial Supreme Court voided the injunction against a ratification vote, and Murray filed the original copy of the document. At last Governor Frantz called for an election to be held on September 17.

For almost two months the campaign raged. Murray and Haskell, aided by the Great Commoner, William Jennings Bryan, spoke for ratification, saying the vote would be a pronouncement of the people's will. Republicans opposed the document, fearing that it threatened their political dominance in the state, and they were critical of provisions calling for regulation of business and industry. Roosevelt even sent Secretary of War William Howard Taft to Oklahoma to

campaign against the constitution, hoping after a defeat to call a convention that would write a "good" document. Some conservatives stated that ratification of the proposed constitution would lead to economic and social unrest and to the collapse of the financial system of the area.

Unfortunately for the Republicans, theirs had been the dominant party in national politics during the territorial years, and they were associated with carpetbaggers and oppression. Moreover, it had been Republicans who were viewed as having destroyed the Indian nations. In addition, many settlers in Oklahoma had come from the South and were staunchly pro-Democratic, while most newcomers to the territory favored the social reforms and the anti-business features of the progressive constitution. In short, Oklahomans were weary of politicians in Washington making decisions for them, and they wanted statehood in order to end this practice. In nineteenth-century terms, "They were full of roast beef and ice cream,

and spoiling for a fight." They approved the new constitution by a vote of 180,333 to 73,059. The sobs and wails of mourners for the Indian Territory were lost among the hoorays and cheers of those celebrating the coming of statehood.

In that same election the voters chose new state officials. Democrat Charles N. Haskell defeated Republican Frank Frantz for the governorship; four of the five congressional seats were won by Democrats; and both houses of the legislature had a Democratic majority, while members of that party won almost all other state offices. In addition, the voters, by a majority of 130,361 to 112,258, chose statewide prohibition—the same day Oklahoma entered the Union, its saloons would close at midnight. Teddy Roosevelt might not have liked the new constitution, but he had to admit that it met all terms of the Enabling Act. On November 16, 1907, Oklahoma entered the Union, and the forty-sixth star was added to the national flag.

Governor Charles Nathaniel Haskell took the oath of office as Oklahoma's first governor on the steps of the Carnegie Library in Guthrie on November 16, 1907. OHS

CHAPTER XIII

I Promise if Elected

Alice M. Robertson was elected United States representative from Oklahoma in 1921. The descendant of Samuel A. Worcester and a missionary teacher herself, she was the only woman elected to national office from Oklahoma. OHS

Guthrie was filled with celebrating people on the morning of November 16, 1907, as citizens gathered from all parts of the new state to see Charles N. Haskell inaugurated as Oklahoma's first governor. A platform had been built on the steps of the Carnegie Library, and thousands crowded in to view the historic event. The ceremony began with the mock wedding of an Indian girl, dubbed Miss Indian Territory, and a cowboy, representing Mr. Oklahoma Territory. This marriage symbolized the arrival of statehood for the two territories and the union of the two cultures. After Haskell's inaugural speech everyone went to the city park for a barbecue, and then many men swarmed into nearby saloons to drink as much whiskey and beer as they could hold. At midnight all saloons had to close, seal their alcoholic beverages, and ship them out of the state.

Haskell had been a lawyer and railroad promotor in Muskogee prior to his election. At the constitutional convention he was a major force, highly respected by the other delegates. His popularity garnered him over 53 percent of the vote in the gubernatorial election, while opponents Republican Frank Frantz and Socialist C.C. Ross took 42 and 4 percent, respectively.

Haskell, although a businessman and somewhat conservative personally, recognized the political mood of Oklahoma's citizens at the onset of statehood. During the first decade of the twentieth century Oklahomans, along with perhaps a majority of American voters, were caught up in a so-called "progressive" mood that called for an increasingly activist government. Moreover, many Oklahomans were still filled with the zeal of Populism, an agrarian movement of the 1880s and 1890s filled with hatred of business and dedicated to the graduated income tax and to government regulation of railroads and grain elevators. Moreover, there was a significant percentage of Oklahomans in 1907 who were voting the Social-

The first two governors of Oklahoma took their oaths of office on the steps of Carnegie Library in Guthrie. Ironically, the last piece of legislation signed in Guthrie was the bill removing the capital to Oklahoma City, although Lee Cruce took his oath of office in Guthrie to avoid any legal difficulties. Photo by Jim Argo

ist ticket to demand government ownership of banks, railroads, and grain elevators—perhaps even telephone and telegraph companies.

In keeping with this reality, Haskell asked the first legislature to regulate trusts and monopolies, to provide for a compulsory primary election system, and to enforce prohibition. The legislature complied with a host of Populist-Progressive legislation. To pay for running state government, it enacted a 2 percent gross revenue tax on coal mines, oil pipelines, and telegraph lines; a tax of one percent on oil, railroads, and utilities; and a graduated income tax ranging from

one-half of one percent on incomes from $3,500 to $10,000 to three and one-half of one percent on incomes of more than $100,000. It drafted a broad labor law that included a safety code and restrictions on the use of child labor, provided a system for inspecting workplaces, and established an employers' liability fund. To protect Oklahomans from bank failures, such as had happened during the Panic of 1907, a bank guaranty system was established (similar to the Federal Deposit Insurance Corporation of today). In addition, the legislators provided for compulsory free public education, the certification and training of teachers, a

VOTE FOR OKLAHOMA CITY FOR STATE CAPITAL-JUNE 11.
THE MOST SUITABLE CITY ——— THE PRIDE OF THE STATE

REMEMBER YOU HAVE TO STAMP
THE TICKET TWICE TO MAKE YOUR
VOTE VALID
VOTE ☒ YES ON THE BILL
VOTE ☒ YES FOR OKLAHOMA CITY
ELECTION SATURDAY JUNE 11.

OKLAHOMA CITY STANDS FOR THE DEVELOPMENT OF THE ENTIRE STATE

Oklahoma is the Central City of the State
It presents the best appearance, makes the best impression, attracts capital and population to the State.
It is the center of transportation and commerce.
It has the best churches and schools.
Its hotels are best and biggest.
It has the best public and private buildings.
It has over 94 miles of paved streets.
Its building operations are the talk of the country.
Its $6,000,000 packing plant is now being built, will boost farm values all over the State.
The Capital should be located in the city of greatest achievement.
REMEMBER. The law provides that the Capital Building and grounds will cost you nothing.
The sale by the State of 2000 acres adjoining Oklahoma City will bring millions of dollars into the State Treasury.
It has the finest boulevard and park system in the Southwest

This billboard appeared in Oklahoma City, calling for support of the effort to remove the capital from Guthrie to Oklahoma City in 1910. OHS

textbook commission, and additional funding for an expanding number of institutions of higher learning.

Despite their absence from the constitution, Jim Crow laws were enacted by the legislature to curtail the rights of non-white citizens. These were mandated due to the large number of former Southerners in the state, and because some whites disliked Indians. In 1910 the state would adopt the "Grandfather Clause" used in Southern states to prevent voting by those whose ancestors could not vote as of January 1, 1866, unless he could pass a literacy test. These laws, however, led to discontent and even to riots, for blacks did not submit tamely to this discrimination. (Oklahoma at this time was unique in that it contained more than twenty all-black towns.) Finally, after Commissioner of Charities and Corrections Kate Barnard inspected the Kansas State Penitentiary at Lansing and publicized the brutal conditions under which Oklahoma's felons were suffering, the legislature provided for the construction of a state prison at McAlester—which was built with convict labor to save money.

The most controversial issue in Haskell's term as governor was the permanent location of the capital. In the first two meetings of the legislature there was endless argument about where the capital should be located, although most agreed it should be near the geographical center of the state. Some lawmakers wanted to remove it to a point just west of Oklahoma City and start

a new community, to be called New Jerusalem. Democrats were especially anxious to remove the capital from Guthrie, which they believed to be a "Republican nest," while Governor Haskell agreed to move the capital because he was angry with the continued attacks on him by Republican newspapermen in Guthrie, particularly Frank Greer.

In 1910 a petition was circulated and received sufficient signatures to call a referendum on the issue. Voting on July 11 of that year, Oklahomans overwhelmingly chose Oklahoma City as their capital. That city's 96,261 votes easily beat Guthrie's 31,301 and Shawnee's 8,382. That night Haskell sent his secretary of state to Guthrie to get the state seal, and the next morning, the seal in his possession, Haskell declared the Lee Huckins Hotel in Oklahoma City to be the temporary capitol. The state supreme court would remain in Guthrie for a time, and residents of that city would protest mightily, but no one could find a legal way to force the governor to move from Oklahoma City. Thereafter the capital remained.

In 1910 came the election of a new governor. Lee Cruce, a forty-seven-year-old native of Kentucky who had moved to Ardmore in 1891 to practice law and then to work as a cashier in a local bank, had unsuccessfully contested Haskell for the Democratic nomination in 1907. Yet in this election he won despite a spirited primary contest with Alfalfa Bill Murray. In the general election Cruce received 120,318 votes to Republican Joseph W. McNeal's 99,527. During his term he emphasized economy in state government, and pushed for creation of boards of regents for state colleges and the University of Oklahoma to avoid duplication (at this time the Agricultural and Mechanical College and other agricultural schools were administered by the State Board of Agriculture). The Oklahoma State Highway Department was created during Cruce's administration to be financed by a one dollar license on all vehicles.

On two issues Cruce held strong convictions: he opposed capital punishment, and he favored the so-called blue laws. Although he could not convince the legislature to abolish capital punishment, he did commute the sentences of twenty condemned men to life imprisonment. When criticized for these actions, he responded, "I have received thousands of letters praising my actions. I'm perfectly pleased with the result." During his term unruly mobs lynched fifteen murderers before they could be brought to trial or before he could commute their sentences. In 1915, after Cruce left office, the legislature changed the method of execution in the

state from hanging to electrocution, which was considered more humane. In enforcing blue laws—closing businesses on Sunday, outlawing horse racing, enforcing prohibition, and ending prizefighting—Cruce was more successful. When local law enforcement officials could not or would not effect these measures, the governor sent in the state militia to help.

The census of 1910 showed that Oklahoma rated three additional seats in Congress, bringing its total to eight. Democrats wanted to gerrymander the state to allow the election of three additional members of their party, but Cruce said he would veto such a partisan measure. Thus the three seats were elected statewide. This, along with his economizing, led to Cruce's near impeachment in 1913 by an unhappy legislature—and began a period of intense political rivalry between the legislature and subsequent governors.

In 1914 the Democrats nominated Chief Justice of the state supreme court Robert L. Williams for governor after a primary in which he defeated Al Jennings, a former train robber who had served time in prison. Williams, born in 1868, had moved to Du-

Opposite page, top
Governor Charles N. Haskell met with Secretary of State William Cross at the governor's Oklahoma City hotel suite following the removal of the capital from Guthrie in 1910. A vote of the people relocated the capital to Oklahoma City on June 11, 1910. OHS

Opposite page, bottom
As Oklahoma City continued to grow, transportation became one of the city's most important necessities. An interurban line of streetcars was initiated soon after the turn of the century. Courtesy, Oklahoma County Metropolitan Library

Below
When the capital was removed from Guthrie in 1910, Oklahoma City had already experienced a growth in population from 32,000 in 1907 to over 65,000 in 1910. Courtesy, Bob L. Blackburn

rant, Indian Territory, in 1896 from his native Alabama and had been a member of the constitutional convention. In the 1914 general election, Williams defeated Republican challenger John Fields by only 5,000 votes, while Socialist candidate Fred Holt received more than 50,000 votes. During Williams' administration laws were passed to protect the working class, including a labor code for women that contained social welfare provisions and set the maximum number of hours they could work. The state supreme court in 1915 struck down the Grandfather Clause, which prevented some blacks from voting, but the legislature found a new way, a shrewdly devised registration law, to keep most blacks from the polls.

With the outbreak of World War I in 1917, Socialists and radical labor groups began open rebellion against the drafting of

OKLAHOMA: LAND OF THE FAIR GOD

Statewide prohibition had been enacted in 1907, but Governor Cruce increased enforcement during his term of office. It was not until national prohibition in the 1920s that the flow of illegal liquor was effectively shut down. OHS

young men, and property was destroyed in several counties. This so-called "Green Corn Rebellion" was ended by mob and posse action, and many Oklahomans joined the conservative American Protective League to use extralegal and illegal methods to end what they saw as anti-Americanism.

Perhaps the most famous event of Williams' term was moving the state government into the new capitol building in 1917. Because of the wartime shortage of materials, no dome was put atop this building, although the plans called for one (to the present time no dome has been added).

In 1918 Democratic candidate James B. Robertson defeated Republican Horace G. McKeever by a vote of 104,132 to 82,865 following a hard-fought primary against Alfalfa Bill Murray. During Robertson's term more than 1,000 miles of modern highways were constructed, and the colleges were given separate boards of regents, rather than operate under the centralized Board of Education that Governor Williams had secured. Substantial state support for public schools began during Robertson's term. Many new schools were constructed, reforms were made in curriculum and teach-

ers certification, and appropriation of $100,000 was made for public instruction. Also during Robertson's term Oklahoma experienced a serious conflict with the state of Texas over ownership of the Red River bed. Federal courts ruled that the Treaty of 1819 with Spain had set the boundary at the *south* bank of the river and thus the state of Oklahoma owned the entire riverbed, but Texans insisted they owned half of the riverbed. Units of the national guard of both states faced each other across the river, and shooting was about to begin before cooler heads prevailed.

The latter part of Robertson's term was marked by an economic depression at the end of World War I, and in the election of 1920 Republicans swept five of the eight congressional seats, won a majority in the state House of Representatives, and secured a strong minority in the state Senate. Republicans in the House then brought impeachment charges against Lieutenant Governor Martin Trapp (and tried to impeach Robertson), but Democrats in the Senate refused to convict Trapp.

In 1922 John C. "Jack" Walton captured the governor's mansion, defeating Republi-

164

can John Fields by approximately 50,000 votes out of more than half a million votes cast (women voted for the first time in this election). Born in Indiana in 1881, Walton moved to Oklahoma in 1903 as a sales engineer. He was elected commissioner of public works in 1917, mayor of Oklahoma City in 1919, and won the governorship in 1922 with support from the Oklahoma Farm Labor Reconstruction League, a liberal (almost radical) organization formed the previous year by former Socialist Party members and various labor and small farmer organizations. The league favored public ownership of utilities and heavy land taxes based on improvements to property (and thus hardest on city land owners).

Walton opened his inaugural ball to the entire public—the last event of his term where he found much reason to smile. He had risen in politics by his ability to work compromises, but in office this was perceived as vacillation. In addition, wholesale appointment of friends to positions of authority at the university and at the Agricultural and Mechanical College brought strong hostility from the legislature and alumni of these institutions. The wheels of state government almost came to a halt due

to Walton's unsure hand, and then came public excesses, including activity by the Ku Klux Klan. A grand jury was called in Oklahoma City to investigate the governor's actions, whereupon Walton proclaimed martial law in the state, saying the "deadly Invisible Empire" (the Klan) was attempting to destroy Oklahoma. This excess led to

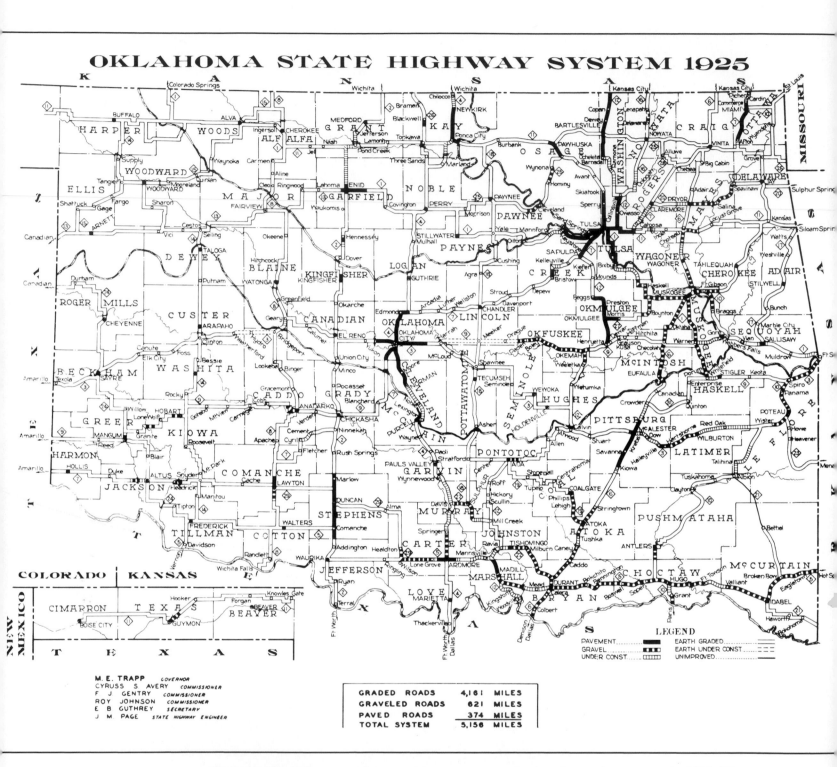

OKLAHOMA STATE HIGHWAY SYSTEM 1925

GRADED ROADS	4,161	MILES
GRAVELED ROADS	621	MILES
PAVED ROADS	374	MILES
TOTAL SYSTEM	5,156	MILES

Walton's impeachment and removal by the Democratic legislature on November 19, 1923. Next year, however, Walton won the Democratic nomination for the United States Senate—only to lose to W.B. Pine, a wealthy Republican businessman from Okmulgee.

Lieutenant Governor Martin Trapp served the remainder of Walton's term. He had served in various offices before becoming lieutenant governor in 1915, and had survived an impeachment vote in 1921. His tenure as governor was marked by little activity, although state spending was cut by one-third, and an anti-mask law severely curtailed Klan activities in the state.

In 1926 Democrats recaptured control of the Oklahoma legislature and continued their monopoly on the governorship. Henry S. Johnston easily defeated Republican Omer Benedict for the governor's seat, although his use of the governor's patronage power in the Highway Department brought his downfall. After his inauguration on January 10, 1927, Johnston quieted the political waters with strong support for hospitals and schools. However, his executive secretary, Mrs. O.O. Hammonds, was fond of ordering legislators out of the governor's office, and some legislators charged that she made all executive decisions—and there were semi-public allegations by Johnston's political enemies that he and Mrs. Hammonds were having an affair. Johnston defended his secretary by saying she was as gentle as a "ewe lamb." Legislators convened in a special session in late 1927 at the Huckins Hotel in Oklahoma City in an attempt to impeach the governor, a move the newspapers called "the ewe lamb rebellion," but the state supreme court ruled the session illegal.

Johnston thus survived this first effort to unseat him, but he angered many legislators by campaigning in 1928 for Democratic presidential nominee Al Smith, a Catholic who favored the repeal of prohibition. When Herbert Hoover and the Republicans swept national offices, Johnston lost control of the state Democratic Party. The legislature, meeting in regular sessions early in 1929, quickly voted articles of impeachment against Johnston, and on March 20 he was removed from office solely on the general charge of "incompetency," his impeachment caused more by political error than any criminal activity.

Lieutenant Governor William J. Holloway had been acting governor since January when impeachment proceedings began against Johnston. During Holloway's years as governor, several educational reforms were enacted, the mining code was strengthened, and the Highway Commission was restructured. Holloway appointed Republican Lew Wentz to the Highway Commission in an effort to promote bipartisanship in that body, leading to some criticism of the governor by fellow Democrats. During his term also came adoption of the runoff primary; this provided that a candidate in a primary election had to receive a majority vote, otherwise a runoff between the top two candidates would be necessary. The beginning of the Great Depression in 1929 did not affect Oklahoma greatly for some months, but Holloway nevertheless tried to keep state spending to a minimum.

Because of the Depression, which hit Oklahoma by the summer of 1930 and which was associated nationally with the Republican Party, the Democrats eyed the 1930 elections confident of victory. Contending for that party's nomination was former governor Martin Trapp, who argued that the constitution did not prevent his candidacy since his previous three-year term came as a result of Walton's impeachment. He was defeated, however, in the primary by Alfalfa Bill Murray, who went on to defeat Republican Ira Hill in the general election by almost 100,000 votes. Murray's candidacy was ridiculed in most state newspapers, for he was crude and dressed poorly. He was born in the community of Toad Suck, Texas, in 1869. After serving as president of the constitutional convention, he had been speaker of the state House of Representatives and then was elected to Congress. In 1924 he went to Bolivia to found an agricultural colony, but when that failed he returned to Oklahoma to reenter politics. Despite Murray's occasionally dishevelled appearance, the common people identified with him and gave him their votes.

When Murray took office on January 12, 1931, Oklahomans faced severe difficulties caused by the Depression. Jobs were disappearing, banks were failing, and individuals were facing bankruptcy—and some of them hunger. Moreover, the state was five million dollars in debt and could find few banks that would honor its warrants. Murray economized by cutting appropriations, and he established a Tax Commission to halt tax evasion. In addition, he raised taxes on gasoline and petroleum products, which increased state revenues by more than two million dollars, and he tried to shift the tax burden away from individuals more heavily onto corporations. His one luxury was to reinstate free textbooks for the public schools, a practice halted during Governor Trapp's administration. Because of Murray's demands for spending cuts, legislators began muttering about impeachment, to which Murray snorted, "It'll be like a bunch of jack rabbits tryin' to get a wildcat out of a hole." Talk of impeachment ceased.

Murray was equally forceful in dealing with other problems. When overproduction caused petroleum prices to fall drastically, he called out the National Guard to force producers to stay within the production limits set by the Corporation Commission.

When the state constructed a free bridge across the Red River to compete with a toll bridge owned by Texans, Murray again used the National Guard to keep the free bridge open—even in the face of a federal court ruling against the free bridge.

In 1932 Murray had visions of getting the Democratic nomination for president, but that prize went to Franklin D. Roosevelt, who instituted the New Deal after he took office. Murray frequently voiced his dislike both for Roosevelt and the New Deal, although in 1933 he did agree to the repeal of prohibition by signing a bill allowing the sale of light beer (3.2 percent alcoholic content). Yet his antics angered voters, and in 1934, despite his support of Tom Anglin of Holdenville for governor, the Democratic nomination went to Ernest W. Marland.

Marland was a former multimillionaire, who lost his fortune in 1929 due to lavish living and free spending. He entered politics and was elected to Congress in 1932 prior to his Democratic nomination for governor. In the general election he defeated Republican candidate W.B. Pine by more than 120,000 votes in a contest in which Marland asked the voters to "Bring the New Deal to Oklahoma."

In office Marland fully embraced New Deal programs, pushing many of them through the legislature despite intense opposition from conservatives led by Speaker of the House Leon C. "Red" Phillips. This bloc argued against deficit spending for New Deal measures. Despite Marland's successes, however, federal relief programs, such as the Works Progress Administration, Civilian Conservation Corps, and Federal Emergency Relief Administration, were continually under-funded. However, in the 1935 legislative session, he secured passage of a 2-percent general sales tax earmarked to aid the aged, the blind, and the indigent. This marked the beginnings of the Department of Human Services, a state agency that would operate as a semi-independent barony, its director secure so long as he dutifully doled out jobs to those recommended to him by legislators.

In the election of 1936 Governor Marland failed to win the United States Senate seat he sought, but his followers did win control of the state legislature. In the legislative session of 1937 this branch of the Democratic Party appropriated millions for relief and reform. Unfortunately, revenue-raising

measures to finance the increased spending were not passed, leaving the state with a massive debt. Lawmakers that year also created the Oklahoma Highway Patrol, a move heavily opposed by many citizens for fear that the organization would be a statewide police force subject to political appointments and political pressures.

In the election of 1938 Marland was succeeded by his principal enemy, Leon C. Phillips. There was some question about the legality of his nomination, for the primary runoff election had been abolished by the legislature in 1937, and Phillips had defeated his closest Democratic opponent, General William S. Key, by only 3,000 votes. His victory in November, however, was unquestioned; he had 355,740 votes to Republican Ross Rizley's 148,861.

Robert S. Kerr, founder of Kerr-McGee Petroleum Company, was governor of Oklahoma from 1943 to 1947 and United States senator from 1949 to 1963. OHS

Due largely to the influence of Senator Robert S. Kerr, the McClellan-Kerr Arkansas River Navigation System was developed to open the Arkansas River to barge traffic. Head of navigation is Catoosa, on the Verdigris River northeast of Tulsa. Photo by Jim Argo

As governor, Phillips demanded that the state budget be balanced, and in 1941 he secured an amendment to the constitution prohibiting the legislature from appropriating more money than there were funds available in any given fiscal year. To cut spending and retire the debt, Phillips halted construction of many projects begun during the Marland years. Budgets for institutions of higher learning were cut by 20 percent, and additional taxes were imposed on tobacco and gasoline. Bonds in the amount of thirty-five million dollars were issued to retire the public debt. With the outbreak of World War II, prosperity returned to Oklahoma, ending the hardships of the Depression and easing the financial posture of the state, but the war placed a heavy burden on Phillips to meet the state's responsibilities in

the war effort.

Another feature of the Phillips' years was the intense fighting between factions of the Democratic Party. Several of Marland's friends, among them Dr. Henry G. Bennett, president of Oklahoma A. & M. College, feared prosecution for alleged irregularities in the state textbook commission. In return, there were ugly accusations against Phillips, but the state's preoccupation with the war effort reduced this feud somewhat.

In 1942 Robert S. Kerr became the state's first native son to be elected governor. Born near Ada, Indian Territory, in 1896, Kerr studied law and, in 1926, founded what was to become the Kerr-McGee Oil Company. After a difficult primary battle, he was nominated by the Democrats, and in the general election defeated Republican

William J. Otjen. Kerr was also committed to reducing the state's debt and was aided in this effort by the wartime boom that brought greater state revenues from rising personal incomes and increased petroleum production; so great was the flood of revenue that the entire thirty-seven million dollar debt was paid off by 1947.

Kerr also pushed for and secured creation of the Pardons and Parole Board, and he convinced the voters to approve a constitutional amendment establishing separate boards of regents for the University of Oklahoma and for the Oklahoma A. and M. system. The runoff primary was reinstated, and free textbooks were again made available in the public schools (which had been halted after a textbooks scandal that had led to the near impeachment of some officials several years before). As wartime governor, Kerr also fought to attract military bases to the state. A total of twenty-eight Army, thirteen Navy, and many Army Air Corps installations were opened during these years and provided employment to tens of

thousands of Oklahomans. By 1946, as the general elections approached, Kerr could look back on a record of solid accomplishment—and a growing national reputation for himself.

Kerr was followed in office by another oil man, Roy J. Turner, who also was a successful rancher. Campaigning for the Democratic nomination, Turner defeated Republican Olney J. Flynn, son of Territorial delegate to Congress Dennis Flynn.

Turner, continuing the tradition of stressing economy in state government, vetoed several bills increasing welfare spending (although he did raise old-age pensions to fifty-eight dollars a month). Moreover, he pushed for reorganization of several state boards and commissions, such as the Planning and Resources Board, the Oklahoma Tax Commission, and the Oklahoma Highway Commission. This move was brought on by the discovery that much state highway money had been wasted through mismanagement and political patronage. To combat this, the department was placed under the state merit system, and turnpikes were authorized to reduce state spending on highways. Another major problem during Turner's administration was skyrocketing enrollment in state colleges caused by World War II veterans returning home and enrolling under the GI Bill. To alleviate the overcrowding that resulted, Turner, working with legislators, financed a building program for colleges by issuing thirty-six million dollars in bonds to be repaid from an increased tax on cigarettes. During Turner's term, the state supreme court ordered integration in some college programs, ending decades of discrimination.

In 1950 Johnston Murray, the son of Alfalfa Bill Murray, became governor. Running for office on a plank of being "just plain folks," Murray won the Democratic primary in a bitter contest, then defeated Republican Jo O. Ferguson in an extremely close contest.

His administration was one of contrasts: stringent economy in some areas, especially welfare (where there was strict enforcement of eligibility), and proposed massive spending in other areas, such as one plan to build a series of canals to move water from the eastern part of the state to the arid western area. He did secure passage of a plan to consolidate rural schools, but a constitutional amendment to allow eighteen-year-olds to vote failed. Murray also tried to reorganize state government by establishing a Governor's Joint Committee on State Government and by forming a "broom brigade" whose task was to rid state government of unneeded personnel. He fulfilled his promise to be just plain folks by maintaining an open-house policy at the governor's mansion, and his elderly father again became a familiar figure in the state capitol as he wandered the corridors and sat in offices.

In 1954 came the election of the first governor born since statehood. Raymond D. Gary, a former teacher, salesman, oil businessman, and senator, defeated Republican Reuben K. Sparks by more that 100,000 votes. In that election Governor Johnston Murray angered many Oklahomans by declaring martial law in several counties and using the National Guard to watch polling places to prevent irregularities.

Gary's administration saw a marked increase in appropriations for both public and higher education, as well as for mental institutions. During his term the public

Henry Louis Bellmon was the first Republican elected governor of Oklahoma, serving from 1963 to 1967. He later became United States senator from 1969 to 1981. OHS

schools were integrated, more than 3,000 miles of highways were constructed (including the start of the Interstate Highway system), the Department of Commerce and Industry was created to stimulate economic growth, and a water code was passed allowing dams to be built to conserve water.

In 1958 J. Howard Edmondson became the youngest man ever to hold office of chief executive. Just thirty-three when he took office, Edmondson received his law degree from the University of Oklahoma, and entered politics after moving to Tulsa. He brought to the statehouse many young and aggressive assistants, and with him they antagonized veteran politicians by trying to accomplish what old-timers saw as "too much too fast." Edmondson's most pronounced victory was the repeal of prohibition in 1959. This was accomplished by strict enforcement of the law, causing many thirsty Oklahomans to decide to vote for repeal. Edmondson also pushed vigorously for county consolidation, a merit system for state employees, centralized purchasing for state agencies, a withholding plan for state income taxes, and expanded construction of turnpikes. While some of these programs were passed, Edmondson failed to win acceptance of legislative reapportionment or a constitutional Highway Commission.

When United States Senator Robert S. Kerr (the former governor) died on January 1, 1963, Edmondson resigned as governor and five days later was appointed to fill the remainder of Kerr's term in the Senate. There were cries that Edmondson had made a "deal" with George P. Nigh, who had been elected lieutenant governor in 1958 and who had been colorful and outspoken during his four years in that office. Nigh served as governor for nine days before Henry L. Bellmon, Oklahoma's first Republican governor, took over the office.

Bellmon, born at Tonkawa, Oklahoma, in 1921, had farmed at Billings and served in the state legislature before winning the Republican nomination for governor in 1962. In a general election that surprised most political observers, Bellmon, thanks to the best organization ever put together by a Republican, defeated Democrat William P. "Bill" Atkinson.

Facing a legislature dominated by Democrats, Bellmon pledged to veto any measure calling for increased taxes. This split the legislative and executive branches and threatened to halt all activity by the state government, but Bellmon managed to secure legislation improving the retirement system for state employees, and additional bonds were authorized for additional turnpike construction. After prolonged debate about teachers' salaries—and the threat of a teacher strike—Bellmon and the legislators agreed to raise the state appropriation for both public and higher education through an increased tax on cigarettes. One scandal marred the Bellmon administration, although neither he nor his staff was touched by it. The scandal involved certain judges who were accused of taking bribes, and Associate Justice N.B. Johnson of the state supreme court was impeached in 1965.

In 1966 voters chose a second Republican governor, former state senator Dewey F. Bartlett. After defeating Democrat Preston J. Moore by more that 80,000 votes in the general election, Bartlett took office on January 9, 1967. During his administration he stressed pride in Oklahoma, encouraging everyone to wear "Okie" pins to demonstrate that this once derisive term had become a proud name. His tenure was marked by rapid increases in population and growth in industry, as he fought to reverse Oklahoma's anti-business attitude.

Bartlett was the first governor eligible to succeed himself, for state voters had recently passed a constitutional amendment removing the old clause restricting governors to one term. Bartlett, however, lost the election by slightly more than 2,000 votes to Democrat David Hall.

Born in Oklahoma City in 1930, Hall had earned a law degree from the University of Tulsa and had been county attorney in Tulsa County before his election. During his early years in office, Oklahoma continued to grow in population and the number of people employed in manufacturing rose to an estimated 200,000 by 1971. However, Hall angered many voters because he pushed for a large tax increase in 1971, part of it on oil and gas and the other on personal income and liquor. Although he argued that these increases would hit only "fat cats," the result was higher taxes for an overwhelming majority of Oklahomans. Much of this revenue went to support public education, including free public kindergartens, and the remainder to the construction of state highways. Late in his term, as Hall campaigned for reelection, rumors circulated that he was involved in a bribery attempt, and shortly after he left office he was arrested and convicted on charges of soliciting a kickback, and was sentenced to three years in federal prison.

Defeating Hall in the Democratic primary was David L. Boren, son of Lyle H. Boren, a former member of Congress from the fourth Oklahoma district. After graduating from Yale University and then studying in England, Boren had returned to Oklahoma to earn a law degree from the University of Oklahoma. While teaching at Oklahoma Baptist University, he also had served in the state House of Representatives. His opponent in the general election was Republican James Inhofe of Tulsa. Elected on a reform platform that utilized Johnston Murray's theme of the "broom brigade," Boren began working to reorganize the state government by making fewer state offices elective, thereby shortening the ballot for state officials, and he was concerned with restoring confidence in state government lost during the Hall administration. He also increased funding for public and higher education, and promoted a better public understanding at the national level for Oklahoma's petroleum industry. The teacher retirement sys-

Governors Dewey Bartlett and David Hall spent extensive effort to attract industry to Oklahoma during their terms of office. This effort was rewarded when the General Motors Assembly Plant was located in southeastern Oklahoma City during the administration of Governor Hall. Photo by Jim Argo

tem was overhauled, and a beginning was made on ending the earmarking of state sales tax revenues for the Department of Human Services.

The 1978 Democratic gubernatorial nomination went to George P. Nigh. A native of McAlester, Nigh taught Oklahoma history in the public schools before serving in the legislature and then becoming lieutenant governor in 1958. He proved extremely popular with state voters because of his wit and his outspoken candor, but failed to win election as governor in 1962. Reelected lieutenant governor in 1966, he continued to hold this office until his 1978 election as governor. Four years later in an era of economic prosperity almost unparalleled in Oklahoma

history, Nigh became the first governor reelected to that office in a victory of stunning proportions. In defeating Republican Tom Dixon, Nigh carried all seventy-seven counties in Oklahoma, a feat never before accomplished.

Nigh's first term in office was marked by an economic boom, high employment, tax cuts, and swelling revenues. Money was appropriated for salary increases of high proportions for state employees and public and higher education, road construction, and the Department of Human Services were appropriated large budget increases. This was possible because of the boom in oil and gas production, swelling state coffers thanks to the tax increases voted during the

administration of David Hall. Oklahoma's economy heated to the point that for several months the state had the lowest unemployment rate in the nation, and job seekers flowed into the state at a rate that triggered a spree of construction—and a reversal of the out-migration of the Depression years. At the end of Nigh's first term, the boom collapsed, and appropriation exceeded state revenues. Cuts in state spending were matched by cries for tax increases by those affected by the reductions. Even longtime director of the Department of Human Services, Lloyd Rader, caught in this dilemma and facing charges of administering a system in need of overhaul, was forced to resign. Early in 1984 the legislature responded to the problem of declining revenues by enacting a "temporary" one-cent increase in the state sales tax and by passing tax hikes in several other areas; in 1985 the "temporary" tax became permanent, and there were other increases in state levies.

Nigh, like his twenty-one predecessors in office as state governor, has received credit for the good things that happened during his administration and has been blamed for the hard times and the scandals. In truth, Oklahoma's chief executive has little real power, for the state has been dominated by its legislature (some observers have argued that the speaker of the House has more real

power than the governor). Like the governorship, the legislature, consisting of forty-eight senators and 101 representatives, has been almost exclusively controlled by the Democratic Party. Republicans have won significant numbers of seats only during years in which their party did well at the national level, as in 1920. In more than seventy-five years of statehood, there has been only one Republican Speaker of the House.

Republicans have been numerous among Oklahoma's representatives in the United States Senate, however. At statehood there was an informal agreement that one senator would be chosen from what had been the Indian Territory, the other from the Oklahoma Territory. Although senators then were appointed by the legislature, there was a referendum in 1907 in which the people voted for their choice. Democrats Robert L. Owen from Muskogee and Henry M. Furman from Ada came in first and second, but, honoring the agreement made earlier, Furman stepped aside to allow Democrat Thomas Gore of Lawton, who had finished third, to be appointed. Gore, who drew the short term, was blind, but he proved to be one of the most colorful and energetic representatives to Washington ever produced by the state. He was succeeded in 1920 by J.W. Harreld, a Republican who held office only one term. In 1926 Democrat Elmer Thomas won election and held the office for twenty-four years. He was succeeded in 1950 by Mike Monroney, also a Democrat, who stayed in office until 1968 when Republican former governor Henry Bellmon won the office. In 1980 Republican Don Nickles, a young businessman from Ponca City, won election.

The other line of succession in the United States Senate has been filled by several men: Robert L. Owen, a Democrat who served from 1907 to 1924; W.B. Pine, a Republican who served one term; Thomas P. Gore, the blind former senator from Lawton, served from 1930 to 1936; Josh Lee, a Democrat, 1936 to 1942; Ed H. Moore, a Republican, held office from 1942 to 1948; Robert S. Kerr, the former governor, served from 1948 until his death on January 1, 1963; J. Howard Edmondson, the Democrat who resigned as governor to assume the office on January 6, 1963, and who served until the general election in 1964; Fred R. Harris, a Democrat, who won the seat for two years in 1964 and then was reelected in 1966 to a full term; Dewey F. Bartlett, the former Republican governor who won office in 1972; and former Democratic Governor David Boren, who was elected to the office in 1978.

At the time of statehood Oklahoma received five seats in the United States House of Representatives. Four of the five elected that year were Democrats. After the census of 1910 the state received three additional seats, which were filled at large until redistricting in 1914. After the census of 1930 the state was given yet another congressional seat, which was elected at large. During the Dust Bowl years, however, Oklahoma's population declined, and in 1940 the state lost one seat, leaving it eight. This was followed by the loss of two more seats in 1950. Today Oklahoma is still represented by six congressmen. Notable among those who have served in this capacity are Alice M. Robertson of Muskogee, elected in 1920 as a Republican (she was the second woman in history to serve in Congress); Carl Albert, born in 1908 and a Rhodes scholar who served as a Democrat in the House from 1946 to 1976 and who in 1971 became speaker of that body; and Tom Sneed, a Democrat first elected to the House in 1950.

Oklahoma today is still divided into seventy-seven counties, each of which by law must be at least 400 square miles of taxable land in area, contain a population of at least 15,000, and have a minimum of four million dollars in taxable wealth. The powers of these counties are only those delegated by the state, and consist almost wholly of administering state laws. The voters in each county select three county commissioners (by district), a county clerk, an assessor, a treasurer, a sheriff, and a surveyor. In addition, many counties still elect a county school superintendent (although most counties no longer have any rural schools to be administered). Prior to 1965, when the legislature created a statewide system of district attorneys, each county also elected a county attorney. In counties other than Oklahoma and Tulsa (where the municipal government provides most services) the county commission is still an influential body controlling local law enforcement and taxation.

A major task of county commissioners is overseeing roadwork in their districts, which involves the expenditure of large sums of

Carl Albert was United States representative from the Third District of Oklahoma from 1947 to 1977. He was named Speaker of the United States House of Representatives in 1971, serving until his retirement from the House in 1977. OHS

money. In the early 1980s came a scandal, prosecuted by the federal government, in which more than 230 persons—commissioners and suppliers—were convicted of taking or giving kickbacks, but despite the widespread proof of corruption the legislature enacted few meaningful reforms. Thanks to the automobile and improved roads, there is no real reason today to have seventy-seven counties in a state the size of Oklahoma, but county officials constitute the second largest lobby (behind teachers) in the state, and no political leader talks seriously about county consolidation. The only modern governor to discuss such reform, J. Howard Edmondson, was unable to accomplish the task and was hurt politically for even talking about the subject.

Oklahoma's politics have been colorful—and promise to remain so in the future. Although the Republican Party in the 1960s managed to elect two governors and to win the presidential race in every contest since 1952, Democrats still dominate among registered voters by a wide margin. Requirements for voting in the state are simple: the citizen must register at least ten days prior to the election. Today the voters seem little concerned with party affiliation, looking instead at the personality and philosophy of candidates. Those who register and go to the polls apparently are as independent as their ancestors who settled the region.

CHAPTER XIV

Riches From the Land

Oklahoma is a land of great contrasts in climate, soils, and elevation. East of U.S. Highway 81 the annual rainfall increases dramatically, approaching forty and even fifty inches a year. To the west of this line, however, the annual rainfall decreases rapidly, often falling below ten inches a year moving west into the panhandle. In the southeastern corner of the state the growing season approaches 230 days, while in the panhandle it can be less than 180 days. In the east the soil often is thin and lacks fertility, while in the west it is rich and deep. These factors make for a diverse agriculture.

Since the days of prehistory there has been farming in eastern Oklahoma by the Indian inhabitants. With the removal of the Five Civilized Tribes to the area, the federal government sent agents to urge the newcomers to plant and harvest, like they had been doing in their old homeland. Through their own hard labor, and that of their slaves, these tribes soon had surpluses of corn and cotton for sale. Because of their methods of farming, however, they soon exhausted the fertility of the soil, and by the post-Civil War period much of the land had been returned to grass used to fatten cattle. The arrival of the railroad made farming profitable once again by expanding the marketplace, and new land was cleared for a return to some cash crop production by the 1880s.

Then came the land runs, auctions, and lotteries, and western Oklahoma was filled with new settlers, most of them farmers. They usually established farms on 160-acre tracts. Their first chore was to break the thick topsoil, usually matted with grass roots. Frequently they plowed open spaces around their quarter sections for protection from prairie fires and as a place to plant fruit trees. Most of the crops they planted had already been tested in Kansas or north Texas. By 1891 Oklahoma's white settlers

This idyllic view of a farm-stead in eastern Oklahoma Territory shows the poten-tial of Oklahoma's rich farmlands. All too often, however, drought, severe winter weather, and insects damaged or destroyed crops, leaving the settler destitute. OHS

This idyllic view of a farm-stead in eastern Oklahoma Territory shows the poten-tial of Oklahoma's rich farmlands. All too often, however, drought, severe winter weather, and insects damaged or destroyed crops, leaving the settler destitute. OHS

were growing wheat, corn, oats, sorghum, and cotton, along with potatoes, peanuts, watermelons, turnips, and many varieties of fruit. The territorial legislature created a Board of Agriculture in 1901 to assist these farmers, while scientists at the Oklahoma Agricultural and Mechanical College intro-duced new techniques and crops. Working together, the board and the scientists pro-vided much appreciated assistance to farm-ers, ranchers, and dairy operators.

In 1909, the first year after statehood, the census bureau began gathering informa-tion concerning Oklahoma agriculture. In that year there were twenty-nine million acres in cultivation, about 65 percent of the state's total of 44,424,960 acres. The aver-age size of Oklahoma's approximately 190,000 farms in 1909 was 151.7 acres—of which only 137 (or .1 percent) were irrigated. Farm land was valued at twenty-two dollars and forty-nine cents per acre, an increase from six dollars and fifty cents per acre in 1899. More than eight million acres were planted in corn, producing slightly less than seventy-two million dollars in income. The third most significant crop was hay and for-age grasses, totaling 1.3 million acres and producing $9.5 million in income. The total value of all crops that year in Oklahoma was estimated at $133,454,405.

The livestock industry, which had flour-ished in Oklahoma since the days of the Cherokee Strip Live Stock Association, was even more valuable than farming to resi-dents of the state. Ninety-seven percent of all farms reported domestic animals. To-gether with ranchers, this totaled almost two million cattle, almost a million horses and mules, and 135,000 hogs. The total value of these animals was $150 million.

By 1910 life on many Oklahoma farms had improved considerably. Few people still lived in dugouts, and for the wealthy there were ornate, comfortable wooden houses with wide porches, stuffed furniture, and many luxuries. For the poor there were log cabins or frame "shotgun shacks." School-houses had been built in most rural areas, and there the children received several months of education throughout the year. Classes were dismissed in the fall during harvest season because everyone, even chil-dren, was needed in the fields. The school-house usually served as a church on Sunday, with some untrained but fervent farmer in the area contributing the preaching. Despite gatherings for church, school recitals, all-night sings, and lectures by professors about agriculture, rural life still was lonely—the winters cold, the summers hot.

Machinery, mostly steam powered, some powered by gasoline motors, gradually was introduced to end some of the hard drudg-ery, making it possible to break the thick prairie sod or harvest wheat or sow grain with fewer laborers and less hand work. Yet farmers needed credit to buy machinery,

This team of oxen prepares to break the prairie sod in western Oklahoma. Often-times crews would contract out to individual farmers to break the sod so that farms could be improved. OHS

and interest rates at banks ranged to a legal high of 24 percent. In years when cotton and corn prices dropped, some farmers were unable to pay their debts and lost their land through mortgage foreclosure. Because of this, tenant farming increased steadily in the state. In 1910, 54 percent of all farms were operated by tenants, a figure that rose to 60 percent by 1935.

In addition to mortgages and debts, farm-ers were also burdened by the freight rates charged by railroads and the storage charges of grain elevator owners. Many farmers came to believe there was a con-spiracy among bankers, railroaders, and elevator operators to keep them poor, espe-cially in years of good harvests when prices fell. It seemed the more the farmer pro-duced, the less money he had. Therefore some farmers flirted with the Socialist Party for several years after statehood. In 1907 the Socialist candidate for governor received 9,740 votes, a figure that grew to 52,703 votes in 1914. The prosperity generated by high prices during World War I and repres-sive policies by government officials caused the Socialist vote to decline to 7,428 in 1918, and thereafter it became insignificant.

The quality of farm life gradually im-proved as farm-to-market roads were graded, as schools were consolidated, and as Model T Ford automobiles became commonplace. Moreover, county agents and agricultural experiment stations demonstrated the value of scientific farming, and dairy herds were slowly upgraded, better types of seed were used, and marketing cooperatives were formed. Soon there was an Oklahoma Grain Growers Union, an Oklahoma Poultry Im-provement Association, an Oklahoma Co-Operative Creameries Association, an Oklahoma Cotton Growers Association, an Oklahoma Livestock Growers Association, and even an Oklahoma Pecan Growers As-sociation. These groups spread knowledge and urged cooperative marketing to achieve better prices. Organizations for young-sters—for boys the Future Farmers of America, for girls the Future Homemakers of America, and for both the 4-H clubs— encouraged scientific farming.

For these reasons the number of farms in Oklahoma, along with the total number of residents in the state, steadily grew. At statehood the population stood at 1,414,177. This increased to 1,657,155 by 1910, to

Right
Oklahoma schoolhouses went through a series of changes as they progressed from untamed frontier to settled countryside. This sod school in northwestern Oklahoma was established in 1893. OHS

Opposite page, top
Cotton emerged as a major cash crop after statehood. It required intensive manual labor, and many families turned out all members to help with the harvest. OHS

Opposite page, bottom
Use of farm machinery increased acreage under cultivation and improved harvests. This early tractor and combine operated in western Oklahoma in the 1920s. OHS

Bottom
The two-story school in Amber marked the beginning of the consolidation of school districts that accelerated during the 1930s. OHS

2,028,283 by 1920, and to 2,396,040 by 1930. One dramatic change during this period was a drop in acreage devoted to cotton farming after 1925 and an equally dramatic rise in the acreage on which wheat was grown.

Then state farmers experienced two major disasters in close succession: the Great Depression and the Dust Bowl. The Depression that began in 1929 caused a sudden drop in prices paid for farm commodities. Prime cotton fell below five cents a pound (and low grade cotton to two cents), while cattle and hogs had little market at any price. The Agricultural Adjustment Act of 1933 paid farmers for limiting production, but was declared unconstitutional by the United States Supreme Court in 1936. In 1938 Congress passed another act of the same name, providing for federal control of acres planted and prices paid for commodities, and it established a form of federal crop insurance. Moreover, the federal government passed legislation designed to extend credit to farmers as well as to tenants who wanted to buy their land.

Yet the greatest disaster for farmers in western Oklahoma was the Dust Bowl. This was the popular name given to a five-state region that included parts of Oklahoma, Texas, New Mexico, Colorado, and Kansas—the Great Plains region originally covered by grass and grazed by buffalo. During World War I millions of acres in this region had been plowed for the first time in order to produce wheat. Much of this area consisted of a thin layer of topsoil that was bone dry, except during the spring and fall rains. Worse still, the farmers or absentee landowners did little to conserve moisture or rebuild the soil. When drought came, as it did periodically, the winds whipped soil loose from plowed land to settle in streambeds crossing the region. Rivers such as the Beaver and Cimarron became sluggish and muddy, flowing over wide, sandy beds. For example, the Washita River during the latter part of the nineteenth century had supported navigation by small boats. After its channel filled with sand, it became useless for commerce.

During 1932 there were dust storms during the spring followed by dry, hot summer days when the temperature often hit 100°— but no rain fell. That fall farmers plowed and planted winter wheat, after which came winds that whipped up dust clouds through

a process known as "saltation." Small particles of soil were dislodged by the wind, displacing other particles until the air was filled with flying topsoil and dust. These blew until they found protection from the wind in a ditch or against the side of a building; there the dust piled up in mounds many feet thick.

As the dust worked loose, plants on the windward side of a field had their roots bared, to then blow over and tangle with an adjoining row, hastening the tearing out of yet more plants. Entire fields were stripped in a day in this manner. Farmers soon came to dread the clouds of dust they saw approaching, some as tall and dark as thunderheads. By the spring of 1934 dust storms were so intense that daylight hours became as black as night. Nowhere was there protection. Dust seeped through cracks around doors and windows, coating everything in houses, killing birds and rabbits, even cattle and horses, by suffocation. Humans kept damp cloths over their noses and mouths. After such a storm passed, the dust would swirl about in small eddies for several more days—as farmers cursed or wept and looked in helpless frustration at what had been their fields.

When the winds came from the west, as they did in the spring of 1934, the dust of Oklahoma was carried eastward, sometimes as far as the Atlantic coast. That year Secretary of Agriculture Henry A. Wallace commented, "On May 12, 1934, for the first time since white men came to America, we had a great dust storm that originated in the plains country near the foot of the Rocky Mountains and swept across the continent and far out to sea."

From 1932 to 1938 farmers in Oklahoma fought the dust. As they plowed and planted, they met dry summers, hot winds, dust storms, and plants that were stripped away by the wind. Tenant farmers and migratory workers were the first to leave, some moving east to join relatives where it still rained, others heading for California and the "Golden West" they had heard about. These were the "Okies" celebrated by John Steinbeck in his *Grapes of Wrath*. Farm values tumbled to near five dollars an acre, while several western counties lost residents. Attendance at Panhandle Agriculture and Mechanical College at Goodwell dropped to ninety-two students—who studied soil conservation through dust-choked eyes. The region lost fewer people, however, than exaggerated newspaper accounts indicated. Nor were all those moving to California actually from Oklahoma. Because the Sooner State charged less for its license plates than any surrounding state, migratory farm laborers usually registered their automobiles in Oklahoma. Thus when they arrived at the California border, to be halted there by state police unless they had proof of a waiting job, reporters saw Oklahoma license tags and mistakenly called these people "Okies," a name that came to be used in derision about the hard-working and proud people displaced by the whims of nature.

Those people who remained in western Oklahoma faced their dilemma armed with a sense of humor. Beaver County residents tested the strength of the wind by nailing a chain to a fence post; the wind could not be

despite such efforts, the dust continued to blow. The federal government would later distribute films and millions of printed words to show that the Dust Bowl had been transformed, but such was not the case. Only when it began to rain again did the Dust Bowl end. In 1938 a little rain fell, enabling some farmers to raise a small crop. Then early in 1939 came a fourteen-inch snow, followed by good rains in April, and the drought at last was broken. The 1939 wheat crop, first estimated at twenty-five million bushels, jumped to 46,763,000 bushels when it was harvested. Farmers thereafter did practice methods of retaining moisture in the soil. New, drought-resistant types of seed helped, as did better techniques of soil management and a method of plowing known as stubble-mulching. Of greater help, however, were years of good

Dust storms, such as this one approaching Keyes in the Oklahoma Panhandle during the 1930s, literally blotted out the sun. Courtesy, Donovan L. Hofsommer

called a stiff breeze until the chain blew straight out. Another story told of a New Mexican farmer who sued an Oklahoman for his farm, which had blown east and settled at Guymon; reportedly the Oklahoman filed a countersuit, saying he had just planted a crop on this land when the wind blew it back to New Mexico. One humorist told—with a straight face—that he had seen a prairie dog digging a hole up in the air ten feet off the ground.

The New Deal administration of Franklin D. Roosevelt established programs to help farmers in affected areas. The Soil Conservation Service and local soil conservation districts demonstrated methods to prevent wind erosion, such as contour plowing and land terracing. The Shelterbelt Project was born, in which rows of trees were planted at government expense to slow the wind and hold down the soil. Farmers were asked to allow half their land to lay fallow each year, allowing moisture to store in the soil, but,

rains and high prices during World War II. These brought prosperity—and the breaking of yet more land and planting it in wheat. Then came dry years during the 1950s that saw a return of blowing dust as great as that of the 1930s—and a growing realization that this area could be productive only if man respected nature's periodic spells of drought.

By 1940 the number of farms in Oklahoma had dropped to 179,687, and the population had fallen to 2,336,434. There the population stabilized, but the number of farms continued to decline to fewer than 143,000 in 1950, fewer than 120,000 in 1960, to fewer than 90,000 in 1970, and to approximately 85,000 by 1980. Yet the number of acres under cultivation grew from some twenty-nine million in 1910 to 36.9 million in 1979, and the average size of a farm increased to almost 450 acres during the same period. There were, however, no corporate farms in Oklahoma because a

Public works projects in the New Deal provided jobs for destitute laborers and helped to reduce erosion caused by a prolonged drought. OHS

rural-dominated legislature early enacted laws allowing only family-owned corporations to engage in agriculture.

During this period a major shift occurred from cotton cultivation to wheat. In 1930 more than four million acres of cotton were cultivated, producing 1,130,415 bales valued at $106,992,573. By 1935 this had dropped significantly to 333,595 bales and by 1974 to 310,000 bales. The annual wheat crop rose as cotton decreased: in 1930 almost forty million bushels were produced, in 1940 more than fifty million bushels, in 1950 more than seventy-eight million bushels, and by 1980 some 175 million bushels. Today wheat is the state's largest cash crop, ranking third nationally and worth more than $300 million annually. The reason for this dramatic change was the introduction of man-made fibers to end the nation's—and the world's—dependency on cotton for clothing. In the early 1980s, however, as denim "blue jeans" became fashionable and cotton prices climbed, farmers began increasing their acreage of that crop while reducing wheat acreage, in line with the federal government's policy to reduce its stockpile of surplus grain.

Farmers at the same time were participating in one of the greatest agricultural revolutions in world history. No longer was the fertility of the soil or the amount of annual rainfall related to the abundance of their harvest. Irrigation wells perforated the land of western Oklahoma, and water could be pumped to the surface and dumped on crops as needed. Chemicals derived from petroleum were used as fertilizers and insecticides. Farm machinery of great sophistication—and cost—enabled one man to do the work that took dozens only a few years before (one man with a two-bottom plow pulled by four horses might, on a good day, plow twenty-five acres. Today a combine operated by one man can move through 100 acres in a day). Oklahoma thereby has become one of the great food-producing states of the Midwest—and will remain so as long as petrochemicals and underground water remain available, and if crop prices allow farmers a decent profit. Unfortunately the water table in western Oklahoma has begun to drop significantly, causing some state politicians and agricultural experts to call for a series of canals to move water from wet eastern Oklahoma to the arid western part of the state.

Livestock production kept pace with farming during these years—and actually brought more income to the state. Okla-

Above
During World War II wheat acreage and harvests increased impressively as Oklahomans sought to combat the Axis powers on the home front. OHS

Right
Irrigation helped offset the unreliability of Oklahoma's precipitation pattern. In Custer County an irrigation well helped this farmer produce bumper crops. Courtesy, United States Bureau of Reclamation

homa ranks fifth nationally in income from cattle and calves, and second in number of head. By 1980 there were six and a half million head of cows and calves on Oklahoma ranches, valued at almost one billion dollars; some 100,000 head of sheep and lambs valued at two and a half million dollars; and 350,000 hogs valued at fifteen million dollars. In addition, Oklahoma ranchers are major producers of the nation's quarter and riding horses, a number that may increase because of a referendum passsed in 1982 allowing pari-mutuel betting at legal racetracks in the state. There are also some 140,000 milk cows producing almost 1.2 bil-

barrels a day—began at Neodesha, Kansas, in 1893. Drillers, however, were slow to enter the Indian Territory because of uncertainty about the ownership of Indian lands. Speculators found oil near Chelsea in 1889, near Muskogee in 1894, and near Bartlesville in 1897, but none of this could be exploited because there was no way to get the petroleum to market. After the Dawes Commission began alloting land to individual Indians, leases could be signed with certainty, and the result was a significant strike in 1904 at Red Fork (just south of Tulsa) on land belonging to a Creek Indian. Although the Red Fork Pool was small,

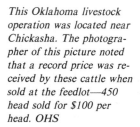

This Oklahoma livestock operation was located near Chickasha. The photographer of this picture noted that a record price was received by these cattle when sold at the feedlot—450 head sold for $100 per head. OHS

lion pounds of milk annually, valued at more than $100 million.

Oklahoma's forestry industry annually produces products valued at some seventy-five million dollars. Approximately 23 percent of the state, some ten million acres, is covered with forests, one-half of it of commercial quality. This mainly centers in seventeen southeastern counties where loblolly pine, short-leafed pine, sweet gum, various oaks, cottonwood, pecan, and walnut trees are grown for commercial use. Lumbermen quickly learned the value of replanting trees cut for timber, and thus forestry has an excellent future in the state.

Life for Oklahoma's farmers and ranchers of today is immeasurably better than for their ancestors. Today, the soil for which the Boomers and Sooners fought has delivered the rich promise they saw, and their descendants help feed a hungry world. Making much of this prosperity has become possible due to chemical fertilizers manufactured from petroleum. Oil men knew early that the Mid-Continent region contained petroleum, for commercial production—twelve

Prairie Oil and Gas Company, a subsidiary of Standard Oil Company, built a pipeline to carry the production to a refinery in Kansas. This strike spurred others to search in the region, and the same year another field was opened near Cleveland, followed in 1905 by a discovery at Glenn Pool. Opened by Robert A. Galbreath and Frank Chesley, Glenn Pool was a major stike that made several millionaires and triggered the modern oil boom in Oklahoma. Another strike at Okmulgee in 1906 further encouraged oil speculators. Tulsa became the center of this activity, and soon what had been a small cattle town and Indian trade center was transformed into the self-proclaimed "Oil Capital of the World." In 1907, thanks largely to Glenn Pool's output, Oklahoma produced forty-three and a half million barrels of oil. The Texas Company (Texaco) and Gulf built pipelines to carry crude to refineries on the Gulf Coast, while Prairie Oil and Gas constructed another pipeline to take Oklahoma oil to a Standard refinery in Louisiana.

The next major strike came in 1912 at

the Cushing Field, because of the determination of several men who believed oil was there. Chief among them was Tom Slick, a Pennsylvanian who learned the oil business in his home state and who boasted that he could smell oil-laden sands before a drill bit touched the earth. For several months he suffered disappointment as he tried to drill a producing well, but finally he and his backers tapped what eventually would prove to be the second largest field in Oklahoma's history.

In the weeks and months that followed Tom Slick's initial discovery, Cushing experienced what other towns would come to know when oil was found nearby. Before Slick's success, Cushing had been a dusty, sleeping village. A few businessmen along the main street kept their doors open by extending liberal credit to farmers who hoped to pay their bills at harvest time. When crops failed, so did some businesses. There was not a single telephone, electric line, paved street, or automobile in town.

Oil brought dramatic and almost immediate change. Telephone lines were quickly

strung, while the noise and fumes from automobiles soon could be heard along dusty streets, scaring horses and starting grass fires. All over town new businesses sprang into existence: storage yards for pipe and the assorted machinery needed to drill oil wells, lumber yards filled with massive derrick timbers, wagons used to transport all this to sites in the countryside, restaurants and hotels catering to the mass of humanity bustling about town, and supply houses carrying a wide assortment of merchandise at inflated prices. Other businesses opened for the sole purpose of separating the newly wealthy from their money: automobile dealerships, jewelry stores carrying a wide assortment of glittering gewgaws, and gift shops carrying "presents" for loved ones left behind. All the businessmen seemed to be doubling their prices almost every hour.

Because of the rapid growth, there was confusion, disorder, and uneven progress. For example, at the height of the boom, Cushing still had no sewer system, nor did it have suitable housing, and food often was in short supply. Housing was in such de-

Livestock production in Oklahoma remains one of the leading cash producers for the state's economy. Cattle still outnumber humans in the state. While technology has improved, roundups on horseback are still necessary. Photo by Jim Argo

Tulsa, pictured in the late 1920s, was the Oil Capital of the World. OHS

mand that enterprising pool hall owners allowed men to sleep on and beneath billiard tables from midnight to sunup for fifty cents (even chairs were rented for sleeping space). More enterprising men erected shanties from packing crates, cardboard, tree limbs, or anything else available on any plot of ground they could defend.

Conditions were made worse by the horde of tramps, vagrants, and hangers-on who swarmed into Cushing, as they did to every boomtown in Oklahoma. Unable to find work, they stood along the streets, sleeping in alleys and begging for food. There were also camp followers of a less desirable nature: gamblers who kept games going at all hours, women with no visible means of support, and whiskey peddlers. One writer referred to this class as "vultures, harpies, and the riffraff of the country . . . ." Crime became rampant, as did disease spread by cramped living conditions, poor food, impure water, and lack of proper sanitation. Meningitis became a dreaded killer, and typhoid was common.

Cushing was no quiet, sober community. It was boisterous and alive, its streets a jumble of humanity. Restaurants, hotels, stores, barbershops, illegal saloons, all brightly lighted, kept open house on both sides of the main street late into the night, while down at the freight yards men could be heard swearing as they sweated to load wagon after wagon with pipe or steam boiler or lumber or wire. The "roughnecks," as oilfield workers were known, arrived at the end of their shift of work and began to spend. And spend they did, for their wages ranged from six to fifteen dollars a day. Oklahoma was officially dry, but in the first week of the boom whiskey peddlers seemed to be on every corner doing a brisk business.

Theirs was a raw, potent product that seared the throat, warmed the stomach, and inflamed the head. One teetotaler commented in disgust, "Every bottle sold seemed to contain a thousand curse words, several arguments, and at least one fist fight."

The countryside around Cushing changed as much as the city during the oil boom. Dirt roads suddenly were crowded with flashy automobiles carrying agents offering fistfuls of money for drilling rights. Farmers and their sons, to whom $100 cash had once seemed a fortune, suddenly were exposed to fast-talking city slickers from Houston or Chicago offering thousands of dollars in return for a signature on a lease. Once the lease was signed, heavy wagons carrying steel, pipe, and timber cut deep ruts into roads that became impassable when it rained, while makeshift roads were torn across once-barren pastures. Such was life in and around a booming Oklahoma oil town.

The year after the discovery at Cushing, another major field opened at Healdton (near Ardmore). The combined production of the two fields swamped the national oil market as tens of thousands of barrels were brought to the surface daily, dropping the price of crude to forty cents a barrel. In fact, when a great fire destroyed more than 500,000 barrels of oil at Cushing, some producers were relieved to be rid of the excess. Eventually some producers tried self-regulation to slow production and stabilize oil prices. When this "gentlemen's agreement" failed to work, the Oklahoma Corporation Commission undertook regulation of the new industry in 1914. Although this attempt was largely a failure, the legislature passed laws the following year to stop the waste and try to bring order to the industry. Thereafter the Corporation Commission exercised some control in the oilfields, although several governors found it necessary to call out the National Guard to enforce the stop-production rulings of the commission to protect oil prices.

The outbreak of World War I increased oil prices after 1914, which, in turn, stimulated the search for new oil. Fields were now being located through geological analysis rather than by evaluating surface formations. Using this new method, three fields were discovered at Tonkawa (Three Sands) and Burbank by E.W. Marland.

In 1926 came the opening of the Greater Seminole Oil Field. The first discovery in this area had been made at Wewoka in 1923, but little development had taken place. When the extent of the field was realized in 1926 and serious production started, more than eight million barrels of oil were pumped within one year. The strike had a dramatic impact on the estate of O.D. Strother, a shoe salesman thought to be "land and lease poor." Regardless, Strother believed that oil was in the area, and when he died in March 1926, oil had been discovered and his estate was conservatively valued at seven and a half million dollars.

Then in December 1928 came the opening of the Oklahoma City Field when, "with a roar like thunder, . . . black gold flowed," as one newsman wrote. As early as 1915 oil men had learned that small deposits of oil and gas were underground in the area, however, most producers believed these were too small to be of commercial potential. In 1928 the Indian Territory Illuminating Oil Company drilled below the first level of production, and the main pool was located. Soon the output of the Seminole and Oklahoma City fields threatened to outdo the disastrous results of overproduction at Cushing and Healdton. To prevent a glut of oil and disastrously low prices, the Corporation Commission attempted to enforce the 1915 laws limiting overproduction—only to find itself disregarded and production increasing. Just at this time came the onset of the Great Depression—and the discovery of the East Texas Oil Field, one of the largest in the nation's history. The Depression slowed industry and slackened oil consumption just when production was greater than ever, and prices tumbled below fifteen cents a barrel. Governor Bill Murray twice declared oil wells under martial law to enforce Corporation Commission rulings. Certain wells were not allowed to produce again until the price of oil reached a dollar a barrel. There was open violence between the National Guard

The Cushing Oil Field was discovered by Tom Slick in 1912. This road ran from Cushing to Oilton through the heart of the field, showing the density of wells in the field, as well as the haphazard development of transportation routes and communication networks. Courtesy, Western History Collections, University of Oklahoma Library

The Greater Seminole Oil Field east of Oklahoma City was one of Oklahoma's largest producing fields from 1925 to the mid-1930s. Over-production from this and other Oklahoma fields led Governor "Alfalfa Bill" Murray to order the Oklahoma National Guard to close Oklahoma's oil fields to enforce proration. Courtesy, Western History Collections, University of Oklahoma Library

and roughnecks during the second period of martial law (1932), and some "hot oil" (illegally pumped) continued to flow through clandestine pipelines.

To remove the need for future declarations of martial law, the legislature in 1933 passed a proration law that provided a staff to oversee production and to halt illegal production. Although this law was imperfect, as when it relied on production potential rather than acreage to determine how much oil could be pumped from a well, it nevertheless became a model followed by other oil-producing states.

After 1935 the Oklahoma oil business began to settle down. The search for new fields became more orderly, as did the conduct of oilfield workers in towns where booms occurred. Major finds were made in the southern and northwestern areas of the state, including the Panhandle Field near Guymon. The discovery of the West Edmond Field in 1943 showed that unknown large pools were still underground, and technical innovations allowed secondary and tertiary methods of oil recovery in fields thought exhausted. When the Organization of Petroleum Exporting Countries (OPEC) embargoed oil shipments to the United States in 1973, intensified efforts to find additional petroleum in the United States led to a drilling rush in Oklahoma, especially

after 1981 when President Ronald Reagan signed legislation deregulating petroleum prices, allowing free market prices to prevail. In addition, this legislation allowed a free market on natural gas discovered at depths greater than 15,000 feet.

When the price of oil soared toward forty dollars a barrel, a boom of historic proportions developed in Oklahoma. This was especially true in the Anadarko Basin where drilling reached record depths of more than 25,000 feet to bring in gas wells of incredible richness. The state's unemployment rate dropped to the lowest in the nation, and migrants flowed into the state at such a rate that some Oklahoma towns experienced growth that rivaled the boom era of the 1920s. Elk City, Woodward, Clinton, and other cities in the western and northwestern portions of the state saw explosive growth with workers living in tents and trailers, while municipal services were stretched almost beyond their limits.

The oil men who created this boom were so successful and their wells so productive that the world price of oil was forced below thirty dollars a barrel, causing the boom to collapse late in 1982. This left in its wake a multitude of bankruptcies and the closing of Penn Square Bank in Oklahoma City, a financial institution that had specialized in financing oil men in their quest for black gold. Its collapse sent shock waves through financial circles across the United States, while the lower prices commanded by oil and gas forced the state of Oklahoma into painful economic retrenchment when the taxes on petroleum production dipped below anticipated levels.

Several giant firms emerged out of the boom-and-bust cycle of Oklahoma's petroleum industry: Phillips Petroleum of Bartlesville, Continental Oil Company (Conoco) at Ponca City (formerly Maryland Oil Company), Champlin at Enid, Skelly at Tulsa, and Kerr-McGee of Oklahoma City. These were large, integrated firms involved in producing, refining, and marketing petroleum products. There were also dozens of independent producing companies in the state involved only in drilling and developing wells, and selling their output to major corporations or to independent refiners and marketers. In the late 1970s and early 1980s, as the consolidation of small firms into larger ones occurred at a rapid pace, some of Oklahoma's better-known companies disappeared. For example, Skelly merged with Getty Oil, which in turn was bought by Texaco. There were, in addition, takeover attempts by other major oil companies that produced headlines across the nation. These firms, large and small, have written a significant portion of the history

of petroleum in both the United States and the world, for the majors and independents who pioneered in Oklahoma took their knowledge and expertise to other states and nations, even to the oceans with offshore drilling technology.

The impact of the petroleum industry in

Above
The Indian Territory Illuminating Oil Company's Oklahoma City discovery well, brought in during 1928, was located near present-day S.E. 59th Street and Shields Boulevard. OHS

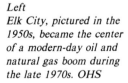

Left
Elk City, pictured in the 1950s, became the center of a modern-day oil and natural gas boom during the late 1970s. OHS

OKLAHOMA: LAND OF THE FAIR GOD

Oklahoma cannot be over-emphasized. The total value of petroleum products, in terms of jobs, wages, dividends, and lease payments, grows each day, amounting to more than forty billion dollars since statehood, while the taxes taken by the state from both production and wages have enabled all Oklahomans to enjoy a far higher standard of living than otherwise would have been possible in a state whose tax structure has not always been favorable to business. Still the search for petroleum proceeds in Oklahoma—the history of the industry is such that other booms doubtless lie ahead.

Oklahoma's petroleum energy has been made available to both residential and business customers by natural gas pipeline companies, and it has been used to fuel electric generators. Many cities in the first years of the twentieth century used diesel generators to produce electricity, but later switched to coal-fired generators. With the building of great dams in eastern Oklahoma, particularly in the 1950s and 1960s, electricity generated by waterpower became widely available through such organizations as the Grand River Dam Authority (GRDA), which sold much of its output to rural electric cooperatives. In the early 1980s, as the cost of energy soared, plans to build a nuclear generator, the Black Fox project in eastern Oklahoma, were abandoned because of soaring costs and public disapproval. A less conventional source of power is also widely available in Oklahoma: wind-turned electric generators. One pioneering firm in Norman specialized in manufacturing "windchargers," as these were known to farmers as early as the 1930s, and were used to power a radio and a few lights.

Other mineral resources of great value to Oklahoma include lead, zinc, coal, copper, cement, granite, gypsum, helium, limestone, sand and gravel, and stone. Oklahoma stands fourth among all states in the production of lead and zinc. This is in a region known as the Tri-State Zinc-Lead Mining District, which encompasses producing centers in southeastern Kansas, northeastern Oklahoma, and southwestern Missouri. Oklahoma coal mining began in the 1870s when J.J. McAlester, an intermarried citizen of the Choctaw Nation, established the Oklahoma Mining Company. Production also occurred at Krebs, Coalgate, and other towns in the Choctaw and Creek regions. Many of the early coal miners were immigrants from Czechoslovakia, Hungary, Germany, and Italy, and the result was the development of towns with a European flavor that has been retained to the present. By 1900 almost two million tons of coal were being mined each year, an amount that grew to almost five million tons by 1920. Production since that time has varied, but by the 1970s, as the energy needs of the nation grew and the price of petroleum soared, Oklahoma's coal reserves increased in importance. Dozens of small strip-mining corporations were formed in Muskogee, Okmulgee, and surrounding counties, but because of the coal's high sulphur content the federal Environmental Protection Agency refused to allow it to be burned in the area. Thus Oklahoma's coal often is exported to foreign countries (by way of the McClellan-Kerr waterway), and electricity is generated in the area with low-sulphur coal from Wyoming and other states.

Oklahoma's rich soil has also been used as a raw resource for two other important products: bricks and glass. Long before statehood, bricks were being made from Oklahoma clay. Mormons who arrived in Tahlequah in 1844 showed the Cherokees how to make the bricks that were used to erect their Male and Female Seminaries. After the land runs, scores of plants in the Oklahoma Territory fired the deep red bricks needed to erect buildings and homes. Today the low cost of bricks in the Sooner State means that even modest homes are attractively faced with Oklahoma-fired bricks. Sand of high quality for glass-making plants is available at many locations, and the abundance of cheap natural gas brought many firms to the state to produce canning jars (at Sand Springs and Okmulgee), sheet glass (at the Ford float plant in Tulsa), bottles and bakeware (at the Corning and Brockway plants in Muskogee), and other types of specialty glass at Sapulpa and Henryetta.

Since statehood the total value of Oklahoma's mineral production, including petroleum, has moved far beyond sixty billion dollars in value. Most experts agree that the amount of oil and natural gas still underground is greater than that taken out in the past. The future promises even greater riches from the soil, and as technology advances Oklahomans will again discover how generously endowed their state is in natural resources.

*Opposite page, top
Oklahoma City was born
on a single day, April 22,
1889. One of the special
events held each year is the
Festival of the Arts. Photo
by Jim Argo*

*Opposite page, bottom left
Steps at the Carnegie Li-
brary were the site of the
swearing in ceremonies for
Oklahoma's last territorial
and first state governor.
Photo by Jim Argo*

*Opposite page, bottom right
The birthplace of Oklaho-
ma humorist Will Rogers is
one of the few structures
on the National Register of
Historic Places to be moved
from its original site and
still remain on the register.
Photo by Jim Argo*

*Above
A giant Old Glory, fifty by
seventy-six feet, slowly
moves through Edmond,
Oklahoma, as part of a
Fourth of July parade. De-
pending on the weather,* *the flag is carried by forty
to sixty people, all mem-
bers of the United States
Naval Reserve Flag Team.
Photo by Jim Argo*

*Top
Oklahoma's domeless state
capitol building was started
in 1914. The cornerstone
was laid on Statehood Day,
November 16, 1915, and
the building was completed* *on June 30, 1917. The
building sits atop a vast oil
trap 6,500 feet below
ground. Photo by Jim Argo*

Above
Each April, Honor Heights Park in Muskogee is the scene of the annual Azalea Festival. In addition to the 625 varieties of azaleas to be found, there are many other types of flowers, shrubs, and trees. Thousands of people come each year to enjoy the floral display. Photo by Jim Argo

Left
Dogwood blooms in the early spring on Talimina Drive in eastern Oklahoma. It is one of sixty-three varieties of trees that can be found along the scenic highway linking Talihina, Oklahoma, with Mena, Arkansas. Photo by Jim Argo

Opposite page
Will Rogers once said, "If you don't like the weather, wait a minute." This is certainly true in Oklahoma's unpredictable climate. A cross-country skier finds an unusually heavy snow just right for practicing his sport in Oklahoma City's Will Rogers Park. Photo by Jim Argo

Above
Oklahoma's water link to the Gulf of Mexico starts at the Port of Catoosa, near Tulsa. These barges, loaded with Oklahoma grain, will go down the Verdigris and Arkansas rivers to the Mississippi River to the gulf to be loaded on boats and shipped to many foreign countries. Photo by Jim Argo

Opposite page
Mazeppa T. Turner of Virginia is credited with being the "discoverer" of Turner Falls near Davis in the Arbuckle Mountains. The seventy-seven-foot falls is located on Honey Creek. The area is owned by the city of Davis and is a popular swimming, picnicking, and camping area. Photo by Jim Argo

Oil is a major Oklahoma industry that has resulted in countless jobs for residents both in the oil industry itself and the related companies. This crew is drilling for oil in Beckham County during the 1980s. Photo by Jim Argo

Like tanks rolling into battle, these combines attack a golden Oklahoma wheat field near Enid. Photo by Jim Argo

Cotton has long been an agricultural staple in southwestern Oklahoma. Fields such as these in Kiowa County can be seen during the fall months. Photo by Jim Argo

Typical of the many rodeos held each year in Oklahoma is the 101 Ranch Rodeo held each August in Ponca City. The rodeo is named for the famous 101 Ranch and Wild West Show that once headquartered a few miles south of Ponca City near Marland. Photo by Jim Argo

*The Oklahoma National
Stockyards Company in
Oklahoma City claims the
title of world's largest cattle market in number of
cattle sold. About 1.2 million are sold there each
year, with most going to
ranches or feedlots for fat-
tening. Photo by Jim Argo*

Enjoying a live concert on a Saturday evening in early summer are a group of central Oklahomans. This performance, on the grounds of the Oklahoma Museum of Art in Oklahoma City, was by Tom McGuire and the New American Ragtime Ensemble. The museum was once the home of oilman Frank Buttram. Photo by Jim Argo

Above
Saturday afternoon this crowd gathered at Owen Stadium to watch a University of Oklahoma football game. The 75,000-seat stadium is almost always sold out for home games. Photo by Jim Argo

Right
Hang gliding enthusiast David Howeth of Oklahoma City is riding the wind at Buffalo Mountain, east of Talihina. A rugged seven-mile ridge overlooking the Potato Hills in LeFlore County is a favorite of area hang glider participants. This picture was taken by a camera mounted on the nose of the glider. Photo by Jim Argo

Above
Little Sahara State Park and Recreation Area, south of Waynoka, is one of Oklahoma's most unusual playgrounds because of the sand dunes found there. Photo by Jim Argo

Left
The American Indian Exposition near Anadarko is one of the nation's top Indian ceremonials and perhaps its most prestigious dancing competition. Photo by Jim Argo

Top, left
This hot-air balloon, owned by Jim Reynolds of Bartlesville, is patterned after the state flag of Oklahoma, a blue background with the shield of the Osage Nation. Photo by Jim Argo

Located in northeastern Oklahoma, Grand Lake of the Cherokees is one of the best developed and most popular resort areas in Oklahoma. It sprawls across three counties and has 1,300 miles of shoreline. Completed in 1941, the lake, which dammed up water of the Grand River, was the first major reservoir in eastern Oklahoma. Photo by Jim Argo

A High Quality of Life

*I*n 1889, on the eve of the first land run, Oklahoma was still largely the way nature had shaped it. Some Indians in the eastern part of the territory were farming and some railroad tracks had been laid, but most of the region was still undisturbed by man. Moreover, the population was small, amounting to fewer than 200,000 people. In the decades that followed towns were built, railroads were joined by highway, river, and air transportation systems, communications improved dramatically, newspapers grew in number, and a modern educational system was erected. The people of the state showed their love for the arts and music, just as they demonstrated an appreciation and awareness of their heritage by establishing museums and joining historical organizations to preserve their unique heritage.

By the date of the first major land run, there were only seven incorporated towns in what would become Oklahoma. The first was in 1873 when the Cherokee Nation approved the incorporation of Downingville (now Vinita)—although residents of Tahlequah claim that their town was incorporated in 1852. Webbers Falls was incorporated in 1885; Mangum, in Greer County, was incorporated under the laws of Texas in 1886; and Chelsea, Chouteau, and Claremore were incorporated in 1889.

Today the most populous city in the state is Oklahoma City, which was born in a single hour on April 22, 1889. Where only a small railroad depot and hotel rested on the prairie that morning, more than 10,000 people had gathered in thousands of tents and wagons by that evening. Confusing the situation were two competing township companies trying to develop the city. Moreover, the federal act opening the Oklahoma District had not authorized city government. Yet the settlers did not worry about the niceties of the law, and on their own initiative organized a local government, elected officials, passed ordinances, and enforced their

Oklahoma City, the largest city in the state and the financial and governmental capital of Oklahoma, has burgeoned from a born-grown town of less than 10,000 in 1889 to a metropolitan area with almost one million inhabitants. Photo by Jim Argo

laws. One township company, the Oklahoma Colony Company, made the run from the south and surveyed south of the railroad tracks. The second, the Seminole Land and Improvement Company, came from Kansas and platted from Clarke (now Sheridan) Avenue northward. After the organization of the territory, the two plattings merged into a town called Oklahoma. The word "City" would not be recognized by the post office for thirty-four more years.

When Oklahoma City was founded, it had no real geographical advantages. Yet because of solid leadership and initiative it grew and prospered, and its future was assured when it became the state capital in 1910. Gradually, thanks to good rail service, it became the wholesaling and jobbing center for much of the state, as well as the major livestock market in the region. The drilling of an oilfield in 1928 inside its corporate limits brought yet another major industry there, while the location of Tinker

Field on its eastern outskirts during World War II provided permanent employment for thousands (and Tinker remains the largest single employer in the state). The Commercial Club, later the Chamber of Commerce—for many years under the leadership of Stanley Draper—played a leading role in attracting industry, securing conventions, and providing cultural activities. Today the city has more than 500,000 residents, while its satellite communities constitute a metropolitan area of approximately 850,000. A pioneering spirit is still evident in Oklahoma City, for in the late 1960s when the downtown area began to deteriorate with age, local leaders began a major urban renewal program that is transforming the face of the city. This rebuilding is scheduled for completion in 1989, the centennial of the run that brought the city into existence.

Oklahoma City's major competitor has been Tulsa, a city started by Creek Indians migrating from the southeastern United

States. In 1836 they founded the community they named Talsi, later called Tulsey Town and then Tulsa. For almost fifty years the community existed as an Indian village. Then in 1882 the Frisco Railroad arrived, and Tulsa became the center of cattle trade in eastern Oklahoma. Under the terms of the Curtis Act of 1898, Tulsa was incorporated and a town survey was made in 1900. Four years later came the discovery of oil at nearby Red Fork, followed in 1905 by drilling at Glenn Pool, and Tulsa changed within a few short years from a sleepy cow town into the "Oil Capital of the World." As a result, the population, which had reached 18,182 in 1910, boomed to 72,075 by 1920. City fathers made a concerted effort to attract oil company corporate headquarters, as well as oil-related manufacturing concerns and refineries. The International Petroleum Exposition, which began in 1923, made oil men everywhere aware that Tulsa, unlike some other cities, wanted their business, and more of them moved to Tulsa. Building on this base, the city grew and prospered, while oil-millionaires-turned-philanthropists beautified and enriched life in the city through selected gifts and donations of parks, museums, and municipal structures. In 1954 *Reader's Digest* named Tulsa "America's Most Beautiful City," and in 1974 *Harper's Magazine* rated it the second-best city in America for livability.

During World War II Tulsa's economy diversified when several non-petroleum-related industries moved to Tulsa, diversifying the area's economic base into aviation (later aerospace) and other concerns. Then in 1971 the McClellan-Kerr Arkansas River Navigation System was opened and provided barge transportation that, in effect, made Tulsa a seaport. All these changes promised to change Tulsa yet again, making it not only a major oil center but also a manufacturing and transportation hub for much of mid-America. Today its population has surpassed 400,000 and its metropolitan area includes almost 600,000.

Another major metropolitan area in Oklahoma is Lawton, born on August 6, 1901, when the Kiowa-Comanche lands were opened to white settlement. Lawton has benefited from the presence of nearby Fort Sill, as well as from the businesses and industrial firms that have located there. Today its population exceeds 80,000, and its future looks bright. Other prominent Oklahoma cities include Norman, home of the University of Oklahoma and aircraft and wind-powered generator industries; Midwest City, a suburb of Oklahoma City and the actual site of Tinker Field; Enid, for many years the home of Champlin Oil Company and now a regional trade and distributing center; Muskogee, former premier city of the Indian Territory and now a center of glass and optical manufacturing; Stillwater, home of Oklahoma State University; Bartlesville, the location of Phillips Petroleum Company; and Ponca City, home of Conti-

Lawton, home of Fort Sill, county seat of Comanche County, and the largest city in southwestern Oklahoma, grew dramatically from a tent city following the lottery of 1901 into Oklahoma's third-largest city in 1980. OHS

Above
Participants at the International Petroleum Exposition met with members of Indian tribes whose lands produced oil and natural gas. Oklahoma's Osage Indians were numbered among the world's wealthiest people in the 1910s and 1920s during the height of the oil boom in Osage County. Courtesy, Tulsa County Historical Society

Right
Depicted circa 1905 is the print shop of the Cherokee Advocate, *staffed by Cherokee Indians. Courtesy, Western History Collections, University of Oklahoma Library*

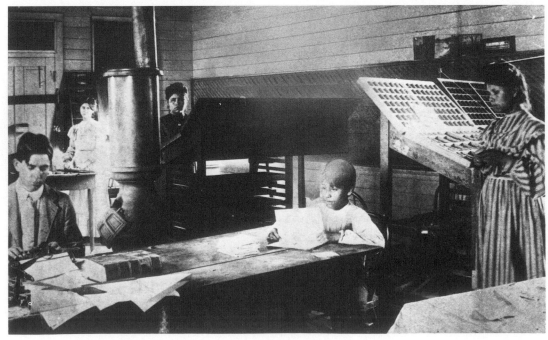

nental Oil Company (Conoco).

Within weeks of the establishment of most towns in newly-opened territories, local newspapers began publication to predict an unlimited future for each community. These joined the *Cherokee Advocate,* which for decades had been the only newspaper in Oklahoma except for religious tracts published by missionaries, and about ten weeklies that began publication in the 1880s with the arrival of the railroads. Most of these early efforts were small and had limited circulation, but gradually a few newspapers emerged to dominate the state. The *Indian Chief* began publication in Tulsa in 1884, and in 1893 came the *Indian Republican;* in 1905 came the *Tulsa Daily World,* which traces its lineage to both these earlier papers. The *World's* major rival, the *Tulsa Tribune,* traces its founding to the *New Era,* a weekly which eventually became the *Tulsa Democrat* and then in 1919 was acquired by Richard Lloyd Jones and renamed the *Tulsa Tribune.* Today the *Tribune* and the *World* are the major daily papers of eastern Oklahoma.

In the Oklahoma District one of the first newspapers was the *Edmond Sun,* founded by Milton Reynolds, but after his death in 1890 it diminished in importance. The *Oklahoma City Times,* later to become the *Oklahoma Journal,* then the *Oklahoma City Times-Journal,* and finally the *Oklahoma Times,* began publication on May 9, 1889, as a weekly under the editorship of Angelo Scott and his brother Winfield W. Scott. The *Daily Oklahoman* began publication in 1889 under the editorship of the Reverend Samuel Small, ceased for a time, and then was reissued by a stock company headed by Whit Grant. Both the *Daily Oklahoman* and the *Times* eventually became part of the Oklahoma Publishing Company of E.K. Gaylord, who arrived in Oklahoma City in 1902 and for more than seventy years was a major force in journalism in the state (in 1984 the two papers were combined into one daily published by E.L. Gaylord, son of the founding publisher).

By 1900 Oklahoma Territory was the home of nine daily papers, 139 weeklies, eighteen monthlies, and four semi-monthlies. These publishers realized early the need for some central organization to represent their interests, and in 1888 at Muskogee they had formed the Indian Territory Press Association, a name changed to the Oklahoma

Press Association after statehood.

The roads over which these first newspapers were delivered were little more than wagon tracks. These had evolved as Indians, especially members of the Five Civilized Tribes, wound through the countryside looking for the easiest way to drive a wagon from one settlement to the next. When they came to rivers and creeks, they sought a place to ford the stream or, failing that, a place where a ferry might profitably be started. These roads usually began in Arkansas and proceeded to Texas or, in the case of the famed Texas Road, started in Kansas and proceeded through eastern Oklahoma to the Lone Star State. Other roads were laid out by soldiers connecting major posts in the territory.

The coming of the railroads eased transportation problems in Oklahoma. The Katy, the Frisco, the Santa Fe, and the Rock Island would remain the principal carriers of freight, mail, and people well into the twen-

Edward K. Gaylord arrived in Oklahoma City after the turn of the century, becoming the business manager of the Daily Oklahoman. *He used this position to build the newspaper into the most widely read tabloid in the state, and expanded his empire into radio, television, and transportation. Courtesy, Bob L. Blackburn*

tieth century. Despite the appearance of automobiles at the start of the twentieth century, little was done to build roads, other than city streets, for a decade. Then in 1909 representatives from six states and Canada gathered at Guthrie to map out a highway to run from Canada to the Gulf (eventually this would become U.S. 77). The immediate effect of the proposed highway was to cause the legislature to create the State Highway Department in 1911—but only after intense lobbying by Governor Lee Cruce. To fund this department the legislature authorized a license fee of one dollar for each automobile in the state. Three years later state records show there were 6,524 automobiles in Oklahoma although only 2,241 owners had paid

geles by way of Tulsa and Oklahoma City; and U.S. 77 crossed the state from north to south, going from Wichita, Kansas, to Dallas, Texas. In addition, the state gradually built hard-surfaced farm-to-market roads in every county. Progress could be seen in the number of highway miles in Oklahoma: in 1916 there were twenty-five and a half miles of surfaced roads; in 1939 the number had grown to 4,804 miles of paved highways and 2,470 miles of graveled roads.

Little could be done during the war years, but in 1947 the legislature authorized the construction of the first turnpike in the state—the Turner Turnpike connecting Oklahoma City and Tulsa. Other turnpikes followed until much of the state was cov-

The Turner Turnpike, linking Oklahoma City with Tulsa, was completed in 1953. Courtesy, Oklahoma Turnpike Authority

the annual fee. In 1915 the legislature enlarged the State Highway Department, authorizing a highway commissioner, a state engineer, an assistant engineer, and a secretary, and it increased the automobile license fee and authorized a tax earmarked for highway construction. Nevertheless, the bulk of all highway construction remained in the hands of the three county commissioners in each of Oklahoma's seventy-seven counties—231 fiefdoms with needless duplication of expensive machinery, haphazard planning, considerable waste, and some corruption.

In 1916 the Federal Aid Road Act was enacted, providing federal matching funds for building national highways, and Oklahoma received $115,139. This was augmented seven years later by passage of a one-cent-per-gallon state gasoline tax. The result was an inflow of sufficient revenue to build national highways across the Sooner State: U.S. 66 ran from Chicago to Los An-

ered, several of them unprofitable because they were born out of intense political pressures rather than sound fiscal analyses. Likewise, automobile tax collection was turned over to private tag agents appointed through senatorial patronage. This also led to waste and some corruption.

Meanwhile the Federal-Aid Highway Act, also known as the Interstate Defense System, became law in 1956, providing 90 percent federal financing for multiple-lane, access-controlled roads. Today this system is virtually complete in Oklahoma. I-35 runs south from the Kansas border to Oklahoma City and Ardmore, then crosses into Texas to Dallas-Fort Worth, while I-44 has replaced old U.S. 66 from the Missouri border to Tulsa and Oklahoma City, and I-40 carries traffic from Fort Smith westward to Oklahoma City and on to Amarillo, Texas.

The Department of Transportation is controlled by an appointive eight-member board funded by earmarked road-user taxes, appropriations from the state general fund, and monies derived from the Federal Highway Trust Fund (which comes from federal taxes on gasoline and other sources). The department cares for a state highway system of more than 12,000 miles of hard-surfaced roads and employs more than 3,000 people, while the Oklahoma Turnpike Authority, a six-member board, oversees six turnpikes of 488 miles.

Another form of transportation as old as the early European exploration of Oklahoma is by way of the Arkansas River. Where Frenchmen once traveled by pirogue and flatboat, the first American settlers moved by steamboat. By the late nineteenth century, however, railroads had supplanted steamboats because of the fickle nature of the Arkansas, which rose and fell depending on each spring's snow melt and rain fall. In 1971, however, after twenty-two years of work, the McClellan-Kerr Waterway opened the Arkansas to barge navigation. Thanks to dredging and an intricate system of locks, river traffic was possible for the 440 miles from the port of Catoosa outside Tulsa to the Mississippi River (and from there to New Orleans and the Gulf of Mexico). Down this artery of commerce passed coal and agriculture commodities, as well as many industrial products. To keep the proper level of water in this waterway, the Corps of Engineers created a series of man-made

lakes: Heyburn (1950), Huhlah (1951), Tenkiller (1952), Fort Gibson (1953), and Robert S. Kerr and Webber Falls (1970). These lakes not only provided water to the largest single civil works project ever undertaken by the Corps of Engineers, but have also become major recreation sites.

Today much of the interstate travel by Oklahomans is done by airplane. The first recorded flight in the state was made in Oklahoma City in 1910 by exhibition pilot Charles F. Willard. For this effort he received $1,000—and crashed. Aviation remained a curiosity until World War I, when a military flying field was created in Oklahoma at Fort Sill. Even after the war ended there was little interest in aviation except among former military fliers, many of whom "barnstormed" across the state, landing in pastures near towns to give local residents a brief flight over the countryside for three to five dollars each.

Then in 1926 Oklahoma City was placed on a transcontinental air mail route, which ran from Dallas to Chicago. To secure this, Stanley Draper of the Oklahoma City Chamber of Commerce guaranteed that an average thirty pounds of air mail would originate in Oklahoma City daily. To meet this quota Draper, on occasion, had to send bricks by air mail to friends in distant parts of the United States. Following Charles Lindbergh's solo flight across the Atlantic

This aerial view pictures the Tulsa Port of Catoosa at the head of navigation on the McClellan-Kerr Arkansas River Navigation System. The system opened the heartland of Oklahoma to river transportation and new economic ties with foreign markets. OHS

215

Wiley Post, Oklahoma's most famous aviator, set several records for trans-world and altitude flights before his death in 1935. OHS

the following summer, interest in aviation soared, and National Air Transport began a passenger and express service from Oklahoma City to Chicago. Tom E. and Paul Braniff began operating what would become Braniff Airways between Oklahoma City and Tulsa in June 1928, while the following November Earle P. Halliburton of Duncan started SAFEway Airlines. Oil men such as Halliburton played an important role in early aviation because they were constantly fighting time and distance, and they learned that airplanes could get them where they needed to go quickly. Frank and L.E. Phillips made important advances in high-test aviation gasoline and pioneered high altitude flying. In 1928 William G. Skelly assumed ownership and management of Spartan Aviation in Tulsa; this firm built airplanes, and its school trained thousands of pilots and mechanics. Aviation in Oklahoma was also aided by the federal Civil Works Administration, which helped finance landing fields, lights, and radio equipment. Oklahoma pilot Wiley Post captured world headlines by setting an around-the-world speed record in 1930 and again in 1933, while Bennett Griffin and James J. Mattern set records in their around-the-world flight that ended in Russia in 1932.

Farmers and ranchers found the airplane to be an excellent tool, and in August 1944 they organized a statewide group known as the Oklahoma Flying Farmers. This soon expanded into the National Flying Farmers Association and then into the International Flying Farmers Association.

World War II brought many military airfields and thousands of young pilot trainees to Oklahoma, further stimulating aviation in the state. Airplane factories were opened in Tulsa, Oklahoma City, and Norman, and these continued to function after the conflict ended, while military airfields and auxiliary landing fields became municipal airports. During the Korean War, when Oklahoman Harold C. Stuart was assistant secretary of the Air Force, bases at Enid and Altus became permanent Air Force fields, and Tinker Field assumed a major role in Air Force planning. Rockwell and McDonnell-Douglas, both at Tulsa, continue to win major military aviation and aerospace contracts employing thousands, while Aero-Commander manufactures corporate aircraft at Bethany (a suburb of Oklahoma City). Oklahoma is in the vanguard of pioneering the next chapter in flying—the move into space. The Sooner State has contributed more astronauts to the efforts of the National Aeronautics and Space Administration than any other state.

The telegraph arrived in Oklahoma around 1871 with the railroad, and it drastically improved links with the outside world. As tracks were laid, additional lines were strung until every railroad station in both Indian and Oklahoma territories had telegraph service. News came over the wires to fill newspapers, and at times of great national sporting events, or national emergency (as during the Spanish-American War and World War I), the telegraph office in each city posted news and game results for the throngs of people gathered outside.

The telephone gradually replaced the telegraph as the main instrument of communication. Apparently the first telephone line in Oklahoma was a military one, strung between Fort Reno and the Darlington Agency. The first commercial telephone service in Oklahoma was organized in 1886 by a twenty-year-old Cherokee, E.D. Hicks, who, after seeing the instrument demonstrated in St. Louis, organized a firm and strung lines between Tahlequah and Fort Gibson, then on to Muskogee. By the time his switchboard opened, he had eighteen customers. Service came slowly to other towns and cities as local firms opened exchanges. For example, the Missouri and Kansas Telephone

Telephones were a recent invention when Oklahoma was opened to non-Indian settlement, but they quickly became indispensable for early settlers. The first telephone line constructed in Tonkawa in the Cherokee Outlet was completed in 1902. Courtesy, Western History Collections, University of Oklahoma Library

Company began service in Oklahoma City in 1893, seven years after Hicks' exchange opened. By 1906 there were a reported 162 telephone companies in Oklahoma, a number that in just two years expanded to 275. The largest of these was Pioneer Telephone Company, which in 1917 joined the Bell System as Southwestern Bell Telephone Company.

The generally accepted date of the first radio broadcast in Oklahoma is November 2, 1920, when Earl Hull, using a twenty-watt transmitter installed in his garage in Oklahoma City, went on the air using call letters WKY. His was the first radio station west of the Mississippi River and the third in the nation to broadcast on a regular basis. Receiving a license in 1923, Hull operated WKY with H.S. Richmond as a partner. In 1928 the station was purchased by the Oklahoma Publishing Company, which has continued to operate it. Next to go on the air was WMAB, which no longer operates; followed by KFJZ (now KOMA) in Oklahoma City; and WNAD, operated in Norman by the University of Oklahoma. Other stations went on the air when individuals across the state decided that a radio

station could do much to promote a city. For example, R.H. Rollestone started KFRU in 1924 in Bristow, telling the audience that the station's letters stood for "Kind Friends, Remember Us." Moving to Tulsa, KFRU was acquired by oil man W.G. Skelly in 1928, and its call letters changed to KVOO (Voice Of Oklahoma). Other pioneers in the field of radio included J.T. Griffin of Muskogee, also known for his food processing and grocery wholesale business; eventually he owned several stations and brought numerous innovations to the radio business.

When these early radio stations went on the air, their audience was small. Few Oklahomans in the mid 1920s had the money (and, in many cases, no available electricity) to purchase expensive radio sets which, at best, picked up little more than static occasionally interrupted by a scratchy voice or a bit of music. By the 1930s, however, most urban Oklahomans had radios in their homes, while rural residents waited for rural electric cooperatives to arrive and power their homes so they could listen to the outside world. A few hardy farmers used "windchargers" (wind-driven generators re-

The first commercial radio station in Oklahoma was WKY of Oklahoma City. This is an early sound effects booth of this communications and entertainment pioneer in the state. Courtesy, WKY Radio

sembling windmills) to operate a radio. By this time Oklahoma's stations had affiliated with national networks, and local residents each evening eagerly awaited a favorite program of news, music, comedy, or drama. There were locally produced programs, many devoted to country music, which might have made Tulsa or Oklahoma City the center of this industry, had there not been a feeling that listening to this music showed a lack of "culture."

The first television station in Oklahoma was owned by the Oklahoma Publishing Company, the same firm that owned the state's first radio station. It also had the call letters WKY, and its 1949 debut was shortly followed by station openings in Tulsa. Not until 1952 were these connected by telephone cable to national network programming, and even in this area Oklahomans

pioneered. For example, KWTV in Oklahoma City began telecasting from a 1,572-foot broadcast tower on January 1, 1954, at that time the tallest man-made structure in the world. Later that same year WKY-TV became the first non-network station in the United States to broadcast color programming. Today the educational potential of television is realized through the Oklahoma Educational Television Authority. Funded by the state and by private donations and using four broadcast towers, this network provides educational programming to all parts of the state.

When Oklahomans, along with other Americans, began listening to radio in large numbers, some educators said that children would stop reading. Similar cries were heard when television stations went on the air. In reality, the number of books circulating from Oklahoma's libraries has increased every year. When the Oklahoma Library Commission was created in 1919, fifty-two of the seventy-seven counties had no public library within their jurisdictions. Now named the Department of Libraries and governed by a seven-member board, this central agency has assisted in promoting public, school, and institutional libraries. Today every county has at least one public library, and many belong to multi-county or city-county library systems supported by a special ad valorem tax.

Oklahoma's public school system has struggled through a difficult infancy. At statehood the rural schools of the Indian Territory were merged with those in Oklahoma Territory to form one system—with scant funds, ill-prepared teachers, and students often kept home to help with planting and harvesting. In what had been the Oklahoma Territory, two sections in each township were reserved as school lands, to provide income to help fund public schools. Such had not been the case in the Indian Territory, and Congress at statehood appropriated five million dollars for the territories' school fund in lieu of such land. This, combined with the value of the reserved school lands, totaled twenty-two million dollars for the state. Very quickly legislators realized that the income from the reserved school lands was inadequate, so annual appropriations for public education were made from the general operating fund, in addition to local property tax assessments. By 1921 this sum had reached $100,000, plus the income derived from school lands.

At first the school term was short, but gradually the length of sessions increased until it reached a full nine months statewide. Moreover, state law, which originally prescribed free public education for all Oklahomans aged eight to seventeen, was changed to guarantee the same right to all citizens from age six to twenty-one, and then free public kindergarten was added.

In the early years after statehood, conditions varied widely from district to district. Some were rich because of valuable property or oil deposits, while some rural districts had only a small tax base. Others had residents unwilling to approve high taxes to support local education. The state founded normal colleges and gradually increased the educational requirements for teacher certification, but in the early years most teachers

began their careers in small, one- or two-room schools that were short of supplies and books. Teachers often had to serve not only as instructors, but also as janitors, nurses, lunch makers, and counselors—all for a salary as low as forty dollars a month. Jennie Hays Higgins of Coweta later recalled her experiences in one school. Although only twenty years old, she had been teaching four years when she arrived there:

I was to get sixty dollars a month for eight months. But they told me it was a "cotton school." I asked what a cotton school was. My schedule included teaching two months during the summer, July and August, then dismissing for three months [so the children could pick cotton] and beginning again in December . . . . Monday morning my father took me to school. When we arrived, the yard was full of children and some grown people. I asked, "Why are all these men and women here?" Father thought they had walked with their children for the first time. When I rang the hand bell, all the children and grown folks came in . . . . I found that I had nine grown girls and seven grown boys [in grades one to eight].

During the next eight years, conditions became worse. Elizabeth Howard of Sapulpa later remembered her teaching experience in that school in 1931:

During the depression, before the federal or state lunch programs were started, mothers would bring vegetables and meat to the school to prepare soup for those children whom the principal found to be in need of food. There were those who fainted in school and who came without lunches.

In 1946 residents of the state approved a constitutional amendment providing for free textbooks (which had been discontinued because of a scandal during the 1930s), and three years later the legislature drafted a school code making all regulations uniform throughout the state. Yet the big crises of the postwar years were school consolidation and desegregation. Governor Roy Turner attempted to consolidate 500 rural schools into several larger districts, but local communities furiously fought to retain their schools' autonomy. Gradually the smaller ones were closed and the children bussed to bigger schools, but to the present day the consolidation of all small schools has not been achieved.

During Turner's administration desegregation came to the forefront in higher education. Ada Lois Sipuel (Fisher), a graduate of Langston University, applied for admission to the University of Oklahoma Law School in January 1946, but was refused admission on the basis of her color. The state supreme court refused to hear her appeal, but the United States Supreme Court ruled on January 12, 1948, that Sipuel had to be admitted. In 1949 the legislature then said that blacks could be admitted to graduate programs in state educational institutions. Then came the Supreme Court ruling in 1954 which ended desegregation in public schools, whereupon such discrimination was dropped not only in colleges and universities, but also in the public schools. Subsequently the state saw the advent of bussing to achieve racial balance in urban schools— along with white flight from urban to suburban areas. This nationally mandated attempt to achieve racial balance also brought skyrocketing costs to public education as well as some public outcries about the courts tampering with what was seen as the sole concern of individual school districts.

Today there are more than 600 school districts in Oklahoma, most of them independent (serving a population base of more than 1,200 students and required to maintain a high school), providing free public education for more than 650,000 students. The teachers who operate this system have developed what many observers agree is the most effective lobby in the state, and, more than 40,000 strong, they annually pressure for more money to be appropriated for education. Changes are coming to Oklahoma's public school system, some of them due to concerns of teachers, some of them a result of public demand. In 1981 the legislature mandated competency testing for all new teachers, and national trends indicate that the concept of merit pay for outstanding teachers may soon become commonplace.

A statewide system of vocational training has been closely connected with the public schools. Authorized by Congress in 1917 in the Smith-Hughes Act, this system provides education for high school students and adults who learn by doing and who usually qualify for jobs immediately after graduation. In 1968 the legislature consolidated this system by creating the State Board of Vocational and Technical Education, which oversees the training of more than 250,000 Oklahomans each year through area "vo-tech" schools. Under Governor Dewey Bartlett, the vo-tech system made a concerted effort to work with prospective manufacturing concerns to train workers for factories, thereby attracting more industry to Oklahoma. The vo-tech system has been one of the bright spots in the state's educational effort.

In the field of higher education, Oklahoma can lay claim to excellence in several fields. The University of Oklahoma, created by an act signed by Governor Steele on December 19, 1890, is recognized worldwide for its efforts in the area of energy, especially in geology and petroleum-related fields. Opening its doors in 1892 on a donated forty-acre tract one-half mile south of Norman, the university today covers more than 1,000 acres and includes the Health Sciences Center in Oklahoma City, the College of Medicine in Tulsa, the Dental College in Oklahoma City, and the State Geological Survey. Its athletic teams have brought national renown to the Sooner State and provided its citizens with many thrills— along with reasons for feeling pride in the accomplishments of its young people. The university is governed by a separate seven-member board of regents appointed by the governor, and today has an enrollment in excess of 20,000 on its main campus.

To the north in Stillwater is Oklahoma State University (OSU), created by an act of the First Legislature which was signed into law by Governor Steele on December 25, 1890. First named Oklahoma Agricultural and Mechanical College, it was the land grant institution in the Sooner State and opened its doors on December 14, 1891, on a donated 200-acre tract. With more than 20,000 students today, it covers 415 acres on its main campus and has one Technical Institute at Okmulgee and another in Oklahoma City, along with a College of Veterinary Medicine in Stillwater and Agricultural Experiment Stations across the state. In addition, all Oklahoma County Agents and Home Demonstration Agents are part of its faculty.

The A & M Board of Regents, appointed by the governor, oversees OSU, Langston University (which began as The Colored Agricultural and Normal University), Cameron University at Lawton, Connors State College at Warner, Northeastern Oklahoma

Agricultural and Mechanical College at Miami (originally the Miami School of Mines), and Oklahoma Panhandle State University at Goodwell.

The third college created in the Oklahoma Territory was originally known as the Territorial Normal School and located at Edmond. This institution is today Central State University. It began classes on November 9, 1891, more than one month before OSU, allowing it to claim to be the oldest public institution of higher learning in the state. In 1897 two additional normal schools were created: Northwestern at Alva and Southwestern at Weatherford. After statehood the legislature determined the former Indian Territory should have an equal number of normal schools, and three new ones were opened: Northeastern at Tahlequah, East Central at Ada, and Southeastern at Durant. The names of each was changed to "Teacher College" in 1919, to "State College" in 1949, and then to "State University" in 1974, and they were placed beneath one board of regents under the title, "Regional State Universities." In addition, in 1908 the state opened the Oklahoma College for Women. Today called the University of Science and Arts of Oklahoma, it is located in Chickasha and is an "innovative institution."

In the 1920s and 1930s some cities began establishing junior colleges, financed through local taxes, as an extension of their high schools. In the 1960s, however, the legislature moved to create a system of state-financed junior colleges: in Tulsa and Oklahoma City in 1968, in Altus in 1969, and again in Oklahoma City in 1971. Two years later, tired of the annual fight to create yet another state junior college, the legislature enacted a law allowing existing municipal junior colleges at Claremore, Poteau, Seminole, El Reno, and Sayre to join the state system.

Governing all these state institutions and coordinating their budgets, programs, and efforts are the State Regents for Higher Education, a nine-member body established by constitutional amendment in 1941. The regents, in turn, appoint a chancellor to serve as their administrative officer.

In addition to a network of state-supported colleges and universities, Oklahoma also boasts several fine private institutions of higher education. Oklahoma City University was founded in 1904 and has remained in Oklahoma City since a brief stay in Guthrie from 1911 to 1919. Courtesy, Oklahoma City University

In addition, the state has fifteen private institutions of higher learning, most of them affiliated with a religious denomination. Oklahoma City University, a Methodist institution, opened in 1904 as Epworth University. Moved to Guthrie in 1911, it returned to Oklahoma City in 1919 and has grown to a position of prominence. Henry Kendall College, which was opened in Muskogee in 1894 by Presbyterians, traces its origins to mission schools for Creek Indians maintained by missionaries from New England. Moved to Tulsa in 1907, it changed its name thirteen years later to the University of Tulsa. Generously supported through the years by Tulsans, this institution has made important contributions, especially in fields related to petroleum.

The Baptists likewise wanted a denominational institution of higher learning, and in 1915 they opened a school in Shawnee. Other Baptist colleges opened in Oklahoma City, Blackwell, and Mangum, but eventually all united with the institution in Shawnee to become Oklahoma Baptist University. The Disciples of Christ founded Oklahoma Christian University in 1906 at Enid, changing the name to Phillips University in 1913 to honor a generous donor. Other private institutions include Oral Roberts University in Tulsa, Bethany Nazarene College in Bethany, Oklahoma Christian College in Oklahoma City, St. Gregory's College in Shawnee, and Bacone College in Muskogee.

Each year approximately 70 percent of Oklahoma's high school graduates enroll in college, public or private, placing the state near the top nationally in this category and reflecting a belief among Oklahomans that education is valuable. Although the Sooner State has more than 175,000 students attending colleges and universities, because of its tax structure and the large number of educational institutions, the state has been unable to support any of these schools at a high level of funding. It has, however, proven politically impossible to close those schools with too few students for efficient operation. In fact, the opposite has been the case. In 1982, owing to a continuing quarrel with federal officials because Langston University still was predominantly black, the state created a University Center at Tulsa, its faculty provided jointly by Langston, the University of Oklahoma, Northeastern State University, and Oklahoma State. Eventually the center at Tulsa may become a free-standing state university due to Tulsan demands for a state-supported institution of higher learning in their city.

Oklahoma's artists and musicians, historical societies and organizations, and public and private museums also serve to educate the public, but in a less structured way than the classroom. Art has always been part of the region. Prehistoric Indians decorated their weapons, pottery, and skin tepees with drawings of animals, battles, and hunts, or with designs of mystical or esthetic appeal. Later, the horse and the buffalo dominated their art, for on these two beasts their culture rested. In 1929 Professor Oscar B. Jacobson at the University of Oklahoma attracted five young Kiowa artists to attend the university: Monroe Tsa-to-ke, Spencer Asah, Steve Mopope, Jack Hokeah, and Bou-ge-tah Smokey. This group gradually attained national acclaim and recognition, holding exhibitions in many parts of the United States and Europe.

Likewise promoting pride in the Indian heritage was the Art Department at Bacone College, where talented instructors and brilliant students began a tradition of excellence in the 1930s. Among those participating in this program were Acee Blue Eagle, Solomon McCombs, C. Terry Saul, Dick West, Fred Beaver, Willard Stone, Dennis Belindo, Enoch Kelly Haney, Jerome Tiger, Ruthe Blalock Jones, Virginia Stroud, and David Williams. Other Indian artists of note include Woodrow Crumbo, Carl Sweezy, Archie Blackowl, Black Bear Bosin, and Troy Anderson. Their styles in one way or another represent a two-dimensional perspective of a world not dominated by technology, and their work has had a two-fold result: it has given Native Americans strength to face the changes that have come into their lives, and it has inspired non-Indian people who are no longer so impressed by the endless conquest of nature.

The first non-Indian artists in Oklahoma were Easterners who paused to use brush and canvas while in the area. In 1834 George Catlin recorded scenes of Indian activity, while Frederick Remington came to Fort Reno and the Darlington agency in 1882 and there made many sketches. The first Oklahoman to attain success with his canvases was John Noble who, after making the run into the Cherokee Outlet, painted *The Run* to capture the excitement of that day. Howell Lewis and Nellie Shepherd did landscapes in an impressionistic style in the early years of the twentieth century, while primitive (untrained) artists such as Augusta Metcalf painted the scenes of ordinary Oklahoma life: fighting a prairie fire, herding cattle, a frontier wedding. Among Oklahoma's modern artists to achieve renown are Charles Banks Wilson, whose work adorns the state capitol; George Miksch Sutton, whose paintings of birds rival (or excel) those of Audubon; Fred Olds, who blends his heritage as a cowboy with his artistic gifts to depict that aspect of the state's past; and James Boren, whose work is nationally known.

Oklahoma's first musicians, like its first artists, also were Indians. Using the flute and drum, they produced a music of complexity and beauty that is understood and appreciated by few non-Indians. In recent years members of the various tribes have rediscovered their rich musical heritage and are preserving it for their children.

Among non-Indian immigrants to Oklahoma, music was usually made with a fiddle or other stringed instrument and used for dances and hoedowns or gospel music sung in church and brush arbor. From this rural tradition sprang the state's rich tradition in country-western folk music. Among the greats in this field have been Woody Guthrie, a native of Okemah who never gained wealth, but whose songs have become part of the American tradition; Bob Wills, known as the "Father of Western Swing," who gained fame over radio station KVOO in Tulsa in the 1930s and 1940s; and Gene Autry, who also performed over KVOO before going on to a great career as a movie star and recording artist.

Less well known is Oklahoma's rich contribution to the field of gospel and jazz music. Alexander Reid, a minister, published two great gospel songs from former slaves in the Choctaw Nation, Wallis Willis and "Aunt" Minerva: *Swing Low, Sweet Chariot* and *Steal Away to Jesus*. The Oklahoma City Blue Devils were performing songs in the genre of jazz and blues before these were popularized in New Orleans and Memphis, and one member of that group went on to world renown as Count Basie. Charles Christian, whose skill on the electric guitar brought him national prominence, and Barney Kessel, a jazz guitarist, made solid contributions in these fields, while Leon Russell, a pianist-singer, cut records that sold in the millions.

Also less known has been Oklahoma's rich tradition of appreciating—and performing—classical music, opera, and ballet. The Tulsa Opera is among the best in the nation, while symphony orchestras perform in Tulsa, Oklahoma City, and Lawton. Five great ballerinas have come from Oklahoma: Maria Tallchief and her sister Marjorie, Yvonne Chouteau, Rosella Hightower, and Moscelyne Larkin. The Tri-State Music Festival at Enid each year attracts thousands of youngsters and encourages an interest in music.

Today the various tribes in Oklahoma celebrate their heritage by holding powwows and dances that attract thousands of Native Americans as well as non-Indian spectators. In some nineteenth-century towns of the Five Civilized Tribes (such as Tahlequah)

Spokesman for the victims of the Great Depression was Okemah's Woody Guthrie. Courtesy, Western History Collections, University of Oklahoma Library

there were theaters where stage productions were regularly presented. The white settlers who participated in runs, lotteries, and auctions likewise had "opera houses" where touring theatrical troupes performed both classical and contemporary plays. Notable among Oklahoma playwrights has been Lynn Riggs, whose *Green Grow the Lilacs* was the basis for the modern stage hit *Oklahoma!* Well-known productions in Oklahoma include the Wichita Mountain Easter Pageant and the reenactment of the Trail of Tears in the Cherokee production at Tsa-La-Gi each summer in Tahlequah. High school, university, and little theater troupes likewise present an annual diversity of drama and comedy in virtually every town and city in Oklahoma, while touring companies bring the latest hits from Broadway to Tulsa and Oklahoma City.

The oldest organization in Oklahoma dedicated to preserving its past is The Oklahoma Historical Society, founded in 1893 by the Oklahoma Territorial Press Association. This became an agency of the territorial

government in 1895 and, after moving several times, assumed its present home in the Wiley Post Building in the state capitol complex in 1930. Its museum interprets the history of the state, its publications preserve that record in print, and its educational division aids Oklahoma teachers of history in myriad ways; moreover, its library is an excellent repository of newspapers, research materials, and genealogical records devoted to the state's past and its people.

It was Joseph B. Thoburn, director of the Historical Society, who in 1924 initiated a statewide contest to change the state flag. In 1911 the legislature had adopted a red banner with a blue-bordered white star in the center. In the middle of the white star were the blue numerals "46" to indicate that Oklahoma was the forty-sixth state. Thoburn thought the order of Oklahoma's admission to the Union was incidental and began a contest to select a better design. Louise Fluke, a thirty-five-year-old artist in Oklahoma City, visited the Historical Society and was impressed by a buffalo-hide war shield with a pendant of eagle feathers and a pecan peace pipe. These she placed on a blue background to represent loyalty and devotion, and the legislature subsequently adopted her design.

Another organization devoted to preserving the past has been the Oklahoma Heritage Association, started in 1927 as the Oklahoma Memorial Association with the legislatively-mandated task of operating the Oklahoma Hall of Fame. Its headquarters, formerly the home of Judge and Mrs. Robert A. Hefner, is a living museum, and its publications program is devoted to preserving in print the lives of Oklahoma's "Trackmakers" and the story of the state's institutions.

Major museums are also operated in Oklahoma by public and private trusts. The National Cowboy Hall of Fame and Western Heritage Center in Oklahoma City, in many ways a testament to its former director, Dean Krakel, is funded by seventeen western states, while the Thomas Gilcrease Institute of American History and Art is owned by the city of Tulsa. Both are national in stature—and deservedly so. Other noteworthy museums include the Museum of the Great Plains at Lawton, the Cherokee Strip Museum in Alva, the Southern Plains Indian Museum and Crafts Center in Anadarko, Woolaroc Museum near Bartles-

The Oklahoma Historical Society was founded in 1893 to "preserve and perpetuate the history of Oklahoma." Its headquarters are in the Wiley Post Historical Building, Oklahoma City. OHS

ville, the Will Rogers Memorial and the Davis Gun Collection at Claremore, the Fort Sill National Historical Landmark and Museum at Lawton, the Five Civilized Tribes Museum at Muskogee, the Stovall Museum of Science and History at Norman, the Oklahoma Firefighters Museum and the 45th Infantry Museum in Oklahoma City, Enterprise Square (operated by Oklahoma Christian College to educate the public about free enterprise), the Pioneer Woman Statue and Museum and the Marland Mansion in Ponca City, the Territorial Museum in Guthrie, the Cherokee Cultural Center at Tahlequah, and the Philbrook Art Center in Tulsa. More recently the Kirkpatrick Center in Oklahoma City (also called the Omniplex) has gained renown as a complex of museums; of special note there is the Oklahoma Air Space Museum, largely the handiwork of pioneer aviator Clarence E. Page.

For most Oklahomans, however, the out-of-doors continues to hold the greatest appeal. For their enjoyment, the Tourism and Recreation Department operates almost eighty recreational properties, including

parks, recreational areas, monuments, museums, and historic lodges, which in 1980 were visited by more than twenty million people. The department also operates seven state resort hotels, all located in state parks (although in 1984 two of these hotels were put up for sale). The department also promotes tourism in Oklahoma, which has become the third-largest source of income for the state (behind agriculture and industry).

A modern Oklahoma wonder is its many man-made lakes. In 1957 the legislature created the Water Resources Board to develop and regulate water reserves. The result has been the building of a huge number of lakes to supply water to the population and for agricultural, industrial, and power generation uses. Oklahoma's 1,137 square miles of lakes are also major recreational sites. Hunting, fishing, boating, and camping are pastimes for many state residents, and the Department of Wildlife Conservation oversees 650,000 acres of public hunting lands. Oklahomans find the climate attractive, fish and game abundant, cultural and recreational activities widely available, and the good life within reach of all.

CHAPTER XVI

Turning Toward Tomorrow

The Oklahoma petroleum industry is one of the important aspects of the state's economy. In the 1970s and 1980s the Arab oil boycott and rapidly rising prices for crude encouraged exploration and production. Courtesy, Western History Collections, University of Oklahoma Library

On the morning of November 17, 1907, the journey home began for the thousands who had jammed into Guthrie the day before to participate in the ceremonies marking statehood. Most Oklahomans felt confident about their future. The land had been settled, farms and ranches were prospering, oil had been discovered, and statehood had been achieved—all in just eighteen years. Through energy and hard work, Oklahoma's settlers had changed the face of the region dramatically—although much remained to be done.

Despite the hard times created by the Panic of 1907, which caused a great scarcity of cash and the issuance of scrip by some banks, the new state government quickly began erecting the machinery necessary to provide services—and to collect the taxes to pay for them. In the next decade Oklahoma witnessed vast new changes as public schools were funded at a higher level, colleges were opened, public buildings were erected, and roads were graded and paved. The new state passed a bank guaranty law to protect depositors from loss in case of bank failure, established an insurance board to protect people from fraud, started a public health service, opened the State University Hospital in Oklahoma City to train physicians, set standards for workman's compensation, and regulated the number of hours and conditions under which women and children could work. Naturally, state expenditures rose accordingly: from $3.9 million in 1907 to $10.5 million in 1913 and $20.5 million by 1921.

During this same period, Kate Barnard, Commissioner of Charities and Corrections, personally inspected conditions at Kansas State Prison at Lansing, where Oklahoma had by contract been sending its prisoners. Her report of the abuses heaped on Oklahomans jailed there was so shocking that in 1909 the legislature appropriated funds to

Jim Thorpe, named the greatest athlete in the world in 1912, was a Sac and Fox Indian from Oklahoma who played football, baseball, and performed in the Olympic Games. OHS

sylvania, from 1907 to 1912, interrupting his education to play semi-professional baseball. At Carlisle he became a national sensation as a football player, but his reputation became international when he won the decathlon and pentathlon in Sweden at the 1912 Olympic Games. King Gustav, in presenting his medals, called Thorpe "the greatest athlete in the world," but later, because he had taken fifteen dollars a week to play baseball, Thorpe was forced to return his medals. Afterward he became a major league baseball player and then a professional football star. Three years before his death in 1953 the Associated Press named Thorpe the best athlete during the first half of the twentieth century. Finally, after years of popular protest, the International Olympic Committee returned Thorpe's medals to his family in 1982 and reinstated him in the record books.

Because many Americans believed the myths about lawlessness and wildness in Oklahoma, as portrayed in dime novels and silent movies, a few enterprising Oklahomans in the first two decades after statehood took Wild West shows on tour in the East and in Europe. Most of the performers in these "exciting extravaganzas" were actually cowboys, as some of Buffalo Bill Cody's employees found out to their sorrow on one occasion. That occurred when both Buffalo Bill's show and that of Colonel Zach Mulhall were performing at the same time but at different locations in New York City. Cody's cowboys decided to "show up them Mulhall fellers" in a contest of cowboy skills. Cody's performers failed to realize that Mulhall's people worked as cowboys all year round, and they were totally outclassed. By the 1920s this kind of show was declining as movies filled part of the public's appetite for knowledge about the "real West." The rodeo gradually became popular, however, and Oklahoma would be home to the top two rodeo events in the nation: the National Finals Rodeo, staged for years in Oklahoma City by the Professional Rodeo Cowboys' Association, and the International Finals Rodeo, staged in Tulsa each year by the International Rodeo Cowboys' Association. Moreover, Oklahoma is home to the Rodeo Historical Society and the Rodeo Hall of Fame, housed in the National Cowboy Hall of Fame in Oklahoma City.

In the years between statehood and World War I Oklahoma was a curious

establish a prison system at McAlester. Oklahoma's prisoners came home by special train under the watchful eyes of heavily armed guards, and they did most of the work of constructing the walls and buildings at the new site. Barnard was also influential in getting other major state institutions established, including schools for delinquents, orphans, the blind, the deaf, and the insane.

Many Americans not familiar with the new state saw it as the home of cowboys and Indians, and the exploits of Jim Thorpe in the 1912 Olympics, which thrilled all Americans, contributed to this image. Born in 1888 at Prague, Oklahoma, Thorpe attended the Indian school at Carlisle, Penn-

The Miller Brothers 101 Ranch Real Wild West Show was popular during the 1910s and 1920s. Hard times during the Great Depression finally forced the show out of business, after years of entertaining millions with rodeo and wild west action. Courtesy, Western History Collections, University of Oklahoma Library

blend of wild frontier and social reform. Prohibition was written into the constitution, but alcoholic beverages were freely available. Gambling was illegal, but horse races, dog fights, and prizefights were scenes of wild betting. On April 14, 1914, Governor Lee Cruce called out the National Guard, after declaring martial law, to halt a horse race in Tulsa, so avid were the fans who wanted to gamble. Almost every town had saloons and a "red light district," but an overwhelming majority of the state's residents belonged to and regularly attended fundamental Protestant churches.

The outbreak of World War I in Europe in 1914 went largely unnoticed in Oklahoma. The following year, however, Oklahomans did take notice when President Wilson called out the Oklahoma National Guard to pursue Mexican bandit-patriot Francisco "Pancho" Villa for his raid on Columbus, New Mexico. The Oklahoma National Guard, commanded by Colonel Roy Hoffman, traveled to Mexico on what proved to be a fruitless exercise, but thereby Oklahomans gained valuable military experience that helped them in the great war that followed.

A cavalry troop of the Oklahoma National Guard was assembled to be transported from Okemah to the Mexican border during the Pancho Villa uprising of 1914. OHS

When the United States entered the global conflict on April 16, 1917, many of Oklahoma's young men rushed to volunteer for service, while those in the National Guard were mobilized for service immediately. Together these numbered more than 91,000 men, a figure that included Indians from most tribes along with some 5,000 blacks. These men fought as part of the famed 36th and 90th divisions, while the Tulsa Ambulance Company was organized within the state. Oklahomans fought in such battles as St. Etienne, Forest Ferme, St. Mihiel, and the Meuse-Argonne. As Louis W. Duncan, who later would enjoy a distinguished banking career in Muskogee, wrote home from the front in the fall of 1918:

To me it seems almost unbelievable that an army that only a few weeks ago were farmers, clerks, lawyers, etc., could come over here and make all of the armies of the world sit up and take notice; but this is just what they did.

Of the Oklahomans involved, 1,064 died in combat, 4,154 were wounded, 502 were missing in action, and 710 died from disease. Oklahoma's surviving servicemen returned to Oklahoma at the end of the conflict to parade in cities and towns across the state—and then to join the American Legion and the Veterans of Foreign Wars.

The draft in Oklahoma was first administered by Adjutant General Ancel Earp, but he resigned in December 1917 to go to Europe to fight. He was succeeded by Adjutant General E.H. Gipson, who was aided by Major Eugene Kerr. Together they saw to the induction of approximately 70,000 Oklahomans. Not everyone in the state believed the government had the right to draft Americans. There were large numbers of Socialists who opposed the draft, as did members of the radical labor union, the International Workers of the World (the IWW or "Wobblies"). These people argued that the conflict in Europe was "a rich man's war," which poor men had to fight. In early August 1917 these protesters, centered in Pottawatomie, Seminole, and Hughes counties, began burning bridges and barns, firing at law officers, and threatening to raid banks, train stations, grain elevators, and stores. Local citizens armed themselves and fought the so-called "Green Corn Rebellion," and hundreds of the protesters

were captured, imprisoned at McAlester for trial, convicted, and sentenced to prison.

For Oklahomans who stayed at home during the war, there was much to be done on the farm, ranch, mine, and oil derrick, for industry was not yet a significant factor in the state's economy. Oklahoma, along with other states, had its Council of Defense, a branch of the National Council of Defense. This agency coordinated Liberty Bond sales and recruited support for the Red Cross. Feelings ran so high in favor of the war effort that many Oklahomans joined the American Protective League or the Knights of Liberty. Sometimes wearing white robes, these patriots watched for people who failed to buy Liberty Bonds, using tar and feathers on "slackers," as they were called. Oklahoma also had its branch of the Food Administration. Headed by Dr. Stratton D. Brooks, it urged food conservation through such devices as "wheatless" and "meatless" days, and by advocating home gardens to conserve food "for the boys at the front." There was some sugar, beef, and flour rationing, and hoarders were visited by members of the American Protective League—or even by angry neighbors.

The war months were especially difficult for Oklahomans of German descent, particularly the Mennonites who conducted church services in the German language. They were warned to speak only English, even in church. Anyone who spoke out for Germany was tarred and feathered, whipped, and even killed on occasion. Civil rights were violated, but opposition to the war ceased, and the state's soldiers were enthusiastically greeted when they returned home.

Most of Oklahoma's 710 servicemen who died of disease had contracted Spanish influenza. This flu epidemic spread into the state in October 1918—at a time when a third of all doctors and half the nurses were away with the armed forces. Within a short time there were reportedly 125,000 cases in the state, and eventually some 7,000 died from it. In an attempt to halt the spread of the epidemic State Health Commissioner John W. Duke ordered all churches, schools, and movies closed, and gatherings of more than twelve people were forbidden—even for funerals. Almost every family had at least one member sick, and soon business activity virtually ceased in the state. Just as the first epidemic eased, a second outbreak came in late November and early December, but it proved less deadly. Then in the spring of 1919 came an epidemic of smallpox, at that time a dreaded killer, and doctors again were called upon to make heroic efforts. In Okmulgee, for example, Dr. Fred S. Watson established a "Pest House" that gained national attention because in admitting patients he did not distinguish between the races—white, black, or red—making this one of the nation's first hospitals operating without segregation or discrimination.

In November 1918 Oklahomans approved the prohibition amendment banning the manufacture and sale of alcoholic beverages, and, by a narrow margin, the state granted women's suffrage. Governor James B. Robertson, taking office in January of 1919, attempted to ease the state's postwar depression by asking voters to approve a fifty-million-dollar bond issue for highway construction. This failed, but Robertson did get funding to build 1,300 miles of paved roads. This was not enough to ease the economic woes of the state, which had enjoyed high prices for its agricultural and petroleum output during the war years. Farmers had gone into debt to plant "fence row to fence row" and to open new acres to cultivation. Labor unions called massive strikes in the coalfields that led to 9,000 miners staying away from their jobs. Governor Robertson declared martial law and sent the National Guard to Henryetta,

This black law firm set up offices under canvas following the disastrous fire of the Tulsa Race Riot of 1921. Courtesy, Tulsa County Historical Society

Coalgate, and McAlester. Foreclosure sales of farms also led to near violence in many counties. When a sheriff came to conduct an auction sale, sympathetic neighbors would often gather and threaten anyone who bid except the bankrupt farmer himself, who thereby was able to buy back his acres at a ridiculously low price.

The strain of this economic distress led to the collapse of Oklahoma's bank deposit guaranty system in 1920, and several banks failed, causing great anguish to depositors (and to bank directors, who were then faced with personal as well as business liability). In Tulsa the situation was especially critical, for bankers there had advanced capital to oil men who, with prices plummeting, could not repay their debts. Early in 1920 the American National Bank closed its doors, causing anxious depositors to mill about in the street and to begin to talk in ugly tones. Across the street at the Exchange National Bank, which had been conservative in its loans and thus was totally solvent, Robert M. McFarlin, a director, saw the mob in front of the American National Bank waving their passbooks and demanding their money. He quickly took action to prevent disaster, for he realized that the failure of one bank would strain the resources of other banks in the city and region. Emerging from the Exchange National Bank, he shouted until the mob quieted. He then calmly told the seething crowd that they could bring their passbooks into the Exchange National Bank and be paid the full amount of savings they had in the collapsing American National Bank. This was a desperate gamble, for if all depositors in the American National accepted his offer it would have bankrupted the Exchange National Bank. After a few minutes of discussion, however, only a few in the mob accepted McFarlin's offer; the others went home, and the banking crisis was over in Tulsa.

Yet violence was not long in coming to that city. During the economic hard times, with jobs scarce and blacks competing with whites for employment, racial hatreds seethed into open conflict on May 31, 1921. Dick Roland, a black, was arrested on charges of assaulting a white girl, and a white mob gathered at dusk at the courthouse where Roland was being held. From the Greenwood section of Tulsa, sometimes called "the Black Wall Street of America"

231

because of its many successful businesses, a large crowd of blacks came by cars intent on preventing what they feared would become a lynching. When a policeman tried to disarm a black and he resisted, the policeman shot him—and a riot of tragic proportions followed. Blacks and whites broke into hardware stores to arm themselves, and shooting became general. Fires then broke out in the Greenwood section, but the melee prevented firemen from fighting the blaze. The result was two miles of burned-out businesses, leaving thousands homeless. The next morning Governor Robertson declared martial law and sent in the National Guard, but it was late afternoon before shooting could be halted and order restored.

Official estimates of the casualties counted seventy black and nine white deaths, but unofficial estimates of the death toll ran as high as 600. In the investigation that followed, the Democratic sheriff blamed the Republican police department, while the Republicans blamed the Democrats—and the citizens blamed their city officials. Blacks were interned at baseball fields and other makeshift centers for several days before being allowed to return to homes and businesses that had been destroyed. The Greenwood section of Tulsa would never regain its former economic status, and several hundred blacks left the city to never return.

The race riot in Tulsa was but one product of what many Oklahomans saw as a lawless era of vice and crime, widespread immorality, and a turning away from traditional Christian virtues. Nationally the decade of the 1920s was a time of marathon dances, flagpole sitting, bathtub gin, flapper dresses, "kissproof" lipstick, cigarette smoking, and bobbed hair. Dresses suddenly seemed too short and too tight, women were smoking and drinking in public, and dances and movies attracted many into the cities. F. Scott Fitzgerald called these years "the gaudiest spree in history" with some truth, but to conservative, Protestant Oklahomans they seemed spawned by the devil to lure young people into sin. If law officers could not enforce prohibition or halt lawlessness, then some Oklahomans were willing to take the law into their own hands.

The organization that took advantage of this feeling was the Ku Klux Klan. Reborn in the South in 1915, the modern Klan was anti-Catholic, anti-Jewish, and anti-black, but as it spread from Texas into Oklahoma just after World War I its stated goals were a return to the old-time virtues and an end to crime. Reportedly the head of the Klan in Oklahoma when it organized was Dr. Edwin DeBarr, a vice-president at the University of Oklahoma. He was succeeded in 1923 by N.C. "Clay" Jewett of Oklahoma City. So great was the attraction of the Klan in those early days that some of its meetings drew huge crowds. At Muskogee in 1922, for example, one rally was attended by 5,000 people. Klan membership at a point reportedly reached 100,000, mostly from the middle and upper classes.

Special efforts were made by Klan leaders to attract church members and ministers into the ranks of the organization. This often was done by having Klan members appear during a church service in full regalia

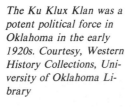

The Ku Klux Klan was a potent political force in Oklahoma in the early 1920s. Courtesy, Western History Collections, University of Oklahoma Library

of robe and hood to make a speech about the organization's goal of enrolling "one hundred percent Americans who believe in law and order." The Klansmen would then make a donation to the church and leave. For example, the pastor of the Baptist Church at Eufaula was given twenty-five dollars one Sunday evening by six masked Klansmen who spoke to the congregation about their group's desire to halt bootlegging, drug selling, crime, and immorality. By 1923 an estimated 60 to 95 percent of all Protestant ministers in the state reportedly were members of the Klan.

Although Oklahoma's Catholic population was small—some 3 percent of the total population—the Klan's bitter denunciation of "Papists" fitted into the tenor of that era. Robert O'Brien, a Catholic oil field worker, later recalled that he was so fearful of Klan violence against his family that whenever anyone knocked on the door of his home after dark his wife would wait to answer the front door until her husband had time to slip out the back door with a shotgun, circle around the house, and set his sights on whoever was at the front of the house. Some teachers were fired when school boards discovered they were Catholic. In addition, women speakers posing as ex-nuns were allowed to use municipal convention halls to "expose" the evils they said existed in Catholic convents—and large crowds came to hear such messages. This was an era of intolerance and bigotry, not only in Oklahoma but across much of America as well.

Robed and masked Klansmen marched in city parades and made other public appearances, and in many towns and cities they had a Klan meeting hall much like other fraternal organizations. Some politicians running for office in 1922 openly sought the endorsement of the Klan. By 1923, however, the brutal nature of the organization was becoming evident, and the better element of Oklahoma society began to withdraw from membership. Some victims of its night-riding efforts, whipped or tarred and feathered and ordered to leave the state, were known lawbreakers, but others were selected on the basis of hearsay evidence and judged guilty of moral violations.

In June 1923 Governor Jack Walton declared martial law in Okmulgee County because of numerous Klan beatings there, quickly followed by martial law in Tulsa for the same reason. Walton, in fact, suspended the writ of habeas corpus in Tulsa, and when a grand jury convened in Oklahoma City to investigate this violation of the state constitution, Walton placed the entire state under martial law, saying this was necessary because of "the deadly Invisible Empire [the Klan]." When the legislature began impeachment proceedings against Walton, he responded by citing evidence of Klan wrongdoing uncovered by military courts where martial law had been declared. The governor asserted, "some of these cases present outrages and heartrending cruelty in the extreme, in the form of mutilation such as cutting off the ear of one man and an attempt made to force him to eat it; burning a woman with acid . . . ; burning houses, striking women with six shooters . . . ." He concluded by offering to resign if the legislature would pass an anti-Klan law. Instead the legislators impeached Walton.

When an Anti-Ku Klux Klan organized in the fall of 1923 and held a statewide convention in Oklahoma City in December, the legislature began a serious investigation of the Invisible Empire. The result was passage of a public anti-mask law on January 14, 1924. Without the right to parade in secret regalia, the Klan gradually lost influence—and membership. As late as the election of 1926, however, the Klan tried to organize political support for some candidates, but by then no politician wanted this public endorsement. By the end of the 1920s the Klan had ceased to exercise an influence, and its membership had shrunk to almost zero.

By that time Oklahomans had other things to worry about, particularly the Great Depression then settling on the land. Factories closed because there was no market for their products, and the price of oil plummeted, as did prices for agricultural commodities (Elma Kilgore of Muskogee later recalled paying only ten dollars for a bale of cotton—two cents a pound—in 1930). Soon soup kitchens were feeding the hungry in Oklahoma City, Tulsa, and other towns, and some city dwellers returned to farms to live with rural kinfolk who had food from their gardens. Organized criminal gangs, such as those of Charles A. "Pretty Boy" Floyd and Matt Kimes, engaged in bank-robbing sprees and seemed to operate with the approval of bank-hating neighbors who helped protect them.

To fight the Depression, in 1932 Oklaho-

mans joined other Americans in electing President Franklin D. Roosevelt, and participated in a variety of New Deal programs. For young men there were Civilian Conservation Corps (CCC) camps, while unemployed adults took jobs with the Works Progress Administration (WPA) raking leaves, laying sidewalks, painting murals on post office walls, and a host of other make-work employment. For businessmen there was the National Recovery Administration (NRA) with its blue eagle symbol displayed in store windows. Yet the New Deal did not end the Depression, for in 1935 there were 150,000 Oklahomans unemployed and 700,000 on relief. The state was steadily losing population, and "Okie" was becoming an ugly word.

Countering this image at both the state and national level was Oklahoma's best-known native son, Will Rogers. Born at Claremore, Indian Territory, in 1879, he was the son of Clem V. Rogers, a mixed-blood Cherokee who ranched near Chelsea and who served with distinction in the Oklahoma Constitutional Convention. Although Will later liked to pose as uneducated, he had more schooling than was average for his day. After working as a cowboy, he began entertaining in Colonel Zach Mulhall's Wild West Show, then traveled in several foreign countries, and finally landed a prominent part in Ziegfeld's Follies in New York City. He later became a movie star and newspaper columnist.

Known as a rural humorist, Rogers laced his remarks with a common sense that the public recognized and appreciated. He was always proud of his Indian heritage and his Oklahoma roots, and he never lost an opportunity to speak on behalf of both. Moreover, he was a philosopher poking fun at the pompous and prosperous. When the Depression hit, he gave benefit performances to raise funds for distressed Oklahomans and other Americans. When Rogers died in an airplane crash at Point Barrow, Alaska, with famed aviator—and fellow Oklahoman—Wiley Post, the state was thrown into mourning. Thousands of people donated to build the Will Rogers Memorial at Claremore, and some five decades later tens of thousands of tourists annually visit this testament to the state's favorite son.

Only the outbreak of World War II in 1939, and the end of the Dust Bowl, brought a return of prosperity. Once again Oklahoma's farm commodities commanded high prices, as did its oil, lead, zinc, and coal. During the war, Oklahoma, because of its mild climate, became the site of many major air training bases, among them Oklahoma City's Tinker Field, named for Major General Clarence L. Tinker, an Osage Indian killed on a bombing raid in the Pacific; and Will Rogers Field at Oklahoma City, named for the Oklahoma philosopher-humorist. British and Canadian pilots trained at air bases at Tulsa, Miami, and Ponca City. The Army had twenty-eight installations and the Navy had thirteen bases in the state, including the Technical Training Center at Norman through which passed some 15,000 aviators. In addition, Oklahoma's colleges and universities became training centers for Army and Navy personnel. Many prisoner-of-war camps were located in Oklahoma, including those at Fort Sill, Fort Reno, Camp Gruber, Tonkawa, Chickasha, Alva, Tipton, and Okmulgee. Prisoners were allowed to work on nearby farms and ranches, earning some money for themselves while helping farmers and ranchers, who were desperately short of manpower.

President Roosevelt's call for volunteers for the armed forces met an enthusiastic response in Oklahoma: more than 212,000 people joined the Army, the Navy, and the Marine Corps. Notable sons of the Sooner State in the war included J.J. "Jocko" Clark, a Cherokee who thereby became the highest ranking person of Indian descent in American military history. Casualties from

Oklahoma included 6,500 killed and 11,000 wounded.

Home-bound Oklahomans faced wartime rationing of gasoline, meat, sugar, coffee, shoes, automobile parts, tires, and many other items. They participated in scrap-metal drives, grew "victory gardens" to conserve food, and took part in war bond drives. Yet at the same time they prospered. The price of wheat, corn, oil, lead, and coal soared, and for the first time large industries came to the state. The Douglas Aircraft Company manufactured bombers in Tulsa and operated a smaller plant in Okla-

homa City. Tinker Field in Oklahoma City employed thousands to repair and rebuild B-24 and B-29 bombers. At Pryor the federal government had a plant manufacturing smokeless powder, while the Navy maintained a large ammunition depot at McAlester. Because such facilities were erected almost overnight, housing was in desperately short supply in most Oklahoma cities during the war.

The end of World War II brought wild celebrations in the Sooner State, along with a host of new problems. Veterans returning to begin or continue their college educations swelled enrollments at state institutions of higher learning, causing rapid growth and the need for larger appropriations. The construction industry struggled to keep pace with the demand for new housing, while farmers prospered from continued high prices for their agricultural goods. The number of Oklahomans employed in industry rose to 55,000 by 1949, with total wages amounting to more than $143 million. The principal industries were refineries (at Bartlesville, Ponca City, Enid, Cushing, Wynnewood, and smaller locations), aircraft manufacturing in Tulsa and in the vicinity of Oklahoma City, flour milling, meatpacking, zinc smelting, and lumber processing plants. By 1953 the state's largest single employer was Tinker Field with 23,650 on its payroll.

By the early 1950s almost every major city and town in the state had created an Industrial Development Board to purchase land and attract industry. Governor Roy Turner (1946 to 1950) pushed the legislature to reduce corporate income taxes by

Oklahoma's famous son, Will Rogers, was an entertainer and writer of world fame. His witty comments on the events of the day brought a ray of hope into the lives of many destitute people. OHS

Bottom, left
Major General Clarence Tinker died during the Battle of Midway in 1942. An airfield, Tinker Field, in Oklahoma City was subsequently named in his memory. Tinker Air Force Base is one of Oklahoma's leading employers. OHS

Below
Raymond S. McLain became the highest ranking Oklahoman during World War II. He commanded the XIX Corps during the final drive into Germany. OHS

manufacturers at several towns, a major meatpacking concern in Oklahoma City, and several petroleum-related industries at many sites in the state, particularly in Tulsa. Between 1950 and 1960 the number of Oklahomans engaged in agriculture dropped from 155,000 to 74,000, while the number in non-agricultural employment jumped from 599,000 to 713,000. By the 1980s agriculture would still be the largest producer of income in the state, industry second, and tourism and recreation third.

The outbreak of the Korean War in 1950 did not slow this new growth and prosperity. The draft returned to take many of Oklahoma's young men to fight, while Marine reserve units in Tulsa and Oklahoma were called to active duty to take part. Almost two decades later these veterans would see their sons drafted to fight in Vietnam, as Oklahomans continued their proud tradition of defending the country whenever called upon by their president.

Despite the growth and prosperity of the state, caused by a prolonged drought in the 1950s, the population declined slightly from 2,333,351 in 1950 to 2,328,284 in 1960. This drop was principally caused by a re-

Above
Wheat elevators, jokingly called "prairie skyscrapers," are often filled to capacity during the bumper harvests enjoyed by farmers in Oklahoma. Photo by Jim Argo

Right
Oklahomans have always enjoyed a good show. When Margaret Mitchell's classic Gone With The Wind *was re-released in the late 1950s, Tulsans waited in 112-degree heat to see Scarlett O'Hara and Rhett Butler. Courtesy, Tulsa County Historical Society*

one-third, and he restructured the Planning and Resources Board, which advertised Oklahoma's industrial potential. Gradually this paid dividends as several major firms moved to the state: Western Electric at Oklahoma City, tire manufacturing concerns at Ardmore and Lawton, a bicycle manufacturer at Enid, clothing and carpet

duction in farm population. Many sons and daughters of farmers went off to college and then sought challenges outside the state. Another cause was farm consolidation. When farmers reached retirement age and sold out to enjoy sunny weather in Texas or Florida, their land was purchased by other farmers and consolidated into larger holdings which, owing to improved farm machinery, employed fewer workers. The decade of the 1960s saw the downward trend in population reversed, however, as increased industrialization attracted thousands of new residents and kept more young people at home. By 1970 the population had reached 2,559,253—surpassing the census of 1930 for the first time.

By the late 1960s certain new trends were evident in the Sooner State. Because of a change in national consciousness about the plight of Indians, many Oklahomans were no longer ashamed to admit that their ancestry included some Indian blood. Moreover, as the federal government stressed the hiring of minorities, many people with no Indian blood whatsoever began claiming to be part Native American (leading some Indians laughingly to call these people "Sycamores"). Thanks to federal legislation in the late 1960s, many Oklahoma tribes began reorganizing tribal governments, acquiring property, and fighting for tribal rights.

In the 1960s and 1970s Oklahoma's young people joined in the national protests against the war in Vietnam, for an end to the draft, and for the right of eighteen-year-olds to vote. There were no major riots on Oklahoma campuses, but there were demonstrations and protest rallies for many causes, including gay liberation. The young began dressing in clothes of any style: overalls, blue jeans, work shirts, Indian headbands, castoff pieces of military uniforms, sandals, and work boots—or no shoes at all—while young men let their hair grow long and their beards sprout. A few enterprising promoters tried to cash in on the popularity of rock music by staging rock festivals, but these generally failed. Illicit drug usage saw a startling increase and became so profitable that many knowledgeable observers estimated that Oklahoma's largest cash crop was marijuana, grown on small plots and harvested to be sold in the cities. Most of Oklahoma's young people retained their basic good sense through this difficult

During the height of the oil boom in the Tulsa area, a popular style of architecture was Art Deco. One of the most beautiful examples of this very ornate style is the Boston Avenue Methodist Church in Tulsa. Designed by Oklahoma architect Bruce Goff, this landmark stands as one of the Oil Capital's finest contributions to the state's architectural heritage. Courtesy, Don Sibley, Metropolitan Tulsa Chamber of Commerce

time, however, working to secure an education, enter the job market, begin families, and worship in the churches of their forefathers.

The OPEC oil embargo brought soaring prices for gasoline and natural gas, while the cost of electricity doubled and then doubled again. Teachers and professors were demanding higher and higher wages, and many Oklahomans believed that government should provide welfare services for everyone, while those who worked and paid the astronomically high taxes saw inflation robbing them of any hope of bettering themselves and their families.

Oklahoma's penal system consumed far more tax dollars than in past years. The prison population soared and prisoners at McAlester rioted in 1973, destroying a significant portion of the facility. Judge Luther Bohanon of Oklahoma City assumed jurisdiction of the system and ran it for some ten years. Despite a second riot at Hominy in 1983, the federal court returned jurisdiction to Oklahoma officials early in 1984. Another source of difficulty was the Department of Human Services, which in the early 1980s was charged by federal officials with abuse of minors in its care. The public was growing restless at the spiraling costs of the social services performed by this agency, an area of concern not yet fully addressed by legislators.

During this period another boom came to Oklahoma; this one—like many in the past—was the result of soaring oil prices caused by petroleum industry deregulation in 1979. The rush to the Sooner State by unemployed people from the Northeast, the northern Midwest, and even from California seemed to match the influx of Boomers in

1889, and by 1980 Oklahoma's population had increased to almost three million. Tax collections soared, thanks to levies on the petroleum industry, and state legislators increased salaries of state employees and boosted the benefits of welfare recipients. By 1982 independent producers had pumped such a volume that the price of oil dropped from a high of forty-two dollars and more to twenty-nine dollars a barrel. Tax revenues dropped proportionately and Oklahoma was in a financial crisis, its revenues no longer able to sustain appropriations made by the legislature. This, in turn, led to another round of tax increases in 1984—but not to any meaningful reform of the tax code that might attract more industry to the state. Nor has there been real reform of other facets of state tax collection, such as automobile license fees. For years this system has been operated on the basis of state senatorial patronage that enriches the favored few while depriving local school districts of revenues intended for educational purposes. Despite obvious and flagrant abuses, the only result has been removal of the tag agents in Tulsa, Oklahoma, and Cleveland counties from senatorial patronage.

By the early 1980s the vast majority of Oklahoma's work force was employed in industry and related businesses and services. In 1981 the state numbered one-and-a-half-million workers, 193,000 of them in industry, but only 50,000 in agriculture. In fact, industry at this time was employing more people than were involved in agriculture and the petroleum industry combined. Then in the economic downturn that began in 1982, the state lost 35,000 jobs in manufacturing that have not been regained. Still the political leaders of the state have not made the legal reforms needed to attract more industry— with concomitant jobs and payroll—to the Sooner State.

In addition, in 1981 Attorney General Jan Eric Cartwright hurt efforts by various cities to attract industry by declaring unconstitutional the tax breaks given to such giant corporations as General Motors. Because surrounding states offer a wide range of subsidies and tax breaks to gain a source of employment for their citizens, the Oklahoma legislature in 1985 proposed and the voters approved giving new industries a five-year tax moritorium. This began paying dividends quickly.

Still more changes need to be made to improve the business climate in Oklahoma, for too much of its agricultural output continues to be shipped elsewhere for processing, its oil and natural gas sent outside the state to be refined into petrochemicals, and its lead and zinc transported to Arkansas and Missouri for smelting. There also have been dramatic changes in agriculture and the petroleum industry, the two areas that Oklahoma relies upon to keep its citizens working.

No longer is there great potential for any meaningful increase in the number of people employed in oil and agriculture. The petroleum industry has experienced numerous cycles of boom and bust, and there will doubtlessly be periods of high employment in the future—but not like in past years, for the world of the mid-1980s faces an oil glut. Similarly the state's farmers are plagued with overproduction, while cattlemen face increasing costs of production and decreasing prices for their beef. In 1981 agriculture employed just 4 percent of the state's work force, and there seems little likelihood that this number will increase. The degree of mechanization in farming and the increasing size of farms means that, even if agriculture enters a boom period in the future, there will be few new jobs created.

Compounding the economic confusion in the early 1980s has been state (and federal) legislation allowing limited chain banking in the Sooner State, merging of some banks into giant financial organizations, and allowing savings and loan institutions to perform many bank functions. Fears of a few giant financial institutions controlling state banking spread, but consolidation nevertheless moved forward—at a time when decreasing prices for petroleum brought an increasing number of bank failures.

This economic dislocation and change has been matched by a dramatic change in social attitudes in what once was described as "the buckle on the Bible Belt." In a 1983 special election, Oklahomans permitted pari-mutuel betting on horse racing, and the following year, in a hotly contested election, authorized liquor-by-the-drink by county-option (ending decades of the illegal sale of mixed drinks so prevalent that many said Oklahoma had "liquor by the wink").

Yet through the turmoil of recent years, as well as the problems associated with out-of-control state and national spending, the people of the Sooner State have remained positive, vibrant, and dynamic. They have remembered the state motto, *Labor Omnia Vincit*—"Labor Conquers All Things"—and they have acted on this premise despite their hardships.

Just before statehood Robert M. McFarlin and James A. Chapman mortgaged their ranch near Holdenville to take a lease in the Glen Pool Oil Field. They subsequently went into the Cushing and Healdton fields with their McMan Oil Company, and through their labor they became titans of independent oil production. In the 1930s three merchants in western Oklahoma— R.E. Tomlinson, E.L. Gosselin, and R.A. Young—joined together to form T G & Y, a merchandising giant now headquartered in Oklahoma City, but stretching across the nation and employing some 30,000 people. In the 1950s O.W. Coburn of Muskogee developed and marketed machinery that revolutionized the optical industry in the United States and around the world. Oklahomans have seen rewarded the inventive genius of Sylvan Goldman of Oklahoma City, who built and patented the grocery store shopping cart, and Virgil Browne of Oklahoma City, who developed the formula for a nationally manufactured soft drink and who devised the "six-pack" as a marketing tool for soft drinks. These are but a few of the Oklahomans who have helped build a state with the highest quality of life in the entire republic and whose deeds inspire today's young men and women to take chances in the marketplace with their ideas in spite of the state's tax structure.

Today's Oklahomans display the same courage and fortitude, generosity and hospitality, informality and openness that characterized the men and women who were forcibly removed to Oklahoma or who made the runs, broke the land to the plow, and erected cities. If these traits of a unique past remain, then the sacrifices of Oklahoma's red, white, and black pioneers will not have been in vain, and the future will continue to be as bright as that envisioned by the Boomers of Oklahoma, such as Milton W. Reynolds, who called this "the Land of the Fair God." November 16 and April 22—Statehood Day and the date of the first land run—are times of celebration and remembrance of the pioneers whose sinew and spirit transformed a wilderness and who built and created "better than they knew." The words inscribed on the bottom of the

famed 89er Statue in downtown Oklahoma City indeed sum up the spirit of those who created—and inherited—this rich legacy:

Strong men and women came upon a raw land with vision ...
They spanned rivers and prairies and mountains with determination ...
They created schools—churches—farms—factories
They lifted great buildings to the skies
They drilled deep wells into the oil rich earth
With thankfulness to their God
They are still pioneering—still achieving
And still exploring future frontiers
Passerby—LOOK ABOUT AND ASK THIS QUESTION
Where else within a single life span
Has Man Built So Mightily.

The 89er statue in Oklahoma City honors the pioneers who made the first and later land runs into the state. Photo by Jim Argo

Partners in Progress

*F*rom the prehistoric era to the twentieth century, the economy of the region that is now Oklahoma has been based on the bounty of the land. Native peoples relied on game—especially the buffalo—and some crops indigenous to the area. When members of the Five Civilized Tribes began arriving in Indian Territory in the 1830s, they brought with them the agricultural traditions they had developed in their original homelands. Most established small subsistence farms, although a few wealthy individuals created large plantations. Later, the area was home for the range cattle industry, as members of the Five Civilized Tribes raised cattle and leased vast areas of their lands to non-Indian cattlemen. The Indians also established a forest industry in southeastern Oklahoma that continues to thrive more than a century later.

Oklahoma's agricultural economy has grown to become the state's single most important industry. At first cotton dominated Oklahoma's agricultural economy; however, it gradually was replaced first by corn and finally by wheat, which by 1982 was contributing $831,105,000 of the $1,221,484,000 annually being pumped into Oklahoma's economy by agribusiness. Cattle-ranching and feedlot operations also were important sectors in the state's economy, as were crops such as peanuts and pecans. The bountiful natural resources beneath the land also have played a major role. Coal mining was important in Indian Territory before and after statehood, bringing immigrants of Italian, Polish, Slavic, and Russian heritage into the area. Moreover, Oklahoma has been a giant among the

oil- and gas-producing states. Indeed, the region's energy industry began as early as 1859, when Lewis Ross completed Oklahoma's first oil well; however, it was not until the Nellie Johnston was brought in near Bartlesville in 1897 that the state's modern oil boom began. During the first three decades of the twentieth century, Oklahoma's oil wells would yield more dollars than the combined wealth of the California Gold Rush and Colorado's silver mines. More than 3,906,012,375 barrels of crude were pulled from the earth during these years. Some of the discoveries were astounding. The Cushing Field, for example, produced 17 percent of the nation's total output of crude in 1917, and the Greater Seminole Field contained five of America's greatest discoveries: Little River, Seminole City, Earlsboro, Bowlegs, and St. Louis. Such a tremendous outpouring of crude made Oklahoma a mecca for oil men and gave birth to several international energy companies. Oil production remains an important factor in the state's economy, with Osage County ranking second among counties in the nation in the number of producing oil wells.

Oklahoma's natural gas industry began with statehood in 1907 with the discovery of the Hogshooter Field, which became the principal supplier of natural gas for the region. In the following decades the industry grew into a billion-dollar-a-year business. Moreover, the vast Anadarko Basin in western Oklahoma is recognized as one of the largest gas fields in the world.

Manufacturing centers and large metropolitan areas were well established in other regions of the United States by the time

Oklahoma began to emerge from the frontier. Thus, with the tremendous agricultural and mineral bounty of the land, agriculture and energy remained the dominant forces in the state's economy into the 1980s. It was these sectors that furnished the capital during the early years of the twentieth century to develop the state's strong financial basis and bring in thousands of new citizens. Yet Oklahomans endeavored to diversify the state's economy as early as the turn of the century. The effort has intensified in recent years as state leaders have attempted to capitalize on the state's resources, interstate highway network, and outstanding aviation facilities to bring new types of economic opportunities to the state. The capital generated by oil, gas, and agriculture made the effort possible, and Oklahoma has made significant progress toward becoming a major Sunbelt manufacturing center. In addition, oil, gas, and agriculture provided many of the necessary raw products for an active manufacturing economy to be established.

Along with various manufacturing operations, tourism has been developed as a major factor in the state's economy. Oklahoma also has developed a national reputation for its outstanding medical centers, which have the potential of spawning a major biotechnological industry in the state. With both the energy and agricultural sectors of the economy in a recession in the mid-1980s, the push for increased diversification of Oklahoma's economy has become even more intense. Yet the traditionally optimistic spirit of the Sooner State remains strong, with its citizens determined to continue the steady improvement in Oklahoma's economy and quality of life that had begun decades earlier.

The organizations whose stories are detailed on the following pages have chosen to support this important literary and civic project. They illustrate the variety of ways in which individuals and their businesses have contributed to the state's growth and development. The civic involvement of Oklahoma's businesses, institutions of learning, and local government, in cooperation with its citizens, has made the state an excellent place to live and work.

OKLAHOMA HISTORICAL SOCIETY

On May 27, 1893, the Oklahoma Press Association, representing the newspapers of Oklahoma Territory, organized the Oklahoma Historical Society (OHS) to preserve the heritage of both Indian and Oklahoma territories. William P. Campbell was named custodian of the Kingfisher-based organization—and within three months began publication of *Mistletoe Leaves,* a small, four-page weekly for members of the society.

Concurrent with the founding of the OHS, another similar group was created at the University of Oklahoma in Norman. Chartered and supported by the Territorial Legislature, the Norman historical society soon overshadowed the activities of the Kingfisher organization. As a result the two historical societies were united in 1895 with headquarters in Norman. In the reorganization, Campbell resigned and publication of *Mistletoe Leaves* was suspended.

In 1902 the OHS was moved from Norman and relocated in the modern, fireproof Carnegie Library in downtown Oklahoma City. Two years later Campbell returned as custodian of the organization. He remained in that position for the following two decades. In 1906 Jasper Sipes became president of the OHS, an office he also held for twenty years. Rejuvenated, the society again began to expand. However, the growth was hindered by the limited confines of the Carnegie Library; and with the completion of the state capitol in 1917, the OHS and its collections were moved to the basement of the new structure.

In 1921 the society launched *The Chronicles of Oklahoma,* devoted to the scholarly investigation of the state's history. Under the later direction of Muriel H. Wright, its longtime editor, the quarterly quickly gained international recognition.

With the expanded publication program and the active acquisition of archival material, the organization's offices in the state capitol soon were overcrowded. A movement was begun to fund an Oklahoma Historical So-

Denzil Garrison, president of the Oklahoma Historical Society.

ciety Building, and in 1929 the state legislature appropriated $500,000 for the construction of the structure. Dedicated on November 15, 1930, the society's permanent headquarters is located at 2100 North Lincoln Boulevard, just to the southeast of the front entrance of the state capitol.

In the following half-century the OHS continued to develop its productivity. A major accomplishment was achieved when the federal government recognized the society as one of three repositories outside of the National Archives to hold federal records. By the mid-1980s—under the direction of president Denzil Garrison and executive director Earle

Metcalf—the OHS emerged as one of the premier historical organizations in the nation, with an active membership in excess of 4,000.

The Administrative Division is responsible for the day-to-day operation of the organization and its internal structure, and extensive research collections are maintained by both the Library Resources and the Indian Archives and Manuscripts divisions. Other visible activities of the society are supervised by its Publications, Museums, Historic Sites, and

Earle Metcalf, executive director of the Oklahoma Historical Society. Courtesy, Oklahoma Historical Society

Historic Preservation divisions. In addition to the production of *The Chronicles of Oklahoma,* the Publications staff is responsible for the publication and distribution of *Mistletoe Leaves,* a monthly newsletter, and a wide variety of books and brochures. The Office of State Historic Preservation is responsible for various educational programs and the identification, preservation, and restoration of Oklahoma's historic buildings and sites. The society's Museums and Historic Sites divisions oversee the operation of twenty-seven museums and historic sites as well as the State Museum in the Oklahoma Historical Building. Millions of tourists visit these facilities annually.

Today the Oklahoma Historical Society works diligently to preserve and interpret the state's rich heritage. Through the efforts of staff, directors, and members, these goals will be achieved for the benefit of future generations.

— Fred Smith Standley

Entrance to the Oklahoma Historical Society on the grounds of the state capitol in Oklahoma City. In addition to containing the organization's offices, the structure houses the State Museum. Courtesy, Oklahoma Historical Society

THE ECONOMY COMPANY

In 1929 David D. Price was completing his education at the University of Oklahoma. To finance his schooling Price had sold yearbooks to high schools throughout the state. During his travels he observed the scarcity of quality teaching materials, especially in the language arts area. Struck by the availability of an untapped market, Price and his wife, Bernice Ford Price, designed a book-report form for use in elementary and secondary schools.

Printing the form in his garage, Price spent the week canvassing the state soliciting sales and then returned home on the weekends to ship the form to his customers. Because of the hard times brought on by the Great Depression, Price named his venture The Economy Company and marketed his initial educational component for eight cents a copy. That first year Price sold 300,000 units.

Under Price's direction The Economy Company continued to grow, creating a multitude of superior, quality products. In the decade between 1929 and 1939, the firm, which moved from Price's garage to its first headquarters at 106 1/2 Northeast Second Street in 1935, published more than fifty titles on such diverse subjects as economics, clothing, food, spelling, geography, history, handwriting, civics, and mathematics. Each was prepared by a professional educator, proven in the classroom, and designed to allow the students to advance at their own pace with a minimum of teacher instruction.

In 1938 The Economy Company published three new English programs, *Keys to Good Language, Keys to Good English,* and *Keys to English Mastery,* which employed a unique text-exercise format. They were an instant success. In 1950 the firm moved into another facility at 24 West Park Place, a site it occupied until 1964 when it moved to 1901 North Walnut. In 1952 The Economy Company revolutionized reading instruction with the release of *Phonetic Keys to Reading,* a program for grades one through three, which taught reading by utilizing phonetic and structural analysis of words. *Keys to Independence in Reading* was released in 1960 for use in grades four through six. By 1970 the combined sale of both series had surpassed thirty million copies.

During the 1970s The Economy Company dominated early childhood education and introduced several innovative language-arts projects, including a series of early childhood programs, a Spanish bilingual/bicultural program, and a basal reading program. In 1980 the firm acquired Bowmar/Noble Publishers, Inc., and assimilated its line, a handwriting and a social studies series. The following year The Economy Company entered the curriculum-based microcomputer software market and established American Educational Computer, Inc.

Dave D. Price headed The Economy Company until 1970, when he was succeeded by his son, David D. Price, Jr., who in turn was succeeded by another son, Ford C. Price, in 1973. A daughter, Lavonna Bernice Rushton, also serves on the firm's board of directors. By 1986 The Economy Company had grown to 225 employees and had established a

Dave D. Price, founder of The Economy Company.

new corporate headquarters at 1200 Northwest Sixty-third Street in Oklahoma City; a shipping facility in Indianapolis, Indiana; and a satellite editorial office in Glendale, California. With sales in fifty states, The Economy Company is the largest privately owned schoolbook publisher in America and offers more than 6,000 titles covering all aspects of reading, language arts, early childhood development, and bilingual education fields.

The Economy Company's corporate headquarters at 1200 Northwest Sixty-third Street, Oklahoma City.

OKLAHOMA GAS AND ELECTRIC COMPANY

As early as 1889 the Oklahoma Ditch and Water Power Company, which was to produce electricity, and the Oklahoma City Light and Power Company, which was to distribute the electricity, were organized to serve central Oklahoma. After an ill-fated attempt to produce hydroelectric power, the two firms placed a steam-generating plant on-line in September 1892 and for the next decade struggled to establish themselves. Finally, in 1902, two of the principal investors in Oklahoma City Light and Power, G.E. Wheeler and E.H. Cooke, sold their interest to F.B. Burbridge and Harry M. Blackmer, who reincorporated the business as the Oklahoma Gas and Electric Company (OG&E).

Established five years before statehood, OG&E is Oklahoma's oldest state-chartered corporation. It received its first franchise from Oklahoma City in February 1902. Two years later, in 1904, C.B. Ames and Dennis Flynn acquired control of OG&E, and brought H.M. Byllesby into the corporation. Under their direction, OG&E increased its generating capability from 700 kilowatts to 4,050 kilowatts and expanded its distribution lines from 76 miles to 227 miles during the following five years. Correspondingly, the number of OG&E's customers jumped from 1,400 to 4,500. Encouraged by this growth, OG&E expanded outside the Oklahoma City metropolitan area in 1910 and purchased the El Reno Gas and Electric Company. Additional expansion extended OG&E's service

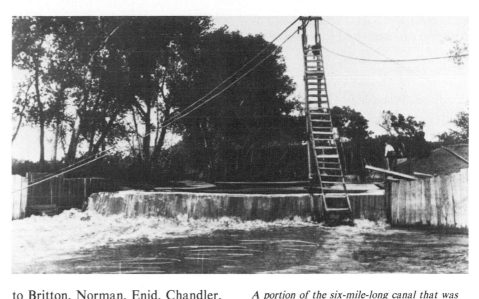

to Britton, Norman, Enid, Chandler, Byng, Shawnee, Ada, Guthrie, and other communities.

OG&E sold its natural gas properties in 1928; however, its name remained the same. That same year the firm expanded into western Arkansas. Also in 1928, OG&E became the first investor-owned electric company to develop performance data on natural lake cooling for generating stations. This was the first of many innovations that characterized the firm in the following decades: In 1935 OG&E was the first in the nation to use recarbonation of circulating water to reduce scale formations in condensers; in 1949 it was the first American company to use gas turbines combined with steam turbines

A portion of the six-mile-long canal that was constructed by the Oklahoma Ditch and Water Power Company and the Oklahoma City Light and Power Company in an ill-fated attempt to produce electricity.

to produce electricity; in 1959 OG&E introduced single-phase service, which was more economical for consumers than any previous method; in 1963 it built the world's largest combined-cycle generating unit at the Horseshoe Lake Station; and in 1971 OG&E became the first electric company in Oklahoma to open one of its cooling reservoirs, Lake Konawa, to the public. Sooner Reservoir, on the Arkansas River north of Stillwater, was opened later.

In the 1970s OG&E established a link between its substations and a central computer, which updated the system and limited the chances of power outages. Also, it placed its first modern coal-fired generating plant into operation, easing its reliance on natural gas and produced fly ash as a by-product. In recognition of the firm's eighty-one years of service to its customers, in 1983 *Electric Light and Power* magazine named OG&E, under the direction of James G. Harlow, Jr., board chairman and president, the "Utility of the Year." Also recognized were OG&E's innovative technological advancements and its contribution to the betterment of the quality of life in the area.

Oklahoma Gas and Electric Company's Muskogee generating plant. The ultramodern facility allowed OG&E to reach a peak production of 4,890,000 kilowatts by the mid-1980s.

OKLAHOMA FIXTURE COMPANY

In 1928 Oscar Nilson and his son, Arthur J., moved from Kansas City, Missouri, to Tulsa, Oklahoma, to open a 15,000-square-foot expansion plant for the Union Wood Products Company. When Union Wood's profits dropped at the onset of the Great Depression, the Nilsons assumed control of the facility located at 623 South Xanthus Avenue. Renaming the enterprise Oklahoma Fixture Company, the two men and their nine to twelve employees concentrated on supplying the fixtures and interior equipment necessary to operate banks, department stores, libraries, museums, and sports facilities. During the following years the firm expanded its operations to serve most of the United States.

When his father died in 1932, Arthur Nilson assumed responsibility for management and design of equipment for Oklahoma Fixture. To oversee the day-to-day operations of the plant, Andy G. Nilson, Oscar Nilson's brother, moved from Kansas City to Tulsa. Two years later Lloyd K. Stephens entered the firm as a draftsman. With Stephens advancing steadily through the ranks, the young proprietor directed the expansion of the company into the interior design of clubs, taverns, grocery stores, and larger retail establishments.

As Oklahoma Fixture continued to grow, Stephens became assistant general manager in 1939 and vice-president shortly afterward. His career was interrupted in 1943 when he entered the military for service in World War II. Upon his return three years later, the organization had grown to thirty employees.

In 1948 the company obtained a contract with the White Auto Store chain of Wichita Falls, Texas, to design and build the interiors of its outlets. Because of the increased demand for additional products created by that negotiation, in addition to the general expansion of the firm, the following year Oklahoma Fixture moved from its location on Xanthus Avenue to a 25,000-square-foot structure at 924 South Hudson. By

1986 the plant had been expanded to 175,000 square feet and employed 460 individuals.

Arthur Nilson was named chairman of the board of directors in 1965, and Stephens—associated with the firm by then for nearly three decades—succeeded him as president and chief executive officer. The third generation of the founding family, John Nilson, after studying architecture for two years at OSU and graduating with a degree in commercial art and business administration from the University of Tulsa, became executive vice-president. Arthur Nilson died on May 9, 1977, leaving a tremendous void in the enterprise that he had helped create and nurture through the early, difficult years. His son's untimely death on January 22, 1979, was another major loss for the firm. Stephens assumed the additional title of chairman of the board in 1977 and continued the tradition of strong leadership.

During the corporation's dramatic

Lloyd K. Stephens, president, chief executive officer, and chairman of the board of directors, Oklahoma Fixture Company.

growth in the 1970s and 1980s, several additional vice-presidents were added. Clarence H. Jones is vice-chairman of the board, Ronnie G. Line is senior vice-president, Larry J. Bishop is first vice-president, and Jim Philp is secretary/treasurer. Duane Walker, Mark Cavins, Mike Raburn, and Faye Parrish also were promoted to vice-presidential status due to the tremendous expansion since 1972.

Key people in the organization's operation are Charles E. Cunningham, plant superintendent; Coy Roy, assistant plant superintendent; and Don Malone, purchasing agent. They are responsible for getting the raw material to the plant on time and the finished fixtures to the customer when specified.

Among the statewide clients served

by Oklahoma Fixture Company are Orbach's, M.M. Cohn, Froug's, Vandevers, Peacock Jewelers, the McFarlin Library at the University of Tulsa, Gray's Jewelers, OTASCO, the Oral Roberts University Library, the F&M Bank and Trust Company of Tulsa, and the Oklahoma State University Library. In addition, the firm has designed and supplied the fixtures for numerous out-of-state customers, including Lazarus in Columbus, Ohio; Macy's in Kansas City, Missouri; Bloomingdale's and Sanger-Harris in Dallas, Texas; and Foley's in Houston, Texas. The interiors of the Eisenhower Library in Abilene, Kansas, and the Wichita, Kansas, Cultural Center (designed by Frank Lloyd Wright) were outfitted by the firm. When Arrowhead Stadium, the home of the Kansas City Chiefs football team and the Kansas City Royals baseball team, was completed, the concession counters and the football team's facilities were provided by Oklahoma Fixture.

The corporation's most significant client has been the Dillard's Department Store chain, headquartered in Little Rock, Arkansas. One of the fastest-growing department store operations in the nation, it has stores in Oklahoma, Arkansas, Texas, New Mexico, Nevada, Missouri, Louisiana, Kansas, Tennessee, and Arizona. Oklahoma Fixture Company has been responsible for new and remodeled interiors for Dillard's stores throughout the retailer's expanding network, and as of 1986 had two years of work with the organization planned for the future.

Oklahoma Fixture Company, known throughout the United States as OFIXCO, provided interiors and fixtures for 2.5 million square feet of retail floor space in 1984. Founded as a small business during the depths of the Great Depression, it has become a prosperous, nationally prominent enterprise.

Oklahoma Fixture Company's modern 175,000-square-foot plant and corporate headquarters at 924 South Hudson in Tulsa.

CAMELOT HOTEL

Opened on October 1, 1965, the Camelot Inn, as it originally was named, was the first convention center located in northeastern Oklahoma and the first high-rise hotel situated outside the downtown Tulsa area. Eight stories in height, and with a Great Hall designed to seat 900, the Camelot—located at the intersection of US-66, now I-44, and Peoria Avenue—quickly became a major Tulsa landmark.

Financed by Ainslie Perrault and Richard O. Wheeler, two Tulsa investors, the structure was designed by Butz, Piland, and Associates, Architects, to resemble the mythical castle at Camelot in the legend of King Arthur. Initially, guests were hosted exclusively on the seventh and eighth floors, with the elevators programmed to stop only on those levels. Soon afterward the second, third,

Designed to resemble the legendary Camelot of King Arthur, the Camelot Hotel, with its drawbridge entrance, is a major tourist attraction.

fourth, and sixth levels were opened to occupancy. The fifth level was utilized for storage, and was the last to be opened. Operated by Master Host, the inn was originally managed by Kendal Hunt.

Shaped to resemble King Arthur's shield, the Camelot pool area occupies the center of the hotel complex.

The Camelot was painted to resemble Neuschwahstein Castle, built by King Ludvig II of Bavaria; and in keeping with its namesake, the inn "rose majestically like a mythical castle in the air" to dominate the southeast Tulsa skyline. Guests traveled through a main drive-in entrance that resembled a castle's drawbridge. The medieval decor was retained throughout, with original furnishings and artifacts created specifically for the structure. Sconces and chandeliers were imported from Spain, and towel bars, dressing table benches, and other items were custom-made. The first bilevel swimming pool in the community, shaped to resemble King Arthur's shield, is located in the center of the complex. The magnificence of the Camelot was so popular that the hostelry quickly became a well-known tourist attraction throughout the Southwest.

In 1968 the inn was purchased by Kinark Corporation in the largest real estate transaction, at that time, in the history of Tulsa. The organization then embarked on an extensive

date 2,000 people, or be subdivided into six smaller rooms. Other meeting rooms are available for smaller gatherings. Located to the northeast of the main building, a separate structure—the Camelot Hall—can accommodate 300 additional guests for receptions, meetings, or private parties. All types of equipment, including high-fidelity public address systems, pianos, lighted lecterns, flags, standards, projectors, screens, and risers, are available, as well as parking spaces for 700 automobiles.

Overlooking the pool, the King's Court Dining Room offers outstanding dining with an emphasis on European cuisine. The King's Room is available for private dining parties, and the hotel's Red Lion Club is a popular Tulsa night spot. Under the direction of general manager L. Gino Starita, the Camelot hosts 113,000 guests and serves 239,000 meals annually.

remodeling and expansion project, completing this endeavor in 1972. The following year the establishment became one of only ninety-four hotels in America to receive a four-star rating from the Mobil Travel Guide Service. In 1981 its name was changed to Camelot Hotel.

Containing 202,000 square feet of floor space, the lodging is fully air conditioned, totally electric, and fireproof. It contains 330 baronial guest rooms as well as 14 multiroom suites that feature single-floor or town house designs. The trilevel and bilevel deluxe suites provide the perfect atmosphere for receptions or small business gatherings and offer private

eighth-floor balconies. The seventh and eighth floors' V.I.P. Crown Service provides guests with turndown service, wine and cheese welcoming bouquets, morning coffee, complimentary editions of the *Wall Street Journal,* and other amenities.

With its proximity to the Tulsa interstate system, the Camelot's location allows its visitors quick and easy access to all parts of the metropolitan area. Offering complete convention facilities, the hotel's Great Hall and Convention Center contains 8,900 square feet and can accommo-

The Camelot's deluxe trilevel suites are popular for receptions and business meetings.

MACKLANBURG-DUNCAN COMPANY

Macklanburg-Duncan employees and their Christmas baskets, which are still distributed by the company for the holidays, posed in front of the Northwest Twenty-third Street plant in 1928.

Prior to the development of central-air systems that cool in the summer and warm in the winter, most Oklahoma homes were heated by floor furnaces, which often were inefficient to operate and awkward to maintain. The heat radiated outward from a centralized furnace. In the more distant areas of a house, much of the heat was lost through cooling and through contact with cold air, which seeped inside through cracks around doors and windows. The problem was obvious, as anyone who sat near a drafty window knew, but until 1920 little was done to alleviate the situation.

In that year L.A. Macklanburg discovered that placing metal strips around doors and windows kept cold air out, thereby allowing a floor furnace to warm an entire house. Macklanburg called his innovative idea "Numetal" weather stripping, a product still manufactured by the company that bears his name. Macklanburg had moved to Oklahoma in 1903, and, after graduating from the University Preparatory School, among other things he worked as a brick mason before becoming involved with the Tradesmen's National Bank of Oklahoma City. He left the banking business after developing Numetal.

Numetal was an instant success. The cost of heating homes and businesses dropped drastically, and the heat was spread more evenly throughout the house. After obtaining a patent for Numetal, Macklanburg opened a small manufacturing plant, 25 by 130 feet, on West Main Street in downtown Oklahoma City. Joining him in the venture were his father, R.L. Macklanburg; three brothers, R.A. Macklanburg, A.F. Macklanburg, and G.W. Macklanburg; and a sister, Alma Macklanburg. While the Macklanburg family oversaw the production portion of the firm, H.M. Duncan became the company's first full-time salesman. The name of the business was taken from a combination of its founder and first salesman—Macklanburg-Duncan.

Canvassing Oklahoma and surrounding states, Duncan quickly built up Numetal's market, while L.A. Macklanburg spent most of his time in the company's plant developing additional products and designing much of the machinery used in their manufacture. As the firm's product line grew, so did its business, and within five years it was necessary to find a larger plant. In 1925 Macklanburg-Duncan moved to a new plant on Northwest Twenty-third Street, in what was then the outskirts of Oklahoma City.

During the following two and a half decades, Macklanburg-Duncan continued to undergo expansion and growth. With the outbreak of World War II, the firm switched to war production and supplied the government with aluminum and plastic aircraft parts. By 1950 the Northwest Twenty-third Street plant was overcrowded and out of date. A new location was selected at North Santa Fe Avenue, just north of the state capitol, and a new 375,000-square-foot plant opened. During this period of rapid expansion, the Macklanburg family acquired complete control of the firm.

In 1973 Macklanburg-Duncan purchased the American Level Manufacturing Company, a leading manufacturer of brass-bound mahogany wood levels for professional crafts people. Four years later the American Level production facility was moved to Oklahoma City. In 1980 Macklanburg-Duncan purchased the Southern Moulding and Hardware Company of Gainesville, Georgia. The firm's name was changed to Macklanburg-Duncan Georgia Division in 1985, and it is recognized as one of the nation's leading manufacturers of extruded aluminum products. Macklanburg-Duncan, which also maintains facilities in Los Angeles, California, and Saddlebrook, New Jersey, requires a sales staff of 100 to handle its extensive marketing network.

L.A. Macklanburg's daughter, Nona Jean, also entered the firm. She married W.W. Hulsey, who served as chairman of the board and chief executive officer of Macklanburg-Duncan until his death in 1982. He was succeeded by Nona Jean Macklanburg Hulsey, who currently serves as chairman of the board. The Hulseys had four daughters, who became the third generation of the family to be

actively involved in the management of Macklanburg-Duncan. Richard L. Gaugler is president and chief operating officer.

By the mid-1980s Macklanburg-Duncan's Oklahoma City operation employed 800 workers who manufacture Numetal and 2,000 additional products divided into eight product families—aluminum shapes and decorative moldings; builders' hardware; caulking, adhesives, and sealants; levels and tools; mailboxes and mail drops; shelving systems; thresholds; and weatherproofing products. It is the only American manufacturer of caulk that produces its own caulk tubes.

Among the aluminum products are angles, channels, bars, tubing, sheets, linoleum binding and edging, packaged carpet metals, and siding trim. The builders' hardware facet of the company produces closet rods and brackets, continuous hinges, door grills, driveway markers, fence post caps, gutter screens and leaf guards, kick plates, mounting boards, num-

bers and letters, push bars for doors, push plates, reflectors, shower curtain rods, signs, sliding door hardware, storm/screen window systems, tapes, foam tapes, and vents and vent covers. Thirty-eight types of caulking, adhesives, and sealants as well as caulking guns are manufactured.

Macklanburg-Duncan also supplies carpenter's squares, cutting guides, kitchen ladders, levels, and measuring tools, in addition to numerous types of mailboxes. The shelving division provides shelves, supports, brackets, and threshold accessories, and the weatherproofing product line offers door and window weather strips and other insulating products. A leader in the nation's home-building and home-improvement industry, Macklanburg-Duncan has outlets in thousands of hardware stores, home centers, and building supply stores throughout the nation.

One of Macklanburg-Duncan's 800 employees operates a control panel at the firm's modern caulk-manufacturing facility.

BANKS OF MID-AMERICA, INC.

In July 1984 Liberty National Bank and Trust Company of Oklahoma City merged with Tulsa's First National Bank and Trust Company to form Banks of Mid-America, Inc. Although Banks of Mid-America is one of Oklahoma's newest financial institutions, it is the state's largest and its legacy covers nine decades of Oklahoma history.

By 1895 Tulsa was an important farming-ranching center in northeastern Oklahoma with no banking facility to serve the region's citizens. To fill the void, on July 29, 1895, Jay Forsythe, B.F. Cooley, and C.W. Brown organized the Tulsa Banking Company. Housed in a two-story building in the 100 block of Main Street, the bank was an overnight success.

The first of a series of mergers took place in 1899 that eventually made the First National Bank of Tulsa one of the state's leading financial institutions. In that year William H. Halsell joined with Forsythe and the others, secured a federal banking charter, and on July 3, 1899, opened the First National Bank of Tulsa. By 1929 the City National Bank, the Oklahoma National Bank, the Union National Bank, the First Trust and Savings Bank, and the Tulsa National Bank had been acquired or merged with the First National Bank of Tulsa. Its present home—First Place—originally was occupied in July 1950.

In 1918 a group of Oklahoma City financial and civic leaders, headed by L.T. Sammons, formed the Liberty National Bank and Trust Company, which opened for business on September 3 in a converted barbershop in the Lee Building at Main Street and Robinson Avenue in downtown Oklahoma City. In 1921 Liberty acquired the Guarantee State Bank, and four years later it purchased the Oklahoma National Bank. In 1960

J.W. McLean, chief executive officer.

Liberty National Bank and Trust Company merged with the Bank of Mid-America, a much younger and smaller institution.

During its first half-century Liberty National occupied a series of sites as it continued its steady growth. By 1968 the bank announced the construction of the 36-floor Liberty Tower, the city's tallest and largest building and the first major structure completed in the revitalization of downtown Oklahoma City. Ten years later work was begun on the Mid-America Tower, which together with the Liberty Tower formed Mid-America Plaza, a major financial center for downtown Oklahoma City.

J.W. McLean, Liberty's chief executive officer since December 1967, played a major role in facilitating the merger that created Banks of Mid-America. From 1948 until 1958 McLean also had been an executive officer of First Tulsa and was quite active in the civic life of that city. He currently serves as chief executive of Banks of Mid-America, Inc.

The heritage of strong leadership of both banks was reflected in the composition of the board of Banks of Mid-America. As of March 1986 the directors were J.W. Bates, Jr.; Donald L. Brawner, M.D.; Jack R. Durland; William Egolf; Jean I. Everest; C.W. Flint, Jr.; Walter H. Helmerica III; John E. Kirkpatrick; Robert F. Long; Burch Mayo; J.W. McLean; John W. Nichols; George O. Nolley; William G. Paul; W.K. Warren, Jr.; and Henry Zarrow.

Mid-America Tower (left, foreground) and Liberty Tower (left, rear), located in Oklahoma City, and Tulsa's First Place (right) form Banks of Mid-America, Inc.

MUSTANG FUEL CORPORATION

Edward C. Joullian III, president and chairman of the board.

E.C. Joullian, founder.

Westoc merged with another firm and thus became a part of Oklahoma Resources Development Company. The two Joullian companies continued to supply OG&E's needs throughout the 1950s. The founder's son, Edward C. Joullian III, returned in 1955 from service as commander of the U.S. Army's Petroleum Laboratory during the Korean War and assumed the responsibility for design, construction, operation, and gas acquisition for Oklahoma Resources.

In 1959 OG&E asked the Joullians to prepare a proposal to supply natural gas to the two remaining power plants the utility company operated in Oklahoma. Realizing that the project would require additional assets, E.C. Joullian merged Oklahoma Resources Development Company and Rock Creek Oil and Gas Company into the Mustang Fuel Corporation. Within a year Mustang Fuel had grown from 184 miles of gas pipeline to 730 miles of pipeline operated by seventy employees. When OG&E's Muskogee and Horseshoe Lake power plants went on-line on November 16, 1960, Mustang Fuel assumed the responsibility of supplying natural gas to the utility's entire Oklahoma operation. That same year Mustang Fuel was given the task of securing OG&E's natural gas reserves, negotiating natural gas contracts, ensuring compliance with delivery contracts, and overseeing payment to OG&E's gas producers.

With the added responsibilities came tremendous expansion for Mustang Fuel. In 1961 the company became the first to build a gas transmission line into western Oklahoma when it completed a pipeline into the Anadarko Basin. Three years later the system was extended to the Arkoma Basin in the eastern part of the state. Mustang Fuel also expanded its supplier role to Public Service Company of Oklahoma in 1964.

When E.C. Joullian died in 1964, Edward C. Joullian III, who previously had been elected president of Mustang Fuel, also was named chairman of the board. Under his direction,

When E.C. Joullian laid the groundwork for the formation of Mustang Fuel Corporation in 1948, he already had two decades of engineering and management experience, including service as president, with the Consolidated Gas Utilities Corporation. When Consolidated rejected a proposal that year from the Oklahoma Gas & Electric Company to supply one of OG&E's gas-fired generating plants, Joullian, with the approval of Consolidated's board of directors, stepped down, secured adequate financing, formed Westoc Oil and Gas, and won the contract to fulfill OG&E's gas needs for its Mustang power plant.

OG&E began construction of its Arbuckle power plant near Sulphur in 1951 and approached Joullian to provide the needed natural gas. Forming a new firm, Rock Creek Oil and Gas Company, Joullian again was the successful bidder. In 1953

in 1968 the firm initiated a diversification program and established Mustang Gas Products Company, which directed the design and construction of a jointly owned gas-processing plant near Calumet. One of the largest gas-processing facilities in Oklahoma, the Calumet plant produces forty-five million gallons of natural gas liquids annually. Three years later Mustang Production Company was formed, and during the remainder of the 1970s participated in more than 400 wells, half of which were operated by the firm.

Mustang's expansion continued into the 1980s as the company pushed its pipeline network into the midwestern and eastern regions of the United States. Through innovation and careful planning, E.C. Joullian and Edward C. Joullian III created one of the most successful natural gas supply and transmission companies in the nation.

GENERAL MOTORS CORPORATION OKLAHOMA CITY ASSEMBLY PLANT

The GM assembly plant in Oklahoma City is part of the worldwide General Motors Corporation and its Chevrolet-Pontiac-Canada (CPC) Group.

General Motors began in 1897 when Charles E. Duryea formed the Olds Motor Vehicle Company, the forerunner of Oldsmobile. Seven years later William C. Durant gained control of Buick Manufacturing Company, and in 1908 organized General Motors Company, which quickly acquired the Olds Motor Corporation.

By 1919 the rapidly growing concern had acquired Cadillac Automotive Company, Chevrolet Motor Company, United Motors Corporation, Fisher Body Corporation, and several overseas corporations, and in 1916 had become General Motors Corporation.

Eventually the corporation offered seven lines of automobiles, a truck company, and several automotive support firms, among which were Champion Spark Plug, Delco, Hyatt Roller Bearing, and Harrison Radiator.

In the following decades General Motors became one of the world's most successful corporations. By 1986 GM operated 142 plants or other properties in 89 cities spread throughout 25 states as well as foreign operations in Canada, West Germany, the United Kingdom, Australia, Brazil, Mexico, Austria, Belgium, and Spain.

In August 1973 GM announced that a new passenger car assembly plant would be built in Oklahoma City as part of the GM Assembly Division. Ground was broken for construction in January 1974. However, the following March, GM announced that it was indefinitely postponing completion of the plant due to the drastic effect of the oil embargo and the general downturn in the economy. The project was reactivated and activities resumed in April 1977.

The plant is located just within the city limits of Oklahoma City on a 436-acre site adjacent to Tinker Air Force Base. The plant structure faces I-240 at Southeast Seventy-fourth Street and Midwest Boulevard, approximately nine miles southeast of the central business district of Oklahoma City.

The plant contains about three million square feet of floor space with seventy acres under roof. It is fully air-conditioned and is one of the larger passenger car plants. The plant contains 14 miles of drainage pipes, 138,000 cubic yards of concrete (enough to pave 32 miles of 24-foot-wide highway), 18 tons of struc-

This October 1977 photograph shows early construction on GM's Oklahoma City assembly plant.

tural steel, 21 miles of conveyor, and 5.6 miles of railroad track on-site. Its powerhouse has three boilers, each of which is capable of generating 150,000 pounds of steam per hour. (This is enough steam to provide heat for a city of 84,000 people.) Coal is the primary fuel used in the powerhouse; however, the facility is also capable of operating with natural gas. The plant's total utility bill is about twelve million dollars per year, or one million dollars each month.

The first car to be completed at the assembly plant on Tuesday, April 24, 1979, was a four-door Chevrolet Citation hatchback sedan. When it first began operating, the plant assembled the front-wheel-drive Chevrolet Citation and Pontiac Phoenix, but it was converted in 1982 to also assemble the front-wheel-drive Chevrolet Celebrity and Buick Century, which it still assembles today in two-door, four-door, and station wagon models.

The plant presently operates on two shifts and produces 75 cars per hour, which equates to 1,200 cars per day or 6,000 cars each week. In the 1985 model year, the plant produced 327,928 cars to be shipped throughout the United States. The plant is

The plant contains about three million square feet of floor space with seventy acres under roof.

The GM plant is located just within the city limits of Oklahoma City on a 436-acre site adjacent to Tinker Air Force Base.

serviced by the Atchison, Topeka and Santa Fe Railroad Company, which transports 70 percent of the vehicles produced at the plant. United Transports provides the truckaway service for the shipment of the remaining 30 percent of completed cars to GM dealers.

General Motors' most important asset is its people. There are about 7,000 people employed at the GM plant in Oklahoma City. Their salaries and wages in 1985 amounted to approximately $225 million.

Assembly of the product takes an average of three eight-hour shifts. The plant in Oklahoma City does not manufacture any parts. It assembles previously manufactured parts from all over the United States and, in some cases, the world.

The assembly of the body starts in the body shop. Body shop employees weld the various parts together using a wide variety of tools, fixtures, and machinery, including twenty-two robots. The floor pan, quarter panels, motor compartment, tail pan, and roof are assembled with special high-precision tools. The doors, fenders, trunk lid, and hood are then bolted onto the welded body frame. After passing through a metal finish area, the body shell then goes to the paint

shop.

In the paint shop, the metal is prepared by cleaning and spraying with a rust-preventive alkaline solution. The entire body is then dipped in Uniprime, which is electrostatically bonded to the body shell. The body then moves into the areas where it is sealed, primed, and baked. After topcoat painting, baking, and an elaborate polish system, the car goes to the trim shop for further assembly.

The freshly painted body is trimmed by adding seats, windshield, carpets, instrument panel, steering wheel, and several other interior components.

Following the trim shop, the body proceeds to the chassis shop. The body becomes a car in this department. The body is linked to the appropriate motor, transmission, brake system, wheels, tires, and a variety of related parts.

As the car moves through the various stations throughout the plant, it is inspected by an elaborate inspection process composed of human and computer checks. Once the car is verified, it is then sent to the United Transports yard to be shipped to the customer—a quality car produced by quality people in Oklahoma City.

GM's CPC assembly plant in Oklahoma City has produced 1,550,787 cars since 1979. The payrolls, services, and products purchased locally; taxes; and other expenditures represent a substantial addition to the local economy. The plant employees' involvement in local community affairs represents a sizable contribution to civic, charitable, and educational organizations. The plant is proud to be located in Oklahoma and plans to continue producing cars here for a long time to come.

An operator performs finish grinding in the body shop.

SKIRVIN PLAZA HOTEL

In 1909, exactly two decades after the opening of the Unassigned Lands and the overnight birth of Oklahoma City, William B. "Bill" Skirvin announced his plans to construct the largest hotel in the state on four lots that he owned at the northeast corner of First Street and Broadway Avenue in downtown Oklahoma City. Governor Charles N. Haskell turned the first shovel of dirt for the ceremonial groundbreaking in March 1910 for the unique ten-story, U-shaped structure designed by Solomon A. Layton, one of the region's foremost architects. When completed, the hotel consisted of two wings, each facing the south, connected by a rounded bay the same height as the wings. In making good his boast, Skirvin spared little expense in the construction. Malakoff red bricks laid in a Flemish bond pattern were used for the upper exterior facade. The lower levels were faced with limestone, which surrounded two covered entryways located at the intersection of First Street and Broadway. In the lobby, ornate marble, offset by inlays of rare woods decorated in English Gothic detail, was a showpiece of elegance.

In a more practical vein, Skirvin planned to make the hotel as self-sufficient as possible. In so doing, it was provided with its own water wells and electric plant so that it would not be dependent on municipal services. Likewise, Skirvin connected the building by a privately constructed pipeline to local natural gas wells for heat and power.

On September 26, 1911, the Skirvin Hotel was opened. Visitors could lounge in the Skirvin Café in the luxury of chilled air ventilation while watching musicians performing on stage. Or they could browse through the retail shops at the west end of the first floor. Two electric elevators conveyed guests to the 225 rooms and suites located on the upper floors. Each room offered a private bath, velvet carpets, hardwood furniture, and a telephone.

The Skirvin became a showplace

Built in 1910, the Skirvin Plaza Hotel is listed on the National Register of Historic Places.

under the direction of its first manager, Frederick Scherubel, who greeted many guests personally. The hostel of choice for most well-known politicians, oil men, celebrities, ranchers, and others, the Skirvin had become so popular by 1923 that an expansion of the original structure was necessary. Under Layton's direction another wing was added to the hotel, this one twelve stories in height, and an additional bay was constructed to the east, on the site of the original Skirvin Garage. This left the original two wings two stories lower than the new addition.

Five years later, in 1928, Skirvin announced plans to raise the original two wings and the 1923 addition to fourteen stories. When the project was completed in April 1930, after an expenditure of three million dollars, the Skirvin boasted a total of 525 rooms, a roof garden, a cabaret club, and an enlarged café. During the expansion an extensive renovation of the lobby, which doubled its size, also was completed. In addition, specially designed Gothic lanterns, costing $1,000 each, were suspended from the ceiling and hand-carved En-

glish fumed oak was added to the walls and doors. The newly remodeled café could seat 300 around three U-shaped counters. Art Deco geometric and floral designs decorated the café, which was complete with cast-iron counter seats, hand-laid tile floors, sunburst light fixtures, carved glass windows, and hand-carved wooden entryways.

On the fourteenth floor of the middle wing, Skirvin constructed a rooftop restaurant, decorated with Italian plaster, a parquet hardwood floor, and in excess of 100 casement windows. Located on the west wing, but connected to the restaurant by a foyer, is the Venetian Room, a supper club featuring live music and dancing. Paneled with American walnut and draped with embroidered mohair, brocatel, and damask, the walls of the Italian Renaissance Room were covered with murals depicting Venetian scenes. The dance floor was made of alternating blocks of red and white oak and above was an arched ceiling covered with acoustic tile. Lending the proper atmosphere to the room were the Venetian lanterns.

In 1931 Skirvin broke ground for the Skirvin Tower. An annex to the original hotel, the Skirvin Tower was located to the west, across Broadway

Avenue from the Skirvin Hotel. Because of the effects of the Great Depression, the tower was not completed until 1938, and was a more modest fourteen stories tall instead of the originally planned 26-story structure. Described as a luxury apartment hotel, the hotel and the tower were connected by a tunnel.

The tower proved to be Skirvin's final project; he died in 1944. The following year the hotel and tower were purchased by Dan W. James, who owned six other hotels in Oklahoma City. In the following decade James modernized the hotel, installed air conditioning, placed wrap-around awnings around the outside, added a drive-in registry, constructed a parking garage, and redecorated many of the meeting rooms. In the tower, James remodeled the Persian Room, opened the Tower Club, and remodeled many of the luxury apartments and suites. In 1959 a swimming pool was added to the north side of the hotel, and the following year the Sun Suite lounge was opened by the poolside. Under his direction, the Skirvin became one of the most successful hotels in the Southwest.

However, beginning with the 1960s, the character of downtown Oklahoma City changed radically as more and more shoppers fled the area for suburban shopping malls. In 1963 James sold the hotel and tower to a group of Chicago businessmen. In 1968 the property was sold to H.T. Griffin, who spent $2.5 million redecorating the Skirvin before declaring bankruptcy in 1971. That same year the Skirvin Tower was sold to a local savings and loan firm, which transformed it into a glass-enclosed office building. In 1972 the Skirvin Hotel was purchased by CLE Corporation, which changed its name to the Skirvin Plaza Hotel and invested eight million dollars in restoration efforts before selling the structure

in 1979 to Skirvin Plaza Investors, composed of a group of local businessmen.

The investors group wasted little time in restoring the Skirvin Plaza to its original finery through a massive renovation project. The ceiling of the lobby was raised to the second story, where it originally was designed to be. Ceiling murals were recreated and highlighted by massive chandeliers from Czechoslavakia. Arches and wooden trim were modeled after an original wooden archway uncovered by workers.

August 1, 1985, saw the beginning

of a renaissance for the hotel with its purchase by SPH Ltd., a group of skilled hoteliers headed by Scott Morrison, Bill Drury, and Gary Engle, all of Boca Raton, Florida. Their plan is to complete the period restoration of this grand dame of the American hotel scene and to return the Skirvin Plaza Hotel to the forefront of the most prestigious United States hotels.

Under the leadership of the new owners, the Skirvin will once again take its place as the "showplace of the Southwest" and its position as one of the finest hotels in the nation.

The hotel's lobby features specially designed Gothic lanterns and hand-carved English fumed oak, which was added to the walls and doors in 1930.

KEN'S RESTAURANT SYSTEMS, INC.

Operating and franchising four different regional pizza restaurant concepts, Ken's Restaurant Systems, Inc., was founded in 1961 by Ken Selby as a privately held, Tulsa-based corporation.

Originally a public school educator, Selby opened his first pizza restaurant in Tulsa to supplement his teaching income. After teaching from 8:00 a.m. to 4:00 p.m., he operated his Ken's Pizza Parlor until midnight. By the time the entrepreneur mopped up and locked the door, it would be 2:00 a.m. He maintained that schedule for four years, until he opened his second restaurant in June 1965. At that time Selby realized that "all of a sudden, I couldn't supervise everything that happened in

Ken Selby in front of his first restaurant in Tulsa in 1961.

By 1985 Ken's Pizza had grown to twenty-six company-owned and eighty-one franchised restaurants in eleven states.

one store." As a solution he decided to let the managers do it themselves, making certain to hire managers of character. "Hire honest people," Selby observed, "and they'll hire honest people." Soon thereafter, utilizing his management system and the secret recipe for sauce he had developed, the founder began offering franchises and launched construction of additional company outlets. Nine years later, in 1974, he opened his 100th Ken's Pizza restaurant.

Ken's Pizza, which provides traditional dine-in table service and specializes in its original thin crust and deep-pan pizza, offers a choice of sixteen toppings—together with spaghetti, rigatoni, nachos, garlic bread, three types of sandwiches, and a 24-item salad bar. By 1985 there were twenty-six company-owned Ken's Pizza outlets and eighty-one franchised

restaurants, operated by twenty-five franchisees, spread throughout Oklahoma, Texas, Arkansas, Missouri, Kansas, Illinois, South Carolina, Nebraska, Georgia, New Mexico, and Iowa. Three of the company-owned restaurants are Ken's Pizza Buy The Slice operations, which sell pizza by the slice in retail shopping malls.

To fill a void in the pizza market and also to broaden the base of the firm, Selby created Mazzio's Pizza in 1979 as an offshoot of Ken's Pizza to serve a younger, more affluent, and mobile customer. In addition to limited-service food, it features video games and a contemporary decor. By 1985 Mazzio's Pizza had grown to 120 individual locations in Oklahoma, Texas, Louisiana, Arkansas, Missouri, Kansas, Illinois, South Carolina, Nebraska, Georgia, Mississippi, Tennessee, Iowa, Florida, and New Mexico.

In 1984 the company again expanded and formed Scooter's Pizza Delivery, which is strictly a pizza-delivery operation catering to customers who want the convenience of having high-quality pizza delivered to their homes. Its unique approach is to guarantee delivery of any order

In order to appeal to a younger, more mobile customer, Mazzio's Pizza was established in 1979. By 1985 there were 120 locations in fourteen states.

utilize the convenient locations and family-oriented atmosphere of Ken's and Mazzio's and the special training given to company employees to entice widespread participation in the program.

Unique in that it operates and franchises four different concepts simultaneously, Ken's Restaurant Systems, Inc., by 1986 had captured 57 percent of the market in the Tulsa area through Ken's and Mazzio's Pizza restaurants. To maintain its position, the organization offers a fifteen-week, intensive training program and an on-site assistant for newly franchised outlets during the initial two weeks of their operations. In addition, updated marketing and sales techniques are offered periodically through a variety of workshops, seminars, and video tapes.

Ken's Restaurant Systems, Inc., employed in excess of 5,500 permanent and part-time individuals in both company-owned and franchised operations in 1985. The remarkable success story of Ken Selby epitomizes the ideal of social and economic opportunity that is unique to this nation.

within thirty minutes or the pizza is free. Serving the Tulsa metropolitan area, Scooter's has eleven outlets, ten of which are company owned.

In an effort to ensure the continued growth of the organization, Selby negotiated a contract with SYGMA, a subsidiary of SYSCO Corporation of Houston, Texas, to establish a distribution center near Stroud, Oklahoma. The facility will be designed to serve the 120 Ken's Pizza, 130 Mazzio's Pizza, and 9 Scooter's Pizza Delivery units in the fifteen-state franchise area of Ken's Restaurant Systems. As the nation's largest food-service distribution company, SYSCO Corporation will supply Ken's and Mazzio's with the more than six million pounds of natural mozzarella cheese and four million pounds of pepperoni, sausage, and other meat items they utilize every year.

As president, chief executive officer, chairman of the board, and director of Ken's Restaurant Systems, Inc., Selby has insisted that the company maintain an active role as a

corporate citizen. Thus it is a regular sponsor of Tulsa's River Run, a five-kilometer benefit for the Cystic Fibrosis Foundation. Ken's Restaurant Systems also actively promotes a number of concerts and professional sports in the Tulsa area. In addition, the firm initiated Operation Fingerprint within all company restaurants, a community-service program designed to help parents record their children's fingerprints. Alarmed by the large number of missing children reported annually, Selby hoped to

Scooter's, exclusively a pizza delivery service, has eleven outlets in the Tulsa area.

UNITED FOUNDERS LIFE INSURANCE COMPANY

The oldest life insurance company in Oklahoma, United Founders Life commenced business on November 16, 1892, as the Grand Lodge of Oklahoma, Ancient Order of United Workmen in Guthrie, Oklahoma, under the direction of Charles Allen. It operated in the Twin Territories—Oklahoma and Indian. Until 1889 the region had been raw frontier, and many of the early payments by the Grand Lodge reflect the hazards of operating a life insurance company in such untamed country. The early records of the Grand Lodge show claims for deaths resulting from gunshot wounds, sometimes listed as "accidental," "died at the hands of desperadoes with fractured skull," and "assassinated" as well as a multitude of deaths attributed to grippe, pneumonia, typhoid, septicemia, tuberculosis, gall stones, alcoholism, asthma, anemia, and numerous accidents. In 1892, 13.62 percent of the Grand Lodge's payments were recorded as "killed in making arrests." With statehood the Grand Lodge of Oklahoma, Ancient Order of United

Workmen was granted a charter on February 8, 1907, to do business in the new state.

Nearly half a century later, on May 4, 1956, the charter was amended to convert from a fraternal to a publicly held corporation. Later that same month the name was changed to United Founders Life Insurance Company. A constituent company, American Founders Life, was merged into United Founders in November 1956, and the firm opened operations at 124 Northwest Tenth Street with attorney L. Karlton Mosteller serving as chairman of the board and chief executive officer.

Throughout the first seven decades of its life, United Founders and its forerunners were an active insurance company; however, in 1960 the company purchased seventy-four acres bounded by Northwest Highway, May Avenue, Independence Avenue, and Sixtieth Street in the northwest quadrant of Oklahoma City and embarked on a two-decade program that involved both insurance and real estate development. The plan was to construct a corporate headquarters on the site and develop the remainder of the property into a combination of office structures, retail establishments, and a hotel.

When it was started in 1961, United Founders Life Tower was surrounded by farmland. Completed in 1964, it contained the world's third revolving restaurant, the Chandelle Club, on its top floor. The tower was followed in 1964 by Founders National Bank, located at May Avenue and United Founders Drive and organized by United Founders Life Insurance Company. In the following two years Local Federal Savings and Loan's first branch office was located nearby, as was Shoppers' World and the Ackerman Building. In 1973 United

Bernard Ille, president of United Founders Life Insurance Company, holding a portrait of L. Karlton Mosteller, the firm's first chairman of the board and chief executive officer.

Founders Life constructed the Hilton Inn Northwest, Oklahoma City's first major hotel constructed outside of the downtown area. In the early 1980s United Founders divested itself of most of its real estate investments and was acquired by the Protective Corporation of Birmingham, Alabama. At that time the firm redirected its energies toward an active policy of insurance company acquisitions.

Under the direction of Bernard Ille, its current president, United Founders made several major acquisitions from 1966 to 1985. Among them were Southern Equitable Life of Little Rock, Arkansas; Investors Security Life of Chicago, Illinois; Republic Investors Life of Moline, Illinois; Georgetown Life of Peoria, Illinois; Franklin National Life of Fort Wayne, Indiana; Stonewall Jackson Life of Huntington, West Virginia; and First American Life of St. Louis, Missouri. By the mid-1980s United Founders had increased its coverage worldwide with 98,000 policyholders.

United Founders Tower as it neared completion in 1964. One of the earliest commercial structures in the region, United Founders Tower was surrounded by farmland when it opened. Its top floor contained the world's third revolving restaurant, the Chandelle Club.

SONIC INDUSTRIES INC.

An exciting era in the fast-food business was born when the Sonic Drive-In system began in the summer of 1953. Troy N. Smith bought into a root beer stand in Shawnee, Oklahoma, called the Top Hat. Within a year Smith had introduced a series of innovations that revolutionized the restaurant industry.

Without compromising quality or service, he constructed a series of slanted stalls under canopies, which created a feeling of privacy around the restaurant, in which customers parked their automobiles. Customers then placed their orders through intercoms that connected the stalls with a central ordering station. After cooks prepared the food, it was delivered to the automobiles by "car hops." Customers could either eat their food from a special tray that attached to the window of the car or take the food home with them—all without leaving their automobile.

At about the same time, Charles W. Pappe decided to open a restaurant in Woodward, Oklahoma. Visiting the Top Hat by chance, Pappe recognized the marketing potential of Smith's innovations and approached Smith with the concept of opening a similar restaurant in Woodward, which Pappe would manage. Agreeing to the proposal, Smith allowed the use of the Top Hat name and provided Pappe with sufficient supplies to open.

The expansion proved successful, and within a short time, Smith and

C. Stephen Lynn, president and chief executive officer.

Pappe owned four separate drive-ins. Because the Top Hat restaurants boasted "Service With the Speed of Sound," in 1958 Smith and Pappe franchised their operation under the name Sonic. The original four Top Hat restaurants were converted to Sonic Drive-Ins the following year.

By 1967, the year Pappe died, there were forty-one Sonic Drive-Ins operating in four states. Under Smith's direction, Sonic's operations continued to expand, and by 1973 there were 130 individual operations: In June of that year Smith and nine major franchisees, in order to provide for additional leadership and expansion, created Sonic Industries Inc.

In 1974 Sonic Industries purchased all rights, trade names, trademarks, and other corporate property from Smith. That same year the new firm absorbed Sonic Supply Inc., owned by Marvin D. Jirous and Matt M. Kinslow. When the purchase arrangement and expansion were completed, Smith was elected chairman of the board of directors for Sonic Industries, Jirous was named president, and Kinslow became vice-president.

Other multifranchisees who were also officers, directors, or major stockholders at the time were James L. Barrett, Ralph L. Mason, Ted V. Robertson, Troy N. Smith, Jr., J. Dwight Van Dorn, James T. Williams, and James C. Winterringer. Under their management, the modern Sonic Industries Inc. franchising system was created and quickly evolved into more than 1,000 individual units in twenty states.

Overseeing Sonic's nationwide operations from the corporate headquarters in Oklahoma City, C. Stephen Lynn, who became president and chief executive officer in 1983, has continued the aggressive franchise sales program. To aid the expansion, Lynn implemented a centralized training program and established a system of local advertising and purchasing cooperatives. As a result, by 1985 Sonic Industries had embarked on an updated look for the future, including both inside and outside service facilities.

Charles W. Pappe (left) and Troy N. Smith, Sr., co-founders of the Sonic Drive-In system.

Sonic Drive-In's original sign complete with slogan: "Service With the Speed of Sound."

HILTON INN NORTHWEST

Oklahoma City's Hilton Inn Northwest is a part of the internationally known Hilton Hotels Corporation originally organized by Conrad N. Hilton in 1919. Famed for its service and attention to detail, the Hilton system began with the purchase of the forty-room Mobley Hotel in Cisco, Texas. From this beginning Hilton expanded his operation throughout Texas, and in 1939 expanded into other nearby states. Within a few years he operated hotels in Texas, New Mexico, California, New York, Illinois, Ohio, and Florida. A decade later Hilton entered the international hotel market.

In 1946 Hilton formed the Hilton Hotels Corporation, and within three years the firm had grown to 13,000 rooms in either corporation-owned or franchised hotels. Hilton's success was based on the promise of "minimum cost and maximum hospitality." In addition, he allowed each hotel to maintain its distinct individuality and made no attempt to establish a standard design. Hilton also established the Carte Blanche credit card system to make payment easier for his guests. When Hilton died in 1979, the Hilton Hotels Corporation controlled 260 establishments.

Located near the intersection of the Northwest Expressway and May Avenue, the Hilton Inn Northwest in Oklahoma City was opened in 1970—the first Hilton operation in the state. Built by United Founders Life Insurance Company, the franchise operation boasted a nine-story tower on the west side with a series of cabanas enclosing a square with a pool on the east side. The combination of the tower and cabanas produced a sense of privacy and solitude for those enjoying the pool. The tower contained 190 rooms and five suites. In the lower level of the tower was the Gusher Club, one of the city's most popular night spots.

In November 1978 a group of local investors led by Ronald Burks began a revitalization effort for the near northwest quadrant of Oklahoma City. As a part of the project,

Burks and the others purchased the Hilton Inn Northwest, with plans to make it the keystone of their revitalization effort. To accomplish the project, Burks implemented an extensive modernization, redecoration, and renovation plan spread over the following three years. Every guest room was redone; the restaurant underwent extensive remodeling; the lobby received a new front desk; the Gusher Club was closed and a new club, McNeeley's, was added; the meeting rooms were renovated to provide ad-

The nine-story tower of the Hilton Inn Northwest, which contains 190 rooms, five suites, the Players Café, the Carmel Café, three meeting rooms, and administrative offices, forms the west side of the secluded pool and cabana area.

ditional space; and the administrative offices were moved and updated.

When the revitalization effort was completed, the Hilton Inn Northwest presented an entirely new and more attractive appearance. To cater to the booming economy of the near

northwest quadrant, it offered three versatile meeting rooms—the Oklahoma Room, the Wildcat Room, and the Derrick Room—which could be divided into areas small enough to accommodate a meeting of six or large enough to handle 300. In addition, an Executive Cabana Suite was added. Located to the east of the pool area, it was segregated from the main facility and offered its occu-

pants a private swimming pool, jacuzzi, wet bar, and separate living room.

Players Café replaced the former restaurant. Divided into two dining rooms, which creates a sense of intimacy while offering an open, airy feeling, the café is furnished with comfortable chairs covered in blue velvet. To offset the muted colors of the rooms, the tables are covered with a light-blue cloth. Presenting an imaginative and varied menu, Players was designed to offer dining with a European flair.

Another remodeling project was

The private jacuzzi is but one of several amenities offered by the Hilton Inn Northwest's Executive Cabana Suite.

implemented in 1985. McNeeley's was closed, redecorated, and reopened as the Carmel Café. Designed with a "California look," the Carmel Café features soothing pastels blended with high-energy neons, accented by a bronzed greenhouse entrance. The Hilton Inn Northwest has continued in Oklahoma City the heritage of service and hospitality established by Conrad Hilton.

The interior of the Carmel Café is accented by leaded, stained-glass dividers depicting colorful parrots.

BLUE CROSS AND BLUE SHIELD OF OKLAHOMA

Projections for 1985 indicated that Blue Cross and Blue Shield would pay $275 million in health care benefits for members. When this amount was combined with the projected $500 million dispensed under the federal Medicare Part A (hospital) program that Blue Cross and Blue Shield administers, the corporation was to be financially responsible for approximately $775 million in health care benefits for that year. Blue Cross and Blue Shield had grown dramatically in forty-five years—it paid $13,878 in benefits in 1940, the year of its establishment.

Following the successful example of prepaid hospital insurance programs in several other states, community leaders in Oklahoma City and Tulsa began to formulate proposals to create a similar organization in the state. Two meetings were held, one in each of the cities previously mentioned. At the meetings the assemblage decided that a minimum of $10,000 would be necessary to establish the Blue Cross Plan in Oklahoma, with each city responsible for raising half the money. It was agreed that whichever community reached its goal first would become the association's Oklahoma headquarters.

On March 22, 1940, the Tulsa group deposited $5,000 in the National Bank of Tulsa; two weeks later the Oklahoma City members successfully completed their fund-raising drive. On April 1 of that year, the Blue Cross Plan was incorporated in Oklahoma, not by an enabling act—which would have removed the agency from the official category of insurance—but under the provisions of the state's Mutual Casualty Act, which placed it under the control of the State Insurance Office. Walter R. McBee, Oklahoma's first Blue Cross Plan executive director, opened the organization's headquarters in the Tulsa Loan Building at Fourth and Main streets. W.E. Hightower, of Oklahoma City, was named president of the board of trustees.

Within a year 140 groups throughout the state had enrolled in the

Ralph S. Rhoades, president and chief executive officer.

health benefit program. The cost was eighteen dollars annually for a semiprivate membership, which included all dependents. In addition there was a one-dollar enrollment fee. To ensure cooperation with the Oklahoma State Hospital Association, Blue Cross required that all member hospitals also be members of the association. Because most of these institutions had outrageous accounts receivable, the greater part of which they did

not expect to recover, Blue Cross' offer of a guaranteed daily payment for their member patients was irresistible. However, to meet its stringent regulations, state hospitals were compelled to maintain adequate records and fulfill the Hospital Association's requirements.

In 1941 N.D. Helland (who headed Oklahoma's Blue Cross Plan for a quarter of a century) became executive director; a year later the number of Blue Cross participants had doubled. Afterward there was no doubt of the organization's financial success, and throughout the following years additional services were added. The cost of outpatient care in accident cases; all drugs, medicines, and surgical dressings; as well as basic metabolism tests, electrocardiograms, oxygen, and physiotherapy were added in 1943. Reciprocity of benefit agreements was made with surrounding states the following year. In 1945 a medical/surgical/benefit program, known as the Blue Shield Plan, was incorporated as a companion to the Blue Cross Plan. General anesthesia coverage was added and the ward policy was discontinued in 1947. Ben-

The founder and first executive director, W.R. McBee (right), is shown here with his successor, N.D. Helland, who served the Plan as executive director from 1941 to 1967.

Blue Cross and Blue Shield of Oklahoma is headquartered at 1215 South Boulder Avenue in Tulsa.

efits were expanded to cover X-ray costs in accident cases, obstetrical care limited to family contracts, and quarantinable and venereal diseases in 1948.

In 1950 Blue Cross and Blue Shield increased its coverage to ninety days and added in-hospital medical costs. Payment to osteopathic physicians was approved in 1952, and within the next year the organization's first nongroup enrollment was held. Land was acquired at 1215 South Boulder in Tulsa and a new three-story headquarters building was ready for occupancy in 1954, the same year that benefits were extended to cover 225 surgical allowances. In 1956 coverage for nervous and mental conditions for thirty days in any year was added, as were microscopic tissue examinations. A $25 deductible contract was offered on an

elective basis in 1958; a year later special plans were implemented for senior citizens and students.

A major change in benefits took place in 1962, when a joint underwriting of major medical coverage was initiated by Blue Cross and Blue Shield. In 1966 the organization was named as the fiscal intermediary for the hospital portion of the Medicare program, and at the same time offered Plan 65 to supplement Medicare coverage. W. Ralph Bethel served as chief executive officer from 1967 to 1977, during which time he oversaw the expansion of the headquarters building to twelve stories and facilitated the merger of the company's boards of trustees.

As the cost of medical care continued to grow, in 1970 Blue Cross and Blue Shield originated a Cost Containment Program. Dental coverage was offered in 1974, and three years later, under the leadership of Ralph S. Rhoades, the incumbent president and chief executive officer, the Mem-

ber Service Life Insurance Company was formed as a subsidiary to provide a comprehensive benefit package of life insurance and disability income. Eventually three other subsidiaries were formed: United Automation Services, Inc., a consulting service, in 1983; Takecare Prepaid Health Service of Oklahoma, Inc., in 1984, as a health maintenance organization; and Member Service Administrators, also in 1984, to serve as a third-party administrator for self-insured groups. GHS Holding Company was organized in 1984 as the parent corporation of the subsidiaries of Blue Cross and Blue Shield of Oklahoma.

By the mid-1980s Blue Cross and Blue Shield was Oklahoma's leading health insurer. To hold down the rising cost of health care, the organization led the way in forming the FAIR (Fixed Allowance Incentive Reimbursement) hospital contract; and by 1985, 121 of Oklahoma's 125 hospitals had joined in the effort. That same year Blue Cross and Blue Shield, with branch offices in Oklahoma City, Ada, Enid, Lawton, and Muskogee, provided insurance coverage to approximately 500,000 Oklahomans.

W.R. Bethel, president and chief executive officer from 1967 to 1977.

265

INDUSTRIAL GASKET, INC.

Formed in December 1948 by Larry B. Renth, C.J. Donovan, and C.A. Huffine, Industrial Gasket and Packing Co., Inc., originally specialized in servicing oil refineries and original-equipment manufacturers servicing the oil industry. Initially the company had only three employees: Huffine, who handled sales; Donovan, who oversaw the office; and Renth, who operated the plant. Huffine left the firm in 1959 and Donovan retired in 1984; however, Renth continues to serve as president and chief executive officer of Industrial Gasket, Inc.

In April 1949 the business was incorporated as Industrial Gasket and Packing Co., Inc. Located in a 4,500-square-foot structure at 801 South Walker Avenue near downtown Oklahoma City, the company proved to be so successful that two adjoining houses were removed and the original structure expanded four times. In addition, the old Mobil Oil Company property, which adjoined the railroad between Walker and Dewey avenues, was rented to provide extra space. Despite these efforts, Industrial Gasket's growth so strained available space that a second plant was opened in 1970 at Northwest Sixty-third Street and Rockwell Avenue. In addition, a sales office was maintained in Tulsa

Industrial Gasket's 80,000-square-foot corporate headquarters and plant in Oklahoma City is capable of producing gaskets from more than one million die patterns.

for thirty years beginning in 1955. By the early 1970s Industrial Gasket's operation had outgrown all existing facilities. As a result, a six-acre site was selected at 8100 Southwest Fifteenth Street for a new corporate headquarters and plant. Completed in 1974, the air-conditioned structure contained 80,000 square feet and enabled the company to centralize its entire operations at one location.

Throughout this period of extensive growth Industrial Gasket operated on the principle of "find a need and fill it." While gasket manufacturing with steel-rule dies—which allowed the firm to provide products manufactured to customer specifications—gave Industrial Gasket access to the numerous gasoline plants located throughout central Oklahoma, the same process quickly was applied to original-equipment manufacturers around the state. As the firm's stamping capabilities were increased to ac-

When organized in 1948, Industrial Gasket and Packing Co., Inc., occupied the building to the right of the photograph. Later, as the company grew, it acquired the adjoining houses and leased the Magnolia Petroleum Building (shown at left).

commodate the growing demand for steel-rule die products, it expanded its operations into metal stamping.

With these increased capabilities, Industrial Gasket acquired a number of contracts to supply equipment for Tinker Field's aircraft maintenance center, Halliburton oil field services, Western Electric communication systems, numerous intricate laboratory units for the petroleum industry, and automotive after-market items. In addition, the company entered the insulation field, manufacturing a line of insulation equipment marketed under the Hoshall and U-Insulate brand names. By the 1980s Industrial Gasket had grown into the region's most complete machine shop, capable of producing virtually any metal stamped or machined part. Its automotive gasket department stocks dies for all makes and models of water pumps, generators, coils, and other automobile items, and its die-cut gasket division can design, produce, and deliver gaskets to customer specification for any project. In addition, the company serves as a manufacturer's distributor for a multitude of additional products needed by the area's industrial manufacturers. More than one million die patterns are maintained on file to fill the demands of 3,800 customers worldwide.

SCRIVNER, INC.

A wholesale distributor of food products supplying more than 2,300 independently owned supermarkets in twenty-three states, Scrivner, Inc., maintains fourteen food distribution centers in Oklahoma, Kansas, Texas, Iowa, Illinois, Tennessee, Alabama, New York, Pennsylvania, and Ohio. In addition, Scrivner owns and operates 135 supermarkets and supplies institutional food-service customers.

The enterprise began with the purchase of 160 acres of farmland near Meshak, Oklahoma—the current site of Tinker Air Force Base in Midwest City—by Enoch Scrivner in 1901. To market their crops he and his wife also purchased a grocery store in nearby Oklahoma City. While Mrs. Scrivner managed the business, her husband hauled wagon loads of produce and wild game from their farm to the store; from there the commodities were distributed to retail markets throughout the city.

Four years later the Scrivners expanded their operations and opened a retail grocery store to sell directly to the public. Forming a partnership with his brother-in-law, J.H. Stevens, Scrivner quickly expanded the venture into one of the largest chains of its kind in the Southwest. However, in 1917, the partners sold their retail operations and used the profits to form the Scrivner Stevens Company, Wholesale Grocers.

A decade later the firm purchased its own warehouse, from which it served a multitude of retail grocery outlets in central Oklahoma. This was soon followed by a similar facility in Shawnee, opened in 1929, and another in Tulsa, opened in 1939.

By the close of the 1930s Scrivner Stevens Company had extended its operations into the surrounding states; in the ensuing years the firm continued to grow. At the time of Scrivner's death in 1955, the company's annual sales exceeded $15 million. Expansion continued during the following three decades, until by the mid-1980s Scrivner, Inc., was one of the nation's major wholesale grocery operations.

Enoch Scrivner, founder.

Jerry D. Metcalf, who succeeded James V. Kunstel in 1985 as chairman and chief executive officer, says volume of sales has now increased to three billion dollars. Metcalf joined the organization when it acquired the S.M. Flickinger Company. D. Clark Ogle has become president and chief operating officer.

GOVERNAIR CORPORATION

Specializing in custom-designed commercial and industrial air-conditioning units, Governair Corporation was organized by W.A. Quinn, D.N. Bell, and H.B. Howery in 1937 to manufacture and market attic fans, designed to "govern the amount of air"—hence the corporate name, Governair. Within a few years the firm had outgrown its original plant on West Main Street and moved to another location at 513 North Blackwelder Avenue. In October 1956 Governair moved again, this time to a modern 60,000-square-foot plant located at 4841 North Sewell Avenue. In 1981 an 8,000-square-foot corporate headquarters was constructed across the street, just to the west of the plant.

During the early years Governair concentrated on the production of attic fans. Placed in the attics of buildings, the exhaust fans forced the hot air, which had risen to the top of the structure, out vents located either in the roof or upper sides of the building and pulled in cooler air from windows. Often sections of excelsior were attached to the windows through which the cooler air was pulled. Streams of water were fed through the excelsior, thus enhancing the cooling effect of the attic fans. In the 1940s Governair marketed a self-contained, evaporative window unit.

With the outbreak of World War II, Governair switched to war production. Through a series of government contracts, the firm supplied the Quartermaster Corps and Medical Corps with cooling systems that were used to prevent food from spoiling, to preserve blood plasma, and to provide comfort control. The technological advances in refrigeration made during World War II led Governair into the custom-designed, specialized and comfort cooling business.

Unlike previous cooling systems, refrigeration chills the air with a recirculated fluid. Hot air is pulled into the system and circulated around coils filled with refrigerant. The refrigerant in the coils boils and removes the heat from the air, thereby

Governair's early plant on North Blackwelder Avenue. By the late 1940s the firm had outgrown the facility and moved to a new location on North Sewell Avenue.

R.J. Merriman, president and chief executive officer.

cooling it.

With the return of peace, Governair quickly became a leader in the refrigeration industry. As the nation's economy returned to consumer production, most retail establishments installed air conditioning to attract customers. To meet the demand, Governair developed large, standardized, self-contained commercial air conditioners that could be installed in previously established businesses and introduced a product line of comfort coolers that were built specifically for customers' needs. Because the standardized line of commercial air conditioners required a distributorship system, Gov-

ernair management soon dropped them from the inventory and concentrated on custom-designed products.

Keying its operation to customer demand, Governair built its reputation on supplying custom-designed units for specific cooling problems. By maintaining its own engineering department, complemented with advanced computer technology, the firm can provide just the right system for any commercial or industrial operation through the entire process from bid to on-site installation. Each unit is specifically designed for the customer's building by considering such factors as use need, climate requirement, cooling area, and building size. After each project is computer analyzed for costs and components, detailed drawings are prepared, and then the custom unit is constructed in Governair's modern plant. To ensure quality control, component parts are assembled, the frame is fabricated, the compressor is mounted, and the piping and wiring is completed under specialized supervision at the company's plant.

In 1956 Governair built the world's first 100-ton-cooling-capacity, completely packaged air-conditioning unit manufactured in the United States, for The Market Place supermarket in Philadelphia, Pennsylva-

The 8,000-square-foot corporate headquarters of Governair is across the street from the firm's plant.

nia. With the rapid growth of the central-air concept during the building boom of the 1960s, Governair filled the marketplace with air-cooled, air-conditioning equipment. At the same time it began catering to the highly specialized needs of high-tech industries and medical institutions, which required manufactured environments, not just cooling.

High-tech industries are dependent on a clean, climate-controlled environment in which microchips can be produced without contamination by minute particles of dust and without being subjected to radical temperature and humidity variations. Modern hospital surgical, intensive care, and isolation units require these same climate-control and filtration systems. Likewise, medical research facilities must have standard control measures and stringent contamination safeguards to ensure the success of research projects. Governair's specialized air-conditioning systems not only guarantee reliable climate control, but also remove 99 percent of airborne particles. By 1985 some 20 percent of Governair's production was tailored to the output of these specialized units.

With the return to evaporative and water-cooled air conditioning brought

on by the energy awareness trend of the 1970s, Governair introduced a new line of energy-efficient commercial and industrial cooling units. In addition, the company designed several specific cooling units for the United States government. For example, the Air Force's F-16 fighter utilizes a Governair-produced air-conditioning system to cool its computer system during ground maintenance.

After Bell died, W.A. Quinn assumed management responsibility for Governair. In 1955 the elder Quinn was succeeded by his son, W.A. Quinn, Jr., who oversaw the firm's operations until his death in 1970.

For the following seven years the Quinn estate managed the corporation, and in 1977 a group of thirteen employees, headed by R.J. Stone and R.J. Merriman, purchased Governair from the Quinn estate. Stone served as president until he died in 1983; Merriman became president and chief executive officer at that time. Under his direction, Governair Corporation has expanded its operations overseas and has become an internationally known supplier of specialized and comfort air-conditioning units.

The interior of Governair's 60,000-square-foot plant with several custom-designed cooling units under construction.

UNARCO COMMERCIAL PRODUCTS

Unarco Commercial Products is a division of UNR Industries, a leader in the manufacturing and marketing of industrial, commercial, and consumer products. While the parent firm is based in Chicago, Unarco Commercial Products is headquartered in Oklahoma City, with additional plants located in Wagoner, Oklahoma; Memphis, Tennessee; Sacramento, California; and Fogelsville, Pennsylvania.

UNR's Oklahoma connection started in 1962, when the corporation acquired the Oklahoma City-based Folding Carrier Company. Unarco Commercial Products was created to manufacture and market the shopping cart, and is under the direction of president Marvin Weiss.

Oklahoma City's Unarco Commercial Products is the leading manufacturer of the supermarket shopping cart in the nation. In addition, the company produces a wide variety of specialized products and carts used throughout the retail merchandising industry. Among them are a modular merchandising system of interlocking baskets that can be stacked on gondolas and used as a substitute for shelving; mobile merchandisers that allow goods to be displayed throughout the store; portable display bins to present prepackaged and bulk merchandise; continuous baskets for wall displays; end and island display merchandisers used for impulse sales. Entirely new concepts in the mass-merchandising field, the VendAll and Vendex lines are designed to allow goods to be bulk-dumped. This cuts costs by eliminating the necessity of handling items individually.

The Commercial Division also makes a number of products utilized to stock merchandise, including stock carts designed for use in either stores or warehouses; utility carts specifically for aisles; and small-item carts

Marvin Weiss, president.

for general merchandise. As well, the firm manufactures several specialty carts such as cigarette carts that can be filled in the back room and then used as a display merchandiser; returned-goods carts that allow those items to be taken back to the shelf in a time-saving manner; bottle carts to hold bottles returned for deposit; mail carts for the mail room; carry-out carts to help customers load heavy products easily; and luggage carts for airports, railroads, and hotels or motels.

Unarco Food Handling, also under the direction of president Marvin Weiss, markets under the McClintock trade name and produces more than 90 varieties of platters, pans, lugs, covers, and drain inserts; 21 types of lug carts and dollies; 6 kinds of chicken dollies; over 40 assorted floor and cooler racks; 17 choices of meat boat racks; 281 various stainless steel boning, preparation, chopping, or processing tables and accessories; 32 variations of cutting boards; 15 different knife sharpeners and accessories; 18 types of paper, film, or foil cutters; 100 models of processing carts and racks, cooler, blooming, dish, spice, and cantilever carts, and can and platter racks; and 56 stock trucks. Other lines include a number of plastic dividers and holders used to merchandise meat and produce, several models of bottle carts, and receiving desks.

Unarco manufactures every item utilized by mass retail businesses from the time goods are delivered until they pass through the checkout

Unarco Commercial Products' Classic Shopping Cart. Produced for general mass merchandise outlets, the cart is designed so that the top tilts up, allowing large objects to be carried on the bottom rack.

Unarco Commercial Products' Model 109 Shopping Cart. Designed for use in supermarkets, the back of each cart is hinged so that the carts fit together for ease of storage.

counter. As the concept of mass merchandising spread, Unarco Commercial Products and the firm's Food Handling Division expanded its marketing worldwide and currently distributes its lines in thirty-six countries spread across five continents—North America, South America, Europe, Africa, and Asia.

Another aspect of Unarco Commercial Products is Brytline DME Medical Equipment, especially de-

signed to fulfill the needs of the nation's senior citizens. By providing specialized health care equipment, the organization presents numerous choices of products that enable senior citizens to enjoy expanded mobility by the use of several different walking aids—such as canes, crutches, walkers, and grab rails. It additionally offers specific supplies designed for the infirm.

Unarco Commercial Products is but one of several UNR divisions. Among the others are Unarco Home Products, offering a large assortment of stainless steel sinks used commercially and in the home; Unarco Rubber Products, a major supplier of

molded solid rubber wheels for recreation and industry; Unarco-Leavitt, which makes more than 75,000 miles of steel tubing annually; and Unarco Lighting, the producer of lighting and venting systems for recreational vehicles and mobile homes. UNR's corporate structure also includes Unarco Material Storage, which manufactures various industrial racks and other storage equipment; Unarco-Midwest Steel, a major supplier of rail, trackwork, and tools used by America's railroads; Unarco Transportation, which provides load-bearing, protected, segregated systems used by the country's railroads and also manufactures, rebuilds, or repairs boxcar side doors, freight-car hand brakes, and freight cars; Unarco-Midwest Tele-Communications, a leader in the sales, engineering, installation, and maintenance service of complete closed-circuit television systems; and Unarco-Rohn, a major producer of residential televisions, CBs, ham radios, microwave towers, lighting towers, and livestock confinement equipment.

Through its diversification, UNR Industries has become one of the most successful and innovative of the multifaceted corporations in America.

Unarco Commercial Products' Wagoner, Oklahoma, plant.

OKLAHOMA PUBLISHING COMPANY

E.K. Gaylord, who oversaw the operation of the Oklahoma Publishing Company from its founding in 1903 until his death in 1974.

Edward L. Gaylord, who previously had managed OPUBCO's myriad investments and operations, became president of the company and editor of The Daily Oklahoman *in 1974.*

From a relatively modest investment in a small, frontier newspaper in 1903, the Oklahoma Publishing Company, or OPUBCO, has grown during the following eight decades into one of the largest privately owned communications companies in America. What began as a minority interest in *The Daily Oklahoman* has blossomed into a nationwide enterprise that also includes television stations in Florida, Texas, Louisiana, Wisconsin, Ohio, and Washington; radio stations in Oklahoma City and Nashville; Opryland USA, which includes a hotel, a theme park, and the Grand Ol' Opry; the Nashville Network, a cable television system that covers the country; Oklahoma Graphics, a printing company that produces high-quality publications for major firms across the United States from its modern plant in Oklahoma

City; Gaylord Productions, Inc., which produces movies and television programs for worldwide distribution; and numerous other companies involved in real estate development, oil and gas exploration, ranching, telecommunications, and information retrieval.

From its inception, the Oklahoma Publishing Company has been under the leadership of the Gaylord family: first, E.K. Gaylord, who purchased *The Daily Oklahoman* and turned it into the state's largest and most influential newspaper; and later, his son, Edward L. Gaylord, who directed the company's expansion and business interests before taking the helm as president and publisher upon the death of his father in 1974.

In December 1902 E.K. Gaylord, then twenty-nine years old, arrived in Oklahoma City in search of a newspaper in which to invest. Drawing on his newspaper experience in Missouri and Colorado, Gaylord decided that *The Daily Oklahoman* was just what he was looking for. Started in 1889

by the Reverend Samuel Small, *The Daily Oklahoman* had passed through several owners during the following years. Initially Gaylord considered purchasing the rival *Times-Journal,* but when its owners declined his offer he joined with Ray M. Dickinson and two other investors to acquire *The Daily Oklahoman.* The purchase was completed on January 29, 1903, and the Oklahoma Publishing Company was formed to oversee the newspaper's operations. Although his health forced him to retire in 1912, Dickinson remained active on OPUBCO's board of directors until his death in 1948. His son, Donald C. Dickinson, and his grandson, Martin C. Dickinson, became members of the board of directors in 1949 and 1974, respectively. Gaylord became president of OPUBCO in

1918 and assumed responsibility for both the business management and editorial policies of the company.

Housed in a 22- by 65-foot building at 18 South Broadway Avenue and printed on a flatbed press with a small case of type, *The Daily Oklahoman*'s readership numbered 3,500. By October 1903 *The Daily Oklahoman* was well on its way to becoming a leader among the state's newspapers. A new two-story office and printing plant building had been completed at the intersection of California and Robinson avenues; a contract had been reached with the Associated Press wire service to give the paper access to national and international news; and a modern $15,000 sixteen-page printing press and additional type had been acquired to increase the newspaper's appeal. As a result, *The Daily Oklahoman*'s circulation had grown to 31,000 by statehood in 1907.

Another $25,000 printing press was purchased to handle the increased readership; however, on January 29, 1909, a fire destroyed *The Daily Oklahoman*'s printing plant and offices. Undaunted, Gaylord, without missing an issue, constructed a new building at the intersection of Northwest Fourth Street and Broadway Avenue in downtown Oklahoma City, which continues to serve as OPUBCO's offices. In 1929 a $1.5-million expansion project calling for the construction of a production and circulation building just to the east of OPUBCO's offices was started. Two decades later, in 1950, a $1.25-million newsprint warehouse was constructed, and in 1963 a new business building was completed. Eventually, OPUBCO occupied virtually the entire block between Broadway Avenue and the Santa Fe Railroad tracks and between Fourth and Fifth streets.

During its first decade OPUBCO began to broaden its operations. In 1911 *The Farmer-Stockman* was established replacing *The Weekly Oklahoman*. In 1916 OPUBCO acquired the *Oklahoma City Times*, an afternoon newspaper. In 1984 *The Daily Oklahoman* and the *Oklahoma City Times* merged into a single newspaper with four daily editions.

As the electronic media entered the news market, OPUBCO wasted little time in expanding into that arena. In 1928 Gaylord purchased WKY-Radio. Boasting a 20-watt transmitter, WKY was the first radio station west of the Mississippi River and the third station in the country to broadcast regular daily programs. A leader in the radio industry, WKY employs one of the largest news staffs in the state and maintains many mobile vans and a helicopter for on-site broadcasts. Two additional AM-FM radio stations were later added to the WKY system—KRKE, in Albuquerque, New Mexico, and KYTE, in Portland, Oregon.

On June 6, 1949, WKY transmitted the first television picture in Oklahoma as WKY-TV, Channel 4. Eleven days later it aired its first network program, and on April 4, 1954, WKY-TV became the first non-network television station in the country to broadcast in color. In 1965 a new 1,602-foot broadcasting tower was placed into service and the following year, 1966, WKY-TV put the state's first all-color newscast on the air.

Although WKY-TV, which now broadcasts as KTVY in Oklahoma City, was sold in 1976, Gaylord Broadcasting continues to operate seven other television stations— WTVT in the Tampa-St. Petersburg, Florida, area; WUAB-TV in Cleveland, Ohio; KSTW in Seattle-Tacoma, Washington; WVUE in New Orleans, Louisiana; WVTV in Milwaukee, Wisconsin; KHTV in Houston, Texas; and KTVT, in Dallas, Texas.

The key to any successful statewide newspaper is rapid distribution of the paper throughout its marketing area. Unwilling to depend on the railroads to handle such an important assignment, Gaylord organized Mistletoe Express Service in 1931. The new corporation not only allowed overnight delivery of newspapers, but guaranteed merchants utilizing its services same-day or overnight delivery of merchandise to any point within 150 miles of Oklahoma City. Eventually its operations were expanded throughout Oklahoma, Kansas, Arkansas, and Texas. OPUBCO divested itself of Mistletoe Express in 1979, to its stockholders.

E.K. Gaylord remained active in the operation of OPUBCO until his death in 1974. Throughout his more than seven decades with OPUBCO he constantly pushed for the growth and development of Oklahoma City and the remainder of the state by making the support of community activities a conscious, continual purpose of the company. His son, E.L. Gaylord, who previously had the responsibility of managing OPUBCO's myriad investments and operations, assumed leadership of the firm as president of Oklahoma Publishing Company and editor and publisher of *The Daily Oklahoman* and the *Oklahoma City Times* in 1974.

Gaylord continued his father's policy of "building a better, more prosperous community, state, and nation," and expanding OPUBCO's operations. He added the *Colorado Springs Sun* newspaper (which was later sold) to the OPUBCO family as well as a real estate development company; a ranching concern; the syndicated television program "Hee Haw"; and Opryland USA, which includes the Grand Ol' Opry, a hotel, and a theme park; a cable television network; and WSM-AM and -FM in Nashville. Recognizing that advancing technology rapidly was changing the newspaper business, he oversaw the completion of a $60-million, 300,000-square-foot plant, complete with Goss Metroliner offset presses. Located at the intersection of Britton Road and Broadway Extension, it is one of the most advanced printing facilities in the world, and, combined with OPUBCO's efficient organization, makes it possible for *The Oklahoman* to reach more than one million readers every Sunday and almost a million every weekday.

OTASCO

In 1906 Herman Sanditen, then seventeen years old, and his fifteen-year-old brother, Maurice, immigrated to America from Lithuania. At first the two teenagers settled in St. Stephen, South Carolina, where they hauled freight, arranged stock, and swept floors in a general store owned by a second cousin, Gus Rittenberg, who had paid their passage across the Atlantic. Although Herman remained in St. Stephen, Maurice moved to Nashville, Tennessee, at the age of twenty-four and opened a grocery store. Afterward they were joined by a third brother, Sam, who briefly settled in Nashville to work in Maurice's grocery store. However, Sam moved to Okmulgee, Oklahoma, in 1916 and took a job as a helper in a local tire store.

The early Oklahoma oil boom was in its heyday, and business opportunities abounded. Within a short time Maurice relocated to Okmulgee and opened a used oil field pipe business; Herman soon followed. In February 1918 the three brothers pooled their entire savings of $2,000, formed a partnership, and opened Oklahoma Tire and Supply (OTASCO) at the intersection of Okmulgee Avenue and Main Street in downtown Okmulgee. Located in a small brick building with a gas pump at the side, it was the first of an eventual network of OTASCO stores spread across fourteen states in the southeast and south-central United States.

Within three years the entrepreneurs opened a second store in Henryetta. It was quickly followed by others in Tulsa and Shawnee and in Fort Smith, Arkansas. During the early expansion a brother-in-law, Gershon Fenster, joined the business. As early as 1923 the Sanditen brothers established a profit-sharing plan for employees. This was one of the first successful employee benefit programs in the nation, and was one of the main reasons behind OTASCO's rapid growth. A few years later the company established a retirement trust fund, a benefit almost unheard of at that time. All costs of the retirement program were and to this date are paid by OTASCO. In addi-

Located at the intersection of Okmulgee Avenue and Main Street in downtown Okmulgee, the first OTASCO store had everything a customer might want for an automobile, including gasoline which was sold from a pump at the side of the building. Herman Sanditen's pickup, in which he made deliveries, is parked in front of the store.

tion, employees were offered stock bonus and stock purchase plans that allowed them to become stockholders in the firm. Such an employee-employer relationship resulted in many longtime workers, which gave OTASCO a sense of stability. As Maurice Sanditen explained, "At the very beginning of its existence, this company took it upon itself to follow the principle of the Golden Rule, of treating everybody, whether they be customers, suppliers, or employees, like we would like to be treated; this sums up in a nutshell our formula for success." Throughout this early period the stores were company owned.

In 1934 the Sanditen brothers implemented a system of independently owned associate stores under the direction of OTASCO's Associate

From left are Maurice Sanditen, Herman Sanditen, and Sam Sanditen, founders.

Division. By 1948 there were 42 company stores and 140 associate stores spread across a four-state area.

The firm's growth continued during the following decades; by 1960 there were a total of 253 company and associate stores, served by two large warehouse complexes, reaching almost thirty-six million dollars in total sales. That same year the owners agreed to merge OTASCO into the McCrory Corporation. The following year McCrory Corporation purchased the Economy Auto Stores and assigned full operating responsibility of the combined chain to the OTASCO management team.

OTASCO's headquarters and distribution center in Tulsa is housed in a 500,000-square-foot building covering ten acres on a 28-acre site. It utilizes a modern computerized inventory system to maintain control over more than 9,500 stock-keeping units sold by OTASCO stores. Additional distribution centers are maintained in Little Rock, Arkansas, and Atlanta, Georgia. Total retail sales in 1985 reached $325 million.

Sam Sanditen died in 1939, Maurice in 1970, and Herman in 1971. Julius Sanditen, a younger brother who later served as president and chairman, passed away in 1977. The youngest and last of the brothers, Ely, who served as chairman of the executive committee, died in 1983.

However, Edgar R. Sanditen, Herman's son, former president and chief executive officer, continues to serve as chairman of the board of OTASCO; Jerry Goodman, who first joined the firm in February 1970, is president and chief executive officer. They oversee more than 600 company and associate stores spread across Oklahoma, Arkansas, Kansas, Texas, Missouri, Mississippi, Florida, Kentucky, Tennessee, Louisiana, Alabama, Georgia, North Carolina, and South Carolina, employing over 4,300 individuals.

On October 23, 1984, a group of OTASCO management personnel and the employees of OTASCO Employee's Retirement Trust, under the chairmanship of Abe Brand (who joined OTASCO in 1931), formed the OTASCO Holding Corporation. The OTASCO Holding Corporation repurchased the firm from the McCrory Corporation in a leveraged buyout. This action created the fourth-largest completely employee-owned organization in America.

This 500,000-square-foot building houses OTASCO's headquarters and distribution center. Located on a 28-acre site in northeast Tulsa, the structure is so large that individual railroad cars are pulled inside for unloading.

ST. ANTHONY HOSPITAL

Serving God through service to others is the ministry of the Sisters of St. Francis and Oklahoma City's St. Anthony Hospital. For almost a century the Sisters of St. Francis have strived to bring the finest health care and medical education to the people of Oklahoma City and the entire Southwest.

The story of St. Anthony Hospital is a saga of the pioneer spirit that founded the Sooner State. In the spring of 1898, less than a decade after the Run of 1889 and the opening of Oklahoma Territory, Sisters Beata Vinson and Clara Schaff traveled to Oklahoma City seeking funds and supplies for their Order's first undertaking—St. Joseph Hospital in Maryville, Missouri. Because Oklahoma had no organized health care facilities of its own, Father D.I. Lanslots, O.S.B., pastor of St. Joseph's Catholic Church in Oklahoma City, asked the Sisters to open a hospital in the future capital city. After a turbulent year of start-up problems and hardships, the first permanent hospital in Oklahoma Territory—St. Anthony—was opened on November 24, 1899, at its present location.

The initial facility housed twenty-four beds, but had few modern conveniences. Water had to be carried four blocks from a nearby school. Telephone service came a year later, in 1900. Electric lights and power was connected in 1902, and natural gas lines were laid in 1904. A well also was drilled that same year and connected to a windmill. In 1911 St. Anthony acquired its first motor-driven ambulance.

During the early years the Sisters mastered the artful science of improvisation. To meet their supply and money needs, they depended heavily on the generosity of the booming community in which they lived. When smallpox and scarlet fever epidemics struck Oklahoma City, the institution's barn was converted into a quarantine facility and renamed the St. Patrick Isolation Hospital. During the hardest years of the Great Depression, the Sisters of St.

Francis and St. Anthony Hospital provided more than two million free meals to Oklahoma City's needy citizens.

St. Anthony's primary mission has remained to provide the best in the rapidly changing field of medical and health care. In 1908 the Sisters of St. Francis opened the state's first school of nursing, graduating its original class three years later. Also in 1908, the initial X-ray machine was installed; and in 1922 Sister Beatrice Merrigan of St. Anthony became the first registered X-ray technician in the United States.

St. Anthony's growth has been an ongoing process, with each new facility creating an opportunity for greater community service. In 1916 a wing was added, bringing to 150 the number of patient beds available. Other expansions included a new surgery room, a clinical laboratory, a medical library, interns' quarters, and classrooms. Two years later the

A late-nineteenth-century view of St. Anthony Hospital. The three-story, half-basement structure housed Oklahoma Territory's first health care facility.

hospital's initial class of interns arrived.

The second major development program began in 1932, when St. Anthony's South Wing was erected. The most ambitious growth effort came in 1955, with a three-phase building program to meet the growing medical needs of the state. Phase I of the program increased the capability of the hospital's School of Nursing and was completed in 1956. Phases II and III added more than 200 beds to the institution and established specialized departments in psychiatry, occupational therapy, pediatrics, and maternity. The 1960s and 1970s also saw unprecedented expansion. The addition of the Northwest Wing, the Annex, and the East Central Tower brought the medical center to its present size of 684 beds and numerous advanced treatment and educational facilities.

St. Anthony Hospital has provided more meaningful "firsts" for Oklahoma's health care industry than any single facility in the state. With the beginning technological improvements came accreditation in 1921 by the American College of Surgeons as the first Class A hospital in Oklahoma. The state's original institutional pharmacy was opened at St. Anthony in 1925. Oklahoma City's initial Intensive Care Unit was established there in 1963, as were in later years the first Mobile Coronary Care Unit, the first inpatient psychiatric facility, the first radioactive isotope laboratory, and the state's first comprehensive alcoholic rehabilitation environment.

Among the most important areas of progress at St. Anthony Hospital has been the development of a highly trained staff of physicians and medi-

cal and lay support specialists. The advent of new health-related technology has brought it some of the finest experts in the many disciplines of modern medical science. Yet, at the same time, the institution has remained dedicated to the prospect of giving all patients the same loving and compassionate care the Sisters of St. Francis first promised in 1898.

In the 1980s the Sisters of St. Francis and the other people of St. Anthony Hospital are preparing to meet the challenge of their second century of service to Oklahoma City and the Sooner State. The Oklahoma Neurological Surgery Institute and the Oklahoma Cardiovascular Institute, both of which are housed at St. Anthony Hospital, are in the forefront of their areas of specialization. In addition, the Second Century Fund—the hospital's first major fund-raising campaign in two decades—was successful in upgrading

and improving St. Anthony's organ transplant program and radiology treatment services, as well as other vital patient care and administrative functions.

From the 1890s to the 1980s and beyond, the Sisters of St. Francis have remained faithful to their pledge "to turn no one away," and to offer the finest medical care available to all Oklahomans. Their proud, living heritage of commitment to the principles of St. Francis pushed St. Anthony—the first health care facility in Oklahoma Territory—to the forefront of the nation's health care and medical education institutions.

Modern-day St. Anthony Hospital. To the left is the institution's emergency department, intensive care units, and the Oklahoma Cardiovascular Institute. The large tower is the facility's East Central Tower. The South Wing of the hospital is on the right. The central portion of the complex forms the West Central Tower.

ONEOK Inc.

ONEOK Inc. is a diversified energy company headquartered in Tulsa, whose roots are in Oklahoma Natural Gas Company—the state's major natural gas utility. Oklahoma Natural was organized before statehood at a time when natural gas had little marketability.

Although manufactured gas was used by numerous towns for fuel and lighting, during the early years of the Oklahoma oil boom, natural gas had received little attention. Viewed as a troublesome by-product of crude oil, natural gas often was vented into the air or burned off. It was not until 1906, with the construction of pipelines to transport it, that Oklahomans began to realize the potential of the state's plentiful supply of natural gas. What later became a billion-dollar-a-year industry was launched.

Recognizing the possibility of substituting natural gas for manufactured gas, Dennis T. Flynn, C.B. Ames, Glenn T. Braden, and Theodore N. Barnsdall proposed a 100-mile-long transmission pipeline from the western terminus of the Caney River Gas Company's pipeline, located about ten miles south of Tulsa, to Oklahoma City. Branch lines would serve Shawnee and Guthrie.

Once financing was assured, the four pioneers founded Oklahoma Natural Gas Company (ONG) on October 12, 1906, and quickly secured a twenty-year charter from Oklahoma Territory. Flynn was elected president; R.H. Bartlett was elected secretary and treasurer; and Ames was named assistant secretary and treasurer. The pipeline was built, and on December 28, 1907, Oklahoma City received its first delivery of natural gas. In 1917 ONG entered the distribution business when it began selling natural gas to retail customers and began an aggressive program to acquire local natural gas distributorships.

On July 31, 1926, the organization moved its corporate headquarters

A showpiece in downtown Tulsa, ONEOK Plaza is the headquarters for ONEOK Inc.

from Oklahoma City to Tulsa, and two years later occupied its General Office Building at Seventh and Boston. ONG continued to expand in the 1920s before undergoing a major reorganization during the Great Depression. With World War II, the firm quickly switched to a wartime economy. Its expansion accelerated, and by 1950 the operation was serving 270,000 customers.

C.C. Ingram, chairman of the board of ONEOK Inc.

In 1980 stockholders voted to change the corporate name from Oklahoma Natural Gas Company to ONEOK Inc. to reflect the company's continuing involvement in many energy businesses.

Today the firm is guided by board chairman C.C. Ingram and president and chief executive officer J.E. Tyree.

ONEOK Inc. has three divisions—Oklahoma Natural Gas Company and ONG Transmission Company (utility) and Energy Companies of ONEOK (nonutility). The corporation has thirteen subsidiaries active in oil and gas exploration and production, pipeline transportation, central cooling and heating, and cold-storage services. Additionally, ONEOK Inc. has interests in sixteen natural gas liquids extraction plants and owns fourteen drilling rigs.

The utility network of natural gas transmission lines stretches from Ardmore to Ponca City and from Stigler to the Panhandle. The utility maintains five underground natural gas storage facilities and has gas reserves estimated at 2.307 trillion cubic feet. Oklahoma Natural serves approximately 650,000 customers, representing a total population of more than two million.

SOUTH WEST PACKAGING, INC.

Formed in February 1972 by Lewis "Lew" L. Narwold, a native of Ohio with an M.B.A. from Harvard; Edward "Ed" D. Hamilton, a native of Marietta and a graduate from the University of Oklahoma; and Richard P. Laster, a native of Iowa and a graduate of the University of Iowa, South West Packaging, Inc., is a leading designer and manufacturer of corrugated containers and displays.

Deciding in mid-life to change from a life-style with the securities of a large, well-respected packaging corporation to that of a spirited entrepreneur, the three founders brought a total of four decades of experience in the packaging industry into the new concern. After spending three weeks planning with attorneys, real estate agents, architects, contractors, machinery salesmen, equipment managers, and bankers, they decided that Oklahoma presented a unique business opportunity for an energetic, aggressive, custom-designed packaging company. Production of attractive, practical, and functional packaging for the needs of individual clients began later that same year.

From its modern plant at 6106 West Sixty-eighth Street South in Tulsa, South West Packaging supplies a myriad of products to the glass, energy, manufacturing, and

South West Packaging's Tulsa plant and corporate headquarters. The facility produces attractive, practical, functional packaging for the needs of individual clients by utilizing state-of-the-art equipment.

From left to right: Edward D. Hamilton, Lewis L. Narwold, and Richard P. Laster, the three founders of South West Packaging, Inc.

consumer goods industries. Utilizing state-of-the-art equipment, the firm provides packaging for every use from bulk shipping to point-of-purchase display.

The experience of building the business and developing lasting relationships with suppliers and customers was gratifying for all three founders. After doubling its dollar sales volume for four consecutive years, South West Packaging opened another plant at 1101 South Metropolitan Avenue in Oklahoma City in 1975. While the Tulsa facility is solely responsible for manufacturing the corrugated materials used by the company, both plants have equal container-production facilities.

In addition to manufacturing the container products, South West Packaging maintains its own fleet of tractor-trailers and diesel trucks—

which along with available railway transportation ensures dependable customer deliveries. With its policy of careful attention to the marketplace and the needs of individual customers, within a decade and a half the firm had become one of the largest custom-designed packaging manufacturers in the Southwest. Under the direction of Narwold, who serves as president and chief executive officer; Hamilton, vice-president of the firm's marketing program; and Laster, vice-president of the procurement and manufacturing, by the mid-1980s South West Packaging had expanded its network of outlets throughout Oklahoma, Kansas, Arkansas, Texas, and Missouri; increased its work force from 60 to 185 employees; and expanded its plant space from 125,000 square feet to 225,000 square feet.

All three founders agree that this tremendous growth would not have been possible without excellent suppliers and a tremendous number of loyal customers. When asked where South West Packaging would go from here, Narwold replied, "Wherever our people will take us!"

TELEX CORPORATION

The Telex Corporation was established by Allen Hempel in October 1936, when he developed the first portable electronic hearing aid. He called his enterprise Telex Products Company. From its modest beginning in the Hempel basement, Telex grew rapidly and established an international reputation in hearing aid technology in the late 1930s. The firm was incorporated as Telex Products Company in Minnesota in 1940 and, at about the same time, moved into its own building in suburban St. Paul. With American entry into World War II, Telex's expertise in miniature electronics was a valuable asset, and the company produced miniature electronic transceivers and other devices for the war effort. After the war the firm changed its name to Telex, Inc., and continued expanding its product line beyond hearing aids into audio devices, head sets, and other electronic products.

In 1959, when the corporation went public, revenues were $4.5 million. The additional capital resources allowed the company to grow through internal development and the acquisition of other related business lines.

During 1959 Telex entered the data-processing marketplace by creating its Data Systems Division, which developed a then-revolutionary computer memory storage device—the fixed-disk memory. In 1961 Telex also entered the computer printer marketplace. The large capital requirements of this expanding market could not be supported by the firm and, therefore, this entity was spun off in 1962. Each shareholder of Telex received a share of a new company, now known as Dataproducts Corporation. That company has continued to grow and prosper and today is a leader in computer printer technology.

In March 1962 Telex acquired Midwestern Instruments, Inc., of Tulsa, Oklahoma, and had combined revenues of approximately thirty million dollars in its fiscal year ending March 31, 1962. After the acquisition the corporate headquarters was moved to Tulsa, and the company

was reincorporated in Delaware. Midwestern was founded in 1950 by M.E. Morrow and E.J. Handley as a geophysical exploration company and also developed a line of galvanometer recording instruments, which it sold to the seismic industry. Midwestern diversified its business in the mid-1950s by introducing the first commercial torque motors and servo valves under a license from the Massachusetts Institute of Technology. These products were used in process control, automatic machine tools, and, later, in aircraft control systems. Simultaneously, the first tape recorder for the geophysical industry was developed internally. The tape recorder program was augmented through the acquisition of Magnecord, which had been acquired in 1956. Magnecord had developed the world's first commercial tape recorder shortly after World War II. The combined technology base enabled the company to expand from analog recorders to digital recorders sold to other computer manufacturers.

Thus, since 1962, the diversity of Telex has been defined by its dual roots. The hearing aids and other acoustical and electronic communications products in Minnesota grew to become Telex Communications, Inc., while the tape and other recording products in Oklahoma grew to become Telex Computer Products, Inc.

The growth of Telex was not all smooth sailing. By 1965 the company was in need of additional capital. Revenues had decreased to about twenty-six million dollars. The additional capital was provided by Roger M. Wheeler, who assumed the leadership of the firm. Wheeler further strengthened the company's management by bringing back Stephen J. Jatras, who joined Midwestern in 1952 from MIT, and was vice-president of engineering when he left in 1956 to join Lockheed Corporation. Jatras became president of Telex in April 1966 and chairman of the board in 1981.

Beginning in 1966, the Midwestern digital tape drives were adapted to

interface with IBM mainframes and, after initial orders from Du Pont and Lockheed, the business grew. As the computer product business grew, the entity's name was changed in 1970 from Midwestern Instruments, Inc., to Telex Computer Products, Inc. The growth in computer tape drives was accompanied by growth in other computer peripherals, such as disk drives, printers, and memories.

The computer business was, in the early 1970s, primarily a lease business. User customers would lease the equipment which, due to its technical complexity, required readily accessible maintenance. To meet such customer needs, Telex Computer Products established an extensive marketing and field service force in the major cities, which grew with the business until it spanned the nation, Canada, and Western Europe.

By 1973 Telex's rapid growth sputtered as the computer peripheral marketplace changed dramatically. As lease revenues dropped, Telex Computer Products retrenched, while the communications segment continued to grow and contribute needed cash to sustain the company through its difficulties.

In 1976, with a field force in place, Telex was actively seeking additional products. An opportunity arose to acquire the assets of Terminal Communications in Raleigh, North Carolina, from United Technologies Corporation. Although Telex was then recovering, with revenues of $106 million, it rapidly took advantage of the opportunity and made the acquisition in December 1976, with the support of the Continental Illinois National Bank and Trust Company of Chicago, Telex's bank for many years.

Thus, Telex Computer Products embarked in a new direction—the computer terminal marketplace. As the peripheral business continued to shrink, by contrast, the terminal business grew. The small entity, which in 1976 produced some 4,000 terminals, controllers, and printers per year, grew steadily. Ten years later the Communication Products Division was producing approximately 15,000 units per month.

Telex Communications also expanded its business lines by internal development and acquisitions under the leadership of Ansel Kleiman, currently the chairman of the board of Telex Communications, Inc., who had joined the company in 1964. Hy-Gain antennae were added in 1978. Turner microphones were acquired in 1979 to complement the head sets and other acoustic products. In 1982 the Caramate slide projectors and audiovisual displays were acquired from The Singer Company.

Having known adversity, Telex carefully concentrated on its business and grew internally. George L. Bragg joined the firm in November 1981 as president of Telex Computer Products, Inc., and continued the momentum of growth. By March 31, 1984, Telex had grown to a business with $325 million in revenues. When Raytheon Company announced in May 1984 that it was withdrawing from the terminal business, Telex moved with great speed to acquire

the business of that entity. This nearly doubled Telex revenues and added a line of airline reservation terminals, as well as an increased international scope. The original entity was integrated into Telex Computer Products' operations and many functions moved to Tulsa.

In December 1985 Telex, through yet another acquisition, added telephone private branch exchange (PBX) product lines to its electronic and computer offerings. This is also being integrated into Telex Computer Products, with a resultant increase in Tulsa employment.

Fifty years since its beginning, Telex still manufactures hearing aids, even though one would be hard pressed to identify the similarity between the bulky vacuum tube devices, although then revolutionary, with the adaptive compression, transceiver devices that are hidden in or behind the ear today. Most of Telex's products today were undreamed of at its beginning, just as the electronic data-processing industry that Telex serves has changed remarkably over the forty years of its existence.

The Telex Corporation maintains its world headquarters in Tulsa, together with the headquarters of its largest subsidiary, Telex Computer Products, Inc. Tulsa is also the home of three of Telex Computer Products' manufacturing divisions: the OEM Division, which continues to supply innovative digital tape drives to the computer industry; the Systems Products Division, which manufactures intelligent work stations; and the Service Support Division, which rebuilds and refurbishes Telex's leased products. In early 1986 Telex had about $750 million in annual revenues with excellent earnings and the potential for future growth. Of some 7,300 employees worldwide, Telex employs 1,450 in Oklahoma.

From its roots in the heartland of America to its reach across the world serving modern industry, Telex has sought to provide quality products and excellent services to improve communications and productivity for its customers worldwide.

Telex is located at 6422 East Forty-first Street, Tulsa.

BAPTIST MEDICAL CENTER OF OKLAHOMA

Baptist Memorial Hospital was founded on April 15, 1959, as a nonsectarian, nonprofit organization of the Baptist General Convention of the State of Oklahoma, and was Oklahoma City's first hospital located outside the downtown area.

For decades the idea of a Baptist hospital had been in the forefront of future planning for Oklahoma's Baptist General Convention, and in 1946 Dr. Andrew Potter—executive secretary/treasurer of the organization—initiated the fund-raising drive that resulted in the construction of the medical institution. Initially, consideration was given to purchasing an older hospital and remodeling it; however, after a thorough study it was decided in 1952 to construct an entirely new facility on a 62-acre site in far northwest Oklahoma City.

Following Potter's death the planning and fund raising continued under Dr. T.B. Lackey, Dr. H.H. Hobbs, Dr. Auguie Henry, the Reverend Anson Justice, United States Senator Robert S. Kerr, Dr. M.E. Ramay, Bryce Twitty, Judge W.R. Wallace, R.A. Young, and former Governor Raymond Gary. Mr. and Mrs. LeRoy Smith donated a portion of the land, and the remaining sixty-two acres were purchased for $260,000. In 1955 the first public fund drive for a hospital in Oklahoma raised one million dollars through an extensive Oklahoma County-wide fund-raising drive, and the Baptist General Convention was able to match these gifts with Oklahoma's Baptist churches raising the money.

Constructed on Oklahoma City's highest point, Baptist Memorial Hospital initially contained 188 patient beds, a maternity ward, laboratory, pediatrics unit, physical therapy area, diagnostic section, emergency room, and surgery unit. John Hendricks administered the facility until 1960, when he was succeeded by James L. Henry. That same year the institution received full accreditation by the Joint Commission on Accreditation of Hospitals; the Women's Auxiliary was formed; and ground-

Baptist Medical Center of Oklahoma.

breaking was held for a four-story Doctors' Medical Building, which was constructed by the Baptist Laymen's Corporation. Henry G. Bennett, Jr., M.D., was appointed to the medical staff for which he served as chief of staff until his death in December 1984.

Within three years of its opening, Baptist Memorial Hospital was operating at 93-percent capacity. To meet the continued demand, in 1962 Senator Kerr headed a fund-raising effort to finance a $2-million Phase II building program. Completed in July 1965, Phase II increased the facility's patient bed count to 376 and added an Intensive Care Unit, a Coronary Care Unit, a radioisotope laboratory, and an additional six stories to the Doctors' Medical Building.

The institution served a wide-ranging area with more than 27 percent of its patients coming from outside the Oklahoma City metropolitan area. Before the close of the 1960s the hospital's occupancy had again passed the 90-percent level. To accommodate the increased patient load, Baptist officials launched Phase III, which was financed by the sale of tax-exempt bonds. With the beginning of Phase III in 1972, Baptist

Memorial Hospital's name was changed to Baptist Medical Center of Oklahoma to more accurately reflect the wide range of health care services it offered. When completed in 1975, Phase III raised the total of patient beds to 563, almost three times the original capacity, and renovated 40 percent of the original structure. As part of its expanded operations, the facility opened Oklahoma's first adult burn center in 1975.

Baptist Medical Center concluded its affiliation with the Baptist General Convention in 1978 and became an independent, nonprofit corporation. At the same time three affiliate corporations were formed to include ProHealth, a for-profit company offering management and shared services to other health care institutions; Baptist Medical Center of Oklahoma Foundation, a fund-raising organization to augment the provision of services and equipment normally financed through patient-care revenue; and Medicol, a medical collection service. Five years later, in 1983, the Oklahoma Health Care Corporation was formed as a parent organization.

Also that year the Oklahoma Ambulatory Care Corporation, Oklahoma Health Care Realty Corporation, and the Oklahoma Heart Center, Inc., were formed. The creation of this health care system provided a comprehensive approach to health problems by offering alternative health delivery programs such as home health care, ambulatory diagnostic and treatment centers, joint ventures with physicians, and preferred provider organizations. In addition, Baptist's Cancer Center of the Southwest was established, providing a comprehensive approach to the treatment of cancer for patients and their families.

Costing $3.5 million, the James Paul Linn Tower was dedicated in 1983 and added three stories to the existing Special Care Tower. In May 1984 the Oklahoma Heart Center was dedicated. Under the direction of Nazih Zuhdi, M.D., and Christiaan Barnard, M.D., Ph.D., the facility

When dedicated in 1983, the James Paul Linn Tower added three stories to the existing Special Care Tower of Baptist Medical Center of Oklahoma.

was designed to promote the advancement of medical science related to the prevention and diagnosis of and the rehabilitation from diseases of the heart and circulatory system. In March 1985 the state's first heart

Nazih Zuhdi, M.D. (left), chairman of the Oklahoma Heart Center at Baptist Medical Center, and Christiaan Barnard, M.D., Ph.D., scientist in residence at the center. Both men are internationally recognized pioneers in the field of heart transplants.

transplant was performed by Dr. Zuhdi, and in May of that year the nation's sixth "piggyback" heterotopic heart transplant was completed.

By the mid-1980s the Oklahoma Health Care Corporation could offer an environment wherein the resources of management, technology, and human endeavor could interact with increased flexibility to present quality programs and services that meet the needs of the people of Oklahoma.

DEACONESS HOSPITAL

Associated with The Free Methodist Church of North America, Deaconess Hospital—a nonprofit organization presenting a strong spiritual emphasis—began as the Oklahoma Rescue Home in Guthrie—Oklahoma's territorial and first state capital. It was founded by William M. and Della Jenkins on December 31, 1900, as a home for unmarried mothers. At the time William Jenkins was secretary of Oklahoma Territory; however, four months after the founding of Deaconess, he was appointed territorial governor. His wife, Della, personally raised $1,000 to allow the home to open. She was aided by Lydia Newberry (the grandmother of Dr. Martin Andrews, who later served on the staff and board of directors of Deaconess Hospital), serving as superintendent; Miss Anna L. Witteman, as secretary; and Mrs. Pearl Holmes, as assistant secretary.

For nine years the Home of Re-

Mrs. Pearl Holmes (left) and Miss Anna L. Witteman, two early supporters of the Home of Redeeming Love, not only acted as officers of the organization, but also served as nurses at the facility.

An aerial view of the Home of Redeeming Love, 1934. In the center is the two-story, 24-bed maternity hospital. On either side are the facility's original three-story brick buildings.

deeming Love, as the facility was renamed in 1909, operated in Guthrie. In that year the home purchased eighty acres of land at the present location of Deaconess Hospital at 5501 North Portland in Oklahoma City, and within a short time completed its move to an unfurnished temporary wooden structure on the site. Shortly afterward, construction was begun on Deaconess' original three-story brick facility. Financed by local businessmen who donated $12,000 in cash and $11,000 in materials and services, the structure was used until 1972.

Although the first building was completed in September 1910, at that time the closest telephone was a mile away and there was no electricity available. Four years later another three-story brick structure was built on the property; it also continued in service until 1972. In 1931 a two-story, 24-bed facility, which served as a maternity unit, was added to the complex. The initial concept of the Home of Redeeming Love was altered in 1944, and the hospital was opened to the public for health care. Two years later the general health care portion of the facility was renamed Deaconess Hospital. The name Home of Redeeming Love

was retained for the unwed mother mission, which continued to occupy the two original brick buildings. Individual budgeting and auditing procedures were established for the now-separate institutions; however, they were administered by the same board of directors.

Within a decade of its creation, Deaconess Hospital had outgrown its facilities. In 1955 the Anna L. Witteman Addition was added to the south of the original hospital building, and the old structure was remodeled and reequipped. When the expansion was completed new medical, surgical, and obstetrical facilities were added and the number of patient beds increased from twenty-four to forty. In 1959 another expansion program added the Emergency Wing, erected on the west of the hospital building, which contained two emergency units. At the same time the bed count was raised to forty-four.

As Oklahoma City's residential area moved to the northwest, Deaconess continued to grow. Almost as

The modern-day Deaconess Hospital. On the right is the Butterfield Wing, completed in 1982, and on the left is the state's first outpatient surgical care unit.

soon as the 1959 improvements were completed, another expansion was necessary. The first phase of the new Deaconess Hospital, containing sixty-six beds, was completed in 1964 at a cost of $1.6 million. At that time the old structure was renamed the Annex. The total capacity of the Annex and the new hospital was 109 beds, plus a five-bed cardiac intensive care unit, and twenty-two bassinets. In 1971 two additional floors were added at a cost of $2.68 million.

The following year the Home of Redeeming Love underwent a $545,000 expansion program that provided a new facility with private suites for the patients and expanded the facility's social service activities. The expansion allowed accredited secondary-level educational programs to be initiated. With this growth the home became the state's only full-service residential facility for unwed mothers, utilizing modern prenatal inpatient training.

In addition, Deaconess produced several medical firsts for the region. In April 1965 it opened the metropolitan area's earliest Intensive Care Unit. It also organized the state's first Outpatient Surgical Facility, Lifeline Emergency Response System, and Daylight X-ray process, as well as Oklahoma City's initial system of immediate computerized interpretations of electrocardiograms and a PRIDE (Parents Responding to Infant Death Experience) Unit.

Deaconess also supports a sister hospital, Deaconess Hospital of Nundu, Zaire, in Africa. Dedicated in 1984, the African facility offers medical care to the general population. For more than 100,000 people in a 100-mile radius it is the only medical care available.

In 1980 work began on another expansion phase, the Butterfield Wing, named for Ralph E. Butterfield, who served as the hospital's administrator

Ralph E. and Gladys Butterfield, for whom the Butterfield Wing of the hospital was named. Ralph served as Deaconess Hospital's administrator for twenty-seven years, and Gladys was superintendent of the Home of Redeeming Love for twenty-two years.

for twenty-seven years, and Gladys Butterfield, the longtime superintendent of the Home of Redeeming Love. Costing more than $7.8 million and containing $1.8 million worth of new equipment, the Butterfield Wing was opened in June 1982. The 63,200-square-foot project increased Deaconess' total of adult and pediatric beds to 250 and new-born bassinets to forty.

As the area's family practice hospital, Deaconess blends its high-touch, individualized care with the latest state-of-the-art technology. Under current administrator Melvin J. Spencer, attorney and formerly general counsel and past chairman of the Oklahoma Hospital Association, the hospital offers a full range of both noninvasive and invasive cardiovascular testing by means of highly sophisticated real-time B-mode ultrasound imaging with gaited, pulsed doppler and in its new angiography

suite. Nuclear diagnostic capabilities, full-body CT scanning, and a sophisticated array of the latest diagnostic and surgical technology and equipment are available. In May 1985 the world's first fully functioning substitute bladder was successfully created at Deaconess Hospital. Deaconess remains on the leading edge of health care technology and service.

NORICK BROTHERS, INC.

When the capital of Oklahoma was moved from Guthrie to Oklahoma City in 1910, it had more horses and buggies on its streets than automobiles, although within a decade the "automobile age" would sweep the nation. That same year George A. "Lon" Norick mortgaged his home, purchased two small hand-fed presses, a hand cutter, and a limited supply of type, and opened a print shop. Once he had secured the necessary equipment, the entrepreneur convinced his brother, Henry, to quit his fifteen-dollar-a-week job and become a printer's devil in his enterprise for three dollars a week. Henry eventually purchased a one-third interest in the company.

The two men first conducted business in a small frame structure next to a blacksmith shop. Only a thin wall separated the two operations, and sometimes when the smithy was shoeing a horse or mule, the animal would kick the wall and send a shower of plaster and dust falling on the printers. However, this was a small problem. Of greater concern was the multitude of small print shops that appeared in the capital city. The abundance of such firms and the limited amount of work available made competition keen. Often the Norick brothers had to mortgage their equipment in order to pay creditors. On other occasions they had to suspend operations and take a job with the Oklahoma Publishing Company until they accumulated sufficient capital to reopen.

The tremendous competition forced the partners to be innovative. They realized that for the business to survive it would have to specialize. The question was, what to specialize in?

While the brothers were pondering the problem, George purchased an automobile in 1917 and discovered that the booming automobile industry lacked a uniform accounting system to handle the upsurge in sales.

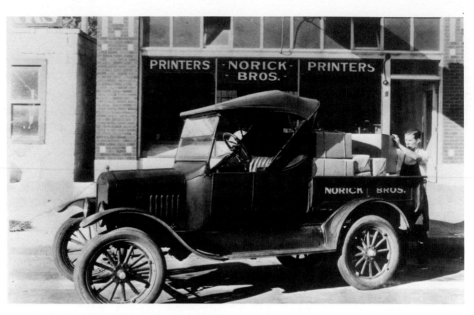

This Model T Ford was one of Norick Brothers' early delivery trucks.

With the question of what to specialize in answered, George and Henry in the following weeks designed a simple form that could be adopted by all automobile agencies. Several months passed before the first forms were printed.

Deciding to market the forms statewide before any competition could develop, the Noricks mailed samples to Oklahoma's 252 Ford dealers. Realizing that many dealers did not bother with records of any kind and therefore might not recognize the potential of their product, George and Henry spent several anxious days awaiting the results. Their fears were unnecessary, for within three days they received their first order. With more following the next

day, it became obvious that the product had filled a vital need. Within a short time the demand for Norick Brothers forms made it imperative to expand the company's operations.

Initially, Norick Brothers was strictly an Oklahoma enterprise—but after officials of Ford Motor Company took notice of the forms and began encouraging its dealers nationwide to adopt the system, orders poured in from across the nation. At the same time, Norick Brothers initiated an aggressive publicity campaign to encourage adoption of the forms by other automobile dealers. The mail campaign was augmented by travel-

The headquarters of Norick Brothers, Inc., is located at 3909 Northwest Thirty-sixth Street in Oklahoma City.

ing salesmen who visited local automobile dealers and demonstrated the advantages of the Norick system.

The major drawback the firm's salesmen reported was the scarcity of adequately trained automobile accountants. Rather than miss the opportunity to acquire a new customer because that particular dealer did not have an efficient accountant, Norick Brothers employed six traveling accountants who offered free training to any bookkeeper whose employer utilized the Norick system. Another endeavor, implemented in 1922 as part of the company's continual training program, was the publication of *Service News,* an automobile dealership periodical that explained new additions to the system and answered common questions. *Service News,* which changed its name to *Motor Dealer,* grew to more than 50,000 subscribers before it was discontinued in 1955.

By the time George retired because of ill health in 1936, Norick Brothers was marketing forms to handle nearly all makes of American and foreign automobiles sold in the United States. Under Henry's direction the organization continued to expand. A series of branch offices and

manufacturing plants were opened, and by the mid-1980s the company had facilities in North Las Vegas, Nevada; Chicago, Illinois; and Kings Mountain, North Carolina, as well as its corporate headquarters in Oklahoma City. To accommodate the extending network of customers, Norick Brothers organized a private trucking system that allowed rapid delivery of orders throughout the country.

In 1953 the firm was reorganized as Norick Brothers, Inc., with Henry Norick retaining the presidency to serve the new corporation. Three of his children—James H. Norick, Marjorie Norick, and Dorothy Norick Patton—were elected vice-presidents, and another daughter, Francis Norick Lilly, was named secretary. Six years later James H. Norick became president, serving in that capacity until 1980, when he was made chairman of the board and his son, Ronald Norick, assumed the position. During his tenure as president of the corporation, James H. Norick also served as mayor of Oklahoma City from 1959 until 1963, and from 1967 until 1971.

In 1959 Norick Brothers, Inc., moved into its current headquarters

The firm's management are shown attending the 1972 NADA convention. Pictured, from left: J.R. McConnell, director of marketing; Ron Norick, vice-president of production; Henry Norick, chairman of the board; James H. Norick, president; and Gerald Roll, sales manager.

at 3909 Northwest Thirty-sixth Street in Oklahoma City. With the adoption of computers for record keeping by many automobile dealers, the firm created Norick Data Systems in 1975 to meet the new demand. The new software was produced in a plant just to the north of the corporate offices.

By the mid-1980s, under the direction of Ronald Norick, the company—whose uniform system of accounting for automobile dealers remains the most widely adopted program among the nation's car dealers—was marketing its automobile accounting forms in all fifty states and several foreign countries. In addition, Norick Data Systems expanded to provide insurance rating systems, which are marketed throughout the Southwest.

Three hundred of the firm's 450 employees work at the Oklahoma City facility; the remainder are spread around the nation.

PRESBYTERIAN HOSPITAL

The roots of Oklahoma City's Presbyterian Hospital were planted in 1910, when Dr. Foster K. Camp and his wife, Janet, purchased the newly established eight-bed St. Luke's Sanitarium. They renamed the institution Wesley Hospital in honor of Mrs. Camp's alma mater, Wesley Hospital Training School for Nurses in Chicago, Illinois.

On December 1, 1910, the new proprietors relocated Wesley Hospital from the ninth floor of the Campbell Building to the eleventh and twelfth floors of the Herskowitz Building on the corner of Broadway and Grand (now Sheridan) avenues near downtown Oklahoma City. The bed capacity of the facility was increased by three times in this move. Within a year the hospital again was relocated—this time to the southwest corner of Northwest Twelfth Street and Harvey Avenue, where it remained for the next sixty-three years.

In 1912 Wesley Training School for Nurses was established as a three-year diploma-granting school under the direction of Janet Camp, a graduate nurse. It remained in operation until 1954.

At the close of World War I six physicians who had been associated with the staff of Wesley Hospital before entering the military—Drs. A.L. Blesh; W.W. Rucks, Sr.; J.C. Mraz; D.D. Paulus; W.H. Bailey; and M.E. Stout—returned to Oklahoma City and organized Oklahoma City Clinic. Because their practice often required the hospitalization of patients, they purchased Wesley Hospital from Dr. Camp. The transfer was completed in October 1919. Shortly afterward Dr. Stout withdrew to resume private practice and was replaced in the partnership by Dr. J.C. McDonald. The clinic maintained offices in the Patterson Building in downtown Oklahoma City until 1927, when it moved across the street north of Wesley Hospital.

From its formation Wesley Hospital had affiliations with the University of Oklahoma School of Medicine as a teaching hospital, with the

founding clinic physicians also members of the faculty. Through this relationship the institution provided intern and residency programs in surgery, internal medicine, gynecology, obstetrics, and radiology. It was the first privately owned hospital in the southwestern United States to receive accreditation for its affiliated teaching programs. The high standards of care adopted by Wesley Hospital attracted the notice of physicians from throughout the state, and as more patients were referred to the facility, numerous expansions were undertaken. Major renovations were completed in 1927, 1929, 1930, 1947, 1951, 1960, and 1964.

In 1961 ownership of the hospital was acquired by the Wesley Hospital Foundation, which had been created for the purpose of promoting charitable, scientific, and educational activities at the institution. Three years later the foundation merged with the Washita Presbytery of the United Presbyterian Church, and the hospital's name was changed to Presbyterian Medical Center of Oklahoma, Inc. This corporate title remained until 1973, when it was changed to Presbyterian Hospital, Inc. These name changes heralded the construction of a new 407-bed facility located in the Oklahoma Health Center at Thirteenth Street and Lincoln Boulevard.

These six physicians formed Oklahoma's first group practice in 1919 and bought Wesley Hospital from Dr. and Mrs. Foster K. Camp. They are (left to right) Dr. W.H. Bailey, pathologist; Dr. A.L. Blesh, surgeon; Dr. D.D. Paulus, internist; Dr. W.W. Rucks, Sr., internist; Dr. M.E. Stout, surgeon; and Dr. J.C. Mraz, urologist. Dr. Stout only stayed with the group a short while before opening a private practice and later built the Oklahoma City Polyclinic Hospital in the 200 block of Northwest Thirteenth Street (now Doctors' General Hospital).

During the mid-1960s the idea of a medical complex was developed. Centered around the University of Oklahoma's School of Medicine and other nearby health care establishments south of the state capitol on Lincoln Boulevard and Thirteenth Street, the planners envisioned one of the most comprehensive medical care and teaching complexes in the country. At the same time, in 1965 Dr. James L. Dennis—the director of the University of Oklahoma's Medical School Center—requested that the directors of Presbyterian Hospital consider relocating the facility near the proposed complex.

In response, a planning committee was appointed. Its members were Drs. Robert C. Lawson, R.B. Carl, Ted Clemens, William L. Hughes, James P. Luton, Edward R. Munnell, and Stanton L. Young. After carefully studying the request, the sixty-eight committee members

Today Presbyterian Hospital can spaciously accommodate hundreds of patients, and visitors are greeted not by a business street scene but a tranquil lake at the hospital's front entrance. Photo by Ric Moore

recommended that Presbyterian Hospital agree to the move and construct a $36-million private, acute care facility in what became the Oklahoma Health Center complex. Construction began in 1972 and on December 1, 1974, the 500 physician staff members admitted the first patients to the new Presbyterian Hospital.

The institution contained 407 beds, as well as thirty-one nursery bassinets, housed in two separate buildings. It also provided thirteen surgery suites, an intensive care unit, a coronary care unit, and complete laboratory services.

The move proved to be a success, and within a year the hospital opened a pulmonary functions laboratory and an electroencephalography laboratory and expanded its patient service and training programs. In addition, an agreement was reached with the Oklahoma Medical Research Foundation that called for Presbyterian Hospital to provide housing for the foundation's inpatients. With the expansion of services and patients, the institution's staff was doubled a year after completing the move.

In 1976 Presbyterian Hospital opened a Sleep Disorders Center; it is one of only twenty-five accredited centers in the nation. Three years later a Genetics Diagnostic Center was opened to offer genetic diagnosis, counseling, and education. In 1982 another $6-million expansion program was launched.

By the mid-1980s Presbyterian Hospital offered services in endocrinology, urology, general medicine, general surgery, cardiovascular and thoracic surgery, microsurgery, neurosurgery, neurology, nuclear medicine, obstetrics/gynecology, oncology, orthopedics, pediatrics, plastic surgery, ophthalmology, otorhinolaryngology, special procedures, X-ray,

In 1910 Wesley Hospital occupied the eleventh and twelfth floors of the Herskowitz Building at Grand (now Sheridan) and Broadway. Fortunately, elevator service was available for visitors around the clock.

gastroenterology, and pulmonary medicine.

Today the state's most comprehensive cancer treatment and research program is available through Presbyterian Hospital. And the hospital is the site of one of only three full-scale brain rehabilitation programs in the world. Presbyterian Hospital also operates chemical dependency treatment centers in three states and family counseling centers in five Oklahoma communities.

The hospital provides its services on a nondenominational basis and is affiliated by covenant with the Indian Nations Presbytery of the United Presbyterian Church (USA). An ecumenical chaplaincy program provides for the patients and their families' spiritual needs as well as a training center for ministers.

Presbyterian Hospital was recently acquired by Hospital Corporation of America (HCA), the world's largest health care provider. HCA Oklahoma City Division provides management services to ten Oklahoma hospitals

and 150 contract services to more than fifty hospitals and clinics statewide. In addition to a staff of 1,700 by the mid-1980s, the facility is served by more than 300 volunteer auxiliary members. The 2,000-plus people involved in providing Oklahomans with the most up-to-date health care available also are devoted to making Presbyterian Hospital a "Patient People Place."

AT&T NETWORK SYSTEMS

The golden anniversary of Oklahoma statehood in 1957 marked the beginning of AT&T's Network Systems', a division of AT&T Technologies, major involvement in the state's economy. Although for years citizens of Oklahoma had relied on AT&T equipment for their telephone service, that year plans were announced for the development of a large facility at 7725 West Reno Avenue in Oklahoma City. A groundbreaking ceremony for the Western Electric plant (a subsidiary of AT&T) was held on December 10, 1958; however, so that adequately trained personnel could be available upon completion, Joseph T. West, the plant's first general manager, organized a pilot plant at Northwest Thirty-ninth Street and Tulsa Avenue.

Housed in a 1.3-million-square-foot building covering more than thirty acres, the Oklahoma City Works was dedicated on May 24, 1960. A state-of-the-art facility when opened, the plant specialized in the construction of electromechanical crossbar switching systems used in automated telephone dialing. During the 1960s nearly 10,000 employees produced in excess of 40,000 crossbar frames annually.

In 1965 the Oklahoma City Works introduced its initial Electronic Switching System (ESS™), designed for large metropolitan areas, and within three years the plant was the highest-volume producer of this equipment in the nation. An ESS system for suburban offices went into production seven years later. The ESS systems revolutionized the American telephone industry and allowed phone companies nationwide to offer such custom-calling features as call waiting, call forwarding, and three-way dialing.

Testers Jerry Buckles (left) and Frank Humphreville put a 5ESS™ office through final system testing at AT&T's Oklahoma City facility. Because lives literally depend on the telephone network, 5ESS™ switches must meet the most stringent reliability standards: fewer than five minutes of downtime in forty years of operation.

Also in 1972 the Oklahoma City Works initiated production of the Remreed switching equipment. The Remreed equipment allowed existing ESS equipment to significantly increase the number of calls that could be handled in a small space.

The ESS systems continued to be expanded in the following years. In 1977 the 1AESS, 2BESS, and the 3ESS, all advanced switching processors, were added to the product line. The 5ESS™ was put into production in 1982. A fully digital communications switching system, the 5ESS is a highly sophisticated instrument designed with a modular architecture, which allows the system to grow from a few hundred telephone lines to a more than 100,000-line capacity.

In March 1984 the Oklahoma City Works introduced its 3B computer family for the general market. The 3B family consisted of five separate systems—the 3B2, 3B5, 3B20S, 3B20A, and the 3B20D. The 3B2 small business computer can connect as many as eighteen terminals at a time, while the 3B5, a mid-range system, can handle sixty-four individual users and offers increased memory storage. The 3B20S is the workhorse of the 3B20 system and is designed to support the heavy-duty needs of data centers, office-service organizations, developers, and manufacturing

The AT&T Network Systems plant, located in Oklahoma City, contains 1.3 million square feet of floor space for manufacturing telephone network switching equipment and computers.

enterprises. An enhanced 3B20S, the 3B20A offers increased speed and capability. The 3B20D, actually two 3B20Ss, is the controlling device for the 5ESS system. Utilizing the most advanced semiconductor memory available, the 3B family allows high-speed, reliable, network interface and automatic calling units for dial access.

By the mid-1980s AT&T Network System's Oklahoma City Works had approximately 6,700 employees. Focusing on the production of ESS and the 3B family of computers, the facility's basic mission is to provide network telephone systems and computers with the highest quality at the lowest cost.

READING & BATES CORPORATION

A multifaceted energy organization, Reading & Bates Corporation is the parent of Reading & Bates Drilling Co., Reading & Bates Petroleum Co., and Resources Conservation Company. Originally a land-based drilling concern formed by J.W. Bates, Sr., and George M. Reading, Reading & Bates Corporation currently is a leader in offshore drilling industry and is also engaged in oil and gas exploration and production and water systems management.

Bates Sr. entered the oil business in 1910 as a teamster in California, and by 1914 had become a drilling superintendent for a predecessor of Shell Oil Company in the mid-continent region. Reading entered the oil business as a trucking operator in Texas, where he and Bates Sr. became friends. Deciding to pool their finances and launch their own drilling venture, in 1937 they formed the nucleus of Reading & Bates Corporation.

After graduating from Dartmouth College in 1941 and serving in the Navy during World War II, J.W.

Bates, Jr., joined with Clyde Baker in 1946 to form B&B Drilling Company, which merged with Reading & Bates in 1949. Two years later another Oklahoma oil man, Charles E. Thornton, joined Reading & Bates.

In 1955 Bates Jr. and Thornton toured drilling operations in the Gulf of Mexico offshore Louisiana and became convinced that the future of the corporation was in a similar endeavor. As a result, that same year they organized Reading & Bates Offshore Drilling Company (later renamed Reading & Bates) and commissioned the building of two drilling tenders, the *J.W. Bates* and the *George M. Reading.* At that time the two units represented the most advanced technology in the new offshore drilling industry. Throughout the following decades Reading & Bates has maintained its technological advances by designing and purchasing a modern fleet of offshore drilling units—including cantilever jackups, drill ships, and severe environmental semisubmersibles. Examples of the company's technologically modern fleet are the semisubmersible *M.G. Hulme Jr.* and the cantilever jackup *Randolph Yost.* The *Hulme,* a severe environment semisubmersible, can work in water depths of 2,250 feet and drill

to depths of 25,000 feet. Its air-conditioned quarters can accommodate 104 crewmen. The *Yost,* which can accommodate 94 men, is rated to drill in water depths of 300 feet. Its cantilever feature allows the drilling equipment to be extended onto or over an existing platform adjacent to the jackup.

Bates Jr. has been the chief executive officer of the company since its organization in 1955. His father, who served as an officer and director of the firm from 1955, retired in 1976 and was director emeritus at the time of his death in 1984.

Reading & Bates has drilled in the Gulf of Mexico and in other offshore waters around the world. It is among the world's largest offshore drilling contractors with assets of approximately one billion dollars. The corporate headquarters is located in Tulsa, Oklahoma.

Reading & Bates' semisubmersible, the M.G. Hulme Jr. *was constructed in 1982. The* Hulme *can operate in 65-knot winds and 50-foot waves. Rated for deep-water drilling, the* Hulme *can work in water depths to 2,250 feet and drill to depths of 25,000 feet.*

Together for the 1956 christening of Reading & Bates' first two offshore drilling units were four of the company's founders: (from left) J.W. Bates, Sr., George M. Reading, J.W. Bates, Jr., and C.E. Thornton.

SOUTHWESTERN BELL TELEPHONE

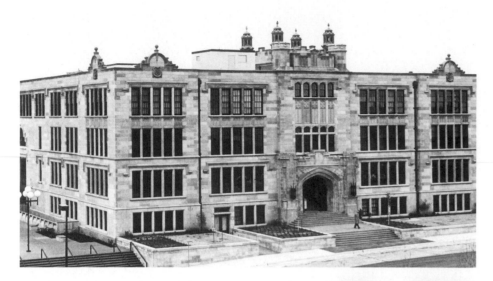

One Bell Central—one of the nation's land-mark historic preservation efforts—houses the headquarters of Southwestern Bell Telephone's Oklahoma operations.

Oklahoma's first telephone conversations were taking place only three years after the invention of the telephone. Telephones were connected at each end of a telegraph line from Fort Sill to Fort Reno, and sometimes the leather-lunged soldiers shouting into the instruments could hear the man at the other end seventy-five miles away. This experiment did not last long, but in 1884 the first full-time telephone connection was built between Fort Reno and the Cheyenne-Arapaho Indian Agency at Darlington, a distance of 1.5 miles.

Two years later the first commercial telephone line was constructed from Tahlequah through Fort Gibson to Muskogee. The Cherokee Council granted authority to the promoters to build the telephone line only after they set up a demonstration line to show the council that the telephone could "speak" Cherokee as well as English.

Long-distance lines grew statewide, but the first telephone exchange in Oklahoma was built in Oklahoma City in 1893 by the Missouri and Kansas Telephone Co. The firm also opened a Guthrie exchange that same year. Then came the organization that was to have the greatest influence on the history of the telephone in Oklahoma—the Arkansas Valley Telephone Co. After successfully completing a Perry to Pawnee line, the firm began expanding service throughout the state. In Feb-

ruary 1902 it became the Pioneer Telephone Company. Two years later Pioneer became a part of the Bell System and acquired all of the Missouri and Kansas Telephone Co.'s properties in Oklahoma. Ten years later its name changed again, this time to Southwestern Bell Telephone.

Then came the Great Depression, followed by World War II. In the eight years after the war the number of telephones in the state increased from 290,000 to 550,000, almost equal to the increase in the first sixty-six years of the industry. Technological advances continued, and in 1952 the first live network television was brought to the state with the installation of microwave relay stations between Dallas, Oklahoma City, and Tulsa. Two years later operators in Oklahoma City began dialing long-distance calls directly to cities throughout the nation, and in 1955 Enid became the first city in Oklahoma and the second in Southwestern

Installation cars belonging to Pioneer Telephone and Telegraph are shown parked in front of the Pioneer Building at Northwest Third Street and Broadway in downtown Oklahoma City in 1913. Southwestern Bell Telephone still uses this building.

Bell's five-state territory where customers could dial their own long-distance calls. More than a decade later, in 1966, Enid became the first city in Southwestern Bell territory to acquire touch-tone service.

By the 1980s Southwestern Bell Telephone's Oklahoma City operations had grown to such an extent that the company was leasing space in several different buildings. The decision was made to centralize operations, and Southwestern Bell purchased Central High School in downtown Oklahoma City. In one of the landmark historic preservation efforts in the nation, Southwestern Bell completely renovated the inside of the structure while maintaining the original external appearance.

Since the Bell System breakup of 1984, Southwestern Bell Telephone has not provided telephones, just the lines to connect them. By the mid-1980s Southwestern Bell served 1,272,451 access lines in 187 cities and towns in Oklahoma. The firm has an annual payroll of $245 million, which is paid to more than 8,000 employees.

MOULDER-OLDHAM COMPANY, INC.

Tulsa's oldest wholesale building-maintenance supply business, Moulder-Oldham Company, Inc., was formed in 1919 by Ethan Moulder and Rahe Oldham—two friends who had served together in the U.S. Army during World War I. They met while undergoing recruit training at Fort Logan, Colorado, became friends, and decided to utilize their experience to open a janitor supply firm when the fighting ended. Released from the military, the partners acquired a small "chicken coop-type" building on West Archer in Tulsa, and began production of a sweeping compound for wood and concrete floors.

Oldham was the firm's salesman. Moulder oversaw the company's only other employee and the production of its single product at that time—floor sweep. As Moulder recalled, the mobilization of the nation for World War I created an awareness for sanitation among most Americans. "They learned to expect clean housing." This change in attitude created a demand for Moulder-Oldham products.

The enterprise continued to grow in the following decades. Floor sweep was supplemented by waxes, polishes, disinfectants, buffers, and carpet sweepers used to clean tile and carpeted floors. Special industrial-strength soaps were developed and paper bathroom products were added to the firm's inventory. With the increased environmental awareness, Moulder-Oldham developed products that could safely be discharged into sewers. In addition, many of the synthetic fabrics used in carpets, drapes, and furniture covers required specialized cleaners that would not harm the material.

Following Rahe Oldham's death in 1954, Ethan Moulder continued to manage the company; he was joined by his former partner's son, Jack Oldham, who remained active with the organization for almost two decades before he died in 1971. Twin brothers G. Gregory Moulder, executive vice-president, and J. Granville Moulder, chief executive officer, pur-

chased their father's company in 1982.

This new management team has continued the philosophy of stocking only quality goods, treating customers honestly, and providing outstanding service. Both partners remain directly involved in sales so they can react immediately to changes in the marketplace, and they aggressively pursue new innovations—such as telephones in all salesmen's cars—to serve their customers more efficiently.

The establishment of regulations on cleanliness has created a multimillion-dollar industry that is highly technical, yet labor intensive. Moulder-Oldham's edge in this market is due to its ability

J. Granville Moulder (left), chief executive officer, and G. Gregory Moulder, executive vice-president, the current management team of Moulder-Oldham Company, Inc.

to reduce customers' overall costs through training and innovative cleaning techniques, and its high level of attention to customers' needs.

By the mid-1980s the Moulders oversaw company operations from a modern 25,000-square-foot plant and office at 216 North Denver, where more than 2,500 cleaning and maintenance products were manufactured and distributed throughout a 35,000-square-mile region in three states.

OKLAHOMA TEACHING HOSPITALS

With an internationally recognized medical staff and outstanding professional personnel, the Oklahoma Teaching Hospitals are recognized as among the premier health care and teaching facilities in the United States. More than 26,000 inpatients and 300,000 outpatients receive treatment annually, and some 500 medical residents and fellows receive all or part of their clinical training at the facilities each year.

Located just south of the state capitol and east of Northeast Thirteenth and Lincoln Boulevard, the Oklahoma Teaching Hospitals include Oklahoma Children's Memorial Hospital, Oklahoma Memorial Hospital, O'Donoghue Rehabilitation Institute, and the Child Study Center.

The Oklahoma Teaching Hospitals are a part of the Oklahoma Health Center, which also includes the University of Oklahoma Health Sciences Center with its Colleges of Medicine, Nursing, Pharmacy, Dentistry, Health, and the Graduate College. As the major adult, children's, and rehabilitative hospitals not only for the College of Medicine but also for all the allied Colleges of the Health Sciences Center, the Oklahoma Teaching Hospitals are responsible for teaching future health providers the important aspects of clinical practice.

In addition, the Oklahoma Teaching Hospitals provide a natural setting for the pursuit of knowledge about disease prevention and treatment. Studies address the real problems of real people who go there for care. Researchers investigate all aspects of health care: the diseases, the illnesses, the injuries, the causes, and the cures. Major areas of research activity include childhood cancer, burn therapy, genetic malformation, organ transplantation, and rehabilitation techniques. Other studies center on the cardiovascular system, hypertension, radiation therapy, lung diseases, and at-risk pregnancies.

The Oklahoma Teaching Hospital's legacy began in 1900 with the establishment of the University of Oklahoma School of Medicine. Some eleven years later a private hospital owned by Dr. J.B. Rolater at 325 Northeast Fourth Street, and an adjoining residence, was leased to the University of Oklahoma Medical School. On October 12, 1911, it was renamed State University Hospital, and began operation with sixty inpatient beds, a dispensary, and a kitchen that was used as a clinical laboratory under the direction of Annette B. Cowles.

On March 21, 1917, the Sixth Oklahoma Legislature appropriated $200,000 for the construction of a hospital and building for the O.U. Medical School on the condition that Oklahoma City sell to the state for $100 the Emergency or Municipal Hospital (formally called Oklahoma City General Hospital or Southwest Postgraduate Hospital) located at the intersection of Stiles Avenue and Third Street. The facilities were to be incorporated into the O.U. Medi-

The MediFlight Oklahoma air ambulance takes off from Oklahoma Children's Memorial.

cal School under the direction of the O.U. board of regents.

Completed in 1919, University Hospital, commonly called "Old Main," contained 57,000 square feet housing 176 inpatient beds. Under the direction of Paul H. Fesler, the facility admitted its first patients on August 1 of that year, and became a charter member of the Oklahoma Hospital Association. The O.U. Medical School then established residencies at University Hospital, and Dr. Raymond L. Murdock was appointed its first resident surgeon.

Following its original construction numerous additions and expansions were made on the Memorial Hospital complex. An outpatient clinic building was constructed in 1951, and a radiology building was completed in 1959.

As the major tertiary care center serving the entire state, the adult facility, now named Oklahoma Memorial Hospital, provides inpatient services for the acute medical needs of adults and newborns as well as outpatient care in more than forty clinics.

Among the specialized services offered at Oklahoma Memorial are comprehensive cancer treatment and

Children's Memorial Hospital before renovation by the Department of Human Services.

rehabilitation including surgery, chemotherapy, radiation therapy, and immunotherapy; kidney transplantation and renal dialysis; pulmonary medicine; a neurosensory program; ultrasound services; and orthopedic surgery. With extensive obstetric services encompassing such specialties as high-risk pregnancy and in-vitro fertilization, Oklahoma Memorial is recognized as the region's major health center for women. The Emergency Medicine and Trauma Center serves as a model for emergency medical services in the state. In addition, because Oklahoma Memorial's comprehensive clinical laboratories are among the most complete available anywhere, specimens from

throughout the world are sent to the facility for examination.

In 1928 another teaching facility, a separate Children's Memorial Hospital with 160 beds, was constructed at the intersection of Kelly Avenue and Northeast Thirteenth Street. Responsibility for the institution was transferred to the Oklahoma Department of Human Services in 1973.

At that time an aggressive expansion program was implemented at a cost of forty-one million dollars. An extension added to the front of the old Children's Memorial Hospital totally changed its appearance, and the core facility was completely reconstructed. Upon completion of the work, the addition was named the Charles M. Bielstein Center. A seven-story annex, the George H. Garrison Tower, was added to the west of the original structure and the Ben H. Nicholson Tower, a five-level addition, was built on the east side.

Providing medical and dental care to patients under twenty-one years of age, Children's Memorial Hospital offers treatment for diseases and abnormalities ranging from ordinary childhood illnesses to more complex and rare medical and surgical problems. Its outstanding programs include a neonatal intensive care unit and transport system, burn center, oncology program, surgery, kidney

Neonatologists care for the smallest and most helpless—premature and critically ill newborns.

dialysis and transplantation, clinical research center, cystic fibrosis center, childhood genetic diseases and genetic counseling program, growth deficiency clinic, birth defects center, cardiology, and cardiac surgery. Additional services include ambulatory surgery, forty outpatient specialty clinics, 24-hour emergency department, a laboratory service capable of the most sophisticated diagnostic procedures, nuclear medicine, ultrasound, and radiology services.

Designed to help ease the fears normally experienced by the young in a medical setting, all programs are geared specifically for children. Equipment and fixtures are scaled to child size, well-stocked playrooms are strategically located throughout the facility, and parents are encouraged to spend as much time as possible with their child. In keeping with this setting, patients are grouped according to age, with wings dedicated to nursery, toddler, preteen, and teenage patients.

A Child Study Center was created by Oklahoma Teaching Hospitals in 1959 as a multidisciplinary unit designed to provide outpatient evaluation and treatment for patients with neurological, developmental, social/emotional, and learning problems. The Child Study Center serves patients from newborns through the age of twenty-one.

Among the Child Study Center's primary services is a comprehensive assessment by a multidisciplinary team of physicians, psychologists, social workers, special-education professionals, and others. Additional services include medical follow-up of problems; social work services for the entire family; a respite aide program for deaf-blind/sensory-impaired, Down's syndrome, and multihandicapped children; and psychoeducational programming of autistic, emotionally disturbed, abused, and language-disordered children. A separate two-story building for the Child Study Center was erected a block east of Children's Memorial Hospital in the fall of 1975, to better

Today's Oklahoma Teaching Hospitals, serving the medical needs of all Oklahomans.

serve both the children and their parents.

With the growth of services offered by Oklahoma Memorial and Children's Memorial hospitals and the construction of a Research Building for the College of Medicine in 1961, plans were formulated for a modern medical complex centered around the two hospitals. By the 1970s actual construction of the complex began. Another upgrading of Children's Memorial Hospital as well as several important additions also were part of the planning. The first major addition took place in 1970 when work began on a $12-million, eight-level hospital structure, named Everett Tower in honor of longtime medical school dean Mark R. Everett. Completed in 1973, it contains 300,000 square feet of space, nine operating suites, patient lounges on each floor, and the largest dietary facility in the state.

Also in 1973, at the same time Children's Memorial Hospital was transferred to the Department of Human Services, control of Memorial Hospital was removed from the University of Oklahoma board of regents and given to University Hospitals and Clinics. Development of the medical complex continued by upgrading the facility's equipment; implementing a sports medicine program; and constructing a ten-unit outpatient kdiney dialysis center, allowing kidney patients to be treated without hospitalization. In 1979 the Everett Tower was renovated to permit expansion in the treatment of heart disease by adding a thirteen-bed coronary care unit. That same year work was started on a new building to house an Emergency Care and Trauma Center and new clinical laboratories as well as a 434-space parking facility, constructed immediately adjacent to the Everett Tower.

In 1974 the Oklahoma Teaching Hospitals implemented a revolution-

ary service—MediFlight of Oklahoma. Serving communities statewide, MediFlight utilizes two helicopters to carry patients whose survival often depends upon rapid transportation to the highly specialized medical treatment facilities available only in a metropolitan area. The service is available to physicians, community hospitals, ambulance services, and law enforcement agencies for stabilizing, treating, and transporting patients to the receiving hospital in Oklahoma City.

Completing the range of services, the Don H. O'Donoghue Rehabilitation Institute opened in 1981 to provide both medical and rehabilitative services to physically disabled children and adults. Named for a pioneering orthopedic surgeon from Oklahoma City, it is a 120-bed multipurpose inpatient and outpatient facility that provides short-range, intermediate medical and rehabilitation services to the physically disabled. Its programs include occupational therapy, orthotics, physical therapy, recreational therapy, respiration therapy, and speech pathology. An important part of the educational aspect of Oklahoma Teaching Hospitals, the Rehabilitation Institute offers frequent clinics on subjects that include the spinal cord, hemophilia, cerebral palsy, urology, myelomeningocele, hand, amputee, orthotics, screening, and neuromuscular care and treatment.

Another unique service is its independent living program. Structured to prepare the handicapped to live independently at home, the program utilizes three self-contained apartments in which clients in the final phase of their rehabilitative treatment practice the activities of daily living while the team evaluates and assists their ability to function independently.

ALEXANDER ENERGY CORPORATION

On March 6, 1980, Bob G. Alexander, a geological engineer with more than a quarter-century of experience, joined Jim L. David, a highly respected geologist, and Ronald T. Riggan, a certified professional landman, to form Alexander Energy Corporation. The firm quickly became a major developer of the Anadarko Basin in Oklahoma and the Arkoma Basin in eastern Oklahoma and western Arkansas. Alexander served as president of the company, while David and Riggan became vice-presidents in charge of exploration and land, respectively. Donna Ports Alexander served as secretary, Jerrel W. Stone as treasurer, and F. Wayne Campbell as chief geologist. Later Alexander's son, Roger, joined the business, thereby representing the fourth generation of his family to be involved in the petroleum industry.

Initially a privately held corporation with its stock divided among its seventeen original employees, the firm managed and developed energy properties held by Towner Petroleum Company. However, in 1981 Alexander Energy went public and discovered the East Binger Field in Caddo County and the East Calumet Field in Canadian County, Oklahoma. The following year the West Cruce Field in Stephens County, Oklahoma, was also discovered.

With this growth came a need for more flexibility. As a result, in September 1983 Alexander Energy terminated its agreement with Towner Petroleum in order to become a fully

Alexander Energy Corporation is a highly motivated group of people with expertise in various disciplines integrated into a small tight organization, and all working in the same direction at the same time. Alexander Energy's management team (left to right): Bob G. Alexander, Jim L. David, David L. Bole, and Ronald T. Riggan.

independent exploration and acquisition company. Three months later the firm acquired Edwards and Leach Oil Company, with a stock value of $3.7 million, as a wholly owned subsidiary. The acquisition, the first of several, increased the company's reserve base and added several potentially productive drilling areas. Also in the transaction, David L. Bole, the president of Edwards and Leach, joined Alexander Energy's management team. Roy V. Edwards, chairman of the board of Edwards and Leach, joined as director.

Alexander Energy continued to grow both through the acquisition of established production companies and through the discovery of new reserves through its active exploration and drilling program. As a part of this effort, in February 1984 the firm concluded a $4-million lease acquisition joint venture with Cliffwood Energy Company. Under the provisions of the agreement, Alexander Energy no longer relied on bank

loans to finance lease purchases. That same year Alexander Energy purchased a group of properties owned by The Brooks Hall Oil Companies in a $19-million transaction that doubled the firm's total proved reserves.

Beginning in 1984 Alexander Energy embarked on an extensive exploration and drilling program that through March 1985 had successfully completed seventy-one of the ninety-five wells in which it participated—a success rate of 75 percent. The 1984-1985 drilling program accounted for 40 percent of the company's increase in proven reserves and almost tripled its crude oil production and doubled its natural gas production.

From 1980 to 1985 Alexander Energy Corporation's revenue grew from $258,000 to $8.575 million. By 1985 the firm controlled 79,393 gross and 11,485 net acres in Oklahoma and 65,200 gross and 7,800 net acres in Arkansas, with a total proven reserve value of $104.5 million, and was expanding its operations into Louisiana, Colorado, Texas, and Kansas.

Alexander Energy Corporation's board of directors (left to right): Samuel G. Hammons, F. Wayne Falkenstein, Ronald T. Riggan, Jim L. David, Bob G. Alexander, James A. Bibler, and DeWayne R. VonFeidt.

FORD MOTOR COMPANY TULSA GLASS PLANT

Plans for the Tulsa Glass Plant, a part of the Ford Motor Company complex, were launched in October 1972. It was to be the third glass plant for Ford, which is the nation's second-largest manufacturer of glass, and the Tulsa facility was designed to produce 30 percent of Ford's requirements.

Work at the 218-acre site located at 5555 South 129th East Avenue, which is one of the costliest manufacturing plants built in Tulsa, began in the spring of 1973. The glass-manufacturing building, which is almost a half-mile long, contains one million square feet and covers approximately twenty-three acres. Almost two years later, on August 19, 1974, at 6:20 p.m., the Tulsa Glass Plant commenced operations. Three days later the facility shipped its first finished product. Henry Ford II formally dedicated the plant to "excellence in glassmaking for the benefit of our customers, our employees, and the community" on October 16 of that year.

Six hundred and fifty tons of silica sand, 160 tons of dolomite limestone, 200 tons of straight limestone, 196 tons of soda ash, and other ingredients are measured in the facility's batch house; mixed with water and cullet, or broken glass; and then stored in twenty-six barn-size silos. Electronically controlled conveyors bring the mixture in five-ton lots to the beginning of one of the plant's two 2,000-foot-long float lines housed in the glass-manufacturing building. Seventeen million cubic feet of natural gas daily is used to heat the mixture in refractory furnaces to almost 3,000 degrees Fahrenheit, at which temperature the sand, limestone, and soda ash are transformed to a liquid state.

Once melted, the mixture flows over 245 tons of molten tin; by the use of gravity, surface tension, and intense heat the glass is formed into a ribbon, the surfaces of which are smooth, flat, and fire-polished. Before it leaves the tin bath, the glass passes through knurl machines. In-vented by Ford, the machine grips the outer edges of the glass ribbon and pulls the surface laterally to a predetermined width and thickness. Each of the two float furnaces in the plant has the capability of producing clear, tinted, bronze or gray, or reflective glass in thicknesses that vary from seven-hundredths of an inch to one-half inch.

When the glass emerges from the tin bath, it enters an annealing lehr, an electrically heated oven that cools rather than heats the glass at the rate of approximately two degrees for each of its 440 feet in length. This gradual cooling prevents the formation of stresses that could weaken the glass. When it leaves the lehr, the glass has dropped in temperature to approximately 170 degrees. The glass is then inspected on a capping line. Each capping line is 600 feet long and can handle more than eighteen miles of glass every twenty-four hours. If the glass meets customer requirements, a primary cutter cuts the glass into as many as sixteen different sizes, ranging from 12 by 16 inches to 204 by 212 inches. Such a multitude of sizes makes the Tulsa Glass Plant an industry leader in "on-line" cutting capabilities. If it does not meet specified requirements, the glass is crushed and returned to the furnace for remelting.

Glass handlers remove a large sheet of glass from the Tulsa Glass Plant's float line. The facility is designed to produce 30 percent of Ford Motor Company's glass requirements.

Within three years the Tulsa Glass Plant had outgrown its original facilities, and in September 1977 a major expansion program was launched to add a 228,000-square-foot building, increasing the plant's size by 25 percent. The new fabrication building, located to the south of the float building, went on-line in October

1978. It is used to cut, paint, bend, and temper glass for use on the side windows and rear windows of virtually every car, truck, and van manufactured by Ford Motor Company. In addition, the plant is a major producer of reflective glass used on the exteriors of buildings throughout the United States. Also, it is the first facility in North America to produce blue glass.

New products, advancing technology, and normal wear and aging necessitate the periodic rebuilding of the float furnaces, at a cost exceeding twenty million dollars each. Furnace number one was rebuilt in 1979 and furnace number two in 1981. In addition, robots and sophisticated manufacturing and material-handling operations are constantly being added. Thus, the plant retains its position of industry leadership through state-of-the-art technology.

In its first decade of operation, the Tulsa Glass Plant melted more than 4.1 million tons of raw materials to produce over 4.5 billion square feet of flat glass—enough to circle the

earth three times with a glass belt eleven feet wide. In 1985 the plant produced sufficient glass daily to glaze the Broken Arrow Expressway from the plant to downtown Tulsa and back. Its products are marketed throughout the United States as well as in Europe, South America, and Central America. Presently the Tulsa Glass Plant, under the direction of S.S. Gambino, employs more than 1,000 persons with an annual payroll of forty-eight million dollars, and produces 300 million square feet of flat glass and five million pieces of

automobile glass annually. Sales between 1974 and 1984 surpassed one billion dollars. The Tulsa plant's efficiency has played a major role in the Glass Division of Ford Motor Company becoming the second-largest producer of glass in the United States by 1985.

Tulsa Mayor Terry Young, plant manager Tod Gambino, and Ford Glass Division sales and marketing manager Bob Terrell (left to right) hold the first piece of blue glass produced in North America, at the Tulsa Glass Plant.

An aerial view of the Tulsa Glass Plant operated by Ford Motor Company. The facility contains one million square feet and covers approximately twenty-three acres.

GARDNER SPRING, INC.

A manufacturer and distributor of stock and custom precision springs and washers, Gardner Spring, Inc., was founded in 1902 as Gardner Wire Company, Inc., of Chicago, Illinois. In 1967 Marshall Jackson, who with his brother, Calvin, owned Oklahoma Spring of Tulsa, bought Gardner Wire Company. However, instead of purchasing just the equipment, Jackson, who was accompanied on the trip by his sister, Katherine Inez Skinner Magrini, acquired the entire stock spring portion of the company. This acquisition included the name "Gardner," the company trademark. Gardner Spring was then relocated at 1115 North Utica in Tulsa, a site it still occupies.

From the beginning, Mrs. Magrini managed the firm for her brothers. Her salary was $100 per week and her duties included everything from sweeping the floors to operating the most complicated machinery used in the manufacture of stock and custom springs. Within a year, in December 1967, the company was acquired by the Barnes Group, Inc., the largest producer of springs in the world. Mrs. Magrini continued as general manager of the company for the new owners. At that time she was the only female manager—as well as the youngest manager with the Barnes Group. A decade later, in 1978, Mrs. Magrini purchased the firm and it became today's Gardner Spring, Inc.

Under her leadership, the company has grown from 7 employees working in approximately 1,000 square feet to 67 employees (including sales representatives) and more than 55,000 square feet of manufacturing/warehouse space. Gardner Spring produces military precision springs for airplanes, rockets, and other government defense equipment. Stock and custom springs are produced and distributed by Gardner for such national firms as Ace Hardware, and True Value Hardware-Cotter & Company. In addition, Gardner springs are sold to national industrial distributors such as McMaster Carr. Gardner Spring products also are

marketed nationwide through trade shows and by factory direct sales.

Born in Drumright, Oklahoma, Mrs. Magrini moved to Tulsa with her parents, Marshall E. and Inez Thornhill Jackson, when she was six weeks old. In addition to being the first woman to hold a position of general manager for the Barnes Group, Mrs. Magrini is the former owner of Gardner Stock, Inc., Santa Fe Springs, California, and of Midwestern Metal Finishing Company of Haskell, Oklahoma. She also was secretary/treasurer of American Wireform, Inc., and was the first woman to become a member of the Tulsa Manufacturers' Association. Mrs. Magrini is a charter member of the Committee of 200, an organization that recognizes female entrepreneurs, and has been honored by the Harvard School of Business, the University of Columbia, and the governors of both Kentucky and Colorado. She is a member of the American

Katherine Skinner Magrini, president and owner of Gardner Spring, Inc., a division of Skinner Industries, Inc., a wholly owned corporation of K.I. Skinner Magrini.

Hardware and Manufacturers' Association, the Southern Hardware and Manufacturers' Association, Spring Manufacturers' Institute, and the Central States Industrial Distributors' Association.

Mrs. Magrini is married to Gary Lee, a special criminal agent for the United States Treasury Department. Her son, Gordon Todd, currently assists in the family business. An active supporter of Tulsa, Mrs. Magrini is a member of the Tulsa Philharmonic Association, the Metropolitan Tulsa Chamber of Commerce, and the Statue of Liberty-Ellis Island Foundation, Inc. She also is a patron of Gilcrease Museum Association, a sustaining member of the Philbrook Art Museum Association, and a member of Mapleridge Association.

PUBLIC SERVICE COMPANY OF OKLAHOMA

Public Service Company of Oklahoma, an industry leader in providing reliable, low-cost energy, originated in 1889, when the Vinita Electric Light and Power Company was chartered in Indian Territory to provide electric service to that community. During the following decades other similar operations appeared in the Twin Territories.

On May 29, 1913, the Public Service Company of Oklahoma (PSO) was incorporated, consisting of the original Vinita firm combined with small electric companies at Tulsa, Atoka, Coalgate, Lehigh, and Guthrie. It was a humble beginning. PSO officials revealed plans to provide electric service twenty-four hours a day. Growth came slowly in those early years. World War I delayed expansion.

During the prosperous 1920s the firm bounded ahead. Power lines were extended to communities without electric service. Small existing electric systems were merged with PSO. By combining smaller systems into a single integrated company, PSO was able to provide electric energy more efficiently and at a lower cost. Expansion continued during

PSO representatives work closely with builders and home owners who wish to build a Good Cents Home or retrofit an existing home to Good Cents Improved Home standards. A home certified "Good Cents" provides the home owner with significant energy savings.

the 1930s and 1940s. By 1947 the 30,000-square-mile area currently served by PSO essentially had been established.

PSO today provides electric service to more than one million people in eastern and southwestern Oklahoma. The company's electric generating capacity exceeds 3.7 million kilowatts, one-fourth provided by coal and three-fourths provided by natural gas. PSO is a wholly owned subsidiary of the Central and South West (CSW) Corporation, an electric utility holding company based in Dallas, Texas. CSW owns four electric utility companies, all of which operate in four states in the Southwest.

PSO is now engaged in an innovative customer-oriented business direction built on a pricing structure that encourages greater energy use in winter while promoting energy efficiency year-round. By achieving these goals, the firm will be able to better use its existing facilities and reduce its need to build additional generating capacity. Attainment of these goals also will restrain the need to increase the price of electricity to its customers.

The company's marketing program is comprehensive and congruent, addressing the needs of residential, commercial, and industrial customers. The Good Cents InCENTive program rewards residential customers who install energy-efficient heat pumps and air conditioners with di-

PSO is headquartered in the renovated building that for more than sixty years served as Tulsa's Central High School.

rect credits on their electric service bills. The Good Cents Home and Good Cents Improved Home programs enable customers to build a new home or retrofit an existing home to certified energy efficiency standards and achieve significant energy savings. Customers whose homes are certified "Good Cents" also receive a price incentive.

Commercial and industrial customers have a wide range of energy options from which to choose. Through PSO's level-of-service price structure, a business may select the price it pays and the investment it makes for electric service to fit its own operating needs. A time-of-day price is offered as an incentive to encourage businesses to shift their electric loads from peak hours to off-peak hours, when PSO can more efficiently serve their needs. An interruptible price option enables PSO to reduce or curtail electric service to a business during a period of peak demand.

Always a leader in economic development activities, PSO believes that its new customer-oriented business direction will enhance the state's attractiveness to new businesses and result in the creation of new jobs for Oklahomans.

PSO is headquartered in the renovated historic building that for more than sixty years housed Tulsa's Central High School. This is appropriate as PSO has played and continues to play a major role in the economic history and development of Oklahoma.

ALBRIGHT STEEL AND WIRE COMPANY

A statewide wholesale distributorship of steel products, Albright Steel and Wire Company is a major supplier for lumberyards, hardware stores, and sheet-metal shops. Organized in 1952 by Clyde Albright, the firm supplies material used in residential and small construction projects as well as the farming and ranching industry. The firm serves 750 retail customers throughout Oklahoma, with the exception of the extreme northeast quadrant of the state.

The founder had been associated with the wholesale steel and wire industry, which includes a multitude of metal products ranging from nails and fencing to steel reinforcing rods and sheet-metal products, since his graduation from the Draughon School of Business in Oklahoma City in 1937. For the following decade and a half, except for a stint in the Pacific with the United States Army in World War II, during which time he maintained contact with his customers through the mail, Albright was a familiar face among the state's lumberyards and hardware stores. As a result, when he returned to Oklahoma after the war, Albright quickly

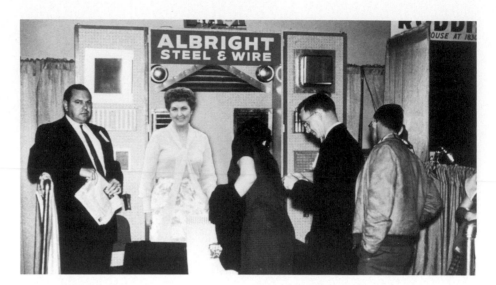

Clyde and Virginia Albright in Albright Steel and Wire's booth at the Oklahoma Lumbermen's Association Convention.

Clyde Albright standing behind a roll of welded wire.

was able to renew his customers' friendship. Possessing a dynamic and outgoing personality, he cultivated a following of loyal customers throughout Oklahoma.

During the economic downturn of the early 1950s, the firm for which Albright worked went out of business. Finding himself with no job but with a vast network of customers, he secured financing and purchased the inventory of his former employer. Incorporated in 1952 as a closed, family-held corporation, Albright Steel and Wire began business with three employees—Albright, who was president, chief executive officer, and salesman; his wife, Virginia, who managed the office and credit department; and a truck driver, who made deliveries. In the following years Albright's three daughters, LaCrecia Albright Lewis, Linda Albright, and Leah Albright Little, also joined the business.

From its organization, Albright Steel and Wire focused on domestically produced steel and wire products. Refusing to compromise on quality, Clyde Albright believed that the strength of his business was built on loyal customers and he personally stood behind every product sold. It was a philosophy that produced three generations of loyal customers.

Combining goodwill and sound business practices, within a year of its organization Albright Steel and Wire had outgrown its original loca-

tion. To provide adequate space for the expanding company, Albright moved its corporate headquarters and distribution center to a new site alongside present-day Interstate 40 between Virginia Avenue and Kentucky Street. In the following two decades the company underwent three major expansions until it occupied the entire city block.

Utilizing a modern computer system, the distribution center, which contains in excess of 50,000 square feet, maintains a 1,500-item inventory that includes such diverse items as an eight-cent ferrell or $285-per-roll V-mesh fence. Among the materials available to customers are galvanized steel, flat copper, stainless steel, and aluminum sheets; joist hangers; louvers; heating and air-conditioning duct work; trolly tracks and fittings; guttering and fittings; sheet-metal accessories, such as screws and pop rivets; poly-film; hot-roofing materials; many varieties of corrugated iron and related building materials; all types of metal fencing and posts for agricultural, residential, or commercial use; concrete reinforcing bars and mesh; channels; 270 varieties of nails; and hot- and cold-rolled, shaped metal items such as angle iron, round and square bars, pipe, and iron plates; and square and rectangular

Board of directors and family members confer. They are (left to right) daughters LaCrecia Albright Lewis and Leah Albright Little, both members of the board. Leah, treasurer, is the only family member involved in the daily operations of the company. On the right is Virginia Albright, president and chairman of the board, who co-founded the company along with her husband, Clyde J. Albright.

tubing.

To provide dependable service to its customers on a regular schedule, Albright Steel and Wire maintains a fleet of nine trucks. In so doing it offers one-day delivery service in the central Oklahoma area and biweekly routes covering the remainder of the state. In addition, a staff of five statewide salesmen calls on every customer at least twice monthly.

Within three decades of its organization, Albright Steel and Wire had moved to the forefront of the state's wholesale building industry. In addition, its expanded sales network had grown to the point that it was necessary to create two branch warehouses—one in Lawton, which was opened in 1966, and the other in Enid, which was established in 1980. With the expansion, the firm was capable of offering its customers in southwestern and northwestern Oklahoma rapid delivery of material while reducing expenses, a savings that was passed on to customers.

A self-made businessman, Clyde Albright was extremely active in civic affairs and an outspoken proponent of the advantages of Oklahoma. He was a charter member and presi-

dent of the South Oklahoma City Rotary Club, in which he maintained a 24-year perfect attendance record. In addition, he served as an elder, treasurer, and member of the board of directors of the First Christian Church of Oklahoma City. His strong handshake and affable personality were well known throughout the state and he often provided extended credit and encouragement to new accounts, knowing that when they succeeded Albright Steel and Wire would acquire another loyal customer.

When Albright died in 1971 many of his customers closed their businesses in tribute. After his death the control of Albright Steel and Wire passed to a trusteeship. Eventually his wife, Virginia, assumed the presidency of Albright Steel and Wire, and two of his three daughters, LaCrecia and Leah, were named to the board of directors. In addition, Leah currently serves as secretary/treasurer, office manager, comptroller, and

head of the credit division. Dan Kimery, who has been with the firm for a quarter of a century, oversees the daily operations as general manager.

In its second generation of family management, Albright Steel and Wire Company continues to serve many of the customers originally contacted by Clyde Albright three and a half decades ago. Throughout this period it has maintained a network of loyal customers by following the founder's business philosophy of providing quality products and dependable services. Knowing that a successful business is built on successful customers, the firm offers steady, reliable service that reflects the contemporary market for wire and steel products just as it did in 1952.

Albright Steel and Wire Company has been at the same location, 12 South Virginia, for over twenty-five years.

T.G.&Y.

Named for R.E. Tomlinson, E.L. Gosselin, and R.A. Young, T.G.&Y. began in 1936 when the three men formed a partnership, leased a former grocery store located on Main Street in Norman, Oklahoma, and opened the first T.G.&Y. outlet. The headquarters for the fledgling business was in an old warehouse on Eleventh Street near downtown Oklahoma City. Tomlinson, Gosselin, and Young individually owned several variety stores throughout the state, and previously the three men had banded together to increase their purchasing power at the wholesale level.

This arrangement not only allowed them to purchase merchandise at a reduced cost, but also to pass the savings on to their customers. This philosophy of "giving the customers what they want, at a price they can afford," Young later recalled, was the springboard that allowed T.G.&Y. to grow from a small Oklahoma-based variety chain to a coast-to-

coast network with outlets in twenty-six states in just a half-century.

Within a year of the opening of the original T.G.&Y. store another outlet was opened in Oklahoma City. Additional expansion followed, and by 1938 growth was so rapid that the Eleventh Street warehouse headquarters was inadequate, and a new facility was acquired on North Broadway. As the business grew, the benefits of incorporating the stores owned individually by Tomlinson, Gosselin, and Young into a 32-store T.G.&Y. chain became obvious.

As a result, a new partnership was organized in 1944. Tomlinson kept his variety stores in Frederick and Grandfield separate, but became partners with the other two men as Gosselin's outlets in Carnegie, Cordell, Hobart, and Elk City; and Young's businesses in Alva, Cherokee, Edmond, Fairview, Kingfisher, Weatherford, Hennessey, Hinton, Crescent, Geary, Watonga, Medford, Sand Springs, Thomas, Woodward,

and three in Tulsa were combined with the existing T.G.&Y. chain. This allowed for the formation of a single management team to oversee the operation of more stores. Two years later, in 1946, T.G.&Y. Stores Company was incorporated.

Shortly afterward, in 1950, it became apparent that the firm had outgrown its downtown Oklahoma City facilities, and a new 70,000-square-foot headquarters complex was constructed at Northwest Thirty-sixth Street and Santa Fe Avenue. In the next fifteen years it was expanded three times to 246,000 square feet. During that same time the concept of regional warehouses was adopted so that whenever the number of T.G.&Y. outlets in a specific area neared fifty, such a facility was established to provide individual service to the stores and to guarantee overnight delivery of stock. The idea of regional warehouses worked so well that in 1977 a system of distribution warehouses was initiated to distribute promotional, seasonal, and new-item

Rawdon E. Tomlinson (1894-1948), co-founder.

Enoch Leslie Gosselin (1901-1977), co-founder.

Raymond Alfred Young (1904-), co-founder.

The Moore, Oklahoma, store with its modern Family Center exterior.

goods to stores that would utilize similar products. An import warehouse was constructed in Oklahoma City in 1979.

During this period of expansion T.G.&Y. underwent several organizational changes. In 1957 it merged with Butler Brothers of Chicago, Illinois. Three years later Butler Brothers was acquired by City Products Corporation. In 1966 Household Finance Corporation purchased City Products. Sixteen years later a holding company, Household International, was created, and in the reorganization T.G.&Y. became a part of the Household Merchandising, Inc., division of Household International.

T.G.&Y. also changed its corporate look by updating its product base to present goods that reflected changing customer demands. At the same time the firm maintained a desirable shopping atmosphere in its outlets, augmented with affordable prices and prompt, courteous service. As a result of its modernized, computerized system, by the mid-1980s T.G.&Y., under the direction of president and chief executive officer Richard C. Rusthoven, consisted of 740 variety stores and family centers nationwide and employed 28,000 people.

Some 5,000 of T.G.&Y.'s workers are located in Oklahoma. In addition, the firm maintains six regional warehouses, located in Edmond, Oklahoma; Lubbock, Texas; La Mirada, California; Montgomery, Alabama; Kansas City, Kansas; and Houston, Texas; with an import warehouse in Long Beach, California. Two distribution warehouses also are operated in Hattiesburg, Mississippi, and Macon, Georgia. With its extensive network of outlets, T.G.&Y. sales surpassed $2.037 billion in 1985.

An artist's concept of an early-day T.G.&Y. storefront. Drawing by Lisa Brown, 1985

FLEMING COMPANIES, INC.

In 1921 Ned N. Fleming entered the food distribution industry when he joined his father, O.A. Fleming, a founder of the Fleming-Wilson Mercantile Company, in the management of a small wholesale grocery firm in Topeka, Kansas. At that time it was not uncommon for the average housewife to spend as many as ten hours each day buying and preparing her family's meals. Most of the food either was homegrown or ordered from a local grocery store, meat market, or bakery, which delivered to her house and extended credit.

But the food system was to undergo tremendous changes in the decades ahead. Chain stores were introduced in the 1920s, threatening the existence of the neighborhood store. In response, independent grocers banded together to form voluntary group organizations to become more competitive by using mass marketing, advertising, and more efficient operational techniques. Ned Fleming was instrumental in developing the voluntary group in the Midwest.

Through the economic downturn brought on by the Great Depression, the new voluntary groups, and Ned Fleming's company, continued to grow. With the outbreak of World War II the trend toward large-volume grocery stores accelerated. The result was the supermarket concept and self-service, offering large inventories and low prices. Keeping pace with this changing marketplace, the Fleming Company, as the firm had been renamed, developed a policy of active acquisition.

As a part of this expansion Fleming acquired the Carroll-Brough-Robinson Company in Oklahoma City during 1941. Three years later the Oklahoma City operation moved to new quarters at 3500 North Santa Fe. That structure, which was to remain the hub of Fleming's Oklahoma operations for thirty-five years, was expanded six times during the decades to follow. During those years Fleming-served retailers gained strong market shares in Oklahoma, and the company became a major economic force in the state.

In 1978 Fleming constructed a new 400,000-square-foot distribution center in far north Oklahoma City. The facility, built at a cost of more than fifteen million dollars, was the first to operate with a mechanized order selection system. It remains a model distribution facility, both in the Fleming Companies and in the food distribution industry. The company's corporate staff also is headquartered in Oklahoma City, with

The firm began operations in Oklahoma when it acquired the Carroll-Brough-Robinson Company in 1941.

national offices at 6301 Waterford Boulevard.

Today Fleming Companies is a national leader in the wholesale food distribution industry, serving more than 3,900 affiliated retailers in 33 states. These retail outlets include some of the nation's most successful and progressive supermarkets. The firm remains a strong supporter of the independent operator and is the largest supplier to IGA stores in the United States. In addition, Fleming serves many nonfranchised independent customers and an increasing number of chain stores.

In the mid-1980s, under the direction of R.D. Harrison, chairman and chief executive officer, and E. Dean Werries, president and chief operating officer, Fleming is the second-largest public corporation, based on sales, in Oklahoma. The firm employs more than 15,000 people in distribution centers that comprise more than 12 million square feet of warehouse space. These centers feature state-of-the-art computer systems that increase productivity and efficiency. In addition to grocery centers, the company's distribution network includes general merchandise facilities, perishable products centers, and institutional food service warehouses.

Fleming's Oklahoma City distribution center features a mechanized order selection system serving retailers across the state.

SOUTHERN SHEET METAL WORKS, INC.

Founded in 1904 by J.W. Tidwell, Southern Sheet Metal Works is one of the state's oldest and most respected sheet-metal fabricators. Originally Southern Cornice Works, the company initially was located at the intersection of First Street and Boulder near downtown Tulsa. Established at the beginning of the Oklahoma oil boom, the enterprise supplied the surrounding oil fields with "everything in sheet metal."

In addition to custom-fabricated equipment, the firm specialized in the manufacture of water tanks used on the thousands of nearby steam-powered drilling rigs and by area farmers and ranchers. Tidwell also produced a series of ventilators designed for installation on the roofs of buildings so that hot inside air could escape. Eventually the company obtained a patent for a counter-balanced revolving ventilator, which was marketed throughout the state for use on industrial and commercial buildings. Before the introduction of air conditioning, it was the most widespread means of cooling the interior of large structures.

During the following decades Southern Sheet Metal developed into one of the state's major producers of both custom-made and standard-designed sheet-metal products. As the company grew, the founder's two sons, J.W. Tidwell, Jr., and Kyle Tidwell became associated. By 1946 the firm had outgrown its original location and was moved to a new site at 1225 East Second Street. Later expansion added adjoining space on East First Street, which increased the company's physical plant to 35,000 square feet. In the mid-1950s J.W. Tidwell, Jr., became president of the company, which he operated with his brother, Kyle C. Tidwell. In the early 1980s third-generation member Michael L. Tidwell, a grandson of the firm's founder, became president of Southern Sheet Metal Works, Inc.

During this period of growth Southern Sheet Metal expanded its operations into climate-control systems. As technology grew so did the corporation's production of industrial/commercial ventilation, dust collection, heating, ventilating, air-conditioning, and hi-tech clean air systems. By the mid-1980s Southern Sheet Metal Works was a major supplier of custom-fabricated metal or

The original Southern Cornice Works near downtown Tulsa. The man in the center behind the wagon is J.W. Tidwell, the company's founder. To the left is one of the models of stock tanks produced for area ranchers. Behind Tidwell is an oil field water tank designed to be mounted on a wagon.

plastic climate-control systems necessary for industries or health care facilities that demanded clean atmospheric conditions, and the firm offered its customers complete engineering, design, installation, and start-up services.

In addition, the company custom fabricates stainless steel, brass, copper, and other specialized products for architects, custom home builders, interior designers, and commercial and industrial contractors. The organization also produces high-quality electrical boxes and wireways for electrical contractors.

With more than eight decades of experience, Southern Sheet Metal Works is recognized as one of the leading fabricators of industrial and commercial ventilation and atmosphere-control equipment in the Southwest.

KVOO RADIO 1170

In early 1924 a permit was granted to Etherical Radio Company for radio station KFRU, owned by E.H. Rollestone. Its first broadcast from the Roland Hotel, Bristow, was midnight, January 12, 1925. Later that year the call letters were changed to KVOO and its name to Voice of Oklahoma, then to Southwestern Sales Corporation.

The station was purchased in 1927 by W.G. Skelly, a leading Tulsan and founder of Skelly Oil Company, then moved to Tulsa. Over the next fifteen years KVOO's power was increased to 50,000 watts day and night, and the firm became one of the country's outstanding radio stations. KVOO also has been the recipient of numerous national awards and citations for its programming and community awareness.

In 1926 KVOO produced Oklahoma's first live broadcast of a football game between Tulsa University and Oklahoma A&M. Often called "Big Country Radio," KVOO has been dominant in the increased popularity

The current facilities of KVOO Radio 1170 with (inset, left) Jon R. Stuart, president, and (right) Harold C. Stuart, chairman of the board.

of country and swing music, catering to such entertainers as Jimmie Wilson and his Catfish String Band, Gene Autry, Bob Wills and the Texas Playboys, Johnnie Lee Wills, and Leon McAuliffe.

Harold C. Stuart, Skelly's son-in-law, became president in 1956. The following year Stuart and his wife, Joan, acquired ownership of the station and constructed new studios at the Broadcast Center in Tulsa.

Operations director Billy Parker was recognized as DJ of the Year in 1974 by the Country Music Association, and in 1975, 1977, 1978, and 1984 was again noted as DJ of the Year by the Academy of Country Music. KVOO was named Radio Station of the Year in 1978 and 1984.

A major factor in KVOO's success has been stability of personnel and strong leadership. Stuart, now chairman of the board, has fostered a friendly, family atmosphere at the station and has developed a proud, dedicated staff. His son, Jon, joined the firm in 1976 and is now president. Stuart also has encouraged public service at KVOO, and the station for decades has been a community and state leader in supporting

Groundbreaking ceremonies for Broadcast Center, the home of KVOO Radio, took place in 1956. Participating are (left to right) Randi Stuart, Harold C. Stuart, Jon R. Stuart, and W.G. Skelly.

worthy civic and charitable causes. One of the most prestigious pioneer radio stations, KVOO has always been prominent on the national scene.

In 1985 the corporate name was changed to First Stuart Corporation, and beautiful new studios were constructed in Tulsa. The dedication on January 23, 1986, started the firm's sixty-second year of broadcasting and the KVOO "family" will continue its dedication to perpetuate the station's heritage of excellence.

SWINSON CHEVROLET, INC.

Located on a fifteen-acre site, Swinson Chevrolet's new car lot contains an average of 750 vehicles. Another 100 used cars and trucks are available. The 100,000-square-foot building contains the parts, service, and new car showroom as well as sales and administrative offices.

Mid-West Chevrolet Corporation was located in downtown Tulsa when it was purchased by N.L. "Bud" Swinson. At the time it was one of the oldest and most successful automobile dealerships in the state.

N.L. "Bud" Swinson first entered the automobile sales business when he was seventeen years old. That many years later, in 1965, he opened Swinson Chevrolet, Inc., near Wichita, Kansas. In 1970 the entrepreneur purchased Mid-West Chevrolet Corporation, located at Seventh Street and Cincinnati Avenue in downtown Tulsa, renamed the company Swinson Chevrolet, and moved to Tulsa.

Founded in 1923 by D.B. Winchell, a longtime northeastern Oklahoma automobile salesman, Mid-West Chevrolet was one of the oldest and most successful Chevrolet dealerships in the state. The new operation occupied the downtown Tulsa location until 1972. There was another such dealership in the immediate area, and—at the urging of General Motors—Swinson decided to relocate to a new site at 8130 East Skelly Drive to take advantage of the shift in Tulsa housing patterns and the development of a community-wide interstate system that had created a large automobile market in the outlying metropolitan area. Situated near the intersection of I-44 and the Broken Arrow Expressway and near the Mingo Valley Expressway, the location boasted a drive-by traffic count of 150,000 automobiles per day within a decade.

Constructed on a fifteen-acre site, the new Swinson Chevrolet complex contained an outdoor new and used car sales lot, which was capable of holding a normal stock of 750 new automobiles and trucks and 100 used vehicles; and a 100,000-square-foot building that housed the company's new car showroom, service department, parts department, sales office, and administrative section. In addition, there was an 8,000-square-foot covered display area for new automobiles.

Employing 140 individuals, Swinson Chevrolet's 28-man sales staff offers customers the entire spectrum of Chevrolet's product line, including more than thirty models of cars and trucks as well as special-order vehicles. Many of the firm's salesmen are longtime employees who have established an extensive list of repeat customers, which the owner emphasizes is a key to the organization's success—customer loyalty and repeat sales. However, Swinson stresses that "sales are secondary; service is first" in a successful automobile dealership. As a part of this policy, the company's thirty service technicians have a total of 396 years of experience. This experience, combined with a consumer-oriented policy of service after sales, made Swinson Chevrolet—with annual average sales of 3,500 new cars and trucks—the top Chevrolet dealership in Oklahoma. Total 1985 new and used car and truck sales reached fifty-three million dollars.

In recognition of his outstanding leadership, Swinson was one of fourteen Chevrolet dealers, out of a nationwide total of 10,000, to be named to General Motors' President's Council, which provides dealer input for GM's long-range corporate planning.

BAMA PIE, LTD.

The story of Bama Pie, Ltd., is as American as homemade pie. It began in Texas when Grandma Bama Marshall, who worked at the fountain of a local drugstore, began baking her homemade pies at work and offering them for sale. They proved to be a popular item; and when her husband lost his job in the late 1920s, she—at his suggestion—began baking pies for him to sell to workers on nearby construction projects.

It quickly became almost impossible for Grandma Bama to keep up with the demand, and her daughters were enlisted to help with the baking; however, Grandma Bama worked out all the recipes. Eventually Bama Pies, Inc., offered pecan pies; apple, cherry, peach, and lemon turnovers; and chocolate chip, butter pecan, oatmeal, and peanut butter cookies.

With the increased output, her husband acquired a Ford automobile, placed a rack in the backseat to hold the pies, and expanded their marketing area. The growth was phenomenal, and within six months it was necessary to purchase another truck to handle the orders. When the truck arrived the couple needed a name for the side panels—and Bama Pie was

Some of the Bama employees and delivery trucks in front of the pie shop in Tulsa, in 1938.

H.C. and Ruby Marshall with one of the first Bama delivery trucks.

born. In 1937 their son, Paul, and his wife, Lilah, moved to Tulsa and expanded Bama Pie's marketing area into Oklahoma.

Throughout the 1940s, 1950s, and 1960s, the family business used routes to cover Oklahoma and parts of Kansas, Missouri, and Arkansas. Fresh pies for the restaurant trade constituted the bulk of the business during these decades of steady growth. In the early 1960s Paul Marshall observed the emergence of the fast-food industry and began providing pies that conveniently could be heated on-site; his early adaptation

to what became a major change in the food-service industry enabled Bama Pie to grow dramatically during the 1960s, 1970s, and the first half of the 1980s. Pies for the fast-food industry quickly became the company's dominant product.

Headquartered at 2745 East Eleventh Street in Tulsa, the 400 employees of Bama Pie, Ltd., operate a custom-built plant equipped with company-designed machines capable

The most popular product Bama Pie makes—a three-inch pecan pie.

Bama Pie takes on a modern look with a more efficient plant.

of producing 100,000 small pies an hour—two million daily. The machine shop not only controls daily maintenance, but designs, assembles, and installs new equipment in the Bama Pie plant. Much of the equipment was built specifically for the production of Bama pies, and the

Bama begins to expand to the west taking more of the block at Eleventh and Delaware.

firm holds patents on its dough rollers and turnover machines.

The custom-manufactured aspect of Bama Pie is followed throughout the production process. Designed for fast-food service, each personal-size Bama pie is sealed in vinyl wrap and flash frozen immediately upon completion. This process allows complete portion control and ease of handling with no cutting or waste. Afterward,

Bama Pie's own fleet of specially designed vehicles delivers fifty truckloads of pies, turnovers, and cookies throughout the United States weekly. Once delivered, they can be thawed quickly or prepared on-site for customer sales.

To ensure the home-cooked quality of more than half a century, Bama pies are consistently examined at random by inspectors. Taste tests are performed three times daily. In addition, a member of the Marshall family works at the plant daily to personally oversee the operation, while a home economist checks the formulation of the recipes. Paul Marshall, who with Lilah retired in January 1985, points out that Bama pies are produced by "a group of people who work hard and choose to make quality pies."

Corporate management was taken over by a partnership of the couple's children—Paula McCarty, John Marshall, and Roger Marshall—thereby perpetuating family management of this quality-oriented company.

Bama Pie expanded with a new plant building, while still using the corner store as a retail outlet.

FACET ENTERPRISES, INC.

Unlike the vast majority of the companies listed on the New York Stock Exchange, Facet Enterprises, Inc., is not the result of the gleam in the eye of an entrepreneur. Rather, a good case can be made that Tulsa-based Facet is the result of a gleam in the eye of a government bureaucrat. For Facet's story begins in 1967, when the Bendix Corporation acquired Fram Corporation, the automotive air, oil, and fuel filter manufacturer.

Almost immediately that acquisition was challenged on antitrust grounds by the Federal Trade Commission. After more than seven years of litigation, the commission's objections were met with an out-of-court settlement that required Bendix to create and then spin off four Bendix and four Fram operations into a separate organization. The arrangement gave Bendix shareholders one share of Facet stock for each five shares of Bendix, and on April 1, 1976, a new enterprise was launched.

Today Facet is a diversified company engaged in the manufacturing and marketing of transportation components, filters and filtration systems, and oil field production equipment. Facet is organized into five operating units—Consumer Filter Group, International Group, Fluid Technology Group, Transportation Components Group, and Woods Energy Products, Inc.

The Consumer Filter Group's General Products Division annually produces in excess of seventy-five million filters for both the home and workplace. This division also manufactures an extensive line of medium- and high-efficiency filters for commercial and industrial uses. In addition, the group's Facet Automotive Filter Company (FAFCO) produces automotive oil, air, and fuel filters marketed under the brand names of thirty-five independent companies. FAFCO's marketing, engineering, and administrative offices are in Tulsa.

Facet's International Group includes four plants located in Europe from which Facet serves the worldwide industrial filtration marketplace. In addition, Facet both exports and licenses various companies to manufacture transportation components for the world market.

Facet's Fluid Technology Group, a leader in research and development of diffusion bonding and fluid mechanics technology, specializes in developing custom products to meet specific needs. In addition to serving the aerospace, fluid power, fuel and chemical processing, marine, medical, and industrial markets, the group is involved in the design and manufacture of environmental systems for treating industrial wastes, and filtration systems for industrial process streams. Tulsa and Stilwell are the home of two of this group's plants.

The Transportation Components Group manufactures starter drives, electronic fuel pumps, carburetors, and electromagnetic clutches and brakes for various transportation, industrial, and aerospace applications.

Woods Energy Products, Inc., produces stuffing boxes, pumping tees, lubricated plug valves, polish rods, clamps, needle valves, casing heads, tubing, and packing at two plants located in Sand Springs and Owasso. A recognized innovator, Woods Energy Products is a leader in the manufacture of oil field production equipment and supplies.

From international headquarters at 7030 South Yale Avenue in Tulsa, Facet's chairman of the board, James B. Treacy, and president and chief executive officer, James R. Malone, direct the operations of 2,200 employees in manufacturing plants in seven states. Sales offices and distributors are located worldwide. By 1984, within a decade of its establishment, Facet Enterprises' annual sales exceeded $150 million.

Facet's heating and air-conditioning filters are but a part of the company's extensive product line of filtration products covering the entire spectrum of industrial and residential filter needs.

CMI CORPORATION

Formed in March 1964 by Bill Swisher, CMI Corporation was organized to develop a machine capable of functioning automatically as a dual-lane subgrader, base material spreader, and fine grader. The company began with just four men—Swisher, an engineer, a mechanic, and an airplane pilot—and an idea to design a machine capable of producing the close tolerances necessary for the building of high-speed, interstate highways and expressway systems. Within a year a prototype was ready, and in 1965 the AUTOGRADE® Trimmer was placed into production.

Revolutionizing the road-building industry, the AUTOGRADE could produce and match grade to within one-eighth of an inch and trim up to thirty feet in width at speeds of up to sixty feet per minute. Beneath a rugged exterior, necessary for the road-construction business, Swisher had installed a simplified electrical system that allowed the AUTOGRADE to be controlled either manually or automatically. Attached to the machine was a series of sensor arms, which, by tracing a stringline, provided electrical signals to control the AUTOGRADE elevation and steering systems. In the following decades the product line was expanded to include a placer-spreader and slipform paver, which laid cement with the same accuracy. By incorporating precision technology and automation, CMI equipment could produce high-quality paving surfaces on any project ranging from sidewalks and tennis courts to interstate highways and airport runways.

The AUTOGRADE proved so successful that by 1970 every state required, by contract specification, its use in highway construction. Not only did it provide contractors with advanced machinery, but it cut the cost of highway construction by eliminating waste and streamlining labor. Thus, the American motorist was provided a smoother, tighter, and safer roadway for less money.

In 1969 CMI entered the asphalt plant business, and in 1972 the com-

Revolutionizing the road-building industry, the CMI AUTOGRADE Slip Form Paver places concrete paving to specifications within 1/8-inch tolerance. This type of paving is now required by all state highway agencies.

pany's engineers completed its first drum-mix asphalt plant. Designed to drop aggregate into an angled drum from the flame end, the system allowed radiant heat to vaporize any surface moisture immediately and heat the aggregate to approximately 300 degrees Fahrenheit before the asphalt cement was added. The result was a less expensive, more maintenance-free, lighter, and more mobile asphalt plant.

CMI again revolutionized the road-building industry in 1976 with the introduction of the ROTO-MILL® Pavement Profiler. Completely altering the maintenance and repair of highways, the ROTO-MILL automatically controlled the cold milling of pavement surfaces to restore a specified grade and slope; remove bumps, ruts, and other imperfections; and leave a textured level surface that was more resistant to skids and hydroplaning. In addition, by utilizing a ROTO-MILL profiler and a CMI-designed recycle asphalt plant, contractors had the capability of producing hot-mix at tremendous savings.

Involved in all aspects of road construction, CMI acquired LOAD KING® Trailers in 1969. By 1975 the firm had acquired 15 percent of the American trailer market and was

The CMI ROTO-MILL Pavement Profiler automatically controls the cold milling of pavement surfaces to restore a specified grade and slope.

a leader in the development and production of sophisticated heavy-hauling trailers. BID-WELL®, which specialized in the finishing of concrete bridge decks and canals, was acquired by CMI in 1970.

Through the innovative leadership of Swisher, by the mid-1980s CMI was a recognized leader in the production of machinery for pavement construction and reconstruction systems. In 1984 the firm entered into a long-term manufacturing and marketing agreement with Caterpillar Tractor Company. Today CMI-built machines are branded Caterpillar and marketed through the worldwide network of Caterpillar construction-equipment dealers.

SOUTH COMMUNITY HOSPITAL

Located at 1001 Southwest Forty-fourth Street, near the intersection of Southwest Forty-fourth and South Western, South Community Hospital is one of Oklahoma City's newest and most modern health care facilities.

In 1962 South Community Hospital, Inc., was formed and South Oklahoma City Hospital Trust organized to raise funds and sell tax-exempt bonds to finance construction of Phase I of South Community Hospital's development plan. Supported by area residents, the fund drive was a success, and a groundbreaking ceremony was held in April 1964 for the institution. South Community Hospital—the largest health care facility between the Canadian River and Dallas, Texas—admitted its first patient the following year on November 1, 1965.

When completed, Phase I of the hospital provided a 73-bed, three-floor acute care facility. Public acceptance was immediate, and constant near-capacity levels led to expansion. Phase II of its develop-

Ground was broken for South Community Hospital in April 1964. Patients were admitted on November 1, 1965, to one of Oklahoma City's newest and most modern health care facilities.

ment plan was completed in 1969, almost tripling the number of beds to 197 and adding three floors. A twelve-bed intensive care unit as well as new support services—such as physical therapy, respiratory therapy, and a 24-hour physician-staffed emergency room—also were added. The emergency room became one of the most utilized in the region.

Despite this rapid physical growth, patient demand resulted in the implementation of Phase III of the development plan. Opened in 1976, the new expansion added four more floors to the existing structure, making a total of ten, and raised the bed count to 391. With the expansion came increased patient services, including intensive medical, surgical, and coronary care; diagnostic and therapeutic radiology; inhalation and respiratory therapy; outpatient respiratory therapy; and extensive social service programs.

South Community Hospital has been a leader in the treatment of cataracts. It was the fourth hospital in the world to offer phaco-emulsification, a technique that eliminated the need for major surgery in cataract removal. The phaco-emulsification process dissolves cataracts and removes them by suction through a tiny incision. This allows

the staff of South Community Hospital to conduct cataract treatment primarily on an outpatient basis.

When the $20-million Phase IV expansion was completed in 1984, it achieved the original architectural plans for South Community Hospital. In addition, it relocated the emergency room and expanded its operations to include X-ray and phlebotomy ser-

Dan E. Tipton, president of South Community Hospital.

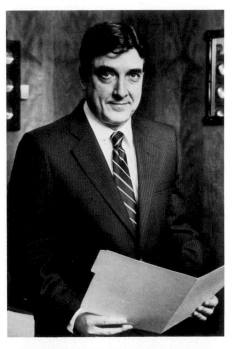

vices, which were situated in close proximity to the laboratory and the newly expanded twenty-bed intensive care units. In addition, all laboratory facilities were strategically placed between the emergency room and these new intensive care/coronary care units. As a part of the effort, the new Jim and Bernice Lookabaugh

James H. Little, M.D., ophthalmology specialist.

Memorial Intensive/Coronary units, featuring complete video monitoring of all patients and the latest in life-support systems, were placed into service. Also, the ninth floor of the hospital was redesigned and designated as the outpatient day surgery unit to handle patients who are treated and discharged on the same day. A new eye surgery suite was constructed; a family health clinic was opened on a seven-day-a-week, 365-day-a-year schedule; and a self-contained energy center was completed. In addition, Phase IV included the redesign and decoration of the public and private dining areas; the renovation and modernization of pulmonary medicine, physical therapy, and radiology units; construction of a redesigned and expanded main entrance and admitting lobby; a new parking lot; and a new helipad.

A senior monitor technician tracks intensive care patients' vital signs on closed-circuit television.

A patient-oriented health care facility, South Community Hospital inaugurated its patient representative program in 1984, which greatly simplified its patients' financial arrangements and established a separate outpatient surgery registration desk to speed paperwork and processing for the large number of South Community Hospital's day surgery procedures, utilized by more than 2,500 individuals annually. The hospital's auxiliary members donated 34,843 hours to patient care. Also in 1984 the hospital's Family Health Clinic was opened to provide trained medical care for minor injuries and illness. Operation Glo Germ was implemented to instruct Oklahoma City schoolchildren on the importance of infection-control methods and germ detection; a new health promotion center was established to offer programs on weight control, stress management, physical assessment, and smoking cessation; an outpatient pharmacy was opened as a convenience to staff and patients; and a Physician Referral Service was established to help consumers find and select a doctor for their health care needs.

By the mid-1980s, under the direction of president Dan E. Tipton, South Community Hospital's staff had grown to more than 1,000 individuals and drew patients from throughout central Oklahoma. From its beginning the institution has stressed its relationship to the south Oklahoma City community. The

close ties between the hospital and the people it serves were enhanced in 1985 when it opened five minor emergency, primary care centers in the region. Called Med Stop, the facilities offer convenient primary medical care on a nonappointment basis.

More than 150 core physicians serve the patients at South Community Hospital, with another 150 having staff privileges at the facility. As well as a nationally recognized cancer treatment program, South Community offers physicians with a wide range of specialties, including emergency medicine, anesthesiology, family practice, cardiology, dermatology, endocrinology, gastroenterology, hematology-oncology, internal medicine, infectious diseases, nephrology, neurology, psychiatry, pulmonary medicine, obstetrics and gynecology, pathology, pediatrics, and radiology. Among the extensive surgical services available are cardiovascular, thoracic, general, neurosurgery, ophthalmology, oral, orthopedics, otolaryngology, urology, and vascular. In addition, the institution offers a sports medicine program and a 20-bed physical rehabilitation unit. Because of its expanded staff specialties, specialized treatment programs, and consumer orientation, South Community Hospital is recognized as one of the health care leaders in the Southwest.

GADDIS-WALKER ELECTRIC, INCORPORATED

Just as Oklahoma became a state in 1907, George A. Gaddis arrived in Oklahoma City, received his union license as an electrician, and went into business for himself. During the early twentieth century electricity was as much a novelty as a source of energy, and Gaddis often followed wagons hauling lumber to new homesites in an effort to persuade the builder to wire the house for electricity instead of installing gas lighting or kerosene lamps.

For almost a decade and a half Gaddis worked as a private electrician in Oklahoma City; then in 1921 he joined his brother-in-law, S.E. Fentress—another electrician—to form Gaddis-Fentress Electric Company. Specializing in residential and commercial contracting, with an emphasis on quality and a responsible yet economical approach, the partners opened their first office on West Main Street near downtown Oklahoma City. They later relocated to 416 North Robinson Avenue and then to 418 North Broadway Avenue, where the company remained until 1969.

In 1934 Fentress left the firm and it was reorganized as Gaddis Electric, Inc., with the founder and his wife, Eva, each receiving 50 percent of the stock. Their son-in-law, Dan E. Walker, joined the company full time in the 1940s, and in 1947 assumed its day-to-day management; however, Gaddis remained active in the business until his death on November 22, 1962. To reflect Walker's involvement in the operation, in 1959 the name was changed to Gaddis-Walker Electric, Incorporated. After his father-in-law died, Walker purchased his share of the stock from the estate; in 1962 he acquired complete ownership by buying Eva Gaddis' stock.

The third generation of the family entered the business in 1970, when James A. Walker became a full-time member of the organization. Dan Walker continued to serve as president and chief executive officer until 1985, at which time his son was named president. However, the elder

George A. Gaddis, founder.

Walker remained chief executive officer and chairman of the board of directors.

With the outbreak of World War II, Gaddis Electric shifted from residential jobs to concentrate on military and industrial-commercial projects—such as wiring the mile-long Douglas Aircraft Plant at Tinker Field in Midwest City. Continuing to emphasize industrial-commercial projects after the war, the company worked on the Hunt Energy Center, Lee-Way Trucking headquarters, Quail Springs Mall, Heritage Park Mall, Lincoln Plaza, First National Center, Oklahoma Christian College, Macklanberg-Duncan Company facilities, and many other office complexes in Oklahoma City.

Offering complete electrical work

from the power source to the finished building, Gaddis-Walker is one of the state's oldest and most respected firms. The organization prides itself on the number of repeat customers, many of which have used its services for more than half a century. Southwestern Bell Telephone Company, for example, was Gaddis-Walker's first customer in 1921; as that enterprise expanded, it continued to utilize the firm as the electrical contractor on its Central Dial Building, on its headquarters in downtown Oklahoma City, and on its historic preservation showpiece, One Bell Central.

In 1969 Gaddis-Walker Electric opened a new 6,000-square-foot

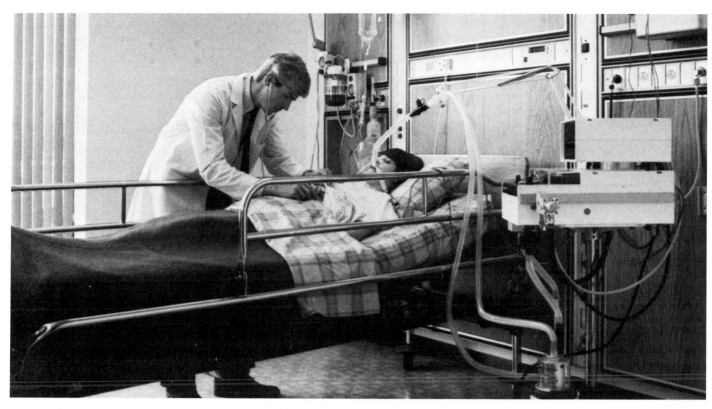

One of the Modular Services Company's completely integrated units offering diagnostic, therapeutic, and support services for individual patient rooms.

office/headquarters complex at 109 Northeast Thirty-eighth Street. Two years later, after a half-century of serving central Oklahoma in electrical contracting, the corporation reorganized into two divisions—Gaddis-Walker Electrical and Modular Services Company. Dan Walker continued to oversee the former operation, and in 1973 James A. Walker assumed management of the latter.

A new concept in hospital care, Modular Services offered prefabricated panels providing electrical and central medical gas systems for health care facilities. As part of the expansion Gaddis-Walker acquired a 15,000-square-foot building at 110 Northeast Thirty-eighth Terrace, just behind the organization's headquarters, to house that division's operations. One of the earliest companies to enter the field, Modular Services supplied custom planning and design to furnish hospitals with custom re-

quirements nationwide. In the following years the Modular Services line—to keep pace with the changing market—became more of a medical product than an electrical prefabricated wall unit, and the firm joined with Ohio Medical (Ohmeda) to offer modular walls that became recognized worldwide.

By the mid-1980s Modular Services, in conjunction with Ohmeda, provided a full line of equipment for patient care and life-support systems. Strategically placed medical gas and electric outlets were combined with a multitude of optional equipment that were ideal for individual patient rooms as well as such specialized hospital units as intensive care, coronary care, trauma, acute dialysis, recovery, and surgery. Almost any combination of equipment could be added to the basic design, including several types of medical gases, lighting units and controls, communication facilities, and therapy equipment.

This versatility allowed for the updating of the system whenever needed. The devices could be added to existing walls or installed as columns or freestanding units, and particular

care was taken to ensure that they created a pleasant patient environment by being aesthetically pleasing. However, the greatest benefit to hospitals was that the systems were not permanent. With complete accessibility from the front, each unit could easily be modified to meet different health care needs—an advantage that permitted the remodeling of rooms, the movement of services, or the construction of new space to exclude the cost of new modular units, as the existing ones simply could be moved to the new location. The diversity of the systems made practical their adoption in both new hospital construction and remodeling projects, as well as their addition to existing rooms for patient care.

During the six and a half decades that Gaddis-Walker Electric has served Oklahomans, it has become one of the state's best-known firms in its field. Its diversification and ability to adapt to the changing marketplace has enabled the corporation not only to become a leading electrical contractor in central Oklahoma, but also to expand its market outlets worldwide.

F.A. HIGHLEY COMPANY, INC.

Fred A. and Lorene Highley standing in a model kitchen displaying the products available from the F.A. Highley Company.

and collection agent; his wife, Lorene, operated the office and served as receptionist and bookkeeper. While calling on potential customers, he quickly realized that anyone interested in wall tiles also would be interested in floor coverings—moreover, few buyers wanted to purchase wall tile from one company and floor tile from another. To fill this void and to provide his clients with a complete package of vinyl and linoleum wall and floor tile coverings, Highley soon added a floor-covering product line. As a natural extension of his provisions, the enterprising businessman added cabinet tops and other accessories to his firm's inventory so that it could supply customers with all materials necessary to carry through their building or remodeling projects.

When plastics were adapted to the home-building industry in the early 1950s, Highley moved quickly to reflect the changing marketplace and expanded his line by establishing a cabinet-top laminating business that manufactured both custom-made and high-volume products. In 1965 the firm again expanded by adding post-forming capabilities that made it possible to offer a complete kitchen or bath modernization package. In addition, a large inventory of tile, floor coverings, kitchen cabinets, and vanities was maintained.

In the fabrication process a particle-board core is cut to specification and fed through a double spindle shaper that cuts a tongue to which the nose of the top is fastened and a groove to which the back of the top is attached. A sheet of lamination is then glued to the board and the two pieces are passed through a heat roller to ensure a satisfactory bond; the glue is allowed to cure, and nails or staples are added for extra strength. Afterward, the laminated covered top is fed through another heat roller that shapes the lamination to fit the

After graduating from New Mexico A&M in the spring of 1940, F.A. Highley enlisted in the Army Air Corps Flying Cadets and completed basic training at Hick Field near Fort Worth, Texas. Assigned to flight training at nearby Kelly Field, the young serviceman piloted military transport aircraft before being sent to Glider School at Joliet, Illinois. Two years later, in 1942, he became a maintenance test pilot. Rising to the rank of lieutenant colonel, Highley test-flew almost 150 different types of aircraft before returning to civilian life in 1946.

Determined to establish his own

business, Highley decided to acquire a metal wall tile franchise and locate somewhere in the Southwest. Having visited Oklahoma City on several occasions during his military career, he returned to the community in early 1946 and on June 3 of that year established the F.A. Highley Company—located on Northwest Twenty-third Street just north of the downtown area. Within a year the entrepreneur changed locations and moved to 819 North Walker, which gave him better access to his customers.

Specializing in the sale and installation of metal wall tile, Highley was the enterprise's installer, salesman,

particle board's edges and sides.

Because of its aggressive marketing techniques, in November 1958 the organization opened a larger plant and sales office at 2405 Northwest Tenth Street, just west of the downtown area. At the same time the founder incorporated the business with himself as president and chairman of the board and his wife as vice-president; both held 50 percent of the stock. In 1971 their son, Larry, graduated from Phillips University in Enid with a degree in business and joined the company on a full-time basis.

Although F.A. Highley Company remained at the new location, the plant underwent several supplementary expansions. In 1965 a 3,000-square-foot annexation provided space for its postforming capabilities. Five years later another 4,200 square feet were added to give more storage and work area. Eventually, the office and plant occupied 18,500 square feet.

During the housing boom of the 1960s, competition from high-volume laminators forced the corporation to revise its sales approach. While continuing to supply Oklahoma City-area builders and contractors with custom-produced or ordered-to-specification kitchen and bathroom furnishings, F.A. Highley Company also began the distribution of the products of its lamination plant throughout the state and the furnishing of company crews to install the materials. As sales grew so did the firm's marketing area, and by the

mid-1980s the organization was offering the installation of a total floor covering, cabinet, and countertop package throughout the United States and in several countries overseas.

In order to further increase business, Highley began to turn his attention to other construction projects that could benefit from the company's product line. Among the most successful of these was custom installations for specialized institutions and offices that required high footage of cabinet space. Performing high-quality work at competitive prices, the corporation utilized both direct bidding practices and subcontract arrangements to enter the market and soon increased its sales throughout the Southwest. With the growth of specialized design work for offices and hospitals came the development of a similar line of custom-laminated cabinet tops for new and remodeled dental offices and medical clinics. Likewise, the firm entered the college and public library market with custom-designed cabinet tops and bookshelves for dormitories.

During this period of expansion F.A. Highley Company retained its supply operation to home builders and remodeling contractors in the central Oklahoma area. In addition, as the luxury housing market began to grow, the company added equipment that allowed the custom laminating and installation of the multitude of exotic shapes utilized by these builders—including U- and G-shaped cabinets.

The corporation's success was built around a manufacturing process sufficiently flexible to permit the production of a wide variety of shapes and sizes. At the same time it retained the high-volume capability necessary to market conventional kitchen and vanity tops. As its founder pointed out, the firm "can easily produce 100 tops per day or make specialized tops with equal ease." By such a process F.A. Highley Company has become a recognized industry leader that prides itself on offering "a good job at a fair price."

In 1984 F.A. Highley retired as president of the organization; however, he remained as chairman of the board. Larry Highley assumed the presidency and with Gorman Newton, who had been with the company for a quarter of a century, formed the corporate management team. As such they oversee a staff of eighteen employees and offer custom-produced cabinet tops, wall and floor coverings, tables, and a myriad of other products used in the home-building industry as well as business, medical, and educational fields.

Accruing annual sales in excess of one million dollars, F.A. Highley Company—maintaining the founder's philosophy of providing the customer with whatever he wants—ships its products worldwide.

F.A. Highley, on the left, taking delivery of a fleet of delivery trucks. The vehicles are used by the company to provide specialized crews for custom installation of the firm's products.

THE BENHAM GROUP

The Benham Group had its beginning in Oklahoma City soon after statehood. Founded in 1909 by Webster Lance Benham as Benham Engineering Company, the firm has served as consulting engineers for hundreds of cities and towns across the state. By its seventy-fifth anniversary in 1984, The Benham Group had grown to a professionally and geographically diversified organization of national reputation—offering services in engineering, architecture, design, and planning. Maintaining corporate headquarters in Oklahoma City, the company serves clients from division offices located across the nation.

Webster Benham came to Oklahoma in 1906 as a young civil engineering graduate of Columbia University. He found Oklahoma City in need of streets, water mains, sewers, bridges, and power structures; municipal engineering projects were the mainstay of the company for many years. In 1917 he accepted a commission as a major in the Quartermaster Corps and built Camp Funston, near Fort Riley, Kansas, where David Blair Benham was born on Armistice Day, 1918. After the war, Webster Benham established an office in Kansas City, Missouri, and moved his family there while still maintaining his Oklahoma City office.

During World War II Benham Engineering Company served as engineers and architects, and subsequently as construction managers, for Army facilities in Louisiana—Camp Livingston, South Camp Polk, North Camp Polk, and Camp Beauregard. Following the war the organization reclaimed its prewar eminence as a consulting engineering operation. In 1946 David Benham joined the company—having graduated from the United States Naval Academy in 1941 and postgraduate school in 1942, then serving as a naval architect in the aircraft carrier program throughout the war.

Webster Benham was made an honorary member of Tau Beta Pi at

Webster Benham (standing), shown in company offices in 1916, was national president of the American Association of Engineers in 1924 and the first Oklahoman elected to the American Society of Civil Engineers' board of directors. ©1985, The Benham Group

the University of Oklahoma. The Associated General Contractors of Oklahoma and the Department of Civil Engineering at Oklahoma A&M College named a civil engineering camp in Colorado for him. David Benham assumed leadership of the firm in 1952 upon the death of his father. In 1956 he was joined by his younger brother, John, who serves as corporate director and officer; and in 1961 by his sister, Margaret Austin, who serves as secretary for the accounting and fiscal department. In 1982 a nephew, Webster Lance Benham III, joined the company and now serves as executive vice-president of The Benham Group East—located in the Washington, D.C., area. Recently, a son, David Blair Benham II, became a member of the graphic arts division of The Benham Group (TBG Graphics). A daughter, Nancy Johnston, serves as a business development specialist.

In the 1950s the corporation strengthened services in all engineering disciplines and established architectural capability. As it expanded it outgrew the building at 215 Northeast Twenty-third Street, built in 1954, and moved into a five-story structure at Northwest Sixty-third Street and Grand Boulevard, which served as corporate headquarters and Oklahoma City Division offices until the completion of One Benham Place

at Britton Road and the Broadway Extension in 1983.

The company has designed major water and wastewater facilities, interstate highways, and bridges throughout Oklahoma and other states. The Benham Group has vigorously pursued professional services for various industrial and commercial corporations in high-technology applications.

The organization has received national recognition in many forms. Six awards came for design of the United Services Automobile Association headquarters in San Antonio. In 1977 the design of a state office building in Sacramento won the first award in the State of California nationwide contest for the design of an energy-efficient building, while another achievement for that design was the Owens-Corning Energy Conservation Award.

Design of the Halliburton Services Research and Development facility in Duncan brought the *Industrial Research & Development* magazine Lab of the Year Award in 1981. Elsewhere in Oklahoma commendation was received for Mercy Health Center, Presbyterian Hospital, and Conoco Laboratory in Ponca City. Among the many other awards given to the company and his numerous personal honors, David Benham—chairman of the board and chief executive officer—was inducted into the Engineering Hall of Fame at Oklahoma State University in 1973. The Newcomen Society in North America came to Oklahoma City to present an award to the company and to David Benham, personally, in 1979.

W.R. HOLWAY AND ASSOCIATES (A DIVISION OF THE BENHAM GROUP)

In 1973 The Benham Group acquired the well-known firm of W.R. Holway and Associates, headquartered in Tulsa, which brought exceptional expertise and experience in water development and power generation. Founded in 1920 by W.R. Holway, it has been actively engaged in consulting engineering since that time. Two sons, W.N. Holway, chief executive officer, and D.K. Holway, vice-president, have applied their working years to the company. In 1967 a daughter of W.N. Holway, Marcia Schaefer, joined the organization and serves as vice-president, manager of support services.

In 1918 W.R. Holway, a 1915 graduate of Massachusetts Institute of Technology, went to Tulsa to supervise the city's Arkansas River Filtration Plant. In the 1920s he de-

signed and supervised construction completion of the original Spavinaw water supply for Tulsa, bringing the water via a 54-mile, gravity-flow pipeline from a dam on Spavinaw Creek. Its first flow to Tulsa was activated on November 17, 1924. Subsequently, W.R. Holway and Associates has been responsible for numerous improvements to the Tulsa water supply and distribution system, including Lake Eucha Dam, the A.B. Jewell Water Treatment Plant, and a 72-inch raw-water pipeline from Oologah Reservoir to the A.B. Jewell plant.

Since the establishment of the Grand River Dam Authority in 1935, W.R. Holway and Associates has served as consulting engineers to the agency. The first GRDA project was the design and construction of Pensacola Dam, the largest multiple-arch dam in the world. GRDA generated and sold its first hydroelectric power in 1941. Since 1976 the company has been involved in engineering, construction management, and start-up

of GRDA's coal-fired generating plants near Pryor. Unit I has been operating since 1981; Unit II began generation of electricity in the fall of 1985.

For forty years the corporation has been active in feasibility analyses, licensing, design, and construction management of hydropower facilities. A recent project was the Lawrence Hydroelectric Project in Massachusetts, in which a hydroelectric plant was added to the dam built in 1848. The firm provided project design and engineering service support, including construction management. For this project W.R. Holway and Associates received awards from the National Society of Professional Engineers and the Association of General Contractors of Massachusetts.

W.R. Holway designed Pensacola Dam, which created Grand Lake O' the Cherokees. The Markham Ferry Dam and the Salina pumped-storage projects were later hydroelectric facilities designed by W.R. Holway and Associates for GRDA. ©1985, The Benham Group

ST. JOHN MEDICAL CENTER

Originating in Bavaria, the Community of the Sisters of the Sorrowful Mother was founded by Mother Mary Frances Streitel in 1884 and charged with operating hospitals, parochial and catechetical schools, orphanages, convalescent homes, and homes for the aged. The following year the Sisters were recognized formally by the Roman Catholic Church. Within four years of the order's founding, the Sisters of the Sorrowful Mother expanded their operations to America, and in 1889 the Sisters opened their first mission, St. Francis Hospital, in Wichita, Kansas.

That same year a portion of present-day Oklahoma was opened to settlement. Inhabitants of the Twin Territories, as Oklahoma and Indian Territory were called, suffered from insufficient medical care. Many of the early pioneers could find medical care only at the various military establishments in the region. Although the Indian Territory Medical Association was formed as early as 1881, it was not until 1904 that the United States Congress passed the National Practice Act for Indian Territory. In 1906, the year before statehood, the Oklahoma State Medical Association was formed, and in 1907 Tulsa's first hospital was opened. That same year the Tulsa County Medical Society was organized.

In the spring of 1914 the members of the Tulsa County Medical Society contacted the Sisters in Wichita, Kansas, concerning the possibility of opening a hospital in Tulsa. Reacting to the request, the Sisters dispatched a delegation to visit the community. Convinced that additional medical facilities were needed, the Sisters approached the Bishop of Oklahoma City for permission to start a hospital in the diocese. In May 1916 the Reverend John J. Heiring approved the request and Sister Mary Cornelia, the Superior of St. Mary's Hospital in Oshkosh, Wisconsin, was given the task of traveling to Tulsa to locate a suitable site for the hospital and oversee its construction.

Working with the Tulsa County Medical Society, the Sisters and the citizens of Tulsa agreed to share the cost of the project. Grant R. McCullough was named chairman and David F. Connolly was selected treasurer of the first fund-raising drive for St. John's Hospital. In March 1916 Wight & Wight Architects of Kansas City, Missouri, was contracted to provide plans for the structure. An option to purchase an eight-acre strawberry farm at what is now 1923 South Utica Avenue in Tulsa was acquired for $25, and a year later, in August 1917, the financing to purchase the tract was completed. The Sisters acquired title to the property for $16,000.

The hospital opened on February 22, 1926. Total admissions reached 1,958 that year, a figure reached each month now.

Work on the building began on February 11, 1920, when General John J. Pershing turned the first shovel of dirt for a five-story building, with a basement, powerhouse, and connecting tunnel. Unfortunately, a nationwide recession caused a postponement. In addition, the actual construction cost proved to be greater than estimated. Although the skeleton of the structure was completed, it was three years before the initial construction project was finished. In the intervening period the Sisters almost abandoned the effort. Fortunately, in 1924 the Sisters of the Sorrowful Mother in Cenville, New Jersey, divested some of their property holdings and made the funds available for the Tulsa project. At the same time it was decided that by slightly altering the original plans, enclosing the skeleton with masonry, and installing windows, it would be possible to complete a fifty-bed hospital with the money at hand. A contract to complete the work was signed with Hutter Construction Company in January 1925.

With the completion of the first two floors, the Sisters opened the facility to the ill. While the building was still being completed, the Sisters

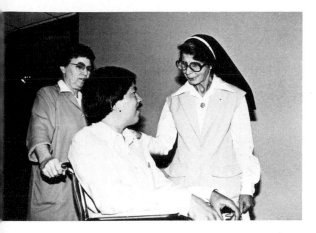

The Sisters of the Sorrowful Mother own and operate St. John Medical Center. Sisters can be found at all times of the day and night comforting patients.

slept at the Holy Family School and commuted daily to the hospital. The facilities at the school were totally inadequate and many of the Sisters were forced to sleep on the floor. Eventually, cots were placed in a house near the hospital for the Sisters.

Early in 1925 a second fund-raising drive raised $550,000, and by May of that year the outside brick walls had been completed, terrazzo floors installed, the roof finished, and much of the interior work finalized. Additional donations allowed the completion of the powerhouse and a laundry, and temporary housing for the Sisters was provided on the second floor. In January 1926 additional Sisters arrived to complete the patients' rooms and on February 22, 1926, St. John's Hospital officially was opened.

Almost immediately, the facility was filled to capacity and extra cots were placed throughout the hospital to care for the overflow. Total admissions in 1926 reached 1,958. The overcrowding was relieved somewhat in the summer of 1926 with the completion of the two floors of St. John's South Wing. During the following months additional floors were completed and opened to occupation. By 1929 the fifth floor was finished and assigned to surgery, a laboratory was functioning, and an X-ray facility completed. An electrocardiogram department was organized in 1929, and

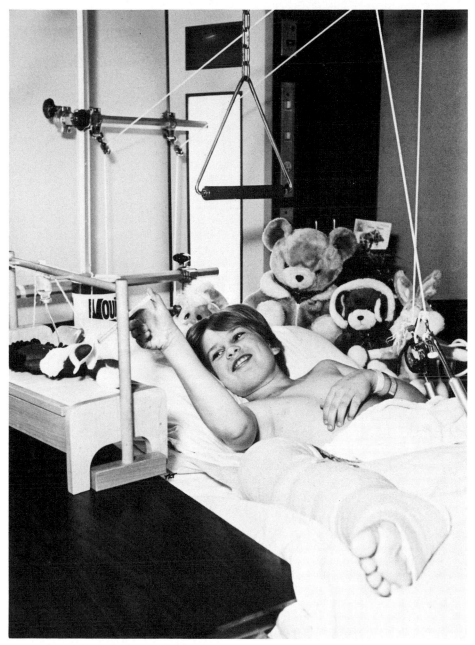

Playing with simulated medical toys can help children overcome their fear of hospitals.

a chapel and a convent were added in 1931.

The same year St. John's was opened, the hospital established a School of Nursing. In 1927 it received state accreditation and during the following years the facility continued to expand. In 1938 a School of Nursing building was dedicated and in 1946 an addition to the nurses' residence was added. Temporary accreditation by the National League for Nursing's Accreditation Board was granted in 1951, and the St. John's School of Nursing received full national accreditation in 1953.

Occupancy continued to outstrip available space. The need for more beds continued to climb, and by 1936 admissions had grown to 5,318. To make room for the patients, the nurses' residence was converted to patient rooms, and a new nurses' residence was added in 1937. In March 1937 work on a radiology building was started thanks to a contribution made by Waite Phillips in memory of his twin brother Wiate. It was

Proud of the past, grateful for the present, and hopeful for the future, St. John Medical Center continues to provide quality health care to Tulsa and the surrounding community.

dedicated in April 1938.

Continued expansion was limited by the outbreak of World War II and the accompanying shortage of building materials. At the same time the booming wartime economy led to a drastic increase in the community's population. By 1945 almost 11,000 patients were seeking care annually at St. John's Hospital. To accommodate the increased patient demand, ground was broken in February 1946 for a T-shaped South Wing to be constructed to the south of the original building. Completed in May 1948, it increased St. John's bed capacity to a total of 440 plus an additional 66 bassinets. To aid in caring for the increased patient load, St. John's Auxiliary was organized in 1951 and through the following decades was a vibrant force in providing nonmedical care.

Once again the expansion soon proved inadequate, and by 1953 patient cots lined the halls in the hospital's obstetrical department. Although waiting rooms were converted to patients' rooms, a countywide survey revealed a shortage of 442 hospital beds. Thus, a $3.5-million fundraising drive was implemented in 1954 to finance a West Wing that would house an additional 202 beds, plus a 52-unit premature infant nursery, new surgical facilities, a psychiatric department, administrative offices, an outpatient department, and a medical library. In addition, the program would expand the area available to St. John's kitchen, laundry, physical therapy, and medical records departments. A groundbreaking ceremony was held on July 19, 1955, and the West Wing was opened in March 1957. Its completion raised St. John's bed count to 600, plus 75 bassinets.

While the West Wing was under construction, a 255-automobile parkade was opened in the summer of 1955. It was expanded to hold 400 automobiles in 1963 and 1964 with the addition of two stories. Continued expansion in 1957 renovated the X-ray building and allowed for the establishment of a cobalt unit.

During the 1960s the implementation of Medicare and other services necessitated the installation of a computerized accounting system and an expansion of the business office. This was the beginning of a building program that carried on throughout the decade. The northeast portion of the hospital was remodeled and a new two-story wing added; the pharmacy was updated and remodeled; an addition was completed to the north side of the X-ray building; and a $70,000 intensive cardiac care unit, made possible by a gift from the Alexander estate, was opened.

To accommodate this expansion program, in 1968 St. John's acquired the property just to the east of the hospital, bounded by Nineteenth and Twenty-first streets and Utica and Wheeling avenues. One year later a new one-story outpatient clinic was leased to the west of St. John's, across Utica Avenue. A new doctors' parking lot was completed on the south side of the hospital and a driveway entrance opened on Utica Avenue that same year. A new chapel was constructed in 1970, and the former facility was converted into the department of radiological sciences.

In 1971 plans were made for the construction of a 603-bed North Tower. Costing $44 million, the fourteen-story facility contained an ultramodern acute care hospital with a capacity of 723 beds. Included in the North Tower were a cancer treatment center, a cardiovascular treatment and rehabilitation center, a trauma treatment unit, a 24-hour emergency room, intensive care units, dining rooms, physical and respiratory therapy areas, cardiopulmonary rehabilitation laboratory, 23 operating rooms, obstetrical-gynecology units, orthopedic services, psychiatry units, and diagnostic and care areas for medical and surgical patients. At that time St. John's Hospital became St. John Medical Center. Its opening on February 22, 1976, half a century after the original opening of St. John's Hospital, makes the St. John Medical Center one of the most complete health care facilities in the Southwest.

BROWN MANUFACTURING COMPANY

The Arapaho-born son of a Sooner, L.G. "Gus" Brown, and his eighteen-year-old bride, Marie Woody Brown of Weatherford, arrived in Oklahoma City in 1925 looking for work. Within six decades the items produced by the company they started were standard equipment on thousands of residences and commercial buildings throughout the world.

However, theirs was not an instant success story. First he worked on the assembly line at Ford Motor Company in Oklahoma City and Dallas; then came their first venture into private enterprise, making spring covers and later adjustable sunshades for side windows of automobiles—followed by adjustable sunshades for residential windows and doors. All the products were created by the inventive mind of Gus Brown and were manufactured by him or under his guidance on machinery and dies, which he either designed or built. All of the private ventures were with partners; however, because of the economic climate of the time, none were successful.

Eventually, in 1943, Gus and Marie decided to go it alone and formed Brown Manufacturing Company as a sole proprietorship. Renting a small shop on North Walker Avenue near downtown Oklahoma City, they were defense contractors until the end of World War II. They then started making Air-O-Blind, an outside venetian-type blind—now known as a jalousie—that Brown had invented for residential windows, doors, and screen porches. Brown was a one-man operation. He sold blinds one day, made them that night, and installed them the following day. His two sons, Russell and Stanley, sometimes worked in the shop when they were not in school.

This was before the days of residential air conditioning, and need for the product was great. Within a

L.G. "Gus" Brown and Marie Woody Brown posed for these portraits on their wedding day, July 4, 1924.

short time, demand for the Air-O-Blind spread beyond Oklahoma City. To satisfy the new market, Brown established "franchised" assembly plants from coast to coast and in Puerto Rico. As the company continued to grow, he built a new 20,000-square-foot plant at the intersection of Linwood and Virginia, just west of downtown Oklahoma City. That same year Brown Manufacturing was incorporated—with Gus, Marie, Russell, Stanley, and Sandra (a daughter) as stockholders.

In the early 1950s architects recognized that the benefits of Air-O-Blind applied to commercial structures as well as residences, and integrated them into plans for school buildings. This led to Brown's current business as an architectural metal manufacturer specializing in sun-control devices, skylight shutters, sunshades, grills, handrails, wall guards, and corner guards for commercial buildings. The success of Brown Manufacturing, known worldwide for its expertise in the field of sun-control devices, is due to the variety of products it offers.

All sun-control devices, whether horizontal or vertical, are a variation of the original Air-O-Blind designed by Gus Brown. Some are small-scale and some large, and they serve a diverse variety of customers—including the control firing rooms at Cape Canaveral, Florida, which are equipped with vertical sun louvers produced by Brown Manufacturing Company with blades that are five feet six inches wide and twenty-eight feet tall. Some are fixed, others are manually adjustable, and some electrically adjustable with an automatic control system that guarantees maximum natural lighting with minimum solar heat gain.

By 1959 the growth of the company necessitated another move. A new 60,000-square-foot plant and corporate headquarters was constructed at 13431 Broadway Extension in north Oklahoma City. Currently, Russell Brown is president of the firm.

Marie and Gus Brown in October 1968. The Browns founded the firm in 1943 as a defense contractor until the end of World War II and then to manufacture Gus Brown's inventions.

THE WESTIN HOTEL, WILLIAMS CENTER

Plans for the Williams Plaza Hotel, Williams Center, were unveiled in November 1975 as a part of the Williams Center in downtown Tulsa. A nine-square-block, $250-million project, the Williams Center—of which the Williams Plaza Hotel was a cornerstone—was intended as a catalyst for the revival of the central-city area. The following month Williams Plaza Hotel, Inc., was formed and on January 8, 1976, Westin Hotels was selected to operate the facility. Groundbreaking ceremonies were held on November 30, 1976. Costing an estimated twenty million dollars, the Westin Hotel officially was opened on July 10, 1978. In 1984 the name was changed to The Westin Hotel, Williams Center.

While the facility is owned by The Williams Companies, it is managed by Westin Hotels—the nation's oldest hotel-management organization—which was founded in 1930 by S.W. Thurston, Frank Dupar, Peter Schmidt, and Adolph Schmidt as Western Hotels. During the 1940s the organization's first management committee—Edward Carlson, Lynn Himmelman, and Gordan Bass—revolutionized the hotel industry by introducing such sweeping innovations

as the substitution of credit cards for cash payment, private wire reservation service, guaranteed and confirmed reservations, a family plan, and 24-hour room service.

Western Hotels continued to grow, and during the 1950s introduced another revolutionary concept in hotel management. If a guest had a confirmed reservation and for any reason there was no room available, Western would secure a room in another hotel at its own expense. Transportation was included in the guarantee. A decade later the firm introduced a computerized reservations system, Hoteltron, to offer its guests the best possible service. Eventually the reservations system was upgraded, and a Central Reservations Center was opened in Omaha, Nebraska, which utilized Westron, an advanced reservations/communications computer system. During this period of expansion Western extended its operations to Hawaii, Guatemala, and Mexico.

In 1963 the company changed its name to Western International Hotels and during the following years opened facilities in Venezuela, Japan, Hong Kong, Australia, and Ecuador. In 1970 Western merged with United Airlines. Under the terms of the merger, Western International operated as an autonomous, wholly

The Westin Hotel, Williams Center, in Tulsa, is Oklahoma's only AAA Five Diamond Award winner.

owned subsidiary of UAL Inc. In 1981 the name again was changed to Westin Hotels. In 1985 Westin Hotels and United Airlines were joined by Hertz Rent A Car.

By the mid-1980s Westin Hotels had grown to thirty establishments within the United States, six in Canada, two in Japan and Korea, and nine in Mexico. Individual facilities also were operated in El Salvador, Guatemala, Hong Kong, the Philippines, Singapore, and South Africa. In addition, the company operated its own Culinary Institute at Costa Mesa, California, to further the kitchen management potential of its sous chefs.

Offering luxury accommodations, The Westin Hotel, Williams Center, contains 450 rooms ranging in size from a deluxe single to the elegant

The parlor of one of five luxurious two-bedroom suites.

A Premier Room.

chairman's suite. Its guests are served by 350 employees. The thirteen-story structure, located between Main Street and Boston Avenue and Second and Third streets, is an integral part of the Williams Center. The hotel is connected to the three-level Williams Center Forum mall, which allows its guests access to the numerous retail outlets, indoor ice rink, and cinema. In addition, a pedestrian skybridge on the east side of the hotel provides access to the Bank of Oklahoma Tower. The east side of the Westin Hotel overlooks The Green, a 2.5-acre park; and the Tulsa Performing Arts Center, which offers opera, ballet, and year-round theater activities. The Tulsa Convention Center is nearby, while easy access to the city's expressway system allows guests of the hotel to quickly reach any place in the city.

Tulsa's Westin Hotel offers several special guest packages designed around special weekends, romance, the performing arts, and family holidays. One of its most luxurious is the Diamond Tradition, which provides accommodations in the hotel's finest suite, champagne limousine service, 24-hour personal valet, and a sumptuous reception. The hotel also provides round-trip transportation, within 1,000 miles, in a private Lear jet or helicopter.

In addition to its glamorous overnight accommodations, the Westin Hotel contains sixteen meeting and banquet areas, numerous dining and entertainment facilities, a large ex-

hibit area, and an underground parking lot. The two exhibit areas/meeting rooms—the Plaza Ballroom, on the west of the Plaza foyer and the Oklahoma Room, on the east of the foyer—can, by utilizing sliding walls, be used as a single room or subdivided. The extreme north end of the Plaza Ballroom can be formed into three small meeting rooms—the Oak, Hickory, and Maple rooms—while the remainder of the ballroom can be divided in half to form two larger rooms. The Oklahoma Room also can be divided into two smaller areas. Dominating the foyer between the two exhibit areas is a large reflecting pool. The diversity of the exhibit area offers a wide range of options available to gatherings as large as 1,500 individuals or as small as a private business meeting.

Smaller gatherings may utilize the Executive Board Room, one of Tulsa's most popular sites for business meetings. In addition to a central boardroom, the area contains a private kitchen and a caucus room. It also has complete audiovisual facilities.

Three restaurants and clubs are located in the facility. Montague's, which offers formal dining in an elegant setting, has been the recipient of the Tulsalite Silver Spoon Award for the best overall restaurant in 1984 and 1985. Its menu features a varied selection of appetizers and entrées. Another award-winning restaurant, Glass on the Green, offers informal, casual dining. Overlooking the landscaped Williams Center Green, Glass on the Green features family fare and the Tulsalite Silver Spoon Award-winning Sunday brunch. Barrister's is a private club with a sophisticated, relaxed atmosphere of dancing and live entertainment. A deli-style lunch is served during the week and light snacks are available during the evening.

The Westin Hotel offers guests an indoor/outdoor swimming pool and hot-tub area for relaxation. In addition, four indoor tennis courts and a health club are available. Color tele-

vision and in-room movies also are provided.

From among the 15,000 American Automobile Association-approved hotels or motels in North America and Mexico, The Westin Hotel, Williams Center, is one of only forty-five that has received the prestigious Five Diamond Award. It is the only hotel in Oklahoma to receive the Five Diamond Award since the honor was initiated in 1977, and has received this recognition for the past seven years. The establishment also has received the Mobil Four Star Award for excellence, and the First Place Award from *Travel/Holiday* magazine for the best small meeting room.

To ensure the hotel's continued reputation for excellence, management completed in 1985 a $3-million refurbishing of the original guest rooms. The hotel operations are governed by a philosophy of five Is: integrity, intestinal fortitude, intelligence, imagination, and initiative. Using this as a guideline, by 1986 The Westin Hotel, Williams Center, had solidly established itself as one of the most outstanding hotels in the United States.

The Westin Hotel maintains four indoor all-weather tennis courts.

HILTON INN WEST

Located at the intersection of I-40 and Meridian Avenue, the Hilton Inn West serves one of the fastest-growing commercial and residential areas of Oklahoma City. Because of its centralized location with easy access to I-40, I-44, and I-240, the Hilton Inn West allows guests to reach any point in the Oklahoma City metropolitan area with ease. To accommodate airline travelers, three vans are on call to shuttle guests from the hotel to nearby Will Rogers World Airport. In addition, the hotel provides facilities for meetings and conventions of any size.

Built in three phases, the Hilton Inn West contains 509 guest rooms, each equipped with king-size or double beds. Phase I, completed and opened to occupancy in 1972, contains 243 rooms spaced around an open courtyard containing two outdoor swimming pools and a paddle tennis court. The Phase I building is divided into thirds, with the western two-thirds of the structure containing the guest rooms and pool area divid-

The hotel's Gazebo Room features an indoor swimming pool, tropical plants, water sculptures, stained-glass lighting, and a gazebo accented with turn-of-the-century antiques.

ed by a central walkway running north and south. In the center of the guest room complex are four town houses and four junior executive suites. Each opens onto one of the two outdoor pools. The town houses contain wet bars, swimming pool-size bathtubs, whirlpools, and king-size beds.

The eastern one-third of the building holds the executive offices, convention facilities, kitchen, Brandy-

Located at the intersection of I-40 and Meridian Avenue, the Hilton Inn West is the largest hotel and conference center in Oklahoma.

wine Room, coffee shop, gift shop, barbershop, and other specialty areas. The coffee shop seats eighty-six customers, and adjoins the Brandywine Room. Specializing in gourmet dining, the Brandywine Room seats another 125 and offers Old

World atmosphere with live entertainment nightly. Also featuring live music and adult entertainment, the Sports Page Club offers a truly upbeat gathering place with cocktails, dancing, and dinner for crowds from throughout the metro area.

The North Ballroom, located at the extreme eastern edge of the Phase I structure, contains 5,000 square feet of meeting space. Designed to be subdivided by movable walls into four smaller rooms—the Allegheny, Blue Ridge, Cumberland, and Shenandoah—each of which measures 25 by 50 feet and contains 1,250 square feet, the North Ballroom allows the Hilton Inn West to offer a variety of room sizes for large, medium, or small meetings. Adjoining the North Ballroom on the east is the East Gallery, which provides additional space for registration, exhibits, or other gatherings. Phase I also contains four presidential meeting rooms for smaller meetings.

An instant success, the Hilton Inn West quickly outgrew its original building. As a result, in 1974 the Phase II building was opened. Located just to the south of Phase I and connected to the older building by a covered walkway, the new expansion added 129 guest rooms to the Hilton Inn's capacity. The rooms are centered around indoor and outdoor recreation areas. The outdoor facility features a wading pool for children and a putting green and is connected to the indoor facility by a flowing waterway. Called the Gazebo Room, the indoor facility presents a special island of refreshment in a tropical setting complete with a gazebo, an indoor swimming pool, tropical plants, water sculptures, and stained-glass lighting, and is accented by turn-of-the century antiques. For evening entertainment, Phase II contains the Bombay Hunt Club, a unique business persons' lounge for quiet conversation and relaxation which features live entertainment nightly, except Sunday.

In addition, the South Ballroom, located on the east side of the Phase II building and separated from the guest rooms and Gazebo Room by the Main Gallery, greatly expands the hotel's convention and meeting facilities. Containing 7,500 square feet, the South Ballroom also can be subdivided by movable walls into four individual rooms—the Quarter Horse, Palomino, Arabian, and Appaloosa rooms—each of which contains 1,800 square feet of floor space. It also contains several presidential meeting rooms for smaller gatherings.

Constructed to the west of the original structure, Hilton Inn West's Phase III building was completed in 1978 and added 137 guest rooms to the hotel's total. In addition, Phase III contains several presidential suites capable of seating up to forty individuals or serving as many as thirty-two guests for banquets. Phase III also contains Chisholm's Club, an old-time dance hall and shuffleboard parlor with the latest in country-western music. Offering one of the largest dance floors in Oklahoma City, Chisholm's seats 175.

The Hilton Inn West also provides numerous athletic facilities for its guests. In addition to the indoor and outdoor swimming pools, paddle tennis court, and putting green, there are two lighted tennis courts, a fitness trail for jogging and physical exercise, and a softball diamond. Saunas and whirlpools are available, as is an exercise room.

With the completion of all three phases, the Hilton Inn West is now the largest hotel and conference center in Oklahoma. Luncheons, dinners, or banquets can be served for from one to 1,000 guests. Complete catering services are available, including food, floral arrangements, and audiovisual requirements for conferences. Staffed by capable and willing sales and catering personnel trained to make meetings a worry-free pleasure, the Hilton Inn West is one of the premier convention centers in central Oklahoma.

Offering complete banquet facilities, the Hilton Inn West is one of central Oklahoma's most popular meeting and convention sites.

Patrons

The following individuals, companies, and organizations have made a valuable commitment to the quality of this publication. Windsor Publications, Inc., and the Oklahoma Historical Society gratefully acknowledge their participation in *Oklahoma: Land of the Fair God.*

AAA Oklahoma
Albright Steel and Wire Company*
Alexander Energy Corporation*
The Apple Tree
AT&T Network Systems*
Bama Pie, Ltd.*
Banks of Mid-America, Inc.*
Baptist Medical Center of Oklahoma*
The Benham Group*
Blue Cross and Blue Shield of Oklahoma*
Barney U. Brown, Jr.
Brown Manufacturing Company*
Camelot Hotel*
Chickasha Cotton Oil Company
CMI Corporation*
Cobb Engineering Company
Crescent Market
Deaconess Hospital*
The Economy Company*
Facet Enterprises, Inc.*
Family Markets-Warehouse Markets, Inc.
W.D. Finney
First National Bank, Sallisaw
The First National Bank of Coweta
Fleming Companies, Inc.*
Ford Motor Company
    Tulsa Glass Plant*
Gaddis-Walker Electric, Incorporated*
Gardner Spring, Inc.*
General Motors Corporation
    Oklahoma City Assembly Plant*
Governair Corporation*
Max E. Harris
F.A. Highley Company, Inc.*
Hilton Inn Northwest*
Hilton Inn West*
HTB, Inc.
Hugh R. Hughes
Industrial Gasket, Inc.*
Ken's Restaurant Systems, Inc.*
Mr. and Mrs. John E. Kirkpatrick
KVOO Radio 1170*
Macklanburg-Duncan Company*
Patricia Montgomery
Moulder-Oldham Company, Inc.*
Mustang Fuel Corporation*
Norick Brothers, Inc.*

Oklahoma Fixture Company*
Oklahoma Gas and Electric Company*
Oklahoma Publishing Company*
Oklahoma Teaching Hospitals*
ONEOK Inc.*
Otasco*
Payne County Historical Society
James C. Pinkerton
Presbyterian Hospital*
Public Service Company of Oklahoma*
Ramsey Winch Company
Reading & Bates Corporation*
St. Anthony Hospital*
St. John Medical Center*
Scrivner, Inc.*
Ralph and Pauline Shebester
Skirvin Plaza Hotel*
Sonic Industries Inc.*
Sooner Builders & Investments, Inc.
South Community Hospital*
Southern Sheet Metal Works, Inc.*
Southwestern Bell Telephone*
South West Packaging, Inc.*
Sun Company, Inc.
Superior Linen Service, Inc.
Swinson Chevrolet, Inc.*
T.G.&Y.*
Telex Corporation*
Turner Corporation (Mortgage Bankers)
Unarco Commercial Products*
United Founders Life Insurance Company*
University of Oklahoma Tulsa Medical College
May Patterson Walley
The Westin Hotel, Williams Center*
Whiteside and Grant, Realtors
Yale Cleaners, Inc.
Yuba Heat Transfer Corporation

*Partners in Progress of *Oklahoma: Land of the Fair God.* The histories of these companies and organizations appear in Chapter XVII, beginning on page 240.

Suggested Readings

The books listed below are not intended to be a complete bibliography of Oklahoma history. Moreover, there is no separate listing of journal articles, which would number in the thousands. There are three categories: previous histories of the state, journals of special interest to Oklahomans, and books on specialized topics. Those volumes in the third category are meant as a starting point, a beginning, for serious students of Oklahoma's long past. A few are fiction, some are reminiscences, some are light, some are scholarly—but all illuminate some aspect of Oklahoma and should be interesting and informative.

STATE HISTORIES

Barrett, Charles F. *Oklahoma After Fifty Years: A history.* 4 vols. Oklahoma City: Historical Record Association, 1940.

Dale, Edward E., and Morris L. Wardell. *History of Oklahoma.* Englewood Cliffs, NJ: Prentice Hall, 1948.

Foreman, Grant. *History of Oklahoma.* Norman: University of Oklahoma Press, 1942.

Gibson, Arrell M. *Oklahoma: A History of Five Centuries.* Second Edition. Norman: University of Oklahoma Press, 1981.

Harlow, Victor E. *Oklahoma History.* Oklahoma City: Harlow Publishing Company, 1961.

Litton, Gaston. *History of Oklahoma.* 4 vols. New York: Lewis History Publishing Company, 1957.

McReynolds, Edwin C. *Oklahoma: A History of the Sooner State.* Norman: University of Oklahoma Press, 1954.

Ruth, Kent, ed. *Oklahoma: A Guide to the Sooner State.* Norman: University of Oklahoma Press, 1957.

Thoburn, Joseph B. *History of Oklahoma.* 5 vols. Chicago: Warden Company, 1916.

_____ and Muriel Wright. *Oklahoma: A History of the State and its People.* 4 vols. New York: Web Publishing Company, 1929.

JOURNALS

Chronicles of Oklahoma
The Oklahoma Historical Society
Historical Building
Oklahoma City, OK 73105

Oklahoma Today
Will Rogers Memorial Building
State Capitol
Oklahoma City, OK 73105

Great Plains Journal
Museum of the Great Plains
P.O. Box 68
Lawton, OK 73502

GENERAL READINGS

Abel, Annie H. *The American Indian as Slave Holder and Secessionist.* Cleveland: A.H. Clark Company, 1915.

Allen, Clinton M. *The Sequoyah Movement.* Oklahoma City: Harlow Publishing Company, 1925.

Alley, John. *City Beginnings in Oklahoma Territory.* Norman: University of Oklahoma Press, 1939.

Bailey, M. Thomas. *Reconstruction in the Indian Territory.* Port Washington: Kennikat, 1972.

Baldwin, Kathlyn. *The 89ers: Oklahoma Land Rush of 1889.* Oklahoma City: Western Heritage Books, 1981.

Barnard, Evan G. *A Rider in the Cherokee Strip.* Boston: Houghton Mifflin, 1935.

Bass, Althea. *The Story of Tullahassee.* Oklahoma City: Semco Color Press, 1960.

_____. *The Arapaho Way.* New York: C.N. Potter, 1966.

Bell, Robert E. *Oklahoma Archaeology: An Annotated Bibliography.* Norman: University of Oklahoma Press, 1978.

Berthrong, Donald J. *The Southern Cheyennes.* Norman: University of Oklahoma Press, 1963.

_____. *The Cheyenne and Arapaho Ordeal.* Norman, 1976.

Bischoff, John P. *Mr. Iba: Basketball's Aggie Iron Duke.* Oklahoma City: Oklahoma Heritage Association, 1980.

Blackburn, Bob L. *Heart of the Promised Land: An Illustrated History of Oklahoma County.* Woodland Hills: Windsor Publications, 1982.

_____. *Images of Oklahoma: A Pictorial History.* Oklahoma City: The Oklahoma Historical Society, 1984.

Blair, Margaret B. *Scalpel in a Saddlebag: The Story of a Physician in Indian Territory.* Oklahoma City: Western Heritage Books, 1979.

Bolton, Herbert E. *Coronado: Knight of Pueblos and Plains.* New York: Whittlsey House, 1949.

Bonnifield, Matthew P. *Oklahoma Innovator: The Life of Virgil Browne.* Norman: University of Oklahoma Press, 1976.

_____. *The Dust Bowl: Men, Dirt, and Depression.* Albuquerque: University of New Mexico Press, 1979.

Boydstun, Q.B. *Growing Up in Oklahoma.* Oklahoma City: The Oklahoma Historical Society, 1982.

Bryant, Keith L. *Alfalfa Bill Murray.* Norman: University of Oklahoma Press, 1968.

Cantrell, M.L., and Mac Harris. *Kepis and Turkey Calls: An Anthology of the War Between the States in Indian Territory.* Oklahoma City: Western Heritage Books, 1982.

Carriker, Robert C. *Fort Supply, In-*

dian Territory: Frontier Outpost on the Plains. Norman: University of Oklahoma Press, 1970.

Carter, L. Edward. *The Story of Oklahoma Newspapers.* Oklahoma City: Oklahoma Heritage Association, 1984.

Chapman, Berlin B. *The Claim of Texas to Greer County.* Oklahoma City: Privately printed, 1950.

——————. *The Otoes and Missouris: A Story of Indian Removal and the Legal Aftermath.* Oklahoma City: Journal-Record Publishing Company, 1965.

Colcord, Charles F. *The Autobiography of Charles Francis Colcord, 1859-1934.* Tulsa: Privately printed, 1970.

Collins, Ellsworth. *The 101 Ranch.* Norman: University of Oklahoma Press, 1971.

Conn, Jack T. *One Man in His Time: The Autobiography of Jack T. Conn.* Edited by O.B. Faulk. Oklahoma City: Oklahoma Heritage Association, 1979.

Constant, Alberta. *Oklahoma Run.* New York: Crowell, 1983.

Dale, Edward E. *The Range Cattle Industry.* Norman: University of Oklahoma Press, 1930.

——————. *Cow Country.* Norman: University Oklahoma Press, 1942.

Debo, Angie. *And Still the Waters Run.* Princeton, NJ: Princeton University Press, 1931.

——————. *The Rise and Fall of the Choctaw Republic.* Norman: University of Oklahoma Press, 1934.

——————. *The Road to Disappearance.* Norman: University of Oklahoma Press, 1941.

Edmunds, R. David. *The Potawatomis: Keepers of the Fire.* Norman: University of Oklahoma Press, 1978.

Ellis, Albert H. *A History of the Constitutional Convention of the State of Oklahoma.* Muskogee: Economy Printing Company, 1923.

Ezell, John S. *Innovations in Energy: The Story of Kerr-McGee.* Norman: University of Oklahoma

Press, 1979.

Faulk, Odie B. *A Man of Vision: The Life and Career of O.W. Coburn.* Oklahoma City: Western Heritage Books, 1979.

——————. *The Making of a Merchant: R.A. Young and T.G.&Y. Stores.* Oklahoma City: Oklahoma Heritage Association, 1980.

——————. *A Full Service Banker: The Life of Louis W. Duncan.* Oklahoma City: Oklahoma Heritage Association, 1981.

——————. *A Specialist in Everything: The Life of Fred S. Watson, M.D.* Oklahoma City: Oklahoma Heritage Association, 1981.

——————. *Dear Everybody: The Life of Henry B. Bass.* Oklahoma City: Oklahoma Heritage Association, 1982.

——————. *Muskogee, City and County.* Muskogee: Five Civilized Tribes Museum, 1982.

——————. *Jennys to Jets: The Life of Clarence E. Page.* Oklahoma City: Oklahoma Heritage Association, 1983.

—————— and B.M. Jones. *Fort Smith: An Illustrated History.* Fort Smith: Old Fort Museum, 1983.

—————— and B.M. Jones. *Tahlequah, NSU, and the Cherokees.* Tahlequah: Northeastern State University Development Foundation, 1984.

——————, J.H. Thomas, and C.N. Tyson. *The Gentleman: The Life of Joseph A. LaFortune.* Oklahoma City: Oklahoma Heritage Association, 1979.

——————, K.A. Franks, and P.F. Lambert, eds. *Early Military Forts and Posts in Oklahoma.* Oklahoma City: The Oklahoma Historical Society, 1978.

Ferber, Edna. *Cimarron.* New York: Bantam, 1929.

Fischer, LeRoy H., ed. *The Civil War Era in the Indian Territory.* Los Angeles: L.L. Morrison, 1974.

——————, ed. *Oklahoma's Governors, 1890-1907: The Terri-*

torial Years. Oklahoma City: The Oklahoma Historical Society, 1975.

——————, ed. *Oklahoma's Governors, 1907-1929: Turbulent Politics.* Oklahoma City: The Oklahoma Historical Society, 1981.

——————, ed. *Oklahoma's Governors, 1929-1955: Depression to Prosperity.* Oklahoma City: The Oklahoma Historical Society, 1983.

——————, ed. *Oklahoma's Governors, 1955-1979: Growth and Reform.* Oklahoma City: The Oklahoma Historical Society, 1985.

Foreman, Carolyn. *Oklahoma Imprints.* Norman: University of Oklahoma Press, 1936.

Foreman, Grant. *The Five Civilized Tribes.* Norman: University of Oklahoma Press, 1934.

——————. *Sequoyah.* Norman: University of Oklahoma Press, 1938.

——————. *Marcy and the Gold Seekers.* Norman: University of Oklahoma Press, 1939.

Franklin, Jimmie L. *Born Sober: Prohibition in Oklahoma, 1907-1959.* Norman: University of Oklahoma Press, 1971.

Franks, Kenny A. *Stand Watie and the Agony of the Cherokee Nation.* Memphis: Memphis State University Press, 1979.

——————. *The Oklahoma Petroleum Industry.* Norman: University of Oklahoma Press, 1980.

——————. *You're Doin' Fine, Oklahoma: A History of the Diamond Jubilee.* Oklahoma City: The Oklahoma Historical Society, 1983.

——————. *The Rush Begins: A History of the Red Fork, Cleveland and Glenn Pool Oil Fields.* Oklahoma City: Oklahoma Heritage Association, 1984.

——————, P.F. Lambert, and C.N. Tyson. *Early Oklahoma Oil: A Photographic History, 1859-1936.* College Station, TX: Texas A & M University Press, 1981.

Gard, Wayne. *The Chisholm Trail.* Norman: University of Oklahoma Press, 1954.

_____. *The Great Buffalo Hunt.* New York: Alfred A. Knopf, Inc., 1959.

Gibson, Arrell M. *The Kickapoos: Lords of the Middle Border.* Norman: University of Oklahoma Press, 1963.

_____. *The Chickasaws.* Norman: University of Oklahoma Press, 1971.

_____. *Wilderness Bonanza: The Tri-State District of Missouri, Kansas and Oklahoma.* Norman: University of Oklahoma Press, 1972.

_____ and E.C. Bearrs. *Fort Smith: Little Gibralter on the Arkansas.* Norman: University of Oklahoma Press, 1969.

_____, ed. *America's Exiles: Indian Colonization in Oklahoma.* Oklahoma City: The Oklahoma Historical Society, 1976.

_____, ed. *Will Rogers: A Centennial Tribute.* Oklahoma City: The Oklahoma Historical Society, 1979.

_____, ed. *The West Wind Blows: The Autobiography of Edward Everett Dale.* Oklahoma City: The Oklahoma Historical Society, 1984.

Gittinger, Roy. *Formation of the State of Oklahoma.* Norman: University of Oklahoma Press, 1939.

Goble, Danney. *Progressive Oklahoma: The Making of a New Kind of State.* Norman: University of Oklahoma Press, 1980.

Gould, Charles N. *Travels Through Oklahoma.* Oklahoma City: Harlow Publishing Company, 1928.

Grady, Charles. Edited by Tim Zwink and Gordon Moore. *County Courthouses of Oklahoma.* Oklahoma City: The Oklahoma Historical Society, 1985.

Green, Donald E. *The Creek People.* Phoenix: Indian Tribal Series, 1973.

_____. *Panhandle Pioneer: Henry C. Hitch, Ranch, and His Family.* Norman: University of Oklahoma Press, 1979.

_____, ed. *Rural Oklahoma.* Oklahoma City: The Oklahoma Historical Society, 1977.

Guthrie, Woody. *Bound for Glory.* New York: E.P. Dutton, 1943.

Hammons, Terry. *Ranching from the Front Seat of a Buick: The Life of Oklahoma's A.A. "Jack" Drummond.* Oklahoma City: The Oklahoma Historical Society, 1980.

Hargrett, Lester. *Oklahoma Imprints, 1835-1890.* New York: Bowker, 1951.

Harlow, Rex F. *Oklahoma Leaders: Biographical Sketches of the Foremost Living Men of Oklahoma.* Oklahoma City: Harlow Publishing Company, 1928.

Harrison, Walter M. *Me and My Big Mouth.* Oklahoma City: Britton, 1954.

Hendrickson, Kenneth E., Jr., ed. *Hard Times in Oklahoma: The Depression Years.* Oklahoma City: The Oklahoma Historical Society, 1983.

Hofsommer, Donovan L. *Katy Northwest: The Story of a Branch Line Railroad.* Boulder, CO: Pruitt Publishing Company, 1976.

_____, ed. *Railroads in Oklahoma.* Oklahoma City: The Oklahoma Historical Society, 1977.

Hoig, Stan. *The Peace Chiefs of the Cheyennes.* Norman, 1979.

_____. *David L. Payne: The Oklahoma Boomer.* Oklahoma City: Western Heritage Books, 1980.

_____. *The Oklahoma Land Rush of 1889.* Oklahoma City: The Oklahoma Historical Society, 1984.

Hurst, Irvin. *The Forty-Sixth Star: A History of Oklahoma's Constitutional Convention and Early Statehood.* Oklahoma City: Western Heritage Books, 1980.

Irving, Washington. *A Tour on the Prairies.* Oklahoma City: University of Oklahoma Press, 1955.

Isern, Thomas. *Custom Combining on the Great Plains: A History.* Norman: University of Oklahoma Press, 1981.

Jones, Billy M. *L.E. Phillips: Banker, Oil Man, Civic Leader.* Oklahoma City: Oklahoma Heritage Association, 1981.

_____ and O.B. Faulk. *The Cherokees: An Illustrated History.* Muskogee: Five Civilized Tribes Museum, 1984.

Jones, Dick. *From Okemah to the State Court of Criminal Appeals: The Autobiography of Dick Jones.* Oklahoma City: The Oklahoma Historical Society, 1983.

Jones, Stephen. *Oklahoma Politics in State and Nation.* Enid: Haymaker Press, 1974.

Kappler, Charles J., comp. and ed. *Indian Affairs: Laws and Treaties.* 3 vols. Washington, DC: Government Printing Office, 1904.

Kirkpatrick, Samuel A. *The Legislative Process in Oklahoma.* Norman: University of Oklahoma Press, 1978.

Lambert, Paul F. *Pioneer Historian and Archaeologist: The Life of Joseph B. Thoburn.* Oklahoma City: Oklahoma Heritage Association, 1980.

_____ and K.A. Franks, eds. *Voices from the Oil Fields.* Norman: University of Oklahoma Press, 1984.

Latrobe, Charles J. *The Rambler in Oklahoma.* Edited by M.H. Wright and George Shirk. Oklahoma City: Harlow Publishing Company, 1955.

Leckie, William H. *The Military Conquest of the Southern Plains.* Norman: University of Oklahoma Press, 1963.

Logsdon, Guy W. *The University of Tulsa: A History, 1882-1972.* Norman: University of Oklahoma Press, 1977.

McReynolds, Edwin C. *The Seminoles.* Norman: University of Oklahoma Press, 1957.

Malone, James H. *The Chickasaw Nation.* Louisville, KY: J.P. Morton, 1922.

Masterson, V.V. *The Katy Railroad and the Last Frontier.* Norman:

University of Oklahoma Press, 1953.

Matthews, John Joseph. *Life and Death of an Oil Man: The Career of E.W. Marland.* Norman: University of Oklahoma Press, 1951.

_____. *The Osages: Children of the Middle Waters.* Norman: University of Oklahoma Press, 1961.

Maxwell, Amos D. *The Sequoyah Constitutional Convention.* Boston: Meador Publishing Company, 1953.

Mayhall, Mildred. *The Kiowas.* Norman: University of Oklahoma Press, 1962.

Meredith, Howard L. and Mary Ellen Meredith. *Mr. Oklahoma History: The Life of George Shirk.* Oklahoma City: Oklahoma Heritage Association, 1982.

_____. *Superior: The Life of B.D. Eddie.* Oklahoma City: Oklahoma Heritage Association, 1982.

_____, eds. *Of the Earth: Oklahoma's Architectural History.* Oklahoma City: The Oklahoma Historical Society, 1980.

Morgan, Anne. *Robert S. Kerr: The Senate Years.* Norman: University of Oklahoma Press, 1977.

_____ and Rennard Strickland, eds. *Oklahoma Memories.* Norman: University of Oklahoma Press, 1981.

Morris, Cheryl H. *The Cutting Edge: The Life of John Rogers.* Norman: University of Oklahoma Press, 1976.

Morris, John W. *Ghost Towns of Oklahoma.* Norman: University of Oklahoma Press, 1977.

_____, ed. *Geography of Oklahoma.* Oklahoma City: The Oklahoma Historical Society, 1977.

_____, ed. *Boundaries of Oklahoma.* Oklahoma City: The Oklahoma Historical Society, 1980.

_____, ed. *Drill Bits, Picks, and Shovels: History of Mineral Resources in Oklahoma.* Oklahoma City: The Oklahoma

Historical Society, 1982.

_____, C.R. Goins, and E.C. McReynolds. *Historical Atlas of Oklahoma.* Norman: University of Oklahoma Press, 1976.

Moulton, Gary. *John Ross: Cherokee Chief.* Athens, GA: University of Georgia Press, 1978.

Murray, William H. *Memoirs of Governor Murray.* 3 vols. Boston: Meador Publishing Company, 1945.

Nye, Wilbur S. *Carbine and Lance.* Norman: University of Oklahoma Press, 1937.

Patterson, Zella J. *Langston University: A History.* Norman: University of Oklahoma Press, 1979.

Rainey, George. *The Cherokee Strip.* Guthrie: Co-operative Publishing Company, 1933.

Rister, Carl C. *No Man's Land.* Norman: University of Oklahoma Press, 1948.

Rosser, Linda K. *Christmas in Oklahoma.* Oklahoma City: Western Heritage Books, 1983.

Ruth, Kent, and Jim Argo. *Window on the Past.* Oklahoma City: Western Heritage Books, 1984.

Savage, William. *The Cherokee Strip Live Stock Association: Federal Regulation and the Cattleman's Last Frontier.* Norman: University of Oklahoma Press, 1973.

_____. *Singing Cowboys and All That Jazz.* Norman: University of Oklahoma Press, 1982.

Scales, James R., and Danney Goble. *Oklahoma Politics: A History.* Norman: University of Oklahoma Press, 1982.

Shirk, George. *Oklahoma Place Names.* Norman: University of Oklahoma Press, 1974.

Shirley, Glenn. *Law West of Fort Smith.* Lincoln: University of Nebraska Press, 1968.

_____. *Heck Thomas: Frontier Marshal.* Philadelphia: Chilton Company, 1962.

_____. *Henry Starr: Last of the Real Badmen.* New York: McKay, 1965.

_____. *West of Hell's Fringe: Crime, Criminals, and the*

Federal Peace Officer in Oklahoma Territory. Norman: University of Oklahoma Press, 1978.

Skaggs, Jimmy. *The Cattle-Trailing Industry: Between Supply and Demand, 1866-1890.* Lawrence, KS: University of Kansas Press, 1973.

_____, ed. *Ranch and Range in Oklahoma.* Oklahoma City: The Oklahoma Historical Society, 1978.

Smallgood, James. *Urban Builder: The Life and Times of Stanley Draper.* Norman: University of Oklahoma Press, 1977.

_____, ed. *And Gladly Teach: Reminiscence Teachers from Frontier Dugout to Modern Module.* Norman: University of Oklahoma Press, 1976.

Smith, Robert, ed. *Oklahoma's Forgotten Indians.* Oklahoma City: The Oklahoma Historical Society, 1979.

Stewart, Roy P. *Born Grown: An Oklahoma City History.* Oklahoma City: Fidelity Bank, 1974.

_____. *Programs for People: Oklahoma Vocational Education.* Oklahoma City: Western Heritage Books, 1982.

_____ and Pendleton Woods. *One of a Kind: The Life of C.R. Anthony.* Oklahoma City: Oklahoma Heritage Association, 1981.

Strickland, Rennad. *Fire and Spirits: Cherokee Law from Clan to Court.* Norman: University of Oklahoma Press, 1975.

Teall, Kay M. *Black History in Oklahoma.* Oklahoma City: Oklahoma City Public Schools, 1971.

Thomas, James H. *The Bunion Derby: Andy Payne and the Great Transcontinental Footrace.* Oklahoma City: Western Heritage Books, 1980.

Thurman, Melvina, ed. *Women in Oklahoma.* Oklahoma City: The Oklahoma Historical Society, 1982.

Tilghman, Zoe A. *Outlaw Days: A True History of Early-Day Oklahoma Characters.* Oklahoma City: Harlow Publishing Company,

1926.

Tolson, A.L. *The Black Oklahomans: A History, 1541-1972.* New Orleans: Edwards Publishing Company, 1972.

Trafzer, Clifford E. *The Judge: The Life of Robert A. Hefner.* Norman: University of Oklahoma Press, 1975.

Tucker, Howard A. *History of Governor Walton's War on the Ku Klux Klan, the Invisible Empire.* Oklahoma City: Southwestern Publishing Company, 1923.

Tyson, Carl N. *The History of Vocational and Technical Education in Oklahoma.* Stillwater: State Department of Vocational-Technical Education, 1976.

——————. *The Pawnee People.* Phoenix: Indian Tribal Series, 1976.

——————. *The Red River in Southwestern History.* Norman: University of Oklahoma Press, 1981.

——————, O.B. Faulk, and J.H. Thomas. *The McMan: The Lives of Robert M. McFarlin and James A. Chapman.* Norman: University of Oklahoma Press, 1977.

Waldby, H.O. *The Patronage System in Oklahoma.* Norman: University of Oklahoma Press, 1950.

Wallace, Allie B. *Frontier Life in Oklahoma.* Washington, DC: Public Affairs Press, 1964.

Wallace, Ernest, and E.A. Hoebel. *The Comanches: Lords of the South Plains.* Norman: University of Oklahoma Press, 1952.

Wardell, Morris L. *A Political History of the Cherokee Nation.* Norman: University of Oklahoma Press, 1938.

Webb, Walter P. *The Great Plains.* Boston: Ginn and Company, 1931.

Welsh, Louise, W.M. Townes, and John W. Morris. *A History of the Greater Seminole Oil Field.* Oklahoma City: Oklahoma Heritage Association, 1981.

West, C.W. *Tahlequah and the Cherokee Nation.* Muskogee: Muskogee Publishing Company, 1978.

Wheeler, Robert W. *Jim Thorpe: The World's Greatest Athlete.* Norman: University of Oklahoma Press, 1979.

Wilson, Steve. *Oklahoma Treasures and Treasure Tales.* Norman: University of Oklahoma Press, 1976.

Wilson, Terry. *The Cart That Changed the World: The Career of Sylvan N. Goldman.* Norman: University of Oklahoma Press, 1978.

Woodward, Grace S. *The Cherokees.* Norman: University of Oklahoma Press, 1963.

Wright, Muriel H. *A Guide to the Indian Tribes of Oklahoma.* Norman: University of Oklahoma Press, 1951.

Wright, Peggy Q., and O.B. Faulk. *Coletta: A Sister of Mercy.* Oklahoma City: Oklahoma Heritage Association, 1981.

Zwink, Timothy A. and B.D. Evans. *The Flying Farmer Organization: First in Oklahoma.* Oklahoma City: Western Heritage Books, 1983.

Index